The New
Propaganda

The New Propaganda

The Dictatorship of Palaver in Contemporary Politics

James E. Combs and Dan Nimmo

Valparaiso University   *University of Oklahoma*

Longman

New York & London

**The New Propaganda: The Dictatorship of
Palaver in Contemporary Politics**

Longman, 10 Bank Street, White Plains, N.Y. 10606

Associated companies:
Longman Group Ltd., London
Longman Cheshire Pty., Melbourne
Longman Paul Pty., Auckland
Copp Clark Pitman, Toronto

Senior acquisitions editor: David J. Estrin
Development editor: Susan Alkana
Production editor: Victoria Mifsud
Cover design: Susan J. Moore
Cover illustration/photo: Susan J. Moore
Production supervisor: Richard C. Bretan

Library of Congress Cataloging-in-Publication Data

Combs, James E.
    The new propaganda : the dictatorship of palaver in contemporary
politics / James E. Combs, Dan Nimmo.
      p.   cm.
    Includes bibliographical references and index.
    ISBN 0-8013-0507-1
    1. Propaganda.   I. Nimmo, Dan D.   II. Title.
HM263.C578   1992
303.3'75—dc20
                                                             92-8091
                                                             CIP

1 2 3 4 5 6 7 8 9 10-AL-9695949392

To
O'Connor Flood
for His Probing Analysis of
and Unsurpassed Artistry in
Palaver!

Contents

**CHAPTER 6   THE MARKETING OF POPULAR CULTURE: PROPAGATING
PERSONAE, NEWS, AND EDUCATION   161**

**PART III   THE ANALYSIS AND CRITIQUE OF POLITICAL
PROPAGANDA   183**

**CHAPTER 7   SCRAPING THE SURFACE: THE TRADITION
OF PROPAGANDA ANALYSIS   185**

**CHAPTER 8   DIGGING BENEATH THE SURFACE: CONTEMPORARY
CRITICAL THINKING ABOUT PROPAGANDA   207**

Preface

Some things in our daily lives we take for granted. We are so accustomed to their presence that we rarely pay them heed—the air we breathe or the water we drink (polluted or not), the ticking of a familiar clock, busy city traffic, waiting in line at amusement parks or the post office. Unless something disrupts the routines of day-to-day living, they continue unnoticed. This is a book about something that routinely fills our daily lives from cradle to grave, now so omnipresent that we take it for granted. This is a book about *propaganda*, and more specifically, what we shall call the *new propaganda*.

In the following pages we explore how propaganda pervades and informs our everyday lives. Indeed, we frequently become propagandists ourselves. It is our thesis here that propaganda is not a marginal or insignificant part of our lives. Quite the contrary, we are all very much in the same condition as the character in French dramatist Jean Molière's *The Bourgeois Gentleman* who was astonished to learn that he had been speaking something called "prose" all of his life! We argue here that we all intuitively know how to "speak" propaganda because it is a familiar and important form of communication that we speak and hear as a native tongue.

Indeed, we will further argue that the new propaganda is indispensable to the way we live in the modern world and the foreseeable future. We could not dispense with propaganda any more than the automobile or the television set. As a matter of fact and forecasting, we believe that the logic of propaganda is inextricably interwoven into the fabric of our civilization. All major forms of contemporary social activity—business, law, politics, culture, academia—require in one way or another the use of propaganda in order to communicate successfully and to achieve organizational purposes.

In this book, we will attempt to demonstrate the principles and uses of the new propaganda in modern society. Further, the thrust of our argument is not only to demonstrate the centrality and indispensability of propaganda as a form of communication, but also to show that in the modern world of mass communications propaganda is ever growing in importance and sophistication, so much so that it may well have become the dominant form of social communication beyond interpersonal discourse. If we are in fact on our way to becoming one of the many modern societies dominated by propaganda, then it behooves us to understand what this may mean for the conduct of our lives. The new propaganda will help determine the way we live, and in some measure even how we think and what we value.

The question we want to bring to attention is, simply put, what is it like to live in a society in which propaganda is an established principle and dominant form of communication?

HOW THIS BOOK IS ORGANIZED

The introductory chapter of this book contains current examples and key concepts of how pervasive and trenchant propaganda is in our everyday lives. These examples and ideas serve as a basis for a historical analysis of propaganda in Chapter 1. Chapters 2 and 3 will give a human face to this history by looking at the careers and thought of several important figures—both past and present—in propaganda. Part II of this book will deal with the social arenas where propaganda plays an influential role. Chapters 4 and 5 discuss how propaganda is both used and abused as a tool for political and economic powers-that-be. Chapter 6 talks about how propaganda helps create our popular culture and brings people together as a "taste culture." Chapter 7 of Part III is aimed at the critical analysis of propaganda and starts with introducing you to the body of social knowledge gleaned from the critical analysis of propaganda, past and present. Chapter 8 concludes by letting you use your newly acquired knowledge by examining some contemporary critical thinking about propaganda.

WHO THIS BOOK IS FOR—AND WHY

This book is designed primarily for undergraduate and graduate courses in political communication, political rhetoric, political socialization, public opinion, and persuasion. Several features distinguish this book from other texts on the market. It integrates political science with communications studies and combines historical and analytical contexts; it also draws out the political implications of apparently nonpolitical phenomena.

The strategy of this book is to rekindle both popular and academic interest in the study of propaganda. Many of the younger readers of this book will live well into the new century, so the nature of that century should be of interest to them.

ACKNOWLEDGMENTS

We would like to thank several colleagues who helped to guide this project with their constructive criticism: Jarol Manheim, George Washington University; Mary Stuckey, University of Mississippi; Henry Kenski, Arizona State University; Charles Larson, Northern Illinois University; and Bob Savage, University of Arkansas. Thanks are also due to the team at Longman who guided the manuscript into book form headed by David Estrin, a book and baseball fan, who supports both authors and athletes (although not on the same pay scale.) He is ably assisted by such stellar performers as Victoria Mifsud, Owen Lancer, Susan Alkana, and Suzanne Davidson, all of whom, like so many Mets players, don't get the credit (nor the salary) they deserve.

The New Propaganda

Introduction
As Ye Sow, So Shall Ye Reap?
Introducing the New Propaganda

We are living in the age of the "new propaganda," and this book will show you how and why. Propaganda is pervasive in everyday life, something we are all familiar with and learn from. Because of its centrality to our lives, propaganda now constitutes a major form of social power with which we should be familiar. Keep in mind as you read this book that propaganda has consequences. It affects your life and society in a variety of ways you may not be aware of. This book should make you aware of the presence and power of propaganda. Let us begin by discussing some ways in which we can feel the presence of propaganda in our lives.

CHRISTMAS WITH SANTA, PROPAGANDA ICON

Christmas, we are told, comes but once a year. Pay attention to another common utterance about Christmas and you learn that it seems to start earlier every year. So perhaps "once a year" will soon be "all year." Be that as it may, Halloween with its ghosts and goblins no sooner ends than myriad signs of Christmas appear. Up go festive Christmas decorations in stores; newspapers, magazines, and television carry stories about the "upcoming season," then fill pages and time with Christmas advertising; soon there are parades, toy drives, charity drives, and other rituals and routines of Christmas; children 6 to 60 are inundated with TV reruns of shows with holiday themes, from "Charlie Brown's Christmas" to multiple versions of Charles Dickens's *A Christmas Carol;* and radio stations and shopping mall sound systems echo the refrains of Christmas songs, hymns, chimes, and carols. What begins in the fall helps create the "Christmas spirit" and culminates in the "Christmas season" amidst feverish rounds of shopping, traveling, visiting, and Yuletide cheer.

Presiding over this lengthy season of joy is a mythical secular deity, Santa Claus. Long since shorn of his religious origins and his punitive functions (such as punishing naughty children by withholding their gifts, a power now even denied the Grinch Who Stole Christmas), Santa Claus is a sanguine and convivial master of ceremonies offering Christmas festivity and cheer. It is correct, of course, that Christmas has long been and remains the religious celebration of the birth of Jesus; millions of Christians across the world exult in the sacred message of the season. (Also, as some skeptics annually remind Christians, the season coincides with the winter solstice celebrated in pagan antiquity). Religious meanings aside for the moment, in our secular society Christmas is the occasion for activities that go beyond the pietistic. For many people, Christmas celebrates an annual ritual of the sale and exchange of material goods, not just the voicing and contemplation of sacred messages. In this milieu Santa Claus is, in the words of one observer, a "symbolic representation of materialism"—a godly if hedonistic figure urging people to join in the festive season through consumption. The message ol' Saint Nick offers to children of all ages is that the acquisition of material items is good, that at an early age they should learn how to buy and know what to consume, for the world is indeed a place of boundless abundance and unlimited consumer choice. Santa, jolly old gent of the holiday season, invites us to join in the Christmas spirit of shopping, giving and getting, and consuming. As an icon of a "consumer culture," Santa Claus is a "uniquely meaningful national hero of American materialism."[1] Kris Kringle is known by many names, but his message has long since ceased to be one of forgiveness and good cheer; rather, he is an *icon of propaganda,* a figure who represents the Christmas spirit that vested interests wish to propagate, and in which many people want to find justification for their seasonal enjoyments. Santa Claus persists as a familiar icon of Christmas not only because children want a gift-god and parents find it all charming; he endures because he is a useful symbol central to the organized propaganda effort that characterizes the holiday season.

By the end of the holidays, with the passing of Christmas Day, then New Year's Day, countless messages of the season have crossed our vision, pierced our ears, invaded our consciousness. They are messages direct and indirect, overt and covert, blatant and subtle. Individually and in combination they have provoked thoughts and acts—of "what to do about Christmas." And they have done more. Business analysts, ever watchful of signs of bolstered or waning "consumer confidence"—a vital element in sustaining a growing economy—read the figures on Christmas sales. Market analysts, ever watchful of signs betokening new trends in consumer spending—a vital element in charting profit and loss—study how well new products (or time-worn products given new appeal) have attracted fickle buyers. A product that becomes a Christmas fad, say the Cabbage Patch doll, can generate fortunes; a product that bombs, say a microwave version of the pop-up toaster, can be a marketing disaster. So crucial to the health of the American and world economies is the Christmas season, there is little surprise that considerable effort and expense enters into promoting the key Yuletide message: CONSUME!

What brings us this message of sanctifying consumption? Propaganda promotes the message—in slogans and jingles, splashy and colorful TV commercials, upbeat music, smiling pitchmen and -women, striking images and haunting phrases, and promises of fulfillment and happiness. And Santa Claus is an icon of propaganda: a mythical authority urging that we have a right, even a duty, to indulge at Christmastime. Christmas in the modern world has been transformed into an occasion of economic importance. Because of that importance, propaganda has become the dominant form of public economic discourse during the lengthy holiday period, the social language of communication that expedites the desired consumer behavior. That behavior is desired not only by economic interests who wish to hype Christmas sales but also by many people who have a "consuming interest" in enjoying the holiday season and respond to propaganda that suggests how they might do so. Propaganda involves both economic interests and ordinary people in a process of social learning, with both parties to the communicative transaction attempting to learn how to shape behavior at Christmastime, and indeed the year round.

KEN AND BARBIE, BARBIE AND KEN: REALLY TAKING PROPAGANDA FOR GRANTED

Yuletime propaganda certainly surrounds us, so much that, like a muted but steady sensation of pain or pleasure, we get used to it. We think it has disappeared, but it hasn't. Consider the shopping mall, certainly a consumer's paradise offering the implicit message Shop 'Till You Drop. Suppose it is Christmas and there wanders through the mall a shopper consumed by, and bent on consuming, the spirit of the season. It is time to purchase a gift for that delightful three-year-old niece. Yelping windup puppies, a stuffed camel, a portly clown—all invite the shopper to enter a toy store. The choices are seemingly endless: war toys from assault rifles to tanks and fighter planes; board and computerized games from the perennial favorite Monopoly to Talking Baseball; and dolls, dolls, dolls, even Flo-Jo attired in a colorful running outfit. Our mall shopper pauses, surveys the multitude of goodies, then fixes a gaze on one doll in particular. It is Barbie, one of the veritable superstars of the toy industry, certainly as deserving of an honored niche in any Toy Hall of Fame as Mickey Mouse, and more so than Snoopy (or certainly Spuds McKenzie!). Let us ponder Barbie for a moment for she (it?) has something to tell us about propaganda.

The Barbie doll is over 30 years old but shows no signs of advancing age. Over 500 million Barbies have been sold by Mattel, a toy manufacturer that claims to control 98 percent of the market for fashion dolls designed for small girls aged three to eight. Barbie is indeed fashionable. Seventy fashion designers, including Bill Blass and Christian Dior, have contributed to Barbie's wardrobe. The Barbie playset incorporates new accessories, friends, and activities each year. There are books on Barbie, a Barbie Fan Club, even a Barbie Hall of Fame. Fans can tour facilities highlighting scenes from the Barbie doll's growth, growing wardrobe, and shifting lifestyle. The Barbie name appears in a wide variety of TV ads—Barbie as rock star, Barbie in her new Ferrari, Barbie hanging out with the gang at the beach or soda shoppe along with Ken, Skipper, Miko, and Teresa. Barbie opened the 1990s by joining the military—as an army captain in a deep blue evening dress with gold braid, as an air force pilot wearing a leather flight jacket, and as a chief petty officer in the navy donning a "Cracker Jack" white uniform with bell-bottoms, navy blue scarf, and V-neck shirt with service ribbons. (Barbie's uniforms were designed to meet Pentagon requirements. Even her hair was shortened to meet military regulations!)

In a toy and game industry that involves many billions in retail sales annually, Barbie is a major creative and marketing success. Not bad for a doll. But is Barbie only a doll? Hardly. As parents know and child psychologists have discovered, toys are often more than toys. Children learn lessons from their toys. This is what bothers critics of the toy industry who fear that playing with toy assault rifles and zapping video fighter planes teaches instant violence as a pleasurable exercise. But what can be learned from Barbie? Does this popular doll transmit a message other than immediate play, a message of propaganda?

Like jolly ol' Saint Nick, Barbie is a cultural icon. The doll represents something more than a plaything or diversion; combined in Barbie's face, figure, and lifestyle are a host of ideas (call them symbols) about how young girls should look, act, and be. Barbie teaches young girls what growing up in American society is all about. Barbie and her boyfriend Ken teach youngsters of both sexes norms of beauty and behavior. In fact, Barbie and Ken represent a version of the American Dream—that youthful beauty never fades, nor should it be allowed to do so. The youthful accessories (wigs, makeup), furnishings, household surroundings, and costumes constitute lifestyles provided by Mattel, suggesting an endless variety of ways to keep Ken and Barbie young, vibrant, and alive! Eternal youth and beauty is to be had through the pursuit of high consumption leisure.

Did anyone, the designers and manufacturers of Barbie, for instance, *intend* to communicate a message of eternal youth through their creation? Probably not. At least, and as yet, there is no evidence of a small group of designers concocting a scheme to teach millions of girls and boys that youth is a privileged state to be preserved forever through expensive fun. No, if intentions alone are at issue, then Barbie's creators succeeded beyond their wildest expectations ($450 million in 1988 sales alone) in achieving a marketing breakthrough. Nor is it likely that those who buy Barbie dolls—parents and relatives— intend through their gifts to communicate a conscious message about eternal youth. Rather they make the purchase out of love, or to please the child, or to provide the same toys "the other kids have." In any case, the motives of both manufacturer and purchaser are likely limited to immediate monetary interests, without a clear agenda of sweeping cultural indoctrination.[2]

Yet, the Barbie Message is there: somehow children should look like, act like, and be like what Ken and Barbie "mean" in youthful imagination. Other questions: Is that the message the kid-consumers of Barbie and Ken receive? Are they recipients of a subtle message that nobody really intended but that nevertheless is there? The answer to those questions is not easily obtained. But since social observers frequently remind us of the numerous consequences that popular icons such as Ken and Barbie can have in a culture, perhaps we should not so quickly and simply take for granted the idea that our doll friends are dolls and nothing more. Consider a few other factors. The Barbie doll is the consequence of an elaborate advertising effort by Mattel designed to promote the doll and all paraphernalia that accompanies her (including Ken). Here the intended message is clear—to boost Barbie sales. As a by-product of the promotional campaign comes a second possibility about the Barbie Message, one not so obvious. Not only was Barbie sold by means of propaganda (advertising), as is any other commercial product; social observers have argued that *Barbie herself* (the doll and all she has come to represent) is implicit propaganda, a message instructing little girls in what they should want to be as they grow up. And what is that Barbie Message? Some critics see in Barbie a uniform and sinister cultural standard—a "role model" for young girls. That standard is impossible to achieve, for very few young girls will grow up flawlessly beautiful and blond. Cultural critics deem the message demeaning to women, for it implies Barbie is subservient to men in the sense of women's defining themselves by how attractive they are to equally handsome members of the opposite sex—the "well-attired and full-bodied sex object." For example, the original feminine ideal implicit in Barbie was that of cheerleader, majorette, and beauty queen, female roles involving male adoration of feminine beauty and athleticism. The Barbie Message, according to critics, is that Barbie is the lovely but dumb consumer whose major interests in life are to look pretty and to shop in order to do so (an all-consuming interest in twin senses).

By contrast, conservative critics of the Barbie phenomenon see something else in the Barbie Message. In this view, Barbie represents dangerous sensuality, a being committed to hedonism and the worship of the body beautiful to be admired and touched my men (many *Playboy* centerfolds bear a striking resemblance to the tall, willowy, blond doll). But here too, ironically, may also be confirmation of feminist ideal: namely female *independence*. Barbie now has her own substantial careers; her own credit cards; equality with males (Barbie the astronaut, the air force pilot, etc.); and achievement (one advertising slogan for Barbie is, We Girls Can Do Anything). Perhaps somewhere between these two versions of the Barbie Message is the one alluded to earlier, that is, the Barbie who never ages, endures misfortune or illness, bears children, or cries.

Whether the Barbie Message be youth, feminism, or antifeminism, it certainly does not seem at first glance to be particularly important or consequential. Yet according to some psychologists and physicians, Barbie may indeed be injurious to health. Such critics trace the fear that some young women have of growing fat in part to the value placed on looking Barbie-like. That fear may contribute to dangerous dieting, bulimia, and anorexia. Research indicates that elementary school children regard obesity as worse than a handicapping or disabling condition; that desperate and unhealthy attempts to stay thin are prevalent among girls (and some boys) even in the lower grades; and that, as measured by public opinion polls, ''getting fat'' is a greater fear among adolescents than nuclear war, economic depression, and parental disapproval.[3]

It is easy to overstate the extent to which Barbie might affect such anxieties in young people. The Barbie Message is not the only carrier of the ideal of beauty as shapely thinness. Quickie diets, diet products, exercise programs, and so on, constitute an ever-growing slimness industry that surely predates Ken and Barbie (witness silent movie stars Douglas Fairbanks and Lillian Gish as svelte, thin role models). Nor do Ken and Barbie alone represent the ideal of ageless youth, that is, young is good, old is bad. Youth-restoring products (facial and body balms for women, hair restorers for men), health spas, and cosmetic surgery profit from a dream promoted long before and independently of Barbie's enduring youthful beauty. (And, it should be noted, there are alternative messages: a firm named High Self-Esteem Toys, Inc., marketed what they called the Happy to Be Me doll, a less beautiful and more ordinary-looking female icon who was not thin, sexy, or rich.) For the moment, however, the Barbie image dominates, in some measure because the Barbie Message was propagated through multiple sources over a long period of time, using endless and pervasive repetition of the message to reinforce that dominance. Barbie's appeal may have been latent in American popular culture, but the manufacturer did not leave that appeal to chance.

The lesson of this extended discussion of Santa Claus and Barbie is that propaganda is not always direct, not always apparent, nor confined to what we might offhand think of as propaganda. When we see a political campaign ad or a prepared statement by a public relations spokesperson or a promotional event staged to hype a new movie, we assume that such communications are propaganda. One can often trace the specific intentions of the sources of these messages, figure that the message itself was structured to maximize its effect and calculate its appeal. But as we have seen with Santa Claus and Barbie, propaganda is not always such a clear-cut thing to identify, if for no other reason than that it is such an integral part of our everyday lives. In the final analysis, we ourselves are the carriers, the propagators, of propaganda. Propaganda works because it has become integrated into our habits of communication, habits that we value and respond to because they promise desirable consequences for our lives. In a larger sense, propaganda has become a form of communication that is inextricably interwoven into the process of social communication in modern society, the persistent ways in which we structure and practice communications in order to perpetuate or change social forms, including structures of power and prestige as well as our common practices. When we go to the mall before Christmas and buy a Barbie doll, or wear a Hard Rock Cafe T-shirt, or put a political bumper sticker on our car, or any of innumerable daily actions, we have become part of the process of *social propagandizing*. Even though we all would like to believe that we are immune to the appeals and practices of propaganda, the very ubiquity and success of propaganda suggests that we are not. It may be the case that we are a part of the propaganda process without being aware of it and all that it entails. This may be a large burden to put upon Barbie and Santa Claus, not to mention ourselves; nevertheless, in order to understand propaganda we have to grasp the fact that it is not exotic or remote but is a part of the way of life of modern society. With that in mind, let us do a thought experiment using a familiar metaphor that will clarify what we mean by the process of propagandizing.

PROPAGANDA AS PROPAGATING COMMUNICATION

A convenient way to describe the character of propaganda is to use a *metaphor*, a figure of speech that transfers a term from one object or activity it ordinarily designates to another that it may hint at by implication or analogy. Such figures of speech help us understand something that seems vague, ambiguous, or abstract by comparing it to the familiar and concrete.[4] Care to propagandize while courting? Try this metaphor provided by Elizabeth Barrett Browning:

> How do I love thee? Let me count the ways.
> I love thee to the depth and breadth and height
> My soul can reach, when feeling out of sight.[5]

Here is love, certainly a vague word, given measureless depth, breadth, and height. (One can scarcely love more than that!) Ageless Ken and Barbie are made so by metaphors presented to us to signify that they are as always in the "morning," never the "evening," of life. A metaphor offers an imaginative analogue that orients us toward the nature and significance of something or someone. Barbie is "youthful and willowy," Santa is "jolly and generous," love is an emotion beyond measure or limit.

In Chapter 1 we discuss the history of propaganda and show that the term itself has been around for a long time. Its precise origins are hard to pin down, but scholars generally credit 1622 as being when it first came into use. In that year Pope Gregory XV established the Congregatio de Propaganda Fide, an organization of the Catholic church established to spread Catholicism among non-Christian populations. Propaganda was the *organization* that delivered a message. By that characterization Mattel, the toy company, would be the agency of propaganda involved in promoting the Barbie doll. However, after 1622 the term *propaganda* began to take on other meanings. For instance, propaganda ceased to refer solely to organizations and instead designated the *message* spread by the organization, that is, in the case of the Congregatio the message of *Fide,* or "faith," was propaganda. In our Christmas example, the sales pitch, rather than the organization, used by Mattel to promote Ken and Barbie is the locus of propaganda. A third dimension of propaganda came into play as a defining characteristic. That consisted of the *techniques* used to spread the message, for example, sending missionaries to convert non-Christians. TV ads, jingles, cartoons, and so on are the techniques used to market the Barbie doll, to spread the Barbie Message. As time passed, other meanings and definitions were attached to the word so that before long propaganda became like the elephant in the fable of the blind men trying to determine what the beast actually was by feeling different parts of its anatomy—a rope (the elephant's trunk), a palm tree (the ears), a great oak (the legs), and so on.[6] A useful body of information developed about propaganda, but this was limited by the lack of a root metaphor that could incorporate the entirety of the process of propaganda communication.

We're Not Promising You a Rose Garden: Propagation as a Root Metaphor

Perhaps it is time to go back to the roots of propaganda, or more precisely, the *root metaphor*. A root metaphor encompasses several related metaphors. For example, three politicians explain themselves: former president Richard Nixon said, "Let me make this perfectly clear," former president Ronald Reagan compared America to a "shining City on the Hill," and President George Bush spoke of a "thousand points of light." What makes things clear, shines, and lights? The sun. The root metaphor for all three is heliocentric, that is, it has the sun at its center. Like the "Sun King" of old, Louis XIV, in different ways the image of political light is to make us believe that it will lead us out of the darkness. Other politicians use similar vague root metaphors in an attempt to include a variety of interests and desires: Jesse Jackson speaks of America as a "many-colored patchwork quilt," and Mario Cuomo, of the country as an "extended family."

The word *propaganda* comes originally from the Latin for *propagate*. Pope Gregory's 1622 decree established a Congregation for the Propagation of the Faith. Propagation, and the process of propagating, is our root metaphor. The word *propagate* has several overlapping definitions: to cause animals or plants to multiply or breed; to breed offspring; to transmit characteristics from one generation to another; to make known, publicize; to transmit, move through a medium—as to propagate radio or TV signals. Before there was publicity, radio, or TV signals, there was the first of these definitions—propagation of animals and plants by nature's processes. We will explore that definition for a moment.

We are all familiar with the cycle of natural life: birth (coming to life); growth to maturity (unless nipped in the bud); multiplication (breeding that creates new life); withering; death. Such is the fate of a rose, a dandelion, a dog, a cockroach, a man or a woman (except Ken and Barbie!). Sometimes the multiplication or breeding (propagation) is random; thus, seeds borne by wind or water find new soil and take root. Which ones reproduce is a matter of what Italian political philosopher Niccolò Machiavelli called *fortuna,* or chance.[7] At other times propagation is intentional rather than fortuitous. For example, through horticulture, the cultivation of the earth, propagation is deliberate. A farmer or gardener plants seeds with the intent of growing and harvesting a crop. There are two ways of doing this. One is to take the seed and plant it in the soil—dig a hole, cover it up, and nurture it. The other is to sow the seed (also called broadcasting) by throwing the seed on ground prepared to accept it. (Note: animal breeding also may occur by chance, as when stallions move through a herd of wild mares; by seeding through selective artificial insemination; or by sowing, as when breeding several mares in estrous, or "heat," to a stallion.)

Whether the horticulturist's intent is carried out by planting or sowing, the success of the endeavor depends on factors similar to those involved when seeds are borne by wind or water. A key question is: Do the seeds germinate, take root, spread, and yield a crop of offspring? If the answer is yes, then whether intentional or not, propagation has occurred. An affirmative answer depends upon many different conditions. There is, of course, the unexpected. Diseases, insects, drought, floods, and all forms of pestilence have been the plight of the farmer throughout history. And don't discount bad farming: using damaging fertilizers and chemical sprays and faulty tilling methods; foolishly burning brush next to one's ripening wheat field; permitting the crop to "jump the fence," spreading to the field of a neighbor who, seeing its potential, harvests it and reaps the profit.

Nor should we forget the culture in which the seeding or breeding occurs. With respect to propagation the term *culture,* like propagation itself, has several overlapping meanings: the cultivation, or tillage, of soil; the breeding of animals or growing of plants; and the growing of microorganisms in a nutrient medium, such as a liquid. Propagation occurs and thrives in a hospitable culture, in an environment that nurtures and sustains its growth. If a particular form of propagation produces desirable results, then it may well become a permanent part of the culture of cultivation, a "natural" and expected part of the social process.

Cultivating Ideas: Seedbeds of Propaganda

> And when the woman saw that the tree was good for food, and that it was pleasant to the eyes, and a tree to be desired to make one wise, she took the fruit thereof, and did eat, and gave also unto her husband with her; and he did eat.

If this is a book about propaganda, why dwell on horticulture and animal husbandry? A fair question, and the passage above from Genesis (3:6) suggests an answer. Genesis records perhaps the earliest propaganda campaign as Eve gives the apple to Adam. She takes the harvest of the tree, which will please the eyes and make one wise, eats it, and so does her husband—just as the serpent importuned. We need no reminders that Adam and Eve ate bitter fruit, that the consequences of their snack went far beyond Eve's intentions (although not beyond the serpent's). Gone was a world of eternal paradise (although Ken and Barbie have reclaimed it) in exchange for a world of "wisdom" through contending ideas.

W. Phillips Davison has described how the communication of ideas relates to propagation and, thereby, shows how propagation describes propaganda.[8] Davison points out that "a familiar allegory uses the analogy of seeds to illustrate the growth of ideas." In this metaphor "the seeds are numbered in the thousands, and are scattered over the land-scape." Being scattered rather than planted, "some fall on the rocks and fail to germi-nate" and "others start to take root but soon die because they lack soil in sufficient depth or because they are smothered by faster-growing weeds." Hence, "only a few fall on earth where the conditions are right for continued growth and multiplication." Drawing the parallel to the propagation of ideas, Davison notes that "similarly, there are many more issues that might prove the basis for mass movements than ever see the light of day." For, "all men have grievances, inspirations, and ideas for improving society, but most of these die away in mutterings or casual conversation." Thus, "most potential is-sues disappear from attention before this human chain grows to an appreciable length, but the few that survive form the basis for public opinion."

The propagation of ideas (and actions) is analogous to that of seeds. Like seeds, some ideas may come and go as if borne on the wind. Some rumors have that quality. For example, during World War II the United States, in order to conserve supplies of copper for the war effort, switched from minting copper pennies to copper alloy and/or lead pen-nies. A rumor began, source unknown, that a person who could discover a 1943 copper penny could exchange it for a new Ford automobile after the war. No copper pennies were minted in 1943, yet that did not prevent periodic hording of pennies during the war and for several postwar years as Americans poked eagerly through penny collections in search of the coveted prize. That rumor died out when it was disconfirmed after the war, but other rumors, again like seeds borne on winds that carry the weeds everywhere, seem to go on forever—for example, the tale of the vanishing hitchhiker, the recurrent UFO ap-pearances, and Elvis sightings.

Other ideas may be deliberately planted in specific people's minds. In Chapter 2 we will discuss several individuals who were masters of propaganda. One of those was Jo-seph Goebbels, minister of propaganda in the Nazi regime of Adolf Hitler from 1933 until 1945. One of his propaganda techniques was the "whisper," or person-to-person propa-ganda (Mundpropaganda). For instance, to mask Hitler's planned invasion of the Soviet Union in 1941, Goebbels planted a rumor with several well-known figures that he knew would pass it along. The rumor was that troops with special training in amphibious war-fare were massing on the English Channel "for the imminent landing against England."[9] Soviets who believed it were diverted from the real threat to Russia by the faked threat to England. A contemporary example of the whisper campaign is the "leaking" of informa-tion by "official" sources in Washington, D.C. Leaks are employed to plant facts, gos-sip, rumors, allegations, and so on, diverting rival politicians and investigative reporters from what is going on to what is not.

Finally, as Davison wrote, other ideas are simply scattered over the landscape by pol-iticians making speeches, advertisers marketing goods, press agents publicizing movie and TV stars, and weekly tabloids promoting sales (e.g., the headline, "Astonishing Fact: 300 lb. Woman Gives Birth to Hippopotamus!"). Whether by chance, planting, or scat-tering, according to Davison, "only a few fall on earth where the conditions are right for continued growth and multiplication." The culture for effective propagation, as with seeds, must be supportive; in horticulture the term culture itself implies a nutrient medium that supports growth. In speaking of ideoculture—the art and science of growing ideas—culture refers to a nutrient of values, beliefs, acts, and institutions conducive to growth. If soil is a key component of physical culture in propagating seeds, people and the contexts they live in constitute key components of human culture in propagating ideas. Soil propagates seeds, people propagate ideas, and both propagate a type of culture that is sometimes random, sometimes intentional. As a contemporary practitioner of the multiple arts of communication recently noted,

> I operate according to the Gospel parable of the sower. Throw that seed out everywhere. Some of it falls on rocky ground, some the wind blows back in your face, but a lot of it falls on fertile ground and germinates. And what germinates is sufficient so as not to miss what hit the rocks and wind.[10] —Jesse Jackson

Sociation: Active Culture and the Necessity of Suasion

Let us explore in greater detail this notion that people are the seedbed, or culture, of ideas and ideoculture, for it is key to our entire discussion of propaganda. The composition of soil—minerals, acids, moisture, organisms—provides a physical *active culture* for the reception of seeds. If the seed finds that active culture receptive, it germinates; if not, germination fails. The active soil receives the seed and sustains or rejects it. The soil culture thereby changes the seed and, if the seed germinates, by drawing on the soil it changes that portion of the earth where it grows. So it is with the propagation of ideas and actions. People constitute a human active culture composed of their beliefs, values, and experiences. They actively, not passively, encounter ideas, liking or disliking them, using or disusing them, discussing or forgetting them, propagating or not propagating them. Human cultures receive ideas and sustain or reject them. As a soil culture changes the seed, a human culture changes the idea (by interpreting it, providing the idea's meaning and modifying that meaning). And if the idea germinates, by drawing upon human energy and imagination, it changes the social and political culture where it grows.

Propagation, therefore, whether of seeds or of ideas, is a transaction, an exchange. In exchange for the soil's nourishment, the flourishing seed changes the landscape. In exchange for acceptance (via interpretation and modification), the flourishing idea changes the social and political landscape. In horticulture, such a relationship of exchange is called *symbiosis,* "the relationship of two or more different organisms in a close association that may be but is not necessarily of benefit to each."[11] Propaganda, the process of human propagation of ideas and actions by *fortuna* and intent, is symbiotic. Both those who originate, modify, and transmit ideas and those who receive, modify, and act (or do not act) on those ideas are propagators in a political symbiosis that "may be but is not necessarily of benefit to each."

A noted sociologist, Georg Simmel, described the type of relationship we are talking about. He wrote of *sociation,* the cultivation of social relationships that help people define, and thereby do, what they want. We associate daily with both real persons (parents, friends, etc.) and imagined ones (Santa Claus, Ken and Barbie), and learn from them the content of what we should do and the form of how we should do it. Parents, for instance, offer tips about what to do generally (how to behave in conversation) and in concrete situations (arguing with a policeman). A TV soap opera heroine demonstrates attitudes toward sexuality in general, and how to handle specific encounters ("Erica" in "All My Children" is notorious for this). Sometimes real and fictional persons intend to teach us what to do and how to do it (we expect that when sitting in the classroom or viewing *Hamlet* on stage). But frequently others who are significant in our eyes suggest indirectly the content and form of behavior for us rather than teach direct lessons. When we learn indi-rectly via suggestion to size up situations, define them, and try to cope with them, the lessons result from suasion. *Suasion* is the root term for the process of sociative communi-cation, of how we are "swayed" through social learning. We learn through sociation how to learn—often through "play-learning" (such as "pretend like" games in childhood)—and through that learning we use our suasive powers to choose, or to allow someone else to influence our choices. In any case, suasion suggests that we can act and react to ideas in different ways.

Beliefs, values, and acts we learn through suasion are often "caught, not taught," to use a figure of speech. Ideas that we acquire by suasion, as we do in learning a large por-tion of our everyday behavior, are those sometimes borne by the wind of chance *(fortuna)* or deliberately "scattered over the landscape." Depending upon our unique individual cultures, we provide seedbeds of support or rejection. There are, of course, persons, orga-nizations, news sources, and others who deliberately try to sway us. This is surely the case in politics. In contrast with being swayed by informal suggestions, that is, sociative sua-sion, we are targets of formal *persuasion*. The prefix *per* is significant when added to *suasion*. It indicates, as dictionaries say, to "cause," "lead over," "press forward." No longer are we swayed by suggestion and indirection, but by urging and direction. Here, to use our horticultural metaphor, is propagation by the direct planting of the seed in selected soil, not via wind/water-borne movement or sowing by Johnny Appleseed.

From what we have said it would be easy to draw a distinction between suasion and persuasion. In suasion, we could say, whether a person heeds, plays with (interprets), and responds to an idea depends on the individual's image of what the idea suggests. Does the young girl model herself on Barbie's suggested lifestyle? That depends on the little girl. In persuasion, whether a person heeds, ponders, and responds to an idea depends on whether those transmitting the message "get through" (say, by dressing up the idea in ap-pealing ways, having a rock star like Michael Jackson endorse it, etc.). Does the young girl model herself on Barbie's promoted lifestyle? That depends on the promotion. Such a contrast between suasion and persuasion, however, would lead us astray. A student of persuasion, Charles Larson, points out that "*all* persuasion is self-persuasion—we are rarely persuaded unless we *participate* in the process."[12] Hence, whether in suasion or persuasion, each person's individual culture, or seedbed, plays a key part in influencing whether the idea germinates. If enough people participate in suasive learning, the idea be-comes a part, sometimes temporarily and other times permanently, of the larger ideocul-ture, since the idea has found ways of "chaining out" and becoming accepted. If not, it atrophies and disappears.

Viewed in this respect, propagation, and by extension propaganda, derives as much from the culture (i.e., people) as from the source of the seeds, be the source fortuitous or intentional seedings (i.e., messages of suasive or persuasive ideas). Thus, people may re-sist an intentional propagandistic appeal, saying to the pitchman, "Forget it; I'm not buy-ing your pitch." Such *contrasuasion,* or "sales resistance," is common. (Just ask officials at the United States Mint, who in 1979 issued the heavily promoted Susan B. An-thony dollar, a coin that was to make the dollar bill obsolete; seen a Susan B. Anthony lately?) Sometimes, promoters encountering contrasuasion "get the message" and quickly adjust their appeals to meet the resistance. (Remember when Coca-Cola tried to abandon their classic formula and sell New Coke?) Such *transuasion* occurred in Texas in 1989. Seeking in part to change the state's image so as to attract out-of-state tourists, officials proposed The Friendly State as the new logo for the Texas automobile license plate. Talk radio shows, letters to the editor in newspapers, and barbershop conversations voiced outrage at abandoning the cherished Lone Star State motto. Officials compromised and a mutual accommodation produced auto tags with no motto. Terms like *contrasuasion* and *transuasion*, however jargony, do help us understand the suasive process, how both producers and consumers of messages are part of the complex ways in which we seek and find guidance in learning reliable dispositions of thinking about, and acting in, the world.

The Propaganda Habit: "Just Say No" Versus Suspending Disbelief

Hence, in dealing with the propagation of ideas and actions—propaganda—we must not overlook self-suasion and contrasuasion no matter what is the persuasive intent and message of the promoter, advertiser, public relations specialist, or other propagandist. Propagation involves individuals, alone and in concert, as seedbeds deciding what ideas and images propagate or do not. In their everyday lives, people develop different patterns, routines, or habits that they employ again and again in responding to ideas, proposals, problems, novel situations, and so on. We will call these routines *habits of suasion*, that is, means regularly used in adjusting to messages by self-suasion and/or self-persuasion. What are these habits?

Some people, probably not a large portion of the populace, develop the *habit of science*. They endeavor to reach decisions on the basis of identification and examination of evidence. Suppose a parent pondering what to buy a twin daughter and son for Christmas discovers a newspaper article reporting a psychologist's finding that the Barbie doll has detrimental effects on little girls (say, for instance, produces fat anxiety), or the GI Joe doll inclines young boys to admire violence. The concerned parent trots off to the library and consults a variety of articles and books on what toys do to children. Weighing the pros and cons, the parent decides on the basis of the evidence accumulated and analyzed to avoid such dolls, buying instead alternative dolls such as the Happy to Be Me doll for the girl, and an environmentally conscious forest ranger doll for the boy. In other words, the parent attempts to decide something in the best interest of the children on the basis of sound behavioral scientific data and rationally chosen criteria (it is not good for children to overvalue physical beauty or violence). The children, of course, may respond with a contrasuasive message on Christmas morning ("Why didn't I get Barbie or GI Joe?"), causing a quick transuasive adjustment on the part of the parent who desired to propagate a valued message without consulting the kids! However, the habit of science is one approach to deciding things, and indeed to deciding what messages one wishes to propagate. Although it is difficult, it has the merit of trying to establish conceptual and empirical grounds for choosing one thing over another, using principles of logic and evidence, and calculating what alternative results might be obtained and which results are most desirable.

The habit of science is obviously demanding and time consuming, sometimes cumbersome, and as the case of the disgruntled children may indicate, does not always produce happy results. As a habit of suasion, it may be difficult for many people to sustain. Some people instead feel more comfortable with the *habit of rhetorical argument*. A search for good reasons to accept or reject an idea takes priority over empirical evidence. That search may take place in a monologue as one argues with one's self, in a dialogue trying arguments out on others, or by listening to the rhetoric of other people. Let us assume that the above parent's children have grown up and are ready to select a college. Both are National Merit Scholars, so both are highly recruited by major universities. How do they reach a decision? Perhaps they have the habit of science as suggested by parental example. But assume each follows the habit of rhetorical argument. Each comes up with good reasons to select a particular university. They can also discuss the matter. Finally, assume college recruiters appear, each making a rhetorical argument for the benefits of the particular school. To be sure, the argument may contain facts about school rankings, facilities, financial aid, faculty qualifications, and so on, but the rhetoric consists overall of strategic assertions, perhaps drawing a critical response, perhaps not. The facts are "framed" in the logic of argument rather than the logic of science. Typically, such a rhetorical pitch is an attempt at persuasion through portraying for the prospective student the benefits, real or imaginary, that will accrue from attending that particular school. This may include all the rhetorical resources—flattery, cajolery, appeal to emotion, identification, indeed all the tricks of the rhetorician's argumentative trade. Here the habit of suasion that is appealed to uses the rhetorical arts rather than the rigors of scientific analysis. This is not to say that it is necessarily inferior to scientific inquiry, only that it is a very different kind of communicative habit used to make decisions. The core of the rhetorician's skill is argument and not evidence, but the tradition of argumentative advocacy goes back to figures such as Socrates and Demosthenes, formidable arguers indeed.

People habitually inclined to science suspend judgments until they have weighed the empirical evidence; those inclined to rhetorical argument ponder reasons and the intent of those making arguments. Both habits involve some degree of rigor in sorting wheat from chaff. But for some other people critical thinking seems to play no part at all, either in considering ideas or in propagating them. There are people who hear and pass on rumors, sometimes vicious, without thinking whether they are true or false, or whether they will damage another's reputation; who are swayed by the emotional pleas for money by an unscrupulous TV evangelist; who are duped by a deliberate campaign smear of one candidate against another; who believe advertising campaigns saying that now is the time to buy for a once in a lifetime opportunity; and so on. Such people accept and propagate messages without submitting them or their sources to scientific investigation or rhetorical criticism. For many people there is a willingness to believe, a readiness to trust "what everybody's saying," "common sense," and what "they say." This is the *habit of credulity*, whereby people make leaps of faith at the slightest provocation and on the most uncertain and possibly biased of grounds. Such people commonly seem to be characterized by their ready openness to suasion and their lack of critical acumen. They are unfamiliar with and unresponsive to scientific presentations as a way of deciding, and are similarly unacquainted with sophisticated rhetorical argumentation. So they get into the habit of being credulous, responding to suasive communication without demanding scientific scrutiny or rhetorical criticism. Those who cultivate the habit of credulity are especially amenable to persuasive messages that circumvent critical thought and appeal to magical or mythical thinking that requires the suppression of doubt.

Building upon the romantic poet Samuel Taylor Coleridge, who wrote that poetry should "transfer from our inward nature a human interest and a semblance of truth sufficient to procure for those shadows of imagination that willing suspension of disbelief for the moment, which constitutes poetic faith," Milton Richards has commented on the workings of one form of propaganda, advertising:

> There is, I submit, evidence on all sides of the ways in which we practice in our daily lives the willing suspension of disbelief. It is part of "our inward nature," is it not, to exhibit constantly a tendency to believe? Advertising people seek always for the small "semblance of truth" that will "procure for [their] shadows of imagination—called advertisements—the willing suspension of disbelief" on the part of consumers without which advertising cannot succeed. It is for this reason that advertising works, and not because of some manipulation by wizards in their Madison Avenue lairs.[13]

Richards speaks of the "beguiling poetry of advertising," a poetry that as much as the ad's surface content sways people through the "truism" that "people do not act on reality; rather they act upon their own perceptions of reality." If people wish to believe in magical or mythical realities, then their desires for credulity can and will be discovered and appealed to. In suasive transactions, the beguiler needs those who are willing to be beguiled in order to succeed at beguiling.

It is our contention that propaganda germinates, flourishes, and thrives best with those who practice the habit of credulity. The habits of science and of rhetorical argument, although often congenial to promotional appeals, are more hostile seedbeds for propaganda's seeds than is an ideoculture that cultivates the habit of credulity. Credible "semblances of truth" often provide meanings in people's everyday lives that they are reluctant to question. It simply seems better and easier for them to suspend disbelief than engage in scientific or rhetorical skepticism and inquiry. "Despite the experiences of life that teach us to disbelieve the poetry and fiction of our existence," writes Richards, we suspend that disbelief; we don't "just say 'No'." In an ideoculture wherein propaganda becomes the form of communication that appeals to the widespread habit of credulity, we are more likely to be asked to say, and apt to respond by saying, yes.

To put this another way, when we are all engaged in the process of suasive communication, we have to decide (or allow it to be decided for us) how we are going to approach making choices. Since presumably choices (where we go to school, what we buy, whom we marry) matter to us, we engage in pragmatic learning about how to decide. Some few of us choose the method of science, or learning through inquiry. Others, again perhaps a relatively few, find congenial the method of rhetorical advocacy, or learning through argument. But many others prefer *learning through propaganda*, allowing their choices to be guided by the "beguiling poetry" of suasive messages that appeal to credulous belief. In that sense, the new propaganda is a distinctive and beguiling modern form of suasive communication that cultivates and propagates the widespread habit of credulous belief, with enormous consequences for both the individual who learns from it and the ideoculture that values and practices that kind of learning rather than more critical modes of inquiry.

OFF WITH THE OLD (PROPAGANDA),
ON WITH THE NEW (PROPAGANDA)

We have compared propaganda to the propagation of ideas and actions metaphorically akin to the propagation of seeds (or of animals for that matter), seeds spread by chance, planting, or scattering in cultural climes that nurture or retard germination and growth. We argued that an ideoculture that favors the practice of credulity is most congenial for the propagation of this form of communication. Yet the credulous have always been with us, as has the attempt to successfully propagate messages. The premodern history of the world abounds with the use of propaganda. So why talk about the "new" propaganda? What distinguishes the new from, presumably, something that preceded it? In Chapter 1 we will discuss the history and development of propaganda and elaborate on the general characteristics of propaganda. Here, however, it is appropriate to consider a few of the features that set the new propaganda off from much of what we will discuss in Chapter 1. It is our argument here that in the modern age, propaganda has become increasingly integral to our way of life, to the extent that as a form of communication it is now the model form of suasive learning, appropriate for and distinctive to the civilization in which we live.

Alfred Landon was the Republican candidate for president of the United States in 1936. He lost in a landslide to incumbent Franklin D. Roosevelt, carrying only the states of Maine and Vermont. Years later an interviewer asked Landon what he recalled about that defeat. The former Kansas governor pondered a moment, then told a story about an old farmer. After a Kansas tornado swept over the farmer's house, destroying everything, but leaving the old man sitting in his rocking chair, the farmer began to laugh. His wife, who also had survived the disaster, said, "What are you laughing at, you ol' coot?" The farmer replied, "The completeness of it all." We can borrow Landon's lament from the old farmer to describe a distinguishing feature of the new propaganda, that is, "the completeness of it all." For propaganda today is complete. It surrounds us like the air we breathe. Propaganda is everywhere, is all pervasive and all penetrating. To live in contemporary times is to be showered with the seeds of suasive ideas, seeds encountered by chance, seeds planted in us, seeds scattered over us.

Walk through a shopping mall. Passersby wear T-shirts touting all manner of soft drinks, beers, amusement parks, restaurants, universities, rock stars—even political candidates and causes. Turn as they pass and find other products advertised on the bottoms of their jeans. Billed caps display logos of not only athletic teams but also hardware stores, paints, tool sets, construction firms, tractor manufacturers, and so on. The people who walk the malls are themselves "carriers" of propaganda. The telephone rings in the home. Is it a friend, family member, or someone else you like to talk to? Perhaps. But often it is a voice (often recorded) soliciting for a charity, campaigning for a cause or candidate, selling aluminum siding for the house, or offering a great bargain on carpet cleaning while "we're in your neighborhood." The mail arrives. There may be welcome letters from friends and relatives, but likely much more: solicitations from a host of interests, charitable, commercial, political. Even the envelope or the stamp cancel may have a slogan included. Radio, television, newspapers, magazines, even academic journals are all vehicles for propaganda as much as for entertainment and public information. Indeed, such publications are partially supported by advertisers, publicists, and others interested in propagating a message. Suppose one tries to escape this daily shower of ideocultural seeds, say by going to a movie. What do the lead characters of the film do? They drink from Coca-Cola cans, wear Air Jordan sweatshirts, drop in at McDonald's, fly United Airlines, and drive Hertz rental cars, all examples of *product placement*, wherein the moviemakers are paid by interested parties to feature their product or service in the film. (Products given a negative image can be excluded: when the film *Rain Man* was shown on some airlines, they cut out the scene in which Dustin Hoffman's character refused to get on a commercial airplane, citing crash statistics). Finally, try to get away from all this to the unspoiled wilderness. There on the hiking trail is a sign informing campers that all this majestic beauty is managed by the National Park Service, and as you enter the park you are given propaganda extolling the work of the service and see icons (such as the now retired Smokey Bear) urging that only you can prevent forest fires. Once you begin to look around and realize how much a part of our lives propaganda is, you become impressed by the completeness of it all.

It was not always this way. Propaganda so all pervasive and penetrating in everyday life as to be taken for granted is a relatively recent phenomenon. As we will see in Chapter 1, forms of propaganda have always been with us. But today propaganda is not simply *with* us; to a large degree propaganda *is* us. This is not to say that everything that we think, say, or do is propaganda. Rather, what we emphasize is that the volume and sophistication of the new propaganda is so vast, and growing, that we increasingly take it for granted as natural and, thereby, we find it exceedingly difficult to distinguish what is propaganda from what is not. Thus we often even fail to contemplate how influential propaganda is on our lives, how much we rely on it for learning, and the extent to which it defines the modern ideoculture in which we live.

Observers of recent history have long noted the growing importance of propaganda, and a large literature on the subject now exists. This book does differ from much of that invaluable previous work in at least one important respect. Heretofore, the feature of propaganda most frequently emphasized by scholars has been that of intentionality, that is, propaganda defined as communication intentionally designed and propagated to have a desired effect (often subversive and nefarious) upon an audience, and executed with more or less the desired impact (e.g., sales campaign to induce people to buy a product succeeds in increasing purchases). Below are typical scholarly definitions of propaganda we have gathered to illustrate the "intentional" approach:

> "the deliberate and systematic attempt . . . to achieve a response that furthers the desired intent of the propagandist"[14]
>
> "an attempt to influence opinion and conduct"[15]
>
> "the typical propaganda situation is that A by one method or another communicates with B so as to tend to affect B's behavior"[16]
>
> "any attempt to persuade anyone to a belief or to a form of action"[17]
>
> "the attempt to affect the personalities and control the behavior of individuals toward ends considered unscientific or of doubtful value in a society at a given time"[18]

With the new propaganda, however, there is a blurring of intent and effects. These older conceptions of propaganda tend to be unidirectional, using a "hypodermic" or "billiard ball" metaphor: Propaganda begins with intent, those intentions are introduced into society, the needle is injected or the balls are struck, and the impact is made. A major difficulty with these definitions is that the intentions of propaganda sources are not always clear in either intent or impact. Certainly Mattel wished to sell the Barbie doll, but was it also the intent to promote a lifestyle young girls should adopt as well? Seeking reelection in 1940, President Franklin Roosevelt reiterated that he would not send "American boys" to a foreign war. Was the intent of his message to win votes, to convince combatants in the war in Europe they could expect no U.S. intervention, to mask a plan to get America into war, to placate pacifists, or what? Intentions are not only ambiguous, they are often mixed, multiple, and sometimes contradictory. If a surly, scowling waitress serves a patron a cup of coffee, slopping a good portion into the saucer, slaps down the bill, then says ''Have a nice day!'' what motive is one to suspect? Intentions are often concealed—witness the serpent's professed intentions in hustling Adam and Eve! Certainly intentions can change. A suitor courting a date may intend merely to have a good time, swell the ego, or even guarantee a bedmate for the evening; but if love blossoms, marriage may become the intention. It is often the case that people are not at all clear as to what they in fact do intend. Finally, whatever one's intentions in trying to sway others, the fact that people constitute the seedbed that promotes or inhibits the germination of ideas can produce unintended, unexpected consequences.

With these ideas in mind, think again of how intentions are only a part, and sometimes the least important part, of the propagation of communication. What is in all cases really important is what communications propagate: What is the outcome, the *consequence,* of what is said and done? Consider a fictional example from a movie entitled *The Fisher King* (1991). In that film, Jeff Bridges plays a late-night talk radio show host who is a master of the type of banter with callers that many people seem to enjoy—baiting them, insulting them, agreeing with them that people they hate are rotten, and so on. As he is about to go off the air late one night, a frequent caller calls again. The young man, named Edwin, often calls to tell Bridges of his troubled life. This evening, he had gone to a fashionable upscale night spot and had seen a girl he immediately had fallen in love with. Bridges flippantly and contemptuously tells Edwin that the people who frequent such a place are ''yuppies'' (young urban professionals), people who are self-centered and arrogant and would find him contemptible. Edwin is crushed, and Bridges, in a hurry to quit, cuts him off. The show host arises the next day to discover that after their radio talk Edwin had gone to that yuppie hangout and killed seven people with a shotgun, including the beautiful girl he spoke of, then turned the gun on himself. The point of this story is that action has consequences, and often consequences that you did not anticipate or intend. Once you do something, often fortuitous and unplanned things follow in its path, outcomes that may surprise you and even backfire on you, and in this case, get you into trouble you surely didn't intend. The talk show host didn't intend to get those people killed, but his offhand comments to an unstable personality had consequences that were terrible and could not be undone.

Consider another example that is drawn directly from the world of propaganda. When Coca-Cola in 1985 introduced New Coke, the avowed intention was to promote Coke sales, which apparently the powers-that-be at Coca-Cola thought would increase with this new product. What no one seemed able to anticipate was that many people liked the old Coke, and quickly they were getting *feedback* (contrasuasion) that people demanded the retention and availability of the older version of Coca-Cola. The soft drink company, which had for some time employed the propaganda pitch Coke is It!, quickly relented (transuasion) by repackaging the old Coke in new bottles as Coca-Cola Classic while at the same time trying to sell the new Coke the consumers didn't much like (prompting the amused president of rival Pepsi Cola to ask, does that mean ''Coke are it''?). More seriously, Pepsi countered with ''comparative'' ads showing people trying New Coke and Pepsi, and of course preferring Pepsi. Although New Coke sales have steadily dropped since its introduction, the unintended consequence has a positive side for the company: Coca-Cola Classic leads the soft drink industry with 20 percent of total sales. There was even a lame attempt to reattach the fig leaf by Coca-Cola executives who claimed that the introduction of New Coke was a brilliant marketing strategy to promote interest in the varieties of Coke. Many observers were skeptical as to whether such cunning intentions ascribed after the fiasco were present at the creation, since often intentions are pointed to after the fact (''I never intended to defraud the IRS''; ''I intended New Coke to flop in order to hype interest in Old Coke''; ''We never dreamed that I would get pregnant''; ''I never dreamed that Edwin would go on a shooting spree''). The road to hell is indeed paved with good (and bad) intentions, simply because so much of what we say and do propagates messages with consequences we neither fully understand nor control. A good bit of what happens in society is unintended in the sense that no one could either anticipate or control the consequences of Edwin, New Coke, or Barbie. Intentions not only are a part of the communication process, they also fail to tell us what is ultimately important: what changes are wrought through communication, producing what results, with what meaning for the conduct of our lives?

To understand the new propaganda we must stress the *consequences* of social actions as much as the intentions that underlie them. If we think of communications as a social process, we then realize we cannot fully, or even adequately, explain why propaganda has become so powerful. For the power of the new propaganda lies in its potential for consequences, whether clearly intended or not. And those consequences are very much influenced by the people who attend to those messages—whether because the messages reach them by chance, or by being targeted to them (planted), or by being scattered (broadcast) across the population. In an insightful article, J. Michael Sproule contrasts public persuasion in the pre-twentieth-century with that of today.[19] A major difference he finds is that in an earlier era persuasive efforts were directed at elite audiences composed of interested, informed, knowledgeable persons. Speakers, orators, and persuaders of all kinds appealed to audiences by offering arguments, reasons, facts, and logic. Persuaders relied upon their reputations for expertise, reliability, and candor to sway people. Intentions, good or bad, counted for a great deal.

But with the advent of such modern innovations as mass media (mass circulation newspapers and magazines, radio, television, etc.), jet travel, growing and migrating populations, mass democratic politics, and consumer economies, mass publics and audiences replaced elite publics and audiences as seedbeds of propagation. Mass audiences, although by no means passive, are not overly well informed, display sporadic interest in politics, have little direct political experience, are caught up in everyday routines of producing (children as well as goods and services), working, and consuming. They are busy people. As Sproule notes, mass audiences respond to conclusions, not reasons; to slogans, not complexities; to images, not ideas; to pleasing, attractive personages, not expertise or intellect; and to facts created *through* suasion, not suasion *based on* facts:

> . . . no longer aiming to activate commercial and political elites, modern communication is beamed to the harried modern consumer who, among other limited selections of the day, hurriedly chooses from among a few truncated commercial and political images.[20]

The very fact that the mass audience is active rather than passive (even the so-called couch potato chooses to switch channels and select what she or he wants to watch on television) and harried rather than reflective renders the mass culture for propaganda an ephemeral nutrient sustaining and retarding intended results. The shelf life of products, political figures, clothing styles, automotive designs, popular TV shows, major news stories, pop groups, or anything else *consumed* by mass audiences is brief and transient. Modern people have often been characterized as consumers of existence. Unless there are sustained efforts to keep personae and products in the public eye, they become yesterday's interests. Modernity is a condition of constant innovation and change. In that condition, propaganda becomes the dominant mode of social learning for all parties to the communication process (producers, publicists, advertisers, consumers, voters, etc.), a way of learning that is so often found because it is so often sought, and is available and useful. Propaganda is popular precisely because it is truncated, beguiling, and interesting to those many who consume communication for its pragmatic purposes. Propaganda is the most powerful means of modern social learning simply because it is widely understandable, appeals to social interests, and helps us learn how to cope with the constant presence of innovation and change.

The new propaganda, then, is pervasive instead of sporadic, complete instead of partial, dynamic rather than static. In the new propaganda intentions are ambiguous, mixed, sometimes contradictory, often concealed, and shifting; and since they are often tied in to organizational purposes, it is hard to pin intentions to a particular individual. Further, the new propaganda addresses ephemeral and changing mass interests. The dialectic of suasion in the modern world is an ongoing one of adaptation to ever-changing circumstances, with both propagandists and propagandees seeking and finding adaptive messages, propagating the practice of propagandizing itself. Finally, the new propaganda arouses and addresses the *poetic imagination* in all of us, the desire to allow our imaginations to soar unbounded by cold facts and reasons. Much more so than propaganda in former times, the new propaganda operates through what we have already described as the suspension of disbelief. It strikes a responsive chord in the poetic scale of our beings, without the necessity of reliance on scientific or rhetorical logics that might produce doubt rather than belief. "Believing is a disposition," says W. V. Quine.[21] The new propaganda thrives in cultures where that disposition is central to the operational code, the modal ways of learning and doing. That disposition, in turn, flourishes where poetic imaginations are addressed in dramatic, entertaining ways. Today, as Sproule comments, pure entertainment is a "staple" of efforts to sway people, not a mere appendage as when speakers introduce their remarks with a joke or monarchs surround themselves with pomp and ceremony. "In the contemporary milieu of sloganistic conclusions and images, appeals presented as entertainment will serve as well or better than ones oriented to conveying information," writes Sproule, and "today's political rhetoric is conveyed chiefly through forms in which entertainment figures are central, in snappy paid 'spot' ads and in short news clips often highlighting the dramatic or human interest aspects of politics."[22]

The new propaganda is not so much a matter of deceptive communication nor informative communication as it is communications play, social learning through a combination of poetic and pragmatic messages that appeal to our imagination and our interests. For great masses of people, then, propaganda has an evocative power denied to scientific and rhetorical communication. Indeed, in the modern world, power is increasingly defined as the ability to understand, appeal to, and mobilize social learning through the use of communication, especially powerful forms of communication such as propaganda. If socially necessary communications—campaigning for office, selling products, promoting a movie, convincing students to come to a particular school—can be presented as play, the interests of all parties to the transaction are more likely to be well served, and imaginations aroused and focused, if the communication is aesthetically pleasing. In such a world, power accrues to those who know how to use the new propaganda.

In conclusion, the new propaganda is a manifestation of what sociologist Hugh D. Duncan called the "dramatic model of sociation," a major form of which he called the "drama of courtship."[23] Our poetic imaginations frame ourselves, our everyday lives, and the world around us as if we are in a drama. We live out stories, play roles on a social stage, act with other players in daily tragedies, comedies, burlesques, farces, and melodramas—ever courting, or attempting to influence, one another. And through such poetic experience we learn how to suspend critical disbelief learning the habit of selectively seeing and caring about what we find pleasing and useful. Our beloved has no facial blemishes, no oversized ears or nose, no receding hairline, no crooked teeth; our enemies are so malign as to hate dogs, cats, and little children. I will always be young, will always be desirable, will never age and die. Because of my desires to believe, I am willing to be courted, and to court, those messengers and messages that tell me the stories I want to hear, and assure me that my own drama is a good play. The new propaganda capitalizes on that courting disposition and exploits, no matter what the intentions may be, all dramatic trappings—actors and actresses, stage, props, lines, and plots. In the new propaganda, "the play's the thing," to borrow from Shakespeare.

The new propaganda effectively expresses not only our sense of drama, but also our expectation of drama—that our lives can be exciting, that we are destined to have good things, that we are vital, sensual, and even immortal, that we are doing the right thing. Further, the new propaganda caters to our desire for dramatically framed actions and explanations. Propagandists find it useful to tell their story in dramatic terms in order to get their message across, because dramatic representations are entertaining, insightful, and playful, thereby likely having a more widespread and lasting impression than more painful forms of communication (such as school!). The histrionic resources of drama are at the core of what propagandists do, what propagandees seek, and how the propagandizing process works. TV advertising, movie promotion, public relations campaigns, and so on are all at heart languages of popular drama, propagating a story (such as the minidramas of the spot ad that offer us parables on how to use products to make us admirable, prosperous, and desirable) that is at once poetic and pragmatic. The successful use of dramatic communications in propagandizing activities is now a permanent feature of the new propaganda, something that makes propaganda one of the major modern languages of communication.

PROPAGANDA AS THE PALAVER OF CONTEMPORARY POLITICS

Although the new propaganda pervades and envelopes our social world so that it seems to be the communication environment rather than a portion of it, recall that we said earlier that propaganda is not *everything*. To set the new propaganda off from other means of communicating, let us consider various ways we talk with one another. Note that we say "with" one another, not "to" one another. For talk, be it informal chattering, a formal speech, or even mass communication such as a TV ad or movie preview, involves an exchange, that is, some degree of reciprocity. In conversation or oratory, a person talks, others listen, and, even as listeners, talk back by being attentive or inattentive. Gestures, nods, frowns, smiles, and other nonverbal means "talk" as well as do comments, questions, and oral expressions. Barbie and Ken advertised on television to an unseen audience of millions yield a delayed response—in the form of sales or nonsales—that is the transuasional two-way street of the Barbie Message. Similarly, a president of the United States addresses the nation on television; citizens talk back via public opinion polls, letters of opposition or support, discussion or nondiscussion of the speech, indeed even by not watching and by ignoring a president trying hard to be taken seriously. We "talk" to each other both intimately and remotely, and get and give "feedback" to the eternal conversation we as social beings are engaged in all our lives.

In what ways, then, do we talk with one another? Political scientist David V. J. Bell has noted that potentially all talk affects others; when it does, he writes, it by definition has political overtones and, thereby, is political talk. Bell describes three forms of political talk.[24] One is *power talk,* but it is more aptly labeled *force talk.* Here an individual, group, organization, or other "talker" wants another to do or not to do something. The message, according to Bell, is phrased as "If you do X, I will do Y." Implied in the utterance is that the *I* has the resources to promise or threaten the *you* into compliance. In short, one person can force another to comply. "Memorize my lectures and talk (write) them back to me on the exam and I will give you an A in the course; fail to do so and you get an F." "Obey the law or go to jail" carries a more obvious political sanction.

Sometimes people have such complete faith in a talker that promises or threats are unnecessary. "Do X" or "Don't do X" are sufficient statements. Such *authority talk* derives from an unquestioned devotion to authority. Consider the French emperor Napoleon or Nazi Germany's Adolf Hitler at the zenith of their respective regimes. So devoted were many of their followers that any wish from either was a literal command to the populace. Or think back to our old Christmas friend, Santa Claus, during an earlier era when children regarded him as an omniscient, omnipresent observer of their behavior. The words of a popular Christmas ditty spoke the message of authority talk: "Better not cry, better not pout" for "he's making a list and checking it twice, going to find out who's naughty and nice." Beware; "Santa Claus is coming to town."

Napoleon and Hitler are dead, and Santa all jolly and forgiving, not stern. But we still encounter a great deal of authority talk. A reputation for expertise and popularity derived from it—acquired in, say, movies, professional sports, or rock music—provides authority to speak on other matters, including political matters. Athletes, TV weathercasters, movie stars, and other celebrities attempt to associate their popular authority ("This is good because you all know me and can believe me that it is") with not only products and services, but also causes, cultural events, and political candidates. Indeed, Ronald Reagan began as a movie star, who then utilized his considerable celebrity to endorse products (General Electric) and then candidates (Barry Goldwater), paving the way for his successful effort to become a political authority himself, as candidate, governor of California, and president.

As the above examples indicate, force and authority talk can be enlisted to propagate ideas and actions. Still, the talk emphasized in propaganda is usually neither that of force nor authority per se, but rather *influence talk*—David Bell's third form. "If you do X, *you* will [get, have, feel, experience, gain, etc.] Y'' is the message of influence. Unlike force talk where the *I* has the capacity to reward or punish, in influence talk the *you* can supply Y but the *I* cannot. The choice is up to the *you*. That is a key point, for influence talk does involve choice. ''Memorize my lectures or fail'' is at best a hollow choice; ''don't cry, don't pout'' leaves no choice for the youngster's childlike faith in Santa's omnipotence. ''*If* you memorize,'' ''*if* you behave,'' ''*if* you vote for me,'' then you will get an A, Christmas gifts, or a reduction in income taxes, leaves it up to *you* without force or command. Rather than suasive force or suasive authority, the suasion of influence emphasizes that you can choose good things for yourself if you will only make the right choice. Rather than the voice of force that propagates the message ''Do as I say or else,'' or the voice of authority that says ''Do as I say because I'm to be believed and obeyed,'' the voice of influence says ''If you choose to do as I say, your choice will be a wise one that will pay off for you.'' Traditionally, propaganda talk can involve all three messages. A military ruler can use the mass media to help enforce martial law by communicating to people that if they oppose such rule they will be shot. A retired politician may go on the air in days before an election to endorse a candidate, attempting to associate his past authority with the new aspirant to office. But a moment's reflection also makes clear that *in the new propaganda, influence talk has gained a new primacy.*

As *primarily* influence talk, the new propaganda brings both *I* and *you,* both the seed and the culture, into prominent roles in propagating ideas and actions. In horticulture neither seed nor culture alone is sufficient. Seed and culture, mutually reinforcing growth, become one. In influence talk *I* and *you* become one, that is, *we.* In this respect influence talk incorporates precisely the type of persuasion (explicit shaping of beliefs) and suasion (implicit suspension of disbelief) we described previously. One writer on propaganda, Paul Kecskemeti, puts it thus:

> In other words, persuasion requires, ideally speaking, complete emotional and affective resonance between the persuader and the audience. As the propagandist develops his master theme, ''There are the sources of your deprivations, and here are the means for removing them,'' he must not encounter any emotional or affective resistance.[25]

And, emphasizing that what we call the *I* and *you* become *we,* he says ''the propagandist voices the propagandees' own feelings.'' For, in language that sets propaganda apart from force/authority talk,

> ''Resonance'' implies that the recipient does not experience the master theme or propaganda myth as a belief imposed upon him by an outside authority to which he is required or committed to defer. To be persuasive, the propaganda theme has to be perceived as *coming from within.* The propagandist's ideal role in relation to the propagandee is that of alter ego, someone giving expression to the recipient's own concerns, tensions, aspirations, and hopes.[26]

What sets the new propaganda off from being *everything,* thus, is that now the dominant form of talk in propagating ideas and actions is influence talk. Influence talk comes in many varieties; one variety is particularly present in the new propaganda. Any form of talk consists of symbols, that is, something—a word, gesture, picture, object, person, and so on—that stands for, or represents, something else. The word *dog* represents a four-footed canine. Ken and Barbie represent dolls, lifestyles, and profits. The ideas, objects, places, or whatever symbols represent can be specific or ambiguous. A dog is a dog, but

Barbie's referent is more ambiguous and may be one or all of the three mentioned in the above sentence. Whether the symbols are specific or vague in what they represent, they compose, singularly or in combination, talk, or to use the American vernacular, *palaver*.

PALAVER AS THE STYLE OF THE NEW PROPAGANDA

Talk itself has contrasting styles. That is, someone may speak to us in terse, clipped, brief utterances. "We have known since man first landed on the moon that it is not made of green cheese." That is a succinct way of saying what could be expressed in a long, rambling, qualified, utterance replete with confusing allusions. Talk, influence talk included, thus consists of specific and/or ambiguous symbols couched in succinct and/or confusing styles.[27] Using these contrasts in symbols and styles we can say that propaganda as influence talk comes in four major varieties:

- *Informative:* succinct, specific comments.
- *Evaluative:* extended, perhaps confusing, specific utterances.
- *Expressive:* succinct, but ambiguous statements.
- *Palaver:* extended, often confusing, messages.

"Congressman Clark is 28 years old; the U.S. Constitution sets a minimum age of 35 to be president; the congressman cannot seek the office now." The message is to the point and informative. People may or may not pay attention, so its propagation is not guaranteed. In either event, Clark is ineligible for the presidency at the moment. Clark ages 10 years and a political organization distributes a 30-page document opposing his candidacy for president; it characterizes him as a communist fascist, free-trading protectionist, workaholic malingerer, gay womanizer, ascetic libertine, and on and on. The document is, in this instance, contradictory and, hence, confusing. But even if all the contradictions were removed, its extended account of why one should not support Clark is evaluative. "We are the world, we are the children," sing Clark supporters, expressing in vague, terse lyrics what they are, but informing us little about Clark's qualifications, an example of expressive propaganda. Finally, Clark wins. In his inaugural address—lasting 45 minutes—he rambles on in vague ways that his administration will seek the "New Society: retaining in millions of ways (unspecified) the heritage of the old, the future of the past, and the past of the present!" That is palaver, defined as dictionaries do, as *talk that charms or beguiles*.

Just as propaganda incorporates force and authority talk into an overarching form of influence talk, so does the new propaganda employ informative, evaluative, and expressive messages, but as adjuncts *primarily* of palaver. The palaver emphasis thus joins the characteristics—pervasiveness, intended and unintended consequences, dramas of courtship—that distinguish the new propaganda. One of the first persons to examine propaganda in a scholarly way, Harold Lasswell, writing in 1927 of earlier forms of propaganda, said, "Democracy has proclaimed the dictatorship of palaver, and the technique of dictating to the dictator is named propaganda."[28] Techniques of new propaganda practice, exalt, and deify palaver while courting, beguiling, and charming people in their everyday lives. Palaver does so with people's willing cooperation, and often at their own instigation. For palaver is the form of talk that engages us in profusions of big talk, circular reasoning, circumlocutions, jawboning and babbling, parleying and cajoling, speaking in riddles, talking our way out of trouble, and so on endlessly. The word *palaver* is apparently derived from the Latin *parabola* (parable, speech, circle), connoting the profusion of talking. In the modern age, palavering is the kind of talk appropriate to the conduct of the new propaganda.

Political, cultural, and commercial palaver thus abound in the world of talk we inhabit. Thus we (the union of *I* and *you*) propagate a daily crop of political spectacles that include dramas of presidential visits to Tokyo, Beijing, Moscow, Warsaw, Paris; of pageants, celebrations, campaign hoopla, the ecstacy of political victory, and the agony of defeat; of officeholders and officeseekers driven from public life because of illicit love affairs, scandals, or gossip; of an inexhaustible supply of congressional hearings full of endless talk and bickering; and of terrorist kidnappings, murder, bombings, accompanied by the profusion of talk about how to deal with terrorists, how to get hostages released, and how to solve the terrorist problem. We are the cultural host of daily talk about school, not to mention talk in school: what's wrong with school, why we need more schooling, the role of school in international competition, whether the German or Japanese schools are better, and so on. *We* are the seedbeds for commercial advertising, as witness this ad for the Barbie We Girls Can Do Anything Game:

> WE GIRLS CAN DO ANYTHING! What will you be when you grow up? That's what young girls learn, playing this fun game. An astronaut, a movie star, a lawyer, a singer or maybe a dancer? Young girls work their way around this board to fulfill their goals and dreams! Join Barbie for lots of imaginative and learning fun. For 2–4 players, ages 5 and up.[29]

Barbie doll advertising may have originated to sell dolls to little girls; now it sells little girls to the "Anything" of imagination. All in all, in this babble of voices that rains upon us daily is propaganda, which has become the modern form of communication that often emerges from social palaver as the kind of talk that has the most influence, produces the most effect, and has the most social consequences. Talk is cheap, but some talk, especially well-said propaganda, can emerge from the torrent as influential beyond any other way of saying. In that case, such a form of talk becomes a valuable and indispensable part of the ideoculture, defining what we communicate by how we communicate. Propaganda is the palaver of the present that charms and beguiles us more than any other kind of public talk. In such a world, propaganda propagates itself, since it is seen as equal to the task of successful propagation.

In retrospect, this chapter has introduced the interested reader to a diverse crop of ideas about the modern ideoculture of propagation (the process of spreading ideas that may or may not take root), the concomitant practice of propagandizing (the interested activity of propagation), and the form of communication called propaganda (how we most successfully communicate ideas to large groups of people in the modern world). We attempted to avoid confining the process to the putative intentions of the propagator, in part because that tends to restrict propaganda to a rational intender who deceives us into believing his or her palaver. The deception model has its merits, since propaganda is oftentimes deceptive; but it is inadequate, because of the problems with imputing intention we have pointed out, and also because propaganda is in many cases anything but deceptive. Sometimes propaganda messages are quite straightforward (we sell pork chops at price

X), and indeed that is often the best strategy. We have also tried to avoid the information model, the notion—usually put forward by the defenders, and beneficiaries, of propaganda—that it simply provides information to consumers, potential students, voters, and so on, and is a valuable form of social advice and advocacy. This implies that propaganda is either harmless or undeceptive, and we cannot here accept the argument that it has no consequences, positive or negative, nor that it cannot be used by clever propagators to achieve results that are hidden from those "targeted" for a desired effect.

Instead, we have emphasized that the new propaganda is a modern process of learning, involving us in an imaginative activity of social learning that directs and mobilizes our poetic natures and pragmatic interests toward objects in our environment that we learn to desire. A massive propaganda industry has arisen in the modern world to help us in that learning, but in the final analysis propaganda exists, and succeeds, because we are both used to it and find it useful, understand its poetry and find that poetry both enjoyable and instructive. Once we see ourselves as part of the propaganda process, we can then know that our complicit understanding of propaganda has helped make it the most powerful medium of social learning in the modern world. And we are well on the way toward self-knowledge, learning how to make ourselves more autonomous from the influences of such a powerful medium, or at least to understand one of the major communicative forces at work in the modern world.

We noted above that much of propaganda works because it is "communication-pleasure," something that is enjoyable in itself but also speaks to our interests. A TV spot ad, a movie preview, a promotional tape may impress us because it is fun to watch, complemented by the fact that we come to believe that we will get something out of it. It should be noted that propaganda can also involve messages that are "communication-pain." Children subjected to patriotic or religious instruction often find such learning painful. Similarly, much school, military, or commercial propaganda is painful, although sometimes it is effective (making you a better student or soldier, and breaking down "sales resistance" to buying a car or insurance), and sometimes it is ineffective (decades of communist indoctrination that pervaded Eastern European and Soviet society apparently didn't take).[30] But it should also be said that understanding a subject such as propaganda is not all pleasurable. Readers will find some of this book fun and entertaining, and will learn from it. But ultimately coming to understand, and in a sense thereby freeing oneself from, propaganda, involves a modicum of work, self-analysis, and "real-world" application, which is more or less painful. The authors contend that the effort is worth it. Perhaps you cannot escape propaganda, or even make yourself totally immune to it, but at least through effort you can understand what it means to be a part of the propaganda process that characterizes the time and place in which you live, and what it would mean to know enough about propaganda to be freed from it.

BECOMING PROPAGANDA-WISE
IN A WORLD OF PALAVER

"Propaganda begets propaganda," wrote Lasswell.[31] And new propaganda begets newer. In the remaining chapters of this text we will see why and how this is so. Our aim, we reiterate, is to make you conscious of the taken-for-granted new propaganda that surrounds you. Some of that propaganda is political on the surface. But propaganda may be seemingly nonpolitical, even antipolitical, yet result in political consequences. We shall examine those types of new propaganda as well. Even though our primary interest is in political propaganda, the practice of propaganda in modern society is a mosaic. An advertising firm, for instance, may have commercial accounts (advertising a product, promoting a shopping mall), cultural accounts (developing brochures for a fund-raising drive for a university), and political accounts (managing a political candidate). It is unwise to exclude the related, and ostensibly nonpolitical, forms of propaganda, since they are all part of the new propaganda. You should then expect to see a wide variety of propagandas, all begetting each other in the propagation of the practice of propaganda.

Vital to the development of an awareness of how the new propaganda penetrates our everyday lives is an understanding of how it has emerged as a suasive and persuasive activity. The three chapters that constitute Part I of *The New Propaganda* deal with that emergence. Chapter 1 examines the growth of propaganda in general and traces the sociopolitical changes and technological innovations in modern life, especially in mass media, that have contributed to new means to sway people. Key to the development of the new propaganda has been contributions by selected masters of the art. Chapter 2 is an intellectual biography of the careers and thoughts of the foremost practitioners of propaganda from a variety of fields—politics, public relations, advertising, and show business. Finally, the new propaganda, when done well (as with all activities ranging from algebra to zoology), possesses a logic of its own. In Chapter 3 we delve further into the logic of the new political propaganda, moving beyond matters already touched on, such as emphases on suasion, drama, and palaver.

Part II consists of three chapters dealing with the cultures of propaganda. As the culture, or seedbed, is a significant factor in whether the seed takes root and propagates, so also are cultures where ideas and actions germinate. Chapter 4 looks at various political cultures that are the soil of the new propaganda, specifically electoral, bureaucratic, and diplomatic cultures. Certainly the commercial world of production and merchandising constitutes an important propaganda culture (witness the role played by advertising); we see that it is a culture with major political implications in Chapter 5. Myriad social organizations in competition and cooperation with one another employ propaganda to advance their interests through image management, another variant of the new propaganda. In Chapter 6 we examine the high, middle, and popular cultures of propaganda.

With an understanding of where the new propaganda comes from, how it works, and where it flourishes, we believe you can critique modern methods for swaying people. This is the subject of Part III. Chapter 7 provides a background in the traditions of propaganda analysis including those that developed out of World Wars I and II. Chapter 8 presents more recent views on how any communication, whether overtly intended as propaganda or not, may be analyzed. Our concluding discussion in Chapter 9 deals with the future of propaganda and what we may look forward to as new propaganda begets the newer in a world of flourishing palaver.

It is the objective of this introductory chapter to impress upon you both the extent and depth of propaganda in modern society. We argue that the new propaganda has helped determine the way we live now, even affecting the ways we think, feel, and act. And we point to some examples of the observable consequences, intended and unintended, of propaganda. You should not think of propaganda as necessarily sinister or conspiratorial, something imposed on us by evil forces. Rather propaganda is popular because it is a familiar part of the modern ideoculture and is a reliable form of communication that is truncated, beguiling, and interesting for the many who consume messages for their pragmatic, and at times their aesthetic, value. Throughout the book, recall that to understand the new propaganda you must see it as a powerful and pervasive form of social learning that we constantly use in order to cope. The functions of propaganda are not confined just to their overt and immediate purposes, but rather includes social consequences that are often far-reaching and innovative. In order to see this, we must now turn to the emergence of propaganda. The new propaganda developed out of innovations associated with the growth of modernity, so now it has a discernible history that we can trace to our present condition. With that in mind, let us now look backward at modern history as the new propaganda becomes increasingly an integral and indispensable part of our lives.

NOTES

1. Russell W. Belk, "A Child's Christmas in America: Santa Claus as Deity, Consumption as Religion," *Journal of American Culture* (forthcoming).
2. BillyBoy Collection, *Barbie: Her Life and Times with Dolls and Documents from the BillyBoy Collection* (New York: Crown, 1987); Jeanne Marie Laskas, "Our Barbies, Our Selves," *Chicago Tribune Magazine,* May 7, 1989, 37–40, 42; Robert Goldsborough, "Billion-Dollar Barbie the Biggest Hit with Kids," *Advertising Age* 58 (November 8, 1988): 22; *Barbie: The Magazine for Girls,* Winter 1989 (Welsh Publishing).
3. Robert Goldsborough, "Billion-Dollar Barbie the Biggest Hit with Kids," *Advertising Age* 58 (November 8, 1988): 22; Jeanne Marie Laskas, "Our Barbies, Our Selves," *Chicago Tribune Magazine,* May 7, 1989, 37–42; Terrence H. Witkowski, "Advertising Images of Thinness" (Paper presented at the annual conference of the Popular Culture Association, 1985); Linda Lazier-Smith, "Media Images, Advertising, and Ideal Body Shapes: Marketing Eating Disorders" (Paper presented at the annual conference of the Popular Culture Association, 1987).
4. A readable discussion of the nature of metaphor in everyday life is George Lakoff and Mark Johnson, *Metaphors We Live By* (Chicago: University of Chicago Press, 1980).
5. Elizabeth Barrett Browning, "Sonnets from the Portuguese," Sonnet 43, in M. H. Abrams, ed., *The Norton Anthology of English Literature,* rev. ed., vol. 2 (New York: Norton, 1968), p. 1149.
6. For a review of conventional definitions of propaganda see Warren Roberts, "Propaganda," in Julius Gould and William L. Kolb, eds., *A Dictionary of the Social Sciences* (New York: Free Press of Glencoe, 1964), pp. 547–548.
7. Niccolò Machiavelli, *The Prince,* Robert M. Adams, ed. and trans. (New York: Norton, 1977).
8. W. Phillips Davison, "The Public Opinion Process," *Public Opinion Quarterly* 22 (Summer 1958): 91–106.
9. Jay W. Baird, *The Mythical World of Nazi War Propaganda, 1939–1945* (Minneapolis: University of Minnesota Press, 1974), p. 25.
10. Quoted in Marshall Frady, "Outsider I—The Gift," *The New Yorker,* February 3, 1992, 53.
11. William Morris, ed., *The American Heritage Dictionary of the English Language* (New York: American Heritage, 1969), p. 1302.
12. Charles U. Larson, *Persuasion* (Belmont, CA: Wadsworth, 1989), p. 10.
13. Milton Richards, "Why Advertising Works: The Willing Suspension of Disbelief" (Paper

presented at the 15th annual meeting of the Popular Culture Association, Louisville, KY, April 3–7, 1985).

14. Garth S. Jowett and Victoria O'Donnell, *Propaganda and Persuasion* (Newbury Park, CA: Sage, 1986), p. 16.

15. F. C. Bartlett, "The Aims of Propaganda," in Daniel Katz, Dorwin Cartwright, Samuel Eldersveld, and Alfred McClung Lee, eds., *Public Opinion and Propaganda* (New York: Henry Holt, 1954), p. 464.

16. Malcolm G. Mitchell, *Propaganda, Polls, and Public Opinion* (Englewood Cliffs, NJ: Prentice-Hall, 1970), p. 23.

17. William Hummell and Keith Huntress, *The Analysis of Propaganda* (New York: Holt, Rinehart and Winston, 1949), p. 2.

18. Leonard W. Doob, *Public Opinion and Propaganda* (Hamden, CT: Archon Books, 1966), p. 240.

19. J. Michael Sproule, "The New Managerial Rhetoric and the Old Criticism," *Quarterly Journal of Speech* 74 (November 1988): 468–486. See also J. Michael Sproule, "Organizational Rhetoric and the Public Sphere," *Communication Studies* 40 (Winter 1989): 258–265.

20. Sproule, "The New Managerial Rhetoric," p. 474.

21. W. V. Quine, "Belief (excerpt from Quiddities)," *ETC.: A Review of General Semantics* (Winter 1987): 371.

22. Sproule, "The New Managerial Rhetoric," pp. 474–475.

23. Hugh D. Duncan, *Communication and the Social Order* (New York: Oxford University Press, 1962).

24. David V. J. Bell, *Power, Influence, and Authority* (New York: Oxford University Press, 1975).

25. Paul Kecskemeti, "Propaganda" in Ithiel de Sola Pool, Frederick W. Frey, Wilbur Schramm, Nathan Maccoby, and Edwin B. Parker, eds., *Handbook of Communication* (Chicago: Rand McNally, 1975), p. 864. Compare Kecskemeti's forms of talk with those of David Bell, and with those employed here.

26. Kecskemeti, "Propaganda," p. 864 (emphasis added).

27. Compare Harold D. Lasswell and Nathan Leites, *Language of Politics* (Cambridge: MIT Press, 1949), chap. 2.

28. Harold D. Lasswell, "The Theory of Political Propaganda," *American Political Science Review* 21 (1927): 631.

29. The ad appears in a mail-order catalog, "Pan-Orama Gifts," (Fall, 1989), p. 33.

30. William Stephenson, *The Play Theory of Mass Communication* (Chicago: University of Chicago Press, 1967).

31. Harold D. Lasswell, "The Person: Subject and Object of Propaganda," *Annals of the American Academy of Political and Social Science* 197 (1935): 187–193.

PART I

The Emergence of the New Propaganda

CHAPTER 1

"From Small Acorns Do Mighty Oaks Grow"

The Germination of the New Propaganda

In the previous introductory chapter, we familiarized you with both key concepts and illustrative stories that underscored our assertion that we are living in a world of constant propagandizing. These ideas alert you to the derivative argument of subsequent chapters, including how the current situation came about. Here we wish to augment that discussion with historically rooted treatment of how modern arrangements of power came into being. This historical panorama will be supplemented with analytical tools that help you understand the nature of modernity. We will argue that propaganda was a crucial generic force in the creation and culmination of modernity. Even though propaganda is as old as civilization, it did not become a prominent part of ruling until the rise of modern ideocultures and the new forms of power associated with it. Here we will demonstrate how propaganda became the distinctive form of modern suasion, an integral part of the information society. You should come away from the chapter with a sense of how the present in which you live is the historical outcome of a major development in modern communications.

We are all familiar with the idea that we live in "the modern age." Most of us think of ourselves as modern people and take for granted the habits of thought and action that mark us and our world as modern. But as students of history know, the world was not always modern; nor is it likely to be considered so in the future. In fact, the label *postmodern society* is even now in vogue in learned lectures, scholarly and popular books, editorial pages, and weekly newsmagazines. But as baseball great and social sage Yogi Berra reminds us, "It ain't over till it's over." The powerful historical force known as modernity will likely persist into the twenty-first century, so let us assume that this force, and the characteristic form of communication we call the new propaganda, will persist for a while longer. So let us begin our inquiry into modern propaganda by attempting to delineate just what it is about modernity that made the world we live in now so susceptible to the pervasiveness of propaganda.

We will initiate our study of propaganda by addressing two questions: What are the defining political and related characteristics of modernity? What was, and is, the role of propaganda in the modern, and perhaps in the future, the postmodern, world? We will not, however, try to provide here a blow-by-blow account of every development that constituted the shift from premodern times politically, socially, economically, or technologically. It would take volumes of print to do that. Nor will we concern ourselves with every innovation in the evolution of propaganda techniques. That too would take volumes and, besides, would add little to our goal of surveying the conditions that led to the arrival of the new propaganda that is the subject of this book. Rather, we will look at (1) the historical seeds of propaganda, (2) the views of a key political thinker who provided insights into how the new era of modernity was preparing a seedbed for the growth of propaganda, and (3) how the acorns of conventional propaganda took root in economic, cultural, and political seedbeds so that the mighty oaks of the new propaganda could germinate in the advanced or ''late'' modern world of today.

Even though we now take modernity for granted, the world we live in is the result of a long struggle involving institutional and attitudinal changes. Over the past several centuries, newly introduced institutional arrangements—parliamentary democracy, large corporations, universities, and school systems—all eventually brought a new way of life in the world. The innovation of new thinking, such as science, new ideologies, and new art and literature underscored the break with the traditional past. More fundamentally, modernity came to be characterized by new attitudes, especially the idea that innovation itself was not only acceptable but actually contributed toward a better life through progress. Scientific and technological innovation, new laws and rules, new freedoms and choices, new products and services, new proposals and discussions—all contribute to the advance of progress.

But such a new world requires concomitant advances in the quality and speed of communication in order to facilitate innovation. Thus the modern world increasingly was characterized by new media of communication and by the expanding need to use those media to spread the ideas that contributed to the newfound power of innovation. Scientific and technological data spread, as well as the scientific attitude and methods, which were quickly applied to social relations, as in the ''science of management'' and the ''science of communication.'' Rhetoric spread through newspapers, radio and television, books, mass meetings, and spectacles, making arguments to an increasingly literate populace.

The old form of communication that was given the greatest impetus by modernity was propaganda. Modern science and rhetoric became part of the new ideoculture, but propaganda became important as the form of suasion that proved to be most indispensable to the requirements of innovation. The constancy of change required human adaptation and compliance through social learning, and propaganda increasingly proved to be an effective and convenient way of communicating those seeds that needed to germinate in order for modern institutions and practices to continue the process of innovation. Modernity came to be characterized by innovation in the forms of communication needed to sustain its institutions and practices, and propaganda was the form that proved most amenable to communicating the sort of adaptive learning required in the new world of innovation. Although very old, in the modern world propaganda became very new and very innovative. Propaganda as we know it is very much a property and practice of modernity.

EARLY PRECURSORS OF PROPAGANDA
IN THE MODERN AGE

Our general thesis is twofold: first, propaganda, as conventionally understood, was a key and generic force in the creation of modernity; second, the conditions and innovations of modernity worked gradually to prepare the ground for developing new forms of propaganda. As a method of political communication, propaganda has grown ever more influential through the introduction of various innovations and the genius of numerous innovators (as we shall see in detail in Chapter 2). Today propaganda is central to the conduct of modern societies, so central that it now is the most prominent discursive habit of the public ideoculture.

We are not saying, however, that propagandistic communication is a creature specific to the modern world alone. In politics, for instance, there has been propaganda as long as there has been government. The pomp and circumstance of royal courts, public rituals such as royal coronations, the rhetorical exaltation of the personage of the king or queen, the badges and insignia of political office—all are as ancient as the city-states of the Near East, yet as recent as any White House attempt to shore up the image of a U.S. president through the use of spectacle (to be explored in depth in Chapter 4). What we are saying is that even though many of the primary features of propaganda are as old as the ancient world, what has evolved from the old propaganda is something that differs in both quantity and quality from the past. The old propaganda was not so much a principle of power and rule as it is now. It tended to be occasional rather than habitual, dependent on whether a particular ruler recognized its potential rather than an institutional practice regardless of regime, and dimly rather than well understood. The traditional ideocultures of the world tended not to have the propensity or the mechanisms to spread ideas systematically (as a practitioner of modern horticulture would). It is only with advanced modernity that propaganda truly becomes a central principle of power, so essential that it is practiced by all regimes and rulers regardless of political culture and ideology.

As a measure of propaganda's antiquity consider the story in the Bible of the enmity between King Saul and his protégé and son-in-law, David. The tale illustrates well the distinction we developed in the preceding chapter between intended and unintended propaganda. When Saul and David won a great victory over the Philistines, they returned in triumph through the cities of Israel. Saul no doubt intended the officially sponsored praise he would receive to be excellent propaganda for his regime: the public rejoicing at triumphant marches in his honor would surely accrue to his political benefit. Not so! He discovered to his dismay that "the women came out of the cities of Israel, singing and dancing, to meet King Saul, with timbrels, with songs of joy, and with instruments of music." But they were singing not about Saul; instead they sang of David. This propagated message, which Saul certainly did not intend, celebrated David as the popular hero: "Saul has slain his thousands, and David his ten thousands." Saul correctly saw that the seed of an idea that threatened his rule had been sown. He angrily mused, "They have ascribed to David ten thousands, and to me they have ascribed thousands; and what more can he have but the kingdom?"

Saul clearly understood how propagating a heroic public image contributes to holding and wielding political power. Witnessing the outpouring of acclaim for David persuaded Saul that his young protégé was now a rival for the throne of Israel. David's present for Saul's daughter Michal at their marriage confirmed Saul's fears that David's reputation as a greater slayer of Philistines had indeed made him a man to be reckoned with—two hundred Philistine foreskins![1]

There are, of course, numerous other illustrations of the practice of propaganda long before the advent of the modern world. Their number suggests that propaganda appears as a universal fact of social existence imbedded in the very nature of communication. For example, the unearthed ruins of Roman cities such as Pompeii (destroyed by an eruption of Mount Vesuvius in A.D. 79) reveal campaign slogans chalked on walls facing once-busy streets; these early political ads urged citizens to vote for a particular candidate for local magistrate on the promise that he would reduce taxes. Citizens of Pompeii may not have read the candidate's lips, as candidate George Bush asked Americans to do in 1988, but they read his graffiti! (Graffito—scratching messages in public places—was also practiced by Roman prostitutes and others who were politically voiceless, a practice that continues today).

Additional confirmation of propaganda's ancient roots lies in the fact that the deliberate cultivation of image management on behalf of a political leader goes back at least to Alexander the Great. Alexander coined money depicting his personage alongside that of his alleged divine father, Zeus, and his profile with the heroic god Heracles. Similarly, the use of organized efforts to proselytize (that is, trying to convince people to change their thoughts, feelings, or actions) can be traced back at least to the dynamic initial phases of the great religions of Christianity and Islam. Missionary Christian preachers, such as Saint Paul, brought a message of hope and love for converts to the faith; the spread of Islam was propagated through the "holy war" *(jihad)* that sought widespread conversion. Finally, consider the great orators of ancient Greece. They were well aware of the power of political speech not only to sway attitudes but also to spur people to act. A legend about the renowned Greek orator Demosthenes says that when a rival spoke to the Athenians they remarked, "How well he spoke!" but when Demosthenes spoke, they said to one another, "Let us march."

We need not belabor the fact that suasion has always been an aspect of human communication, and political communication in particular. People attempting to propagate an idea found that persuasion—directing a relevant group's attention and approval toward an idea—was important in swaying thought and action. Scientific ideas were presented on the basis of method and evidence, trying to persuade the guardians of truth of its verisimilitude. (Galileo tried and failed with the Church authorities, since they did not understand or trust science!) Rhetorical arguments were used to try to sway audiences and publics through persuasion that they should accept one course of action over another, marching to the beat of the rhetorician's drum.

As the practice of propaganda was slowly refined, people begin to notice that it was different, a form of suasion that did not rely necessarily on persuasive discourse such as scientific presentation or rhetorical argument. This form of communication, it was learned, involved propagandizing, propagating messages with effect, and persuasion was only one way that those effects could be achieved. An appeal to credulity—that, say, the king ruled through divine right, and thus was never mistaken—was often a way of learning that was not so much persuasive (intentionally convincing or inducing people to do something they might not otherwise do) as acquiescent (communicating that people may acquiesce in the benign rule of the king, or "let us not march." Similarly, a ruler might authoritatively communicate to his subjects that "X or Y is obvious" because I say so. A specific authoritative message would propagate the idea (for instance) that "it is obvious that the king must confiscate half of everyone's crops for the war effort." If there is a general agreement communicated that courses X or Y are obvious, persuasion has not occurred as much as the authoritative propagation of a suasive message that involves no persuasive inducement but does suggest "obvious" consensus on passive compliance. Although over the centuries persuasion has been a major component and method of propaganda, they are not identical, since propaganda has evolved and grown into a form of communication that subsumes and utilizes communicative qualities and practices (both scientific and rhetorical methods of persuasion have been used in modern propaganda). Propaganda in its modern form mobilizes the gamut of suasion, indeed all communicative resources, for its purposes.

Propaganda, then, like death and taxes, has been with us always. (A cynic might say that ads for funeral homes, or the U.S. Internal Revenue Service, leave the impression that death and taxes obtain respectability through propaganda!) But it is with the advent of the modern world that the use of political communication to sway large populations became all the more important. Let us now turn to how this happened.

TOO MANY PEOPLE, TOO MANY VOICES: PROPAGANDA TRANSLATED TO MODERN POLITICAL SEEDBEDS

We begin our look at the rising influence of propaganda in an era that foreshadowed our modern world, the Renaissance. Like other eras of great change and innovation, the Renaissance was a period of turbulent politics, politics made unsettling because of newly emergent forces in the world that sought both knowledge and power. This was especially so in the city-states of Italy. Those principalities veered through periods of rapid political changes that witnessed conquest by political adventurers, despotism by tyrants and martinets, and demands for political power by new middle classes and artisans.

The seeds of modern politics were being sown in such city-states as Florence, where there emerged political ideas that enhanced the impetus to political modernization. It was in the stormy political atmosphere of Florence that an innovative political thinker appeared, Niccolò Machiavelli (1469–1527). Machiavelli has acquired an undeserved reputation as a teacher of evil, a purveyor of deceit, machination, and trickery. Open a typical dictionary and look up the word *Machiavellianism*. You will find "the political doctrine of Machiavelli, which denies the relevance of morality in political affairs and holds that craft and deceit are justified in pursuing and maintaining political power; political opportunism."

If we set aside such a propagandistic definition we find that, more accurately, Machiavelli was one of the first analysts to grasp the nature, and requirements, of modern politics. He foresaw that the nation-state would eventually become the prototypical modern political organization at the center of the coming world. In his call for the unification of Italy at the close of his political classic, *The Prince*, he envisioned that the nation-state would be the future locus of power. Since ruling the increasingly secular world of the future (that is, the emerging modern world) would be problematic, thought Machiavelli, then the fundamental political task was to discover adaptive techniques for governing under shifting conditions. In other words, a new and expanded social and political ideoculture was emerging, one that would call for fresh approaches to governing.

In the past, Machiavelli theorized, politics was conducted in small, relatively self-contained states (such as the Italian city-states or medieval fiefdoms) and was restricted to the interest and participation of only the few. That era was coming to an end. With populations increasing in size and diversity, modern politics would mean large-sized states with demands for participation by more and more people with different, and perhaps not always satisfiable, interests. Thus, the people of Machiavelli's age experienced the rise of republican ideas along with the emergence of a new educated and monied merchant and middle class. Moreover, the spread of literacy and learning after the invention of the printing press stimulated the birth of the idea of what we now call the public (and of public opinion), composed of those interested in politics who wanted to know what was going on and who clamored for power over officeholders and policy making. In short, as we argued in the preceding chapter, people are the seedbeds of propaganda, and the modern era ushered in an ever-widening diverse and turbulent population of fertile seedbeds. How then could effective governance be achieved in the face of mounting demands and potential disruption, instability, and turbulence?

Machiavelli argued that in earlier political eras the two cardinal means of power had been force *(forza)* and cunning or fraud *(fraoda),* corresponding with his view that the princely ruler is both lion and fox. For princes attempting to rule in small states with relatively few political actors and interests, political force and guile may have been enough. *Forza* and *fraoda* were especially necessary to institute order in a corrupt and chaotic state; without order one could scarcely hope to achieve a politics of morality.

But all of that was the old politics, claimed Machiavelli, inadequate for the world to come. The new politics of the modern world, suggested Machiavelli, would, like all politics, be oriented toward the successful exercise of power. But in these new circumstances of large centralized states and politically involved populations, aspiring rulers would have to adjust. Brute force (armies, police) cannot entirely quell the demands of restless populations, and the use of fraudulent connivance (palace intrigues, secret deals) among the few sparks the suspicions of the many. How then does the prince incorporate the populace into his princedom; how does a ruler gain their support, meet their insatiable demands, and achieve their acquiescence in princely governance?

Machiavelli found the answer in ruling through, and over, public opinion. If the ruler could but appeal to and sway favorably the opinions of the many, then it would be possible to convince them of the necessity and wisdom of allowing governors to govern. Rulers therefore must learn that the modern base of power lies in its understanding and cultivation of public opinion. The study of the techniques of wielding power must include those of commanding opinion by propagating ideas that appeal to and shape political imagination. For Machiavelli, the political logic of creating mass political opinion was an imperative for successful ruling, what he called *necessita,* or political necessity. Politics is in this sense the "engineering of necessity." Future princes of the modern world must learn how to engineer political consent. The prince's task is to understand suasion, including both those waves of opinions that are extant at a given moment and those that might be created, and manipulated, in the future.

Even though the minds of the many consist of unique, individual viewpoints, they can be momentarily unified and satisfied by an astute prince who can successfully define the political situation for them. Rulers must master the skill of communicating to each and every relevant human imagination, thereby shaping multiple private realities into a singular public reality. Machiavelli was impressed with the mercurial and changing nature of political reality, and how the unwary political actor is readily victim to the whims of fortune *(fortuna)* if he or she loses control of the situation. Yet, since situations are dynamic, they are not only a danger but also an opportunity *(occasione),* a moment the astute prince can seize to advantage. Fortune can thus be mastered by grasping people's imaginations through what Machiavelli termed *fantasia,* or seizing the occasion and orchestrating people, places, and events to create popular expectations, then meet them or provide the illusion of having done so. To the extent that one can direct individual imaginations into a common vision, one momentarily gains power over opinion. Thus, the "Machiavellian moment" in the conduct of politics is decisive. At that precise time there is a "concordance of the public imagination" centering around and making the political leader the beneficiary. This does not mean that the prince can create or control public imagination at will; indeed, he or she is often in the position of having to try to anticipate, ride out, or get out of the way of suasive forces that are out of control (as in the many political events that immediately arouse a "firestorm of controversy"). To use another Machiavellian metaphor, collective *fantasia* is like a torrential river in a storm that you hope you can channel and divert as you wish, but doing so is quite problematic.

Machiavelli, then, was one of the first to see the malleability of the modern mind as the major feature of the innovative and dynamic politics that was to come. Future governability would derive from the ability to sway the mass mind. As usual, Machiavelli was blunt about it, as these passages from *The Prince* reveal:

> Men are so simple of mind, and so much dominated by their immediate needs, that a deceitful man will always find plenty who are ready to be deceived. . . . The masses are always impressed by the superficial appearance of things, and by the outcome of an enterprise. And the world consists of nothing but the masses; the few have no influence when the many feel secure. *(The Prince,* Chapter 18)

And again:

> The great majority of mankind are satisfied with appearances, as though they were realities, and are often even more influenced by the things that seem than by those that are. *(The Discourses I,* Chapter 25)

Machiavelli, who had once been an engineer, understood that building a governing regime on the engineering of popular imaginations is risky. It is much like constructing an edifice on quicksand. For people's imaginations are fickle, ever shifting and often contradictory. If one does not "have a mind ready to shift as the winds of fortune and the various circumstances of life may dictate" *(The Prince,* Chapter 18), then someone more crafty may step in to exploit the new fantasies that supersede the old. It is this unending play of political imagination or imaginative fantasy, rather than reason, that is the stuff of politics: "Political activity," writes K. R. Minogue, "is thus not the copying of some rational order, nor is it the establishment of an agreed belief on the ends of public order. It is simply a constantly changing concordance of the public imagination, and the business of politics is to maintain that concordance by any means available.''[2]

This, then, is the core of modern ruling—be it political, economic, or cultural—envisioned by Machiavelli. It is a core that involves the engineering of imagination through propagation of ideas. As Machiavelli recognized and we shall have ample opportunity to illustrate in the remainder of this book, the propagation itself may work as intended, but frequently it may not. Propaganda is thus like the annual problem faced by the horticulturist who may propagate seeds in a field or a garden. Despite all the planning and care, the crop doesn't grow or is destroyed by forces (storms, locusts) beyond control, a wild crop grows instead and chokes out the plants, or if the crop grows successfully there is no demand for what has been produced (the plants are illegal, poisonous, not nutritious, or just taste bad). Like horticulture, attempting to understand, propagate, and direct propaganda is risky business, fraught with the uncertainties of dynamic forces at work and the chance of failure.

MASS MEDIA: AN EMERGING CULTURE NURTURING PROPAGANDA'S GROWTH

So far we have followed Machiavelli's argument that rule in the modern world has shifted its emphasis from governing through the few by force and fraud to governing the many through fantasy. This is not to say that force and fraud have disappeared; there is obviously ample evidence that they have not. Rather it is to say that the arrival of rule by fantasy laid the groundwork for the emergence of a new form of propaganda not necessarily beholden to force and fraud for success. As the consequences of modernity have expanded over the centuries since Machiavelli, the elite's recognition of the necessity for ruling through public opinion has made the use of propaganda more central and sophisticated. Force and fraud are still important, but increasingly they are sustained by the use of fantasy. Force can be taken, and fraud perpetuated, only if they can be justified through the mobilization of opinion.

One of the reasons for this enormous change is simply the great increase in population. When electorates, publics, or the mass number in the many millions, propagating messages that successfully affect the attitudes and behavior of such a vast population is difficult, to be sure, but also potentially rewarding and just downright practical, as the line of least resistance in reaching as large an audience as possible. Populations certainly have grown enormously over the past several centuries. In the census of 1790, the American population was a widely dispersed 4 million people, largely illiterate and isolated from each other and the centers of power. In the census of 1990, the national population is over 250 million largely literate an with almost universal access to mass communication. (Other countries are even larger: China has about 1.1 billion people, India about 850 million, and the former Soviet Union about 290 million). The population of the world exceeds 5.3 billion and is also increasingly literate and ''wired'' to the mass media. The mass media became the only practical way to propagate messages, and was the carrier of the new propaganda as it developed.

Modern Communicative Power

As the potential of the mass media emerged at an ever-quickening pace as a disseminator of communication—printing press, telegraphy, telephones, wireless, movies, broadcasting, satellites, and so on—it became clear that those who would exercise power could do so by controlling these media and the nature of what was communicated. Control of those organizational and communication resources could enrich the possibilities of seizing Machiavellian moments in exercising power. The mass media offered the opportunity for the propagation of messages to great populations, becoming a necessary condition and vehicle for the new propaganda. Now keep in mind that power always "is distinguished by the fact that it involves *asymmetrical* interaction: the source exercises greater control over the behavior of the target than the reverse. . . . It is asymmetrical because the outcome value and outcome scarcity favors the source."[3] In the modern world, asymmetrical relations are vast and multiple, so the potential for upheaval is great. The distribution of wealth, status and class position, and power and influence itself is often drastically unequal. Thus the holders of power are faced with the problem of how to influence and control those great asymmetries, maintaining order and power relations among large populations.

Using the mass media, and the communicative resources of propaganda, thus acquires for ruling elites a high degree of political logic: it makes sense in these circumstances to use propaganda in order to exercise power well. In the complex and large-scale societies of modernity, political, social, and economic asymmetry are always there and often both visible and conflictual. But given the limits of what can realistically be done to alleviate differences or resolve conflicts, propaganda then becomes a primary communicative means to deal with asymmetrical conditions, oftentimes by convincing people that asymmetry doesn't exist or is being overcome through progress. Wealth, for instance, may be unequally distributed across a population, but envy and resentment may be forestalled by the propagandists of the "haves" convincing the "have-nots" that the rich are just like them (see Chapter 5, on John D. Rockefeller's refurbished image), or that mass property "is just around the corner" (this propagated message didn't work for President Hoover during the Depression).

However, power is also *bilateral,* that is, the "target" has to be convinced to comply, thereby constraining the means of suasion and providing the target with other courses of action than that urged by the allegedly powerful. Since the many potentially have the power of numbers, they can exercise a reciprocal constraint on the behavior of the powerful, as in the choice of elites in elections. As the modern era unfolded politicians looked increasingly toward the mass media as means of convincing every target to comply—individuals, publics, crowds, or groups within the mass—by means of "a restructuring of the target's attitudes strictly by means of symbolic manipulation."[4]

As we noted with force and fraud, however, modern populations do not easily submit to power just because the powerful tell them they should or must. The target populace or group must be made to feel that they are part of the bilateral equation. Thus the logic of propaganda involves courting those who would be influenced, attempting to convince people that power is either symmetrical (inequalities or injustices do not exist) or that whatever asymmetries do exist are either just or skewed toward their group because of the beneficence of the powerful. Propaganda is both necessary and problematic in the bilateral relations between the few and the many, since the latter may reciprocate in contrasuasive response by rejecting or reinterpreting the message. Because the modern power of public opinion was, and is, deemed so great, it became clear as the mass media developed that public opinion was not something that could be safely left to the public. Propaganda would become the communicative means to maintain bilateral relations with publics and other emergent social groupings (such as members of movements).

Finally, it should be kept in mind that power also involves the ability to make decisions, and to make those decisions acceptable, or at least palatable, to the masses. In the modern mass-mediated world, propaganda became the instrument that accompanied elite decisions: once something was decided, propaganda machines attempted to propagate the message of the wisdom of the decision, the extent to which the decision had worked well and was producing benefits, how much the mass public or group approved of it, and so on. Since people might be suspicious that a decision was designed to sustain asymmetries and was thus not in their best interest, such potential distrust had to be overcome through appeal to the bilateral nature of interest, suggesting that elite and mass are identified as one. Thus a decision to cut the capital gains tax is justified through propaganda as not something that primarily benefits the rich, but rather as something that really has larger social benefits and applications, such as creating general prosperity. The ability to decide something is in itself not enough; that ability has to be supplemented by justification. In the modern world, propaganda is the most important form of communication used to justify decisions. A policy decision may wither and die on the vine if it is not followed by a vigorous campaign to sell it, and even then it may not find mass root (like President Ford's WIN—Whip Inflation Now—campaign).

The Post–World War I Propaganda Menace

Although passing generations of modern politicians have exploited each new innovation in mass communication as offering ever-widening opportunities for symbolic manipulation, the growing opportunities to mold public opinion via mass propaganda did not go unnoticed by critics fearful of such ''Machiavellian tricks.'' It was not, however, until after World War I that eminent detractors suddenly grew acutely aware of, and vocal about, the newfound power of propaganda communicated through what were by that time truly mass media—widely distributed and cheap books, magazines, and newspapers; billboards and poster art; the movies; and radio. Both academics and journalists voiced concern about ''the propaganda menace.'' In 1918 philosopher John Dewey wrote an article entitled ''New Paternalism: Molding Public Opinion,'' arguing that ''democracies are controlled through their opinions, that opinions are formed by the material upon which they feed, and that propaganda disguised as the distribution of the news is the cheapest and most effective way of developing the required tone of public sentiment.'' He speculated whether ''the word 'news' is not destined to be replaced by the word 'propaganda'.'' Like other early critics, Dewey was suddenly aware that something had changed: power and propaganda had always been around, and the powerful had always used propaganda in an effort to exercise influence over opinion; but now, the newfound disseminative and interesting features of the mass media were making propaganda into the preponderant communicative influence of the modern era.[5]

A 1919 editorial in *The Nation* wondered whether the experience of the war "had revealed to the groups of men who govern . . . new and hitherto undreamed of ways of fortifying their control over the masses of the people." A writer in *The Dial* the same year predicted that since "governments and other interested agencies" had found that propaganda "can be readily utilized to sway and control democratic masses," then, "hereafter no government will confront its electorate without a secret or open bureau of propaganda, and every 'great interest' will organize propaganda as an essential activity." Popular author Will Irwin at the same time said it more bluntly: we now lived in an "age of lies" wherein the "propagandist attacks the foundations of public opinion." Thus, the immediate aftermath of the first big success of the new propaganda—mobilizing opinion for World War I—was the sober reflection that perhaps propaganda had been too successful, and now ironically constituted an innovation that threatened the very ideals of democracy that it had used during the war to defend.[6] These writers were correct in their assessment that at this point the new propaganda was being implemented by every "great interest" (government, corporations, industries, unions, and so on), and that propagandists were at work attempting to understand, and hopefully mold, the "foundations" of public opinion.

Throughout the 1920s in this country analysts of propaganda divided over the nature of the beast. One of the foremost students of propaganda, Harold Lasswell, had by 1927 started to point to possible negative consequences: "We live among more people than ever who are puzzled, uneasy, or vexed at the unknown cunning which seems to have duped and degraded them."[7] Another student, and practitioner, of propaganda, Edward Bernays (see Chapter 2) was more approving. He argued that propaganda is not "the effort of some reprehensible person to poison our minds with lies"; rather it was "an organized effort to spread a particular belief or opinion." The new propaganda was "something far more subtle, more intensely powerful, and more vital than the mere spread of information." Indeed, Bernays argued, "whatever of social importance is done today . . . must be done with the help of propaganda." Rather than being victims of propaganda, we require it to have "increased general knowledge"; propaganda, said Bernays, is "indispensable to this civilization."[8] Whether critics or proponents of propaganda, by the 1920s all serious observers recognized what Machiavelli had suggested four centuries earlier, namely, propaganda was a major communicative force, central to the way we would live in the modern world. By the twentieth century, the new propaganda was becoming that force. Lasswell saw its potential for deception, and Bernays saw its potential for spreading necessary information; all seemed to sense that there was something new and important in the social world, something that truly would be indispensable to advanced modern civilization.

It was at this crucial juncture in modern history that social critics began the great debate about the nature and power of propaganda, a debate that would continue down to the present. The defenders of propaganda, such as Bernays, saw nothing particularly sinister or improper about propaganda. Quite the contrary, they saw it, and still see it, as informative and indispensable, indeed one of the primary features of modern society that makes it different and superior to past civilizations. The other school of thought was more dubious. Figures such as Dewey and Lasswell agreed on the importance and efficacy of propaganda, but saw it as a force that could undermine democratic ideals and political rationality. Both agreed on the power of the new propaganda, and even the fact that it was new:

not only more subtle and important, but really a vital part of how modernity worked. For good or ill, the new propaganda was now at the center of powerful social communication, that is, communications in order to propagate desirable messages to large populations, in an attempt to rule a world of asymmetrical relations, convincing people that they are a bilateral component of rule (sometimes called "identification" of rulers and ruled), and justifying decision making and the impact of decisions. By the 1920s, both defenders and critics of the new propaganda acknowledged that it was a powerful new social force to be reckoned with.

CORPORATE ORGANIZATION AS A NUTRIENT FOR PROPAGANDA'S GROWTH

The popularization of politics and the emergence of the mass media, both of which began at the dawn of the modern era at the time of Machiavelli, contributed to the growth of propaganda as a force to be reckoned with in the centuries to come. But something else had happened that also stimulated that growth over the centuries. As modernity developed, the size and capacity of organizations increased.

Surveying the major changes that had occurred in the previous centuries since the end of the Middle Ages, the German sociologist Max Weber (1864–1920) argued that the world was losing its faith in traditional and "sacred" authority. In the emerging modern era, the world was becoming "disenchanted" from tradition and increasingly "rationalized" instead.[9] Appearing on the scene were large-scale, coordinated, corporate entities of organizational power (the nation-state, the administrative bureaucracy, the industrial corporation, the university, the military and police) that ruled and served the populace. These organizations made the world more "rationalized" in the sense of being more committed to objective criteria and procedures, and able to set and realize objective goals.

In a bureaucracy, the hierarchy of the organization demands measured production on the job, stresses conformity to rules, relies on paperwork (today computerized), and makes periodic evaluations of personnel and performance. Students reading this chapter, for instance, work in a bureaucracy with an organized hierarchy and division of labor; there are standardized rules ("red tape") that each must follow, rules allegedly applied equally to everyone; each must deal with countless forms and office procedures; and "grades" based on academic performance are evaluations duly recorded in transcripts. School is a modern manifestation of organizational power, and students have a role in the organization, which is to learn what the organization deems proper and be rewarded eventually with a degree, if not an "education"!

Although there are obviously many human variations, organizational rationality is the modern norm. Weber thought that modern societies would be increasingly characterized by the rule of such organizations, to the point that they would stifle individuality and perhaps make the world into an "iron cage" of conformity. In any case, there is no doubt that the modern world is marked as much by organizational proliferation, consolidation, and growth as by increasing populations and innovations in media of mass communication. Large organizations tend to overwhelm small ones ("mom-and-pop" restaurants and stores have a tough time competing with McDonald's, Wendy's, or Hardee's), concentrating power in ever more rationalized ways and extensive organizational networks. Dissenters from the trends of modernity may be correct that "small is beautiful," but the tendency has been almost altogether the other way, toward bigness and vastness—the growth of the national state, bank mergers, international corporations, large multinational media conglomerates, and so on, many with a global reach. On the whole, modernity has been characterized by the consistent growth of organizational power and activity, increasingly extending and refining the ability to influence and control things. This process may be termed "the Weberian imperative": the gradual extension of the principle of organizational control as a way of doing things that is considered legitimate, effective, and reliable.

One scholar, James R. Beninger, has extended Weber's notions to speculate about "the control revolution" that has led us to "the information society." In the modern world the ability of organizaions to expand their control over things and people has been enhanced by advances in technique. The manager of large organizations—Sears, Walt Disney Enterprises, IBM, the Pentagon, the Republican party, the University of California, and so on—face the task of using organizational and communication technology to refine their ability to exercise control. The need for speedy and accurate information gives impetus to the creation and use of increasingly efficient information technologies, including those media of communication with which we are all familiar—movies, radio, television, books, magazines, newspapers, and so on—as well as more recent innovations such as satellite communication, computers, fax machines, cellular phones, and interactive media. All these innovations enhance the rationalized reach of those seeking control via electronic mail, computer networking, even computerized espionage. The "wired" world we live in is the result of organizational necessity, but with large-scale consequences (again, unintended) for our lives, including the potential for the exercise of organizational controls through communications over what we think, feel, and do. Machiavelli's "few" (elites) still rule the "many" (masses), but now they do it with modern organizational and communications skills and techniques.

Since the many to be managed by the few include voters, consumers, taxpayers, workers, students, and myriad others, there is little surprise that the development of new techniques of propagating ideas has paralleled new techniques in information control. Unlike earlier eras, the marriage of large-scale organizations with the means of mass communication did not mean the expansion of brute force, or the predominance of fraudulent conspiring. It did mean that to the extent one had a possibility of ruling in mass society, it could only be accomplished in large measure through the control of mass communication, using suasion to direct large clusters of behavior in ways managers deemed acceptable. In the modern world, power increasingly resides in the ability of organizational managers to propagate messages that become fertile for large populations. The control revolution includes the control of discourse, with the ongoing effort to develop and refine the means, the messages, and the effects of communication.

The communications revolution of modernity gave impetus to the new propaganda industry. As Beninger notes, "increases in the volume of production, for example, have brought additional advantages to increased consumption, which manufacturers have sought to control using the information technologies of market research and mass advertising."[10] In the twentieth century, rationalized organizations regularly began to hire other organizations, such as market research and advertising agencies, to enhance their communication expertise, expand their influence with audiences, and control potential consumers. Publicity agencies and agents specializing in promoting products or persons' public images on behalf of paying clients became commonplace in various walks of life. Movie studios, for instance, developed a symbiotic relationship with publicity firms creating, promoting, and protecting the images of their widely known and idolized stars. Corporations, universities, and labor unions utilized the professional talents of public relations experts who propagated events, ideas, and impressions favorable to clients (see Chapter 6). Governmental institutions, such as the U.S. presidency and the U.S. Army employed press secretaries and spokesmen to embellish their coverage by newspapers, magazines, and the broadcast media (see Chapters 4 and 5). Finally, candidates for elective office gradually turned away from the political bosses of old and looked to professional media consultants, opinion pollsters, and public relations specialists to promote their candidacies. Increasingly, those interested in exercising control have turned to the expertise of the new propaganda industry.

All these innovations undertaken in the service of large-scale organizations helped make propaganda the most innovative and consequential form of communication of the modern age. Although, as we have seen, propaganda had its critics earlier in the twentieth century, the artistry behind organizationally based promotional, public relations, and related propaganda campaigns impressed both clients and the mass public. Proponents of propaganda, such as Edward Bernays, argued that the new agencies of mass propaganda provided indispensable and valuable information essential to the operation of a modern society. Yes, propaganda was a form of social advocacy, and it did use tactics such as control over the flow and direction of information, puffery, and subtle suggestion. But for Bernays, the role of the new suasive arts was to create consent among the governed, since that "consent" otherwise would be unformed and undirected. This, he insisted, did not mean manipulation of the governed but rather recognized the governed as sovereign: "The public today demands information and expects also to be accepted as judge and jury in matters that have a wide public import."[11] The many may be sovereign, but it was propaganda in the service of the few that gave them the information that let them learn what it was they were consenting to. In terms of communication, propaganda was the new authority, the source of knowledge of what one is supposed to think, feel, and do. And as technique increasingly established itself as important, propaganda became the communications technique it was legitimate to use in order to achieve desired effects. As a way of propagating messages, propaganda over time proved itself a reliable method of social propagation.

This legitimation of propaganda can be illustrated by the modern penchant to justify practices in the present by reference to a revered figure from the past. A pioneer advertising executive named Bruce Barton gave modern propaganda a religious aura through his widely read book, *The Man Nobody Knows* (1924). Jesus Christ, he wrote, was really the founder of modern business, a master of promotion and salesmanship, who "picked up twelve men from the bottom ranks" of society and "forged them into an organization which conquered the world" with a new and exciting product. Barton was an advertising genius who popularized Betty Crocker as a familiar icon for General Mills and did a public relations campaign for U.S. Steel that portrayed the profit-seeking giant as a great public benefactor. Barton viewed Jesus as a prototypical propagandist whose parables are exemplary advertising copy: "Jesus was a great advertising man," went the magazine advertisement for Barton's book. "He knew how to make words effective." Barton concludes that "the parables are the greatest advertisements of all times"; and "Jesus preached in the market place.'' The only difference, however, is now ''the modern market places are the advertising pages of newspapers and magazines, where the sellers of the nation display their wares before the millions of buyers.''[12] Such a justification strikes many Christians as blasphemous, but that wasn't Barton's aim. Rather what he wanted to convey was that propaganda was something practiced by the founder of the faith in order to propagate the church, and thus what is being done now through the use of the new propaganda is legitimate and proper. This may be dubious logic, but Barton's success in propagating his message suggests that in the modern age the practitioners of propaganda were seeking legitimating grounds for what they were doing, and could find it—as good propagandists always can—in sources that underscore the idea of propaganda as an authoritative mode of communication.

FEATURES OF A NEW PROPAGANDA: THE EMERGING DICTATORSHIP OF PALAVER

The thoroughly modern view of propaganda that developed in the twentieth century was consistent with the explosive growth of its use in a media age characterized by mass societies, innovations in mass communication, and large-scale corporate enclaves. Propaganda engendered an admiring attitude among its practitioners as an indispensable form of communication because it was deemed effective, even though that had not been conclusively demonstrated. Propaganda was becoming the new language of economic, cultural, and political innovation, flowing from the new organizational powers who managed mass communication. In this modern milieu, pioneer propaganda analyst Harold Lasswell amended his notion of people being duped by propaganda by appending a thought that hinted at things to come: ''The ever-present function of propaganda in modern life is in large measure attributable to the social disorganization which has been precipitated by the rapid advent of technological changes. . . . Literacy and the physical channels of communication have quickened the connection between those who rule and the ruled.'' Then appears Lasswell's closing statement (already cited in our preceding chapter): ''Democracy has proclaimed the dictatorship of palaver, and the technique of dictating to the dictator is named propaganda.''[13]

Let us ponder for a moment what Lasswell meant by that last statement. Modern propaganda emerged as a major form of public discourse because it spoke to what modern people wanted, or were told they wanted, through mass communication. Palaver involves, as we saw in our opening chapter, the use of guile and charm. And it implies talking profusely. Modern propaganda certainly grew profusely after the Renaissance. But what did Lasswell mean by the ''dictatorship of palaver''? In modern democracies widespread talk is ascendant, with economic, cultural, and political choices made amid multiple voices of pluralistic advocacy. The dictators are those who can best gain control of, to paraphrase Lasswell's phrase, ''who says what to whom in what channel.'' With the possibility of so many voices drowning each other out, the struggle for power becomes one to gain control over the channels of discourse: who dictates what discourse will be communicated? The new propaganda involved the mastery of all modern forms of palaver, so much so that in the effort to reach and sway large populations, propaganda no longer served as simply a *tool* of those bidding for control. No, propaganda gradually became *the sovereign form of public communication*. Once its bottle was uncorked by the emergence of mass populations, mass media, and organizational interests, the genie of propaganda could no longer be compelled to quietly return. Propaganda eventually achieved the status of sovereignity: it had become the expected form of public communication, with great powers attributed to it. A new propaganda that gradually emerged took on a life of its own and created, shaped, and dictated the options of propagandists themselves—as well as the options of those who were targets of persuasive and suasive messages. If palaver was king, then the palaverer who could dictate discourse exercised power through palaver.

As its title suggests, much of the remainder of this book is devoted to spelling out the distinctive character of the new propaganda. However, to give a preliminary but concrete idea of the difference between the new propaganda that was germinating and earlier forms, let us take some examples from print advertising. (We explore the palaver of advertising in much greater detail in Chapter 5). Consider this typical advertisement from the *Hampshire Gazette* of September 26, 1804:

ORANGE WRIGHT,

INFORMS his friends and customers, that he carries on the

BUTCHERING business; & by his experience in purchasing cattle

and sheep, he flatters himself that he can afford his meat

as cheap as any butcher, for cash or short credit.

Or a patent medicine ad in various publications (circa 1870–1880):

Allen's Cocaine Tablets

POSITIVELY

not injurious

For the Throat and Nerves

Cure Sore Throat, Neuralgia,

Nervousness, Headaches, Colds,

and Sleeplessness

Price .50 a Box at Druggists or by Mail

Allen Cocaine MFG Co.,

1254 Broadway, N.Y.

Now compare those straightforward ads with this classic magazine ad from the 1920s, one of the first great "soft sell" ads. The magazine picture shows a young and attractive woman staring off in the distance with a forlorn look on her face. The ad copy begins:

OFTEN A BRIDESMAID BUT NEVER A BRIDE

Edna's case was really a pathetic one. Like every woman, her primary ambition was to marry. Most of the girls of her set were married—or about to be. Yet not one possessed more grace or charm or loveliness than she. And as her birth-days crept gradually toward that tragic thirty-mark marriage seemed farther from her life than ever. She was often a bridesmaid but never a bride.

* * *

That's the insidious thing about halitosis (unpleasant breath). You, yourself, rarely know when you have it. And even your closest friends won't tell you.

This 1923 ad then goes on to extol the medicinal virtues of a new mouthwash named Listerine.

Now think about the differences in these three advertisements. All of them are instructive, for they provide information about a product. The first is a "pork chop ad," a forerunner of the kind of newspaper ads common in hawking the products of a local supermarket: we can sell you good meat cheaper than anyone else. The second ad too provides information but promises a valuable commodity: it will cure a variety of physical ailments and provide health. The third ad, however, is quite different: it tells a story. The Listerine ad places the product in an aesthetic context. The ad is instructive, providing information about the product; it also promises that the product will temporarily abate an evil, that is, "halitosis." But the ad also has the aesthetic quality of a parable, one that not only instructs and promises but also delights. The mythical Edna represents a common fear latent in many young women of her generation about marriage. Her story is an abbreviated version of a cultural folktale such as Cinderella or Sleeping Beauty except that it is incomplete. The imaginative reader can infer that Listerine will resolve the dilemma posed—why she doesn't have a husband—and let us fill in the blank: through the use of Listerine, bad breath becomes good breath, good-breathed people find suitable spouses, and thus they live happily ever after.

A reader's experience with such an ad, though brief and fleeting, nevertheless may record a lasting impression. A pleasantly told tale holding out hope of a happy ending exploits a logic more fully developed than in earlier ads: the product is a dramatic character, every bit as much as the woman, that solves a mystery regarding a widely feared individual problem. By the 1920s such logic appealed to people willing to suspend disbelief (on the face of it the ad's dramatic claim may be spurious). For those willing to make the leap of faith, such propaganda via advertising held out the lure of wishes fulfilled that might otherwise be denied by cold logic. But people do not live by cold logic alone. They share desires for acceptance and pleasure, like to see happy endings, and wish to believe in the efficacy of help. So a "pitch" like Listerine's little parable may make an impression that overcomes the strictures of logical proof. The logic of propaganda is not that of the syllogism, but rather of suasive palaver that people find fertile for their interests and desires. (The Listerine campaign of the 1920s was successful.)

This Listerine ad but hints at the fully sophisticated forms that the germinating new propaganda would take. In spite of its dramatic portrayal, the ad still emphasizes conventional modes of influence talk (recall our discussion in the preceding chapter) as well as palaver—namely, informative, evaluative, and expressive. But it is in the beauty, the aesthetic merit of the ad, that it approaches the art of palaver and masks blatant efforts to inform, evaluate, or express. The pictured image of a forlorn woman accompanying a folktale of pathos, grace, charm, love, a tragic flaw, and a redeeming resolution yields a message sufficiently ambiguous in content and even a little confusing in style for readers to draw their own conclusions—the essential character of palaver described in the last chapter.

Thus, the new propaganda that started to germinate in the early twentieth century differed from previous forms in its appeal to our aesthetic sensibility. At first the appeal was to engage our imaginations and hold our attentions on behalf of a product like Listerine. Then, as Machiavelli foresaw, appeals turned to creating our imaginations, indeed providing through entertainment imaginary worlds where we could interact with propagated products, people, places, and events. The new propaganda provided us with a vast and ever-renewed theater of the imagination, wherein a wide range of plays paraded before us in review for our delight and instruction.

After all these decades of propaganda, how effective have been these efforts to create imaginations? Research on that topic is vast in quantity, mixed in quality, and often contradictory in findings. However, as a case for effectiveness consider this example. In 1990 the Center for Science in the Public Interest reported a survey of 180 boys and girls, aged 8 to 12 living in Washington, D.C. The survey asked the children to name as many brands of beer or alcohol as they could and to name as many presidents of the United States as they could. The average child named 5.2 alcoholic beverages, 4.8 presidents. Here are typical results:

- A 7-year-old boy named 10 brands of beer and wine coolers, all correct; he named six presidents including ''Aprilham Linchon'' and ''Ragon.''
- A 10-year-old girl named 14 brands of alcoholic beverages, four presidents.
- An 11-year-old boy could accurately spell ''Matilda Bay,'' ''King Cobra,'' and ''Bud Light''; he named two presidents, ''Nickson'' and ''Rosselvet.''
- A 9-year-old boy listed ''gorge Buch'' and ''prestent ragen'' but with perfection wrote ''Molson Golden.''[14]

What this says about the effectiveness of beer ads remains unclear. Nor does one example validate our thesis. But it does suggest that at an early age, people are learning from commercial propaganda, in this case for a product they are too young to legally consume. They are not learning much about presidents, whom they likely tend to see on the news or hear about in school, both ''work'' settings of communication-pain. Alcohol commercials, by contrast, are colorful and exciting ''play'' settings memorable for their entertainment value. Such propaganda palaver has dramatic force, and thus creates an impression on the impressionable. It may even be the case that propaganda such as TV advertising may be a more powerful means of learning than school! (Another popular indicator of the impact of commercials is the extent to which we learn slogans from commercials: ''You've got the right one, baby''; ''Tastes great—less filling!''; ''It's not nice to fool Mother Nature''; and so on. The tale is told of a grade school teacher who gave her students a spelling test, at one point asking them how to spell the word *relief;* the answer came back R-O-L-A-I-D-S.)

The new propaganda, then, emphasizes entertainment values in an age when information, to be palatable, tends to be diverting. As propaganda analyst J. Michael Sproule notes, ''by the 1920s, advertisers were aware of the mass audience's seemingly inexhaustible appetite for messages presented in the form of amusement, an appetite we have not yet lost as entertaining and enticing ads come at us from all directions.''[15] For many people, a pleasant or simple story line (including ''bad news,'' which some people find pleasurable) is more entertaining than an unpleasant or complex fact; a simple and gripping falsehood is often more powerful than a complex and incomprehensible truth. For example, it may be difficult for organizations or leaders to command historical processes or complex events, but they can stage and control dramatic events for publicity purposes that substitute for the inability to control ''the real thing''—they claim the staged event is real, then control it. Like King Canute trying to command the waves to do his bidding, an action designed to focus attention on the symbol rather than the actuality can have dramatic force. Thus, for example, a president unable to stop an event such as the Soviet crackdown on Poland in 1981 instead delivers a solemn speech, then lights a candle in a White House window, commemorating the Poles' love of liberty, as Ronald Reagan did. In such instances, propaganda becomes the policy. The essential response to events is framed as a question of what propaganda message to send. The message is diverting, both in the sense of evoking an emotional and entertaining response, and in the sense of diverting attention away from the inability to affect events. This is not to say, of course, that propaganda is always a substitutionary, or phony, ploy to mask inaction; but that is clearly one of the ways it can be used.

In our time, propagandists of all stripes, but especially advertising and public relations experts, have not only used entertainment formats to increase the appeal of their ideas. They also began (again, really starting in the 1920s) to employ theories and methods of the social and behavioral sciences to understand the social and psychological makeup of the masses of people that were targets of influence talk. Different kinds of appeals targeted different groupings—classes, regions, genders, races, and other interests. The rationales of such targeting were in findings of market and motivational research generating demographic and psychographic data. For example, a current widely used psychographic model called VALS (Values and Lifestyles) breaks potential consumers down into groupings (Belongers, Emulators, Emulator-Achievers, Societally Conscious Achievers, and the Need-Directed); advertisers tailor specific appeals to each. Thus, Belongers have a strong desire to believe in a settled and homey world, so advertisers such as McDonald's appeal to a dinner at the franchise as a latter-day version of family bonding. L. L. Bean, a profitable mail-order enterprise, targets the Societally Conscious Achievers (often young professionals concerned about the environment). These same market segments are targets of manufacturers of sturdy and functional foreign cars (Volvo), trendy wines (Beringer), and casual clothes (Levi Dockers). In the era of the new propaganda, consumers constitute "consumption communities," people bonded together by nothing more than their common use of, or allegiance to, products—designer clothes, stereophonic or computer equipment, guns—that validate a lifestyle common to the community of purchasers (see Chapter 5).[16]

The new propaganda, like the forms of propaganda that preceded it, constitutes languages of power. Rather than a "marketplace of ideas" freely exchanging a wealth of information, power exercised via new propaganda more closely resembles "a supermarket of images in which large establishments offer to their customers a limited number of brands promoted by a few social leviathans."[17] On the other hand, we have an active role in dictating to the dictator what suasion we will accept and what we will reject. However, we cannot help but learn from the powerful languages of propaganda, from identifying beers to using slogans to identifying with consumption communities. Part of the modern condition is to be affected, in ways no one fully understands, by the ever-present and often diverting messages of the new propaganda. For many individuals who are constantly exposed to it, propaganda is *involving*.

Thus, beginning in some measure with the axial period of the 1920s, new languages of suasion emerged from the propaganda that had characterized influence and power from ancient to modern times. Appearing on the scene, albeit in only embryonic form, was a new propaganda—extended in dramatic presentation, often ambiguous in content and intent, sometimes confusing in style—that *involved* people in their own self-suasion. The outcome of this long historical shift has been to make propaganda the distinctive, and dominant, public language of the new information society, and the key normative aspect of modern mass communication.[18] For both those who spread and those who seek suasive messages, propaganda has become the normal language that sustains the relationships between institutions and individuals.

SOWING PROPAGANDA IN FERTILE FIELDS: THE CASE OF ADVERTISING'S PLURAL CONSEQUENCES

In his study of the consumer culture of the 1920s, Stuart Ewen argues that the change from an economy of *needs* to an economy of *wants* in the modern world required educating people in "the logic of consumerism." The language of advertising elevated the consumer economy to the status of a "philosophy of life" that tells people not only what to buy but also what to dream.[19] (Think of how this parallels Machiavelli's *fantasia* and the engineering of imaginations.) For those who live in affluent countries, the culture of consumption is a way of life largely taken for granted. The capacities of large modern organizations for producing a cornucopia of goods and services propagates the idea of a "people of plenty" with a habit of searching for ways to dispose of incomes.

The Economy of Want as a Seedbed of the New Propaganda

The affluence that drives a culture of consumption obviously gives impetus to the palaver of advertising, and the corollary fields of public relations and publicity—forms of propaganda helping to shape our culture and ourselves. No palaver was to be more important in the decades immediately following the 1920s than advertising, which began in the commercial promotion of products but expanded into cultural and political advertising. Advertising was to become one of the principal forms of the new propaganda, and probably the most familiar. As a source of social learning advertising has helped to teach us to see what we want, and want what we see.

We have already noted that the growth and expansion of advertising into different areas of modern life illustrates the power of propaganda to become an integral part of virtually any undertaking—school, sports, art, publishing, politics, and so on. It also illustrates the power of propaganda to have long-term consequences for our lives and society, consequences of which we are often not aware. With the expansion of American business enterprise in the nineteenth century, and the concentration of wealth at the top, economist Thorstein Veblen, in 1900, pointed out how the wealthy few had become a "leisure class" with an abundance of time and money on their hands. To set themselves off from ordinary, nonwealthy folks, according to Veblen, they devoted themselves to "conspicuous leisure" and "conspicuous consumption."[20] The "idle rich" as a class devoted themselves to the art of creatively doing nothing.

In Veblen's time the ability to spend discretionary income on pleasure cruises, jewelry, and mansions made the superrich conspicuous indeed in the ostentatious display of wealth. But as the consumption economy expanded, the same tendencies were soon to appear among members of the new middle class who wanted to pursue leisure and status symbols. Advertising made it possible for them to imagine what it would be like to consume products and services in a lavish way. Advertising propaganda thereby developed one of its standard pitches, one clearly calling for suspension of disbelief: that buying product X made one distinctive, fashionable, successful, romantic, and sometimes just plain erotic. The long-term impact of this successfully created fantasy was to give widespread cultural credence to the principle that *you are what you have*.

It is still true, of course, that the superrich remain conspicuous users of wealth, as illustrated in weekly episodes of the popular syndicated TV series "Lifestyles of the Rich and Famous." But even though most of us cannot live such a lavish life, publicizing of fabulous wealth and "snob appeals" in ads lends credence to the idea of an ideal lifestyle that can be attained by spending and consuming and making certain that others know about it. Veblen labeled this "pecuniary emulation," or what people used to mock as "keeping up with the Joneses."[21] There are obviously risks: in a culture of consumption people may grow obsessed with things (what Karl Marx had called "commodity fetishism") and spend themselves silly trying to shore up their sense of self-worth with possessions, identifying their very being with what they have. Ewen refers to this kind of modern identity as the "commodity self." Such an identity depends on advertising to propagate the idea that anyone can become socially conspicuous—glamorous, fashionable, charming, eternally youthful—and thereby stand out from the crowd of all those other people consuming the same things for precisely the same purpose of also being distinctive.[22] In this way, things become status symbols, shoring up our sense of self-worth: I own, therefore I am.

Commercial advertising as a form of propaganda, then, helped nurture an economy of wants after the 1920s and, in the process, was sowing the seedbeds that would enhance the spread of advertising itself. The wants of the potential consumer did not exist like eggs in a chicken coop to be gathered every morning. Advertising helped *create* as well as *channel* them. As David Potter points out, advertising tends to "minimize information and maximize appeal" and also "tends less to provide the consumer with what he wants then to make him like what he gets."[23] Even products of marginal differentiation—beer, cigarettes, household and body care items—can be portrayed as appealing through TV spot ad minidramas about their use in achieving social acceptance, having fun, and so on, even though "beer's beer" and "soap's soap." (See Chapter 5 for a detailed discussion of marginal differentiation.) Too, since now conspicuous consumption involves many millions of people finding meaning in a wide variety of consumables, advertisers use the Veblen strategy to market a wide variety of objects, putting a high price, and thus high prestige, on something people searching for conspicuousness will buy. A Rolex may not tell time any better than a $2.00 quartz watch, nor a Mercedes-Benz drive any better than a Chevette, but those who purchase the more expensive alternative are not necessarily demanding efficiency or economy but rather status and attention. The advertising-engineered fantasy that "you are what you have" thus stresses cultural values not only of materialism but also of narcissism—people absorbed in themselves and the commodities that define the self.[24]

A historian, T. J. Jackson Lears, has tried to put these various intended and unintended consequences of advertising propaganda in a consumer culture into historical perspective. In this century, he argues, advertisers adopted as their strategy "the therapeutic ethos." More and more, a product was not sold as something merely functional; rather it was a means of self-realization, offering therapeutic help in one's effort to cope with modern life. A product of the new age—canned food, for example—could be portrayed as both reviving nostalgic feelings of the recently lost rural past ("natural food") and also as the height of modern progress ("made in the most hygienic and scientific food laboratory in the world"). Such claims promise not only nourishing food but also warm feelings that link past, present, and future. "The new attention-getting strategies," writes Lears, "particularly the therapeutic emphasis on manipulating feeling rather than presenting information, led advertisers to a nether realm [a world located beneath or below] between truth and falsehood. . . . The world of advertisements gradually acquired an Alice-in-Wonderland quality."[25]

Critics of the culture of consumption point out that the wonderland of advertising so emphasizes materialism that people are captives of the goods they bought because they wanted, wanted because they suspended the disbelief that such goods would really do the trick, and hence thought they *must* have them. Grant McCracken, for instance, speaks of "the Diderot effect." He borrows the term from an essay written by the French Enlightenment philosopher Denis Diderot. Diderot lived in a simple and spare room with few possessions, comfortably working in an old and ragged dressing gown. Then someone gave him a new dressing gown, so elegant that his other paltry possessions seemed drab by comparison. So slowly but surely he acquired new and more lavish things—a desk, a tapestry, chairs, clock, and so on—that complemented his new dressing gown. In his essay Diderot bemoans all this, for he was quite content with his simple complement of goods until the dressing gown made him seek a new, and more expensive, set of possessions that fit with the elegance of the gown.

McCracken argues that the same sort of acquisitiveness occurs in the consumer culture, often perhaps without being fully realized. Suppose that advertising stimulates us to want a new object for our room or house. We buy it and place it in our dwelling; we notice that other things there don't fit with the new and fancier acquisition. So without fully knowing what we are doing, we eventually transform our abode with new purchases that conform with a new "product complement" of our possessions. "The meaning of a good is best (and sometimes only) communicated when this good is surrounded by a complement of goods that carry the same significance. . . . The symbolic properties of material culture are such that things must mean together if they are to mean at all."[26] Thus advertising feeds a kind of expansionary principle of consumption: one new thing is never enough, and even many new things may not be quite enough. In that way, advertising recurrently creates new dissatisfactions, which can be satisfied only by another cycle of consumption.

Popular Culture as a Seedbed of New Propaganda

With or without the Diderot effect, modern advertising provides a classic illustration of a form of new propaganda germinating in the seedbeds of the 1920s that emphasizes guile and charm (palaver) to create, reinforce, and channel people's wants; advertising then flourishes in the seedbed of those wants it has created. In addition to the economic, material, tangible consequences involved in sustaining a culture of consumption, advertising propaganda has also had an impact upon a related area, "popular culture." We explore how the new propaganda operates in today's popular culture in Chapter 6. Here we merely wish to suggest how popular culture provides a rich seedbed for propagandistic appeals.

The modern forces (most notably the rise of the populous nation-state, large corporations, and extensive networks of mass media) that contributed to the economy of wants, and the palaver of economic power that went with it, also advanced the arrival of popular culture. The culture of the populace was, like the mass economy, not imposed from above on unwilling populations by crass elites bent on exploiting the masses. As with the economic culture of consumption, there was a gradual process of cultural producers and consumers creating and nurturing one another. Popular books, movies, radio, newspapers, magazines, television—all the mass media became vehicles for both the organizers and the consumers of popular palaver. The modern organizations operating printing presses, airways, movie theaters, and so forth promoted their cultural products for potentially vast audiences. Concomitantly, modern people actively sought mass media for information, instruction, diversion, entertainment, and other purposes.

The 1920s serves again as a convenient historical takeoff point for the expansion of popular promotion, since it was in that period that identifiable forms of celebrity hype, creative uses of publicity, media evangelism, popular fads such as music (jazz) and musical stars (Rudy Vallee), sensational tabloid newspapers, the spectacle of sports, and other popular fare became prominent. To match an economy of wants in modern society there evolved a culture of wants. No longer was culture—religion, art, literature, music, folklore, sport—the province of either elites (established churches, "high art") or traditional folkways (fairy tales and folk music). Rather culture was created for, and mediated by, mass audiences who wanted to fill leisure time with popular play. No longer was it clear that cultural experiences could be denied those who demanded them and could pay for them regardless of their economic, social, and educational circumstances. Although there were, and are, many powerful constraints on popular culture, it is possible to argue that since the 1920s, mass merchandisers and consumers of desire have opted for wider and often increasingly lurid cultural experiences, including heavy metal music, torrid romance novels, professional wrestling, the demolition derby, slasher/splatter movies, and pornographic films. Popular tastes may not be particularly refined, but in a civilization that legitimates mass cultural expression, they are also hard to deny.

The emergent popular culture was institutionalized through Hollywood film production, book and magazine publishing houses, radio and television networks, and music producers. All had products to merchandise (fantasies, hopes, and dreams as much as tangible goods) through the "channels of desire" they controlled. Since purveyors of popular culture competed with one another for potential customers' discretionary money (the "leisure dollar"), they exploited propagandistic hype to create and sustain audiences. The palaver of popular culture was a descendant of the public hawking of the old-time carnival barker, attracting a crowd by urging people to "Hurry, hurry, hurry, step right up, folks, don't be shy" to see the unbelievable wonders and delights made believable by suspending disbelief.

With the advent of the new propaganda, promotion would become modern and sophisticated. The motion picture industry was a primary seedbed of the new promotion. When people went to the movies, they saw not only a movie but also a "trailer," usually called "Previews of Coming Attractions," that promoted ever more exciting thrills, chills, and spills in new movies "coming soon to a theater near YOU!" Book distributors discovered that the sales of a new novel aimed at a popular audience could be increased not only by advertising (think of the blurbs on paperback edition covers: "pulse-pounding action," "couldn't wait to turn the page," "a puckish spoof of contemporary mores"). The publicity generated by having a book censored or even banned from sale was also a seductive lure ("Banned in Boston," "Too Hot for Cincinnati"). Hollywood, with a large stake in hyping the images of its movie stars, entered into cozy relationships with "fanzines" (*Photoplay* or *Modern Screen* are examples) that fabricated stories about the glamorous offscreen lives and exploits of stars: "That Cagney Cyclone," "Why Gable is King," "Garbo Finds Love," and the contemporary, apparently forever, "Sad Life of Marilyn [Monroe]" or latest report of an "Elvis Sighting." Additionally, the gossip column was a favored channel to propagate the fame of Hollywood stars and starlets.

Another apt illustration of a seedbed for propaganda's growth in popular culture is that of popular religion. Ideally religion and theology invoke the realm of the sacred. In modern society, however, religious faiths, doctrines, and bodies are products promoted and merchandised by cultural entrepreneurs. With radio, then television, churches no longer were confined to sanctuaries or restricted to solemn appeals. One of the pioneers of modern religious promotion and electronic evangelism was Aimee Semple McPherson, who in the 1920s established a "Cathedral of the Air" that broadcast her appeals from her radio station and her Angelus Temple in Los Angeles. Sister Aimee became the first woman to hold a Federal Communications Commission broadcaster's license, in the belief that "to thrive in the present day religion must utilize present-day methods."[27] She was the first modern-day preacher to utilize virtually every medium for the propagation of the faith—radio, records, movies, books, and pamphlets. Just prior to her death she was planning to exploit television in her ministry as well.

Sister Aimee possessed a sense of theater characteristic of the new cultural propaganda. For instance, she delivered sermons on such topics as "What Would Jesus Do if He Were a Great Movie Director like Cecil B. deMille?" from a pulpit in the form of a giant Easter lily. Attired in a stamen-yellow gown, she showcased a huge mock radio that "dialed" changing biblical scenes; a "rock of ages" from whose cleft Aimee emerged; and a grist mill whose water flowed into the baptismal font. In her heyday, she had millions of followers around the world linked together by her International Church of the Foursquare Gospel and by mass media outreach. She was the major precursor of today's televangelists who propagate electronic churches through the adroit use of promotion: television, mass mailings, taped messages, home Bible courses, and so forth. Sister Aimee understood that the "present-day methods" of propaganda were essential for religious entrepreneurship, a lesson that her successors—Oral Roberts, Jerry Falwell, Pat Robertson, Jim and Tammy Bakker—learned from her precedent of "theological entertainment."[28] Popular religion in an age of propaganda is characterized by constant efforts of promotion, not only to rejuvenate the faithful but also to expand the audience and fill the electronically powered collection plate.

The Political Culture of the New Propaganda

Finally, the modern palaver of new propaganda became an integral part of politics. Again the earliest seeds germinated in the 1920s as newly founded political regimes grew increasingly sophisticated at propagating ideas not alone by force and fraud, but by fantasy.

In the new Soviet Union, for example, Lenin created the state propaganda apparatus known as *Agitprop* (the Department of Agitation and Propaganda) that established propaganda as the dominant form of mass communication. Everything from art to circus acts had to conform to standards of "socialist realism," and all media—the press, literature, education—were to conform to the propaganda aims and policies of the regime. In Italy, the new dictator Benito Mussolini mobilized all means of mass communication under the tutelage of a fascist state, a precedent that would be carried to a perverse perfection in Adolf Hitler's Nazi Germany.

In democratic countries, leaders like Franklin D. Roosevelt in the United States and Winston Churchill in Great Britain were masterful in their use of radio; demagogues such as Father Charles Coughlin built huge politico-religious followings through weekly radio broadcasts in America. With the advent of television arrived a telepolitical age marked by mass participation via television in electoral campaigns, presidential spectacles, royal weddings, assassinations of heads of state, wars, space exploration, and numerous events frequently exploited for their propaganda value in the mass media age.

The professionals who mastered the "flack arts" (a derogatory term for advertising, public relations, and publicity) in nonpolitical fields gradually transferred their skills to political management. As the new propaganda developed, show business practices combined with political purposes. An early example came in 1934 when Hollywood moguls joined forces with Republican state leaders and the public relations firm of Whitaker & Baxter (see Chapter 5) to defeat the Democratic candidate for governor of California, Upton Sinclair. Sinclair was an activist, reformist, and muckraking author. The prospect of his becoming governor aroused the ire of Hollywood's leaders—especially Louis B. Mayer of MGM, Harry Cohn of Columbia Studios, and MGM's "Boy Wonder," Irving Thalberg. Sinclair proposed new taxes on the Hollywood studios and the policy of placing unemployed workers in the film industry in positions at other industries. The moguls used force—coercing studio employees to contribute to a fund for Sinclair's opponent, threatening writers and even top stars such as Katherine Hepburn with dismissal if they supported Sinclair.

And they also used propaganda (laced with fraud). Since MGM produced Metronome Newsreels, the studios used the opportunity to make anti-Sinclair pitches in the guise of news. "Seeing is believing," or so audiences of the 1930s who had faith in newsreel reports thought. What better vehicle for dispensing propaganda than seemingly legitimate filmed versions of events? The newsreels, titled *The Inquiring Reporter*, depicted respectable citizens (actually actors) making spontaneous statements that they would be voting for Frank Merriam (Sinclair's opponent); disreputable, unshaven, unwashed "citizens" parroted their support for Sinclair. Said a grandmotherly lady rocking in a chair on her front porch, a vote for Merriam would "save my little home: it's all I have left in the world." A man with beard and boots, affecting a Russian accent, said he favored Sinclair; "his system vorked vell in Russia, vy can't it vork here?" Finally, a newsreel released just prior to the election portrayed hordes and droves of unemployed hobos migrating to California at the prospect of a Sinclair victory. The filmed scenes in the newsreel were actually from a movie, *Wild Boys of the Road,* again using actors straight from Central Casting, the pool of unengaged actors seeking small character and walk-on parts.

Sinclair lost, and the face of electoral politics in California, and later the nation, was markedly changed. Four years later Merriam's opponents used show business techniques to thwart his bid for reelection; they exploited radio shows, endorsements by a host of stars and starlets, and a media blitz of "political humdingery." In the United States and increasingly in other countries of the world the result of such wedding of political and entertainment values has made propaganda the principal form of political communication not only in elections but elsewhere as well. Today we routinely expect messages from the White House, Westminster, the Kremlin, and other political locales across the globe to bear the mark of professional propagandists. Propaganda is now a normal and accepted part of routine politics, not just limited to tailoring messages during a political celebration, campaign, crisis, or war. President Calvin Coolidge said in the 1920s that "the business of government is business." In the 1990s it might more accurately be said to be propaganda.

As with modern economic wants and modern cultural wants, a gradually evolving new propaganda has become the indispensable way of creating, organizing, even fulfilling political wants—if not tangibly then with drama, fantasy, spectacle, and pizazz. Thus, for example, presidential propaganda directs us toward laudable, desirable, yet obtainable aims ("a drug-free America") or away from wanting perhaps equally laudable, desirable, low priority policies (drug rehabilitation). Thereby a politics of wants, of course, may often have very little to do with day-to-day governing, but a great deal to do with maintaining popular political quiescence (reassuring people that the economy is "fundamentally sound" and will soon recover) or inducing popular political arousal (whipping up sentiment to fight a war). A major task of modern ruling is to convince the public that they really want to trust the judgment and assertions of those who rule, and that rulers are actually servants of wants that only they can fulfill.

CONCLUSION: DOES PROPAGANDA PROPAGATE PROPAGANDA?

Political propaganda, like that of the economic marketplace or the cultural showplace, is frequently decried by critics as misleading, deceitful prevarication. Perhaps it is. We shall have many opportunities in the following chapters to explore that claim. However, we conclude this survey of the conditions, yea fertilizer, of modernity that have stimulated the long-term growth of a new propaganda with another thought. Perhaps economic, cultural, religious, political, and other leaders have discovered what Machiavelli spoke of almost five centuries ago: among the many things people want, even need and demand of leaders, for sustenance and for happiness, is propaganda. For propaganda as a form of communication simplifies and directs choices, offering an understandable way of coping based on a leap of faith and on credulity, rather than producing doubt and uncertainty such as so often flows from scientific evidence or rational argument. If that is so, then the most successful thing that the new propaganda propagates is propaganda itself. Let us now turn to examining a few individuals who helped make all of that possible, if indeed it is.

This chapter has demonstrated that propaganda was, and is, an important addition to the practices and institutions associated with the rise of modernity. The modern state, modern economics, modern popular culture would not have become what they are without the communications power of propaganda. The history of propaganda has been one of steady expansion and increased sophistication of message. Now hardly any major enterprise is undertaken without due consideration to what kind of propaganda needs to be generated. Propaganda is no longer a choice, rather it is an expectation. In the history of communications, propaganda has risen to prominence as a palaver of power useful in the mastery of ruling. The reader should now see more clearly how this came about, and how much propaganda has become a dominant and compelling modern force. Now with that in mind, let us humanize this long process by looking at some of the key individuals who both practiced and spoke of the arts of propaganda.

NOTES

1. *The Holy Bible,* 1 Sam. 18:27.
2. K. R. Minogue, "Theatricality and Politics: Machiavelli's Concept of Fantasia," in B. Parekh and R. N. Berki, eds., *The Morality of Politics* (London: George Allen and Unwin, 1972), p. 160.
3. David F. Luckenbill, "Power: A Conceptual Framework," *Symbolic Interaction* 2 (1979): 101–103.
4. Ibid, pp. 101–103.
5. Erika G. King, "Exposing the 'Age of Lies': The Propaganda Menace as Portrayed in American Magazines in the Aftermath of World War I," *Journal of American Culture* 12 (Spring 1989): 35–40.
6. Ibid, pp. 35–40.
7. Harold Lasswell, *Propaganda Techniques in the World War* (London: Kegan, Paul, Trench, Truber, 1927), p. 2.
8. Edward L. Bernays, cited in King, "Exposing the 'Age of Lies,' " pp. 38–39.
9. Max Weber, *The Theory of Social and Economic Organization,* A. H. Henderson, trans., Talcott Parsons, ed. (Glencoe, IL: Free Press, 1947).
10. James R. Beninger, *The Control Revolution: Technological and Economic Origins of the Information Society* (Cambridge: Harvard University Press, 1981).
11. Edward L. Bernays, *Crystallizing Public Opinion* (New York: Liveright, 1923), p. 36.
12. See Edrene S. Montgomery, "Bruce Barton's 'The Man Nobody Knows': A Popular Advertising Illusion," *Journal of Popular Culture* 19(3) (Winter 1985): 21–34.
13. Harold D. Lasswell, "The Theory of Political Propaganda," *American Political Science Review* 21 (1927): 631.
14. Bob Greene, "Beer Makers Draft Their Recruits Early—and Effectively," *The Dallas Morning News,* July 29, 1991, p. 5 J.
15. J. Michael Sproule, "The New Managerial Rhetoric and the Old Criticism," *Quarterly Journal of Speech* 74 (1988): 468–486.
16. Sproule, ibid., pp. 473–474.
17. Sproule, ibid., p. 473; Daniel J. Boorstin, *The Americans: The Democratic Experience* (New York: Random House, 1973), pt. 2, pp. 89–164; William Meyers, *The Image Makers* (New York: Times Books, 1984).
18. Sproule, "The New Managerial Rhetoric," p. 484.
19. Stuart Ewen, *Captains of Consciousness* (New York: McGraw-Hill, 1976), pp. 108–109.
20. Thorstein Veblen, *The Theory of the Leisure Class* (New York: Penguin, 1979).
21. Veblen, ibid., chap. 5.
22. Ewen, *Captains of Consciousness.*

23. David M. Potter, *People of Plenty* (Chicago: University of Chicago Press, 1954), pp. 187–188.

24. Christopher Lasch, *The Culture of Narcissism* (New York: Norton, 1979).

25. T. J. Jackson Lears, "From Salvation to Self-Realization: Advertising and the Therapeutic Roots of the Consumer Culture, 1880–1930," in Richard Wightman Fox and T. J. Jackson Lears, eds., *The Culture of Consumption: Critical Essays in American History, 1880–1980* (New York: Pantheon Books, 1983), p. 21.

26. Grant McCracken, *Culture and Consumption* (Bloomington: Indiana University Press, 1988), p. 121.

27. Gloria Ricci Lothrop, "West of Eden: Pioneer Media Evangelist Aimee Semple McPherson in Los Angeles," *Journal of the West* 27 (April 1988): 50–59.

28. Ibid, pp. 50–59.

CHAPTER **2**

Old Masters and New Propagators

The previous chapters outlined the conceptual basis for the study of propaganda and traced the development of modern propaganda into the form we are familiar with today. This modern innovation of the new propaganda was the outgrowth of a process, but people are the historical agents of social process. The centuries of change brought about the creation of professional propagandists and the organizational power they created in the service of propaganda. The more important of such figures are representative of the emerging philosophy of discursive practices that accompanied the new propaganda and its agencies. In order to humanize the innovative force of modern propaganda, here we wish to look at the careers and thought of several key figures who will illustrate further the power, and the pragmatic philosophy, of the new propagandists. Through such inquiry into the people who made propaganda, you may gain insight into the mentality, and the practice that flows from a way of thinking, of propaganda as a way of life.

P. T. Barnum was one of the best-known figures of nineteenth-century America. As a poor boy growing up, Barnum was fascinated by the arts of entertaining, fooling people, and drawing a crowd. Those carnival (''carny'') arts did not set well with residents in the Calvinist areas of the United States of Barnum's youth, yet he strove to develop them to perfection. An early business partner told him that ''all we need to insure success is notoriety''; and all that takes is any clever publicity trick that ''will be noised all about town.''
Noising plus notoriety spells a paying crowd. This was the first lesson the young Barnum learned. For the rest of his highly public life, Barnum noised a wide variety of entertaining spectacles about town, appealing to people's interest in what he convinced them was extraordinary. He grew famous, and infamous, for ingenious hoaxes, such as displaying what he alleged was the 161-year-old slave nurse of the boy George Washington; unbelievable creatures such as a mermaid; freaks like the diminutive Charles Sherwood Stratton (Barnum gave him the circus name of ''General Tom Thumb''); and such ''monstrosities'' as the elephant Jumbo, billed as the only surviving mastodon! Barnum's Amer-

ican Museum in New York and touring Greatest Show on Earth (eventually becoming the Ringling Brothers, Barnum and Bailey Circus) was world famous. He became a celebrity who in turn made unknown and often bizarre people into other celebrities: "The Swedish Nightingale" Jenny Lind, the original Bearded Lady and the Siamese Twins. If anyone understood the artistry in the craft of publicity, Barnum did—contriving and staging events, exploiting news to stir up fabricated controversies that kept people buzzing, and conjuring up flagrant hoaxes to maximum attention-getting effect; then to keep the pot boiling, admitting they were hoaxes.

"Barnum's great discovery was not how easy it is to deceive the public, but rather, how much the public enjoyed being deceived." Clearly in Barnum echo themes of Machiavelli's sixteenth century *The Prince* discussed in Chapter 1. Here was one who knew all about the engineering of imagination through *fantasia*. Not only was Barnum comfortable with the title Prince of Humbugs, characteristically he claimed that he made it up for the public to apply to himself. After all, he said, his humbuggery and "clap-trap" were "mixed up with the great realities I provide."[1]

In the previous chapter, we outlined how propaganda became a force in the modern world. But as our references to important actors and observers of the process (Edward Bernays, Harold Lasswell, Bruce Barton, Aimee Semple McPherson, the Hollywood moguls of the 1930s, and others) imply, great forces of history are residues of human action. In this chapter we inspect the careers, practices, and thoughts of a selected set of masters of the art of propaganda who sowed the seeds of a crop that flourished and, in the process, opened seedbeds for plantings of the new propaganda. The propagandists we discuss are certainly not the only ones who mastered the art. Rather they compose a group of practitioners who reflected upon their craft and recorded those thoughts in writing. Their ruminations provide a corpus of lore, traditions, habits, and practices essential for understanding the germination of the new propaganda. The figures we scrutinize have been lionized as heroes, damned as villains, and laughed at as fools, but all have been vital in propagating not only propaganda but its art.

IN THE BEGINNING WAS IVY LEDBETTER LEE

We start with an axial generation of new propagandists who experienced World War I, then built their careers in the 1920s. Like the pioneering Barnum who sensed the appeal of humbuggery in a mass society, these innovators realized they too could combine a little humbug, showmanship, and theatrics with information to create "great realities" for a postwar world that was rapidly changing. In the United States particularly, the spread of mass democracy through the popular election of U.S. senators, the extension of the franchise to women, and other progressive reforms introduced new segments of the populace to politics. Those segments wanted to be informed; they also wanted entertainment. Here was the historical opportunity for the germination of a new expertise, that is, professional public relations.

Pioneer public relations counselor Ivy Ledbetter Lee, who we shall see had notable corporate clients, was influential through his speeches, writing, and business in teaching a logic of new organizational thinking about how to relate to the public.[2] Lee deemed it essential in the modern age for organizations and nations to speak loudly, to address the "vast power of the multitude" and their elevation to a status of virtual "divine right." The professional publicist could deal with this new ascendancy of the masses by serving as "courtier to the crowd," one "who molds public sentiment."

Lee argued for the creative use of propaganda (although he didn't use that term) in the "proper adjustment of the inter-relations" between organizations and the public, for in such adjustment "must rest the orderly and healthy development of American business in the future." At first, he called his work publicity, believing (as journalist Bill Moyers said in a PBS series featuring Lee) in "the alchemy of publicity" to refurbish images and spread ideas; by the 1920s this professional undertaking of "adjustment" he began to term public relations. Lee meant the use of all means of propagation, "the entire gamut of expression of an idea or of an institution," not only including newspapers and "fact sheets" but also "the radio, the moving picture, magazine articles, speeches, books, mass meetings, brass bands."

A professional molder of public sentiment, Lee believed, must understand the "psychology of the multitude." In order to gain public acceptance of corporate power, like all great "statesmen, preachers, and soldiers," the modern publicist should recognize the principles of leadership applied to modern mass society. One such principle was to cultivate the art of being believed, mainly by propagating messages in dynamic ways that supplant "erroneous statements." The publicist, however, should avoid open dialectical argument with those who are in error (e.g., unions, reformers, editorialists); it was better to state "the truth," which was apparently the exclusive province of Lee's clients to define. In stating that truth to the public, avoid abstract appeals: "A public to be influenced must feel. . . . To make the public feel, we must be concrete." Fact, he thought, "produces an effect upon the people's imaginations and emotions. It tells its own story, it supplies its own inference."

Like many other successful molders of public sentiment, Lee had a low opinion of human nature and the rationality of the public. The "crowd craves leadership." Don't expect people "merely to reason the case out" on their own. "People are interested in their own affairs, they are not very much interested in your affairs and they will not analyze statistics." The language one must use in communicating with the public is commonplace, featuring simple, appealing phrases and direct sentences. Lee's advice on this point reflects his background as a newspaperman prior to pioneering in the founding of public relations as a profession.

Lee admired evangelist Billy Sunday, who commanded a wide following, because "he speaks the language of the common man." Lee sought to "humanize" one of his clients, the New York subway utility, by doing for the corporation "what Billy Sunday has done for religion." As the popular evangelist humanized religion, so would Lee humanize business by bringing "the personality of the management forward in such a way that the people will realize that the men who run their street cars have red blood in their veins." For instance, Lee instructed the utility company to publish news sheets and post them in the cars of subway trains. These notices expressed the "concern" of the managers for safety and convenience, in language that avoided "unfortunate suggestion(s) to the popular mind." Lee designed his campaign to give the impression to the general public, and especially to the riders of the subway, that the president of the utility was personally concerned for their safety; that the utility was not owned by a small cabal of greedy, gouging capitalists; and that a rate increase was in the public interest, but labor demands were not.

Lee did not confine himself to domestic public relations. In a 1934 speech entitled "The Problem of International Propaganda," Lee stressed that the hostility of wartime propaganda had to be replaced by the give-and-take of mutual propaganda between nations. He based this call on the view that propaganda was not misleading but rather a natural form of communication in a world of pluralistic advocacy. By speaking loudly and clearly, he insisted, propaganda could overcome international barriers and misunderstandings. Rather than rely on the traditional language of protocol and diplomacy, national propaganda should exploit the mass media—print, motion pictures, radio—to convey perspectives to the world. For instance, Lee argued that if Italy—widely regarded at the time as brutally militaristic—would openly present its case to the world in a series of motion pictures prefaced by messages from its ruling dictator Benito Mussolini, who was a moving speaker, the nation's standing in the world's eyes would be enhanced. Lee also opined that everyone could learn from Franklin D. Roosevelt's creative use of the radio in the United States.

The only evil of propaganda, Lee maintained, was not in the effort to propagate ideas, but in hiding the source; if the origin of messages were known (even a dictator such as Mussolini), people could judge their merits. However, Lee's effort to advise first the German chemical combine I. G. Farben and then the German Nazi government on positive public relations shook even Lee's faith in the felicitous consequences of public relations. The success of Nazi propaganda both in mobilizing the blind support of the German masses and in cowing the rest of the European powers profoundly disillusioned Lee. Lee, for example, told the German reichsminister for propaganda Joseph Goebbels (see below) that blatant Nazi propaganda in the United States would fail, and that the Nazis should be more conciliatory toward the foreign press. (When Goebbels then made a conciliatory speech, the American ambassador claimed this was Lee's doing.)

As criticism of public relations and propaganda began to mount (recall the discussion in Chapter 1), Lee was attacked as "Poison Ivy." One historian expressed a widely shared opinion of Lee that "Niccolò Machiavelli could scarcely have given the modern princes more apt advice,"[3] a misreading of both Lee and Machiavelli! But Lee shared with Machiavelli the failure to foresee that the practice of *fantasia* and the engineering of imagination would be regarded as sinister rather than necessary and inevitable. Lee viewed himself as an intermediary between the emergent large organizations of the modern world and the democratic masses who wanted a say in what their leaders did. Historian Foster Rhea Dulles wrote to Lee's biographer that although Lee was a man of great rectitude, the institutionalizing of public relations eventually "weakened the fabric of our society with its emphasis on the image rather than the reality."[4]

Like many propagandists, Ivy Lee took for granted that his practices displayed integrity. He told clients that "the first and most important feature of any plan of publicity should be its absolute frankness; that there should be no devious ways."[5] And Lee, again like most public relations practitioners who venerate their own innovations, railed at the charge that he was a liar who told untruths that served the wealthy and the powerful. Yet as we shall see in Part II of this book, the new propaganda that emerged with figures like Lee rested on a philosophy of discursive practices that made truth something other than, and more than, the "unvarnished truth."

Ivy Lee enjoyed a long and lucrative career; he represented numerous major corporate interests, such as the Rockefellers (see Chapter 5), and built a reputation as a genius in his craft, a craft he virtually founded. Until his death he was diligent in "his careful tending of the fertile Fourth Estate. He was an anxious gardener of the press, pruning and clipping, urging the growth of strong stories in an old plot and stamping out poisonous news in another."[6] Lee was one of the founding masters of the modern art of propagation, combining in his thinking ideas about both the theory and practice of propaganda.

EDWARD L. BERNAYS: THE PROPAGANDIST AS BENEVOLENT SCIENTIST

Edward L. Bernays once remarked that the difference between him and Ivy Lee was that Lee's work was an art and his was a science.[7] If so, perhaps it accounts for the fact that in a society that holds science in higher esteem than art it is Bernays, not Lee, who is regarded as the father of modern public relations. Lee's expertise and sage advice came from his personal experience and contact with the powerful people he counseled as clients. By contrast, Bernays theorized that public relations and propaganda in general could be put on a sounder scientific basis through the study of public opinion, mass psychology, and the basic urges of human desire. He came to this conviction after working in World War I for the Committee on Public Information, the U.S. propaganda arm, and through his family connections (Sigmund Freud was his uncle).

When Bernays's pathbreaking book, *Crystallizing Public Opinion*, was published in 1923, Freud wrote his nephew, "I have received your book. As a truly American product, it interested me greatly." Freud implied that Bernays was a bit too cocksure of his ability to change attitudes, mold opinion, and direct behavior—brash claims he thought typical of Americans. In any case, Freud did little to diminish Bernays's confidence about the power of the propagandist to affect the world in benevolent and socially useful ways. During his long career Bernays lived to see "a scientific attitude" about public relations, and propaganda in general, emerge in the form of an academic subject and practical way of "crystallizing public opinion"[8] (see Chapter 6).

Bernays, like Lee and the others who became "public relations counsels" in the 1920s, viewed the profession as a response to "perhaps the most significant social, political, and industrial fact about the present century," namely, the "increased attention . . . paid to public opinion." Although Bernays rejected the idea that this new profession engaged in "thought control," he was comfortable with calling it "the engineering of consent," arguing that "with the myriad ideas and things in the marketplace competing for the attention and action of the public today, proper engineering becomes a prime requisite to gaining that consent." The propagandist would be that engineer.[9]

Bernays applied the term *engineering* by extension to the practical application of the social sciences. Those who would engineer public opinion must face the fact, according to Bernays, that people in the mass form opinions on the basis of little knowledge, are often intolerant, and are "logic-proof." In dealing with the "established beliefs," the public relations counsel "must either discredit the old authorities or create new authorities by making articulate a mass opinion against the old belief or in favor of the new." People's opinions are both "stubborn and malleable," resting alternatively on existing attitudes or on changeable or nonexistent attitudes. The publicist "must discover what the stimuli are to which public opinion responds most readily." People are members of "the group and herd,'' and their responses follow discernible patterns that are "suggestible." "Propaganda," said Bernays, "is a purposeful, directed effort" to overcome "the inertia of established traditions and prejudices." Applied social science could "scientifically evaluate the hopes, aspiration, ignorances, knowledge, apathy and prejudices of the public,"[10] and the professional propagandist could plan accordingly.

Modern society, wrote Bernays, is a matter of "organizing chaos" by largely "invisible governors," that is, the "new propagandists" charged with "the conscious and intelligent manipulation of the organized habits and opinions of the masses." Left to themselves, voters are confused by competing claims and drawn in a hundred directions by different candidates or ideas. Accordingly, citizens have "voluntarily agreed to let an invisible government" narrow choices and simplify data for the practical purpose of "organizing and focusing" a public opinion "necessary to orderly life." Since "the technical means have been invented and developed by which opinion may be regimented," the "new propaganda" makes it possible "so to mold the mind of the masses that they will throw their newly gained strength in the desired direction." Indeed, whatever of "social importance is done today . . . must be done with the help of propaganda. Propaganda is the executive arm of the invisible government."[11] The engineers of consent now govern.

As an "expert on the public," the public relations counsel is an integral part of "the intelligent few" who have become aware of "the possibilities of regimenting the modern mind." Barnum's "great realities" can be crafted, since reality is not a condition, it is a creation. "The counsel on public relations," wrote Bernays, "not only knows what news value is, but knowing it, he is in a position to make news happen. He is a creator of events." In a world in which publicity is central, it is "news interest which gives him an opportunity to make his ideas travel and get the favorable reaction," to "create news around his ideas." If he can "isolate ideas and develop them into events," the ideas can then be "more readily understood" and "claim attention as news." It is a public relations counsel's "capacity for crystallizing the obscure tendencies of the public mind before they have reached definite expression, which makes him so valuable."[12]

Indeed, the various professions involved in the "consistent, enduring effort to create or shape events to influence the relations of the public to an enterprise, idea, or group" all engage in the "practice of creating circumstances and of creating pictures in the minds of millions of persons." The practice of propagandizing is "universal and continuous." And "virtually no important undertaking is now carried on without . . . regimenting the public mind." Since "approval of the public is essential to any large undertaking," rulers of any sort "find in propaganda a tool which is increasingly powerful in gaining that approval." Bernays makes the "intelligent few," the engineers of consent, sound like a Platonic elite, whose ruling task is to shape and direct the inchoate public mind.[13]

The "new propaganda . . . not infrequently serves to focus and realize the desires of the masses," since any desire, "however widespread, cannot be translated into action until it is made articulate." No matter what it is that groups and masses desire, they have to "call upon propaganda to organize and effectuate their demand." But the fact remains that "small groups of persons"—again the "intelligent few" who understand and use propaganda—"can, and do, make the rest of us think what they please about a given subject."[14] Public opinion is again too important a thing to be left to the public.

Numbered as he was a member of the "invisible government," Bernays had an illustrious career both as an active consultant and as a propagandist for the efficacy of the new propaganda. Bernays helped popularize the use of the *pseudoevent* (an event staged for publicity purposes) as a way to gain favorable news coverage of a person, cause, corporation, or idea on behalf of clients. He smiled upon the use of gimmicks in, for instance, the world of fashion, where clever publicity campaigns create fads and styles. Such popular publicizing cannot be achieved randomly: "Propaganda is not a science in the laboratory sense. . . . It is now scientific in the sense that it seeks to base its operations upon definite knowledge drawn from direct observation of the group mind, and upon the application of principles which have been demonstrated to be consistent and relatively constant." We know from direct observation, Bernays thought, that people are gregarious (identifying with the herd), irrational ("judgement is a melange of impressions stamped on . . . [the] mind by outside influences which unconsciously control . . . thought"), and impressionable (amenable to suasion). People think in cliches, "pat words or images which stand for a whole group of ideas and experiences," and are "rarely aware of the real reasons which motivate their actions," reasons often concealed from them by themselves. People desire many things not for "intrinsic worth or usefulness," but because we "unconsciously come to see" a thing as a "symbol of something else," what Freud's school called a "compensatory substitute."[15] (Recall the slogans, jingles, and status symbols we discussed in Chapter 1.)

Clearly Bernays's major theoretical contribution to the germination of a new propaganda was his postulate that only by understanding the nature of human desire "can the propagandist control that vast, loose-jointed mechanism which is modern society." The new propagandist has "found it possible, by dealing with men in the mass through their group formations, to set up psychological and emotional currents which will work for him" by creating "circumstances which will swing emotional currents so as to make for . . . demands." So, for example, in trying to sell pianos, "the modern propagandist . . . sets to work to create circumstances which will modify . . . custom." Rather than try to sell pianos directly, he will "endeavor to develop public acceptance" of a home music room! How? By organizing an exhibition of well-known decorators, thereby creating "dramatic interest" and staging "an event or ceremony" numbering influential guests who sway public opinion. Or by making a music room part of stylish houses designed by prominent architects, and associating pianos in the home with the height of fashion to "implant the idea of the music room in the mind of the general public." The conventional propagandist asked people to "please buy a piano"; the new propagandist provokes the prospective buyer to say, "please sell me a piano."[16] "The ideas of the new propaganda," insisted Bernays, "are predicated on sound psychology based on enlightened self-interest."[17] Unlike the old-time circus promoters, the new promotion is more subtle and psychological, appealing to the affluent sentiment that you are what you own.

Bernays's reputation as an alchemist of publicity was such that he was in great demand to counsel a wide variety of clients. For example, he arranged one of the first White House pseudoevents designed to enhance—in this case make more charming—the image of President Calvin Coolidge. Since the laconic president of puritan Yankee stock had a public image as aloof and cold, Bernays felt that Coolidge should not be seen only in the company of solemn businessmen and politicians, men of similar serious appearance. To give some jocularity to the dour president, or at least make him seem a "regular fellow," Bernays persuaded the White House to invite famous performer Al Jolson and 40 other show business figures to visit with Coolidge. Jolson and fellow entertainers performed, the press duly reported it (headline the next day: "President Almost Smiles"), and the presidential image now had a lighter touch. "When President Coolidge," wrote Bernays, "invited actors for breakfast, he did so because he realized not only that actors were a group, but that audiences, the large group of people who like amusements, who like people who amuse them, and who like people who can be amused, ought to be aligned with him."[18] Coolidge was now less a stern figure of communication-pain and more an amusing figure of communication-pleasure.

From such simple contrivances evolved the elaborate machinery of presidential public relations, replete with daily press releases and briefings, scheduled and choreographed "spontaneous" appearances, photo opportunities, ceremonies, "spin control," and so forth—all designed for media coverage to portray images of the president being presidential. Indeed, in 1928 Bernays proposed that the government create a cabinet-level secretary of public relations, and later so advised the new president, Franklin Roosevelt. Apparently the rising young Nazi propagandist, Joseph Goebbels, read Bernays's *Propaganda* in 1929–1930 in German translation. If so, Goebbels may have learned considerably from Bernays's chapter on "Propaganda and Political Leadership." Bernays had no illusions that the "voice of the people" includes "any divine or specially wise and lofty idea." No, the public makes up its mind by following "the group leaders in whom it believes and . . . those persons who understand the manipulation of public opinion," knowing full well that "[the public] is composed of inherited prejudices and symbols and cliches and verbal formulas supplied to them by the leaders." In such a situation, "the sincere and gifted politician is able, by the instrument of propaganda, to mold and form the will of the people." In fact, "the only means by which the born leader can lead is the expert use of propaganda." Whatever the political problem or agenda, "the use of propaganda, carefully adjusted to the mentality of the masses, is an essential adjunct of political life." Propaganda has become a modern political necessity, and whatever other skills politicians may possess (bargaining, conquest, administration), they must be complemented with skill in propagandizing.[19]

Bernays wrote also that any political platform should be prepared on "as nearly scientific an analysis as possible of the public and of the needs of the public." In political campaigns, for example, "to appeal to the emotions of the public . . . is sound" and "a charming candidate is the alchemist's secret that can transmute a prosaic campaign into the gold of votes"; however, the modern-day politician should, like Henry Ford, "become known through his product, and not his product through him." Yet "it is essential for the campaign manager to educate the emotions in terms of groups," since "the methods of propaganda can be effective only with the voter who makes up his own mind on the basis of his group prejudices and desires." But the politician need not be "the slave of the public's group prejudices" for "the important thing for the statesman of our age is not so much to know how to please the public, but to know how to sway the public" through "creating circumstances which set up trains of thought, by dramatizing personalities, by establishing contact with the group leaders who control the opinions of their publics." The engineers of consent know how to sway publics through the techniques of suasion.

Similarly, in power, "the expert use of propaganda" aids governing: "Good government can be sold to a community just as any other commodity can be sold." Bernays wondered in *Propaganda* whether "the politicians of the future . . . will not endeavor to train politicians who are at the same time propagandists." He wrote that if he were a political party official, he would have "taken some of my brightest young men and set them to work for Broadway theatrical productions or apprenticed them as assistants to professional propagandists before recruiting them to the service of the party." Politics and propaganda are merging, and entertainment values are all the more important to engineer and display.

With this sense of the dramatic, the political leader must use the media of communication to become "a creator of circumstances, not only a creature of mechanical processes of stereotyping and rubber stamping." The modern propagandist would not only say he or she is for X and argue why you, the public, should be; rather, the political advocate "would create circumstances which would make his contention dramatic and self-evident"—for example, staging an exhibition in major cities, involving prominent citizens in the advocacy, getting interest groups to "institute an agitation," and finding ways to "dramatize the issue" through gestures such as boycotts, or seeking the opinion of experts. Thus "in whatever ways" the political propagandist has "dramatized the issue, the attention of the public would be attracted to the question before he addressed them personally"; with their attention aroused, "he would be answering the spontaneous questions and expressing the emotional demands of a public already keyed to a certain pitch of interest in the subject." The political propagandist, like counterparts in commercial advertising or promotion, must have a dramatic sensibility.

It may be asked "whether . . . the leader makes propaganda, or whether propaganda makes the leader. . . . There has to be fertile ground for the leader and the idea to fall on. But the leader also has to have some vital seed to sow. . . . Propaganda is of no use to the politician unless he has something to say which the public, consciously or unconsciously, wants to hear." Even though propaganda can make political leaders such as the president into an "embodiment of the idea of hero worship, not to say deity worship," this is nonetheless "a condition which very accurately reflects the desires of a certain part of the public." Consequently "the public actions of America's chief executive are . . . stage-managed. But they are chosen to represent and dramatize the man in his function as representative of the people."

In general, "the whole basis of successful propaganda is to have an objective and then to endeavor to arrive at it through an exact knowledge of the public and modifying circumstances to manipulate and sway the public." Bernays saw this skill as essential to modern rule: "The political leader of to-day should be a leader as finely versed in the technique of propaganda as in political economy and civics . . . . If one is dealing with a democracy in which the herd and the group follow those whom they recognize as leaders, why should not the young men training for leadership be trained in its technique as well as in its idealism?" In fact, it is "only through the wise use of propaganda" that a government is "able to maintain that intimate relationship with the public which is necessary in a democracy." Is this, he asks rhetorically, "government by propaganda?" He prefers "government by education." But in any case, "ours must be a leadership democracy administered by the intelligent minority who know how to regiment and guide the masses." If it is education, it is directed education, characterized by "enlightened expert propaganda through the creation of circumstances, through the high-spotting of significant issues, and the dramatization of important issues." Through such direction, "the statesman of the future will thus be enabled to focus the public mind on crucial points of policy, and regiment a vast, heterogeneous mass . . . to clear understanding and intelligent action.''

Bernays remained an active public relations consultant well into his nineties, and continued to write about the new science of propaganda he helped found. Despite the many dubious uses of propaganda since he wrote his pioneering works, he maintained in his later writing a faith in its benevolent uses, distinguishing between ''propaganda'' and ''impropaganda.'' Nor had he lost confidence in the ''intelligent minority'' who he believed could provide guidance for the public. He told Bill Moyers in an interview on PBS that ''people want to be led where they want to go.''[20] With Bernays's blessing, the new propagandists who emerged in modern times have led us in a variety of political, economic, and cultural directions, but whether we wanted, or someone else wanted us, to go where we went is still an open question.

JOSEPH GOEBBELS: THE MINISTER
OF PROPAGANDA

Bernays's conviction that the modern practice of propaganda could be consistent with liberal and progressive democracy was dealt a shattering blow by the rise of totalitarianism. In the Soviet Union under dictator Joseph Stalin, a pervasive state system of official propaganda institutionalized the party line, transforming every form of communication, from school textbooks to circus acts to fairy tales, into messages that were permitted only so long as they conformed to government guidelines. Totalitarian rule had at its core the question: Does this form or text of communication—a movie, poster, radio program, novel, poem, virtually anything that could become a public communication—meet the standards of official propaganda, or alternatively, does it convey the ''correct'' message the state wants to propagate?

At the height of such totalitarian rule, public communication *was* propaganda. The goal was to convince people to believe totally (as in *total*itarian) that what the government said was true and act accordingly, and to develop in citizens a habit of viewing *any* other reasoning as what novelist and essayist George Orwell had called ''thoughtcrime'' (see Chapter 3). There is considerable evidence that the ambitious efforts of official propaganda machines in totalitarian states did not fully succeed, and indeed in some cases— Romania, for instance—may have been a total failure. But the totalitarian experience of the twentieth century provided a major forum for institutionalizing propaganda as *the* central and official mode of political communication.

With that in mind, let us look at a remarkable propagandist in the totalitarian mold, one who reflected on his work in his published diaries (captured and translated after World War II).[21] In his youth, Joseph Goebbels was an unlikely candidate to be one of the ruling circle of Adolf Hitler's Third Reich in Nazi Germany (1933–1945), or in command of a vast propaganda empire that endeavored to convince Germans, their enemies during World War II, and the rest of the world of the destiny of ''a Thousand-Year Reich.'' The young Goebbels was intense, intelligent, small, and crippled—in appearance not at all resembling the ''Aryan'' model of the Nordic master race of Nazi mythology. But like many young Germans after World War I, he was caught up in the intellectual ferment (he earned a Ph.D. from Heidelberg in 1921) and political upheaval of the postwar Weimar

Republic. When in 1923 he offered his services in opposing the French occupation of the Ruhr, he was informed his conspicuous limp disqualified him as a soldier. But he was told "there was work of great importance that I could do: work as an agitator and propagandist."

Soon Goebbels was active in the National Socialist movement, became an intimate of Adolf Hitler, *Gauleiter* of Berlin, and finally in power the *Reichspropagandaminister*. Goebbels put his education to work, reading not only Bernays but also Gustav LeBon's *Psychology of the Masses*; studying the new mass media of communication; and, once in power, organizing and administering a massive official propaganda effort. He proved an odd combination of political fanatic devoted to cause and leader ("Adolf Hitler, I love you, because you are great and simple at the same time," he writes in his diary in 1926; "You are what's called a genius"), and a cynical manipulator ("I took it as my sole objective," the new propaganda chief wrote, "to hammer into the heads of the dunderhead masses acceptance of Hitler as the God of awakening Germany").

In their quest for and exercise of power, Goebbels and Hitler both professed devotion to revival and dominance of German political culture, asserting the racial and national superiority of Deutschland; yet both were willing and adept at formulating and using the new propaganda to move the German masses, of whom they had a low opinion. In his *Mein Kampf, Table Talk,* and private conversations, Hitler expressed his conviction that "propaganda is a truly frightening weapon in the hands of an expert":

> The truth must always be adjusted to fit the need. . . . The aim of propaganda is not to try to pass judgement on conflicting rights, giving each its due, but exclusively to emphasize the right which we are asserting. Propaganda must not investigate the truth objectively, and, in so far as it is favorable to the other side, present it according to the theoretical rules of justice; but it must present only that aspect of the truth which is favorable to its own side.

Goebbels the practitioner had a very similar view of truth, telling a cadre of party members selected for instruction in public speaking that the propagandist must construct his own truth. Whatever is right for the advancement of the party is truth. If it should coincide with factual truth, so much the better; if it doesn't, adjustments must be made. "The great, the absolute truth, is that the Party and the Führer are right. They are always right." (Goebbels also wrote that "truth is what I make it.")

Both Hitler and Goebbels subscribed to the utility of mobilizing public opinion around a political myth so potent and moving—not to mention irrefutable—that it draws people into a movement. Hitler thought that "the great masses of the people will more easily fall victims to a great lie than a small one." Since

> the receptive powers of the masses are very limited, and their understanding is feeble . . . All effective propaganda must be confined to a few bare essentials and these must be expressed as far as possible in stereotyped formulas. These slogans should be persistently repeated until the very last individual has come to grasp the idea that has been put forward . . . the greater the scope of the message that has to be presented, the more necessary it is for the propaganda to discover that plan of action which is psychologically the most efficient.

Hitler's admonition against giving all sides their due and being too abstract and general was echoed by Goebbels when he said, "There is nothing that the masses hate more than two-sidedness, to be called upon to consider this as well as that. They think primitively. They love to generalize complicated situations and from their generalizations to draw clear and uncompromising solutions." Fritz Hippler, one of Goebbels's specialists in charge of motion picture production, said on PBS's "The Public Mind" series that the Reichminister's secret was his ability to simplify complex and complicated things, making them so simple that the least ingenious person can understand them, and keep repeating them until the effect has taken hold. Goebbels devised repeatable slogans ("*Deutschland Erwache!*"), dazzling spectacles (the *Thingspiel*, a quasimilitary parade and gymnastic show), staged pseudoevents (the nighttime pyres for "the burning of the books"), and torchlight parades. Indeed the whole arsenal of propaganda brought under his command at the Ministry of Popular Enlightenment and Propaganda involved simplifying the complex. Goebbels once remarked that he was "to the drama born," and he became the Meistersinger and choreographer of the Nazi drama as it unfolded to the fascination, and horror, of world audiences.

Goebbels was aware of the centrality of propaganda to modern rule, to the point that considerations of propaganda transcended all others. "Propaganda has no policy," he said, "it has a purpose." The Nazi movement, say analysts, had less of an ideology than a mythology, a series of tall tales and cultural stories used to propagate the public basis of rule. Goebbels utilized the myth of "the stab in the back," the widespread notion that Germany had not really lost World War I but rather was betrayed by secret forces at home. These forces centered in the mythical international Jewish conspiracy that allegedly controlled much of German industry and banking. Goebbels, who loved and understood the power of films, made anti-Semitic films to combat the "conspiracy," attempting to "document" Jewish alienness and culpability, such as depicting a Jewish holiday as an occasion for the sadistic torture and murder of animals in ritual sacrifice and as a time of hate prayers against gentiles.

Perhaps the most impressive and influential film of the Nazi period is *Triumph of the Will,* Leni Riefenstahl's documentary of the 1934 annual Nazi party congress at Nuremberg. Riefenstahl, a beautiful actress and one of Hitler's protégés, talked Hitler into letting her make the film. Goebbels disliked Hitler's decision, since Riefenstahl constituted a threat to his control over film propaganda. But once he saw the product, he realized that she had made a propaganda masterpiece that captured the dynamism of the movement at its inception in power. He arranged for it to be virtually obligatory viewing across Germany, and released it for viewing all over the world. The film showcased Hitler and the revived Germany for all to see, intermingling symbols of the old and new Germany, the New Order in the ancient town of Nuremberg.

Goebbels's own greatest achievement, however, was the creation of the Führer myth, of Hitler as a virtual national deity. It was at his insistence, after 1931, that Hitler was referred to only as *Der Führer*. Goebbels insisted on the universal greeting "Heil Hitler," and the shout in unison at rallies, "Sieg Heil." Later, Goebbels coined the slogan "Adolf Hitler is Germany, and Germany is Adolf Hitler." Hitler was rarely seen in public, although frequently photographed in the company of statesmen, beautiful women, children, and dogs. But Hitler was heard. Goebbels understood that the disembodied voice of the Führer could speak to the nation via the new medium of radio. "In that medium,'' said Goebbels, ''we have a great potential for influencing public opinion. I prophesy the day when every factory, every cinema and theatre and restaurant, every market place and store, every railway station, and every home will be within range of the Führer's voice.''

Goebbels studied the technology of radio, learning how it could fade and mingle sounds to dramatize the broadcasts of rallies. The minister of propaganda modified Hitler's often shrill, almost hysterical, speaking style to adapt voice and message to the broadcast medium. Goebbels ordered the manufacture of a cheap ''people's receiver'' to maximize Hitler's audience, and also periods of ''collective listening,'' with virtually every public place and village suspending work at a specified time to listen to Hitler or Goebbels (the latter was himself a compelling speaker, often practicing speeches and gestures in front of a three-way mirror).

''We do not talk to say something,'' said Goebbels, ''but to obtain a certain effect.'' As one who thought of everything in terms of its propaganda value, he analyzed communication practices of bygone eras as exemplars to be applied in Hitler's Reich. For instance, he said of Jesus, ''I cannot think of a more fascinating personality in history than Christ. . . . I know of no more powerful speech than the Sermon on the Mount. Every propagandist ought to study it.'' Goebbels's analyses led him to the view that propagandizing involved two elements: *Stimmung,* or current morale and opinion about politics, and *Haltung,* or behavior and conduct toward politics over time. After a successful Allied air raid against Germany, Goebbels wrote, ''The *Stimmung* is quite low but that means little; the *Haltung* holds well.'' The *Stimmung* is volatile, changing in mood with the vagaries of events; but if the *Haltung* can be maintained in the face of adversity, rule is secure because people's actions haven't changed. Thus, for example, to maintain loyal conduct even in the face of massive Allied bombing during the siege of Berlin in 1945, Goebbels insisted that of all production facilities the breweries must remain open, providing the Germans' beloved beer.

Goebbels was instrumental in obtaining popular acquiescence, if not supporting conduct, in the arrest and disappearance of Germany's (and the rest of occupied Europe's) Jewish population as part of the ''Final Solution.'' The transport of Jews to the infamous death camps Goebbels referred to in official propaganda variously as ''the reorientation of the working population in accordance with the requirements of German industry,'' or ''part of the Führer's plan for the rehabilitation of the Jewish race.'' Since such wordings seemed benign enough, many German people did not question the disappearance of Jews; or if they did, they kept it largely to themselves and did not act upon it.

However, the decline of *Haltung* became obvious in the latter months of World War II as morale fell despite all of Goebbels's efforts in the face of the clear countering evidence of falling bombs, burning cities, and advancing armies. At this point, the myth of the invincible Führer leading Germany to a destined ''Thousand-Year Reich'' collapsed. Goebbels had once said confidently that the face of politics changed every day, but the lines of propaganda must change only imperceptibly, and that ''mere words . . . can be molded until they clothe ideas in disguise.'' But in the end, Goebbels's propaganda could no longer change imperceptibly nor disguise the tattered ideas that fostered the Third Reich. As the Red Army surrounded the *Führerbunker* in 1945, both Hitler and Goebbels committed suicide.

''It may be a good thing to possess power that rests on arms,'' said Goebbels in

1934, "but it is better and more gratifying to win and hold the heart of the people." When the Nazis first came to power, he saw "propaganda as a revolutionary act in so far as the new government no longer intends to leave the people to their own devices." He was quite frank in thinking that propaganda was a substitute "solution" for unresolvable or just bad developments. It was indispensable to reduce popular frustrations, reassure the masses, and condition them to quietly accept their exclusion from power or policy. But propaganda also made people feel as if they were informed, catered to, and part of the "people's government":

> By simplifying the thoughts of the masses and reducing them to primitive patterns, propaganda was able to present the complex process of political and economic life in the simplest terms. . . . We have taken matters previously available only to experts and a small number of specialists, and have carried them into the street and hammered them into the brain of the little man.

The little man was a political spectator of a grandiose national ritual drama, as in the planned "National Moments" when life would come to a standstill to hear a Hitler speech or Nuremberg ceremony, making the individual a participant in collective propaganda. In Goebbels's phrase, the little man was at such moments transformed "from a little worm into part of a large dragon." After the defeat by the Russians at Stalingrad, Goebbels changed the general theme of official propaganda from one of glorious military victory to one of stalwart heroism at home and on the front. The propagandist had to change the colors of the dragon with changing political circumstances, but even in adversity he was able to make the worms feel as if they were part of a noble, if dying, dragon.

Goebbels as master of propaganda used it as an instrument of ruling and thought it to be at the very core of Nazi success. Even though the Nazis suppressed opposition and freely used terror, one observer has concluded that nonetheless "propaganda itself was sufficient to achieve at least passive support for the regime. . . . Nazi propaganda was in tune with the real aspirations of large sections of the German people."[22] In that sense, Goebbels's skillful use of propaganda must be rated a "success" even if it was in defense of a sinister regime and policies. His propaganda machine helped create the condition of a great political reality, even if it was based in a national madness. Perhaps the career of Joseph Goebbels illustrates more than anyone else Hitler's insight that propaganda is a truly frightening weapon in the hands of an expert.

Nazi propaganda, led by Goebbels, was one of the most remarkable early manifestations of the new propaganda. In many ways, for the Nazi regime propaganda was not only at the core of policy, it drove policy. (Once, when a major Allied air raid was under way over Germany, it found little Luftwaffe opposition, because Goebbels had much of the German air force in Poland shooting a film of the "glory days" of the 1939 invasion!) Nazi propaganda was characterized by its magnitude and its blatantness. The mythology of the regime is somewhat reminiscent of Plato's "Noble Lie," but its consequences were far greater and more sinister than the ancient philosopher had in mind. The rhetoric of advocacy was not new either, but it went far beyond what Aristotle or Cicero might have had in mind: for Goebbels, truth was not something to be negotiated or debated, since it was a function of the success of propaganda. If truth is what the propagandist says it is, there is no room for doubt, and if truth is malleable, then there is much room for believing what is expedient today and something else that is equally expedient tomorrow. The Nazis displayed an extreme of a very modern attitude, one from which the rest of the modern world is not entirely exempt.

DAVID OGILVY: THE WIZARD OF MADISON AVENUE

The *Führerbunker* may seem a far distance from New York's Madison Avenue, but perhaps the chasm is not all that great. Madison Avenue has become the street forever identified with advertising. Advertising agencies do not share the political philosophy of Goebbels's Reichsministry, but they do share a commitment to use propaganda in order to affect people's behavior. The creative and well-paid masters of advertising are not to be lumped with the criminals of Nazism, but with a few modifications advertising geniuses share many of Goebbels's assumptions: advertising truth is what they make it; advertising has no policy, it has a purpose; through polling advertisers measure *Stimmung* and *Haltung;* advertisers want to win and hold the hearts of the people.

Mastery of the art and science of advertising has meant the creation of another great reality: a world of propaganda that besets us constantly. Like Goebbels, advertisers think that propaganda works, that people can be induced to believe or do something that they might not otherwise have done. However, even though most advertising people believe that advertising makes a difference, they also tend to combine frank talk about the assumptions and techniques of advertising with a stout defense of its ethics and practices.

Many people in advertising have published their reflections on their mastery and success, but perhaps none with the enthusiasm of David Ogilvy. Ogilvy was both a successful practitioner of the advertising arts and a student of the development of the field. He was fascinated by both the power and beauty of advertising, and wrote vigorously of its achievements. Ogilvy kept 20 reproductions of classic ads in his office and wrote in loving awe of the giants of the field.

Ogilvy was aware of the long debate in advertising thought between the "image" school and the "claim" school, the first featuring the image of a product, the second highlighting a claim for the product, and used both freely. He was responsible for the famous image ad for Hathaway shirts featuring a distinguished gentleman with a black eyepatch ("a sophisticated man with a past") and affordable shirt, and the equally famous claim ad for Rolls-Royce ("At 60 miles an hour the loudest noise in this new Rolls-Royce comes from the electric clock," went the headline, followed by an elaborate claim as to why— "Patient Attention to Detail"). Both Hathaway shirt and Rolls-Royce sales increased, and Ogilvy became a Madison Avenue legend, and soon a spokesman, historian, critic, and interpreter, with attention to the "eternal verities of advertising."[23]

In his various works, David Ogilvy was conversant with the history of advertising, and the masterly figures who made it what it is today. He recounted with relish the accomplishments and insights of these figures. He related tales, for instance, of the long career of Albert Lasker (who was so successful he once claimed, "There is no advertising man in the world but me"). Lasker devised the brilliant marketing idea of advertising Kotex to be sold in plain brown wrappers at drugstores so women wouldn't be embarrassed by public purchase. He also admired Leo Burnett, who claimed that "there is an inherent drama in every product. Our No. 1 job is to dig for it and capitalize on it." Ogilvy pointed to one of the Machiavellian classics in the field, *Scientific Advertising* by Claude Hopkins, who invented test marketing and many other forms of research in marketing products, and who gave such advice as "try to give each advertiser a becoming style. To create the right individuality is a supreme accomplishment." He admired Bill Bernbach, one of the founders of the prestigious firm of Doyle Dane Bernbach, who said in 1982:

> Human nature hasn't changed for a billion years. It won't even vary in the next billion years. Only the superficial things have changed. It is fashionable to talk about *changing* man. A communicator must be concerned with *unchanging* man—what compulsions drive him, what instincts dominate his every action, even though his language too often camouflages what *really* motivates him. For if you know these things about a man, you can touch him at the core of his being. One thing is unchangingly sure. The creative man with an insight into human nature, with the artistry to touch and move people, will succeed. Without them he will fail.[24]

Like most advertising successes, Ogilvy thought of himself as a creative artist who learned how to touch people and could teach us from experience. He belonged to the school of thought, he said, "which holds that a good advertisement is one which sells the product without drawing attention to itself." He continued, "instead of saying 'What a clever advertisement,' the reader says, 'I never knew that before. I must try this product.' " Thus, "it is the professional duty of the advertising agent to conceal his artifice." (One is reminded of Goebbels's thought that once we become conscious of propaganda it ceases to be effective.) This concealment is eminently practical, since through advertising research you "find out how they (the consumers) think about your kind of product, what language they use when they discuss the subject, what attributes are important to them, *and what promises would be most likely to make them buy your brand.*"

Ogilvy fully grasped the importance of selecting the most effective promises in "positioning" a product, advertising "what the product does, and who it is for." (We discuss the relation of brand and positioning advertising in detail in Chapter 5.) Doyle Dane Bernbach, he noted, successfully positioned the Volkswagen Beetle in the early 1960s "as a protest against the vulgarity of Detroit cars in those days, thereby making the Beetle a cult among those Americans who eschew conspicuous consumption." Similarly, the same firm positioned Avis, the second largest car rental company to Hertz, as No. 2 but hustling more than Hertz; out of necessity, said Avis ads, "We Try Harder."

Positioning is complemented by developing a "brand image," meaning "personality" (again, see Chapter 5): "products, like people, have personalities, and they can make or break them in the market place." Sometimes one may simply want a consistent and reliable image (Campbell soup), or a bargain basement image (Wal-Mart), but much of the time "it pays to give most products an image of quality—A First Class ticket." For example, "when you choose a brand of whiskey you are choosing an image. Jack Daniel's is worth its premium price." When people taste another whiskey but are told it's "Jack," they think they are drinking Jack Daniel's: "They are tasting images." Similarly, "Leo Burnett's campaign for Marlboro projects an image which has made it the biggest-selling cigarette in the world.'' (Marlboro ads largely picture weather-beaten, Westerner-clad men in heroic Western settings, with the slogan: Come to where the flavor is. Come to Marlboro Country.) The advertising campaign succeeds if centered on a ''big idea'' that ''attract(s) the attention of consumers and get(s) them to buy your product.'' In other words, the imagery has to be simple and powerful, coming from the unconscious.

Ogilvy developed the long-running Pepperidge Farms ads from a dream he had of ''two white horses pulling a baker's delivery van along a country lane at a smart trot.'' One of his partners developed a TV ad of a herd of bulls running through desert country, with the voice-over saying simply, ''Merrill Lynch is bullish on America.'' (An effective ad, although Ogilvy doesn't mention the fact that the ad was actually shot in Mexico!) The optimal strategy is to ''make the product itself the hero of your advertising'' because ''there are no dull products.'' It may not even be necessary to show a product to be superior to another; rather ''it may be sufficient to convince consumers that your product is *positively good*,'' by simply making the case about ''what's good about your product,'' thereby creating confidence that the ''product is positively good.'' But always remember that consumption is dynamic: ''You aren't advertising to a standing army; you are advertising to a moving parade. . . . A good advertisement can be thought of as a radar sweep, constantly hunting new prospects as they come into the market.''[25]

Ogilvy, like many spokespersons for the advertising industry, felt compelled to defend advertising against criticisms leveled against it—that it creates unneeded wants, is ''intellectual and moral pollution,'' raises prices, corrupts editors, focuses attention on image rather than quality, and all in all, is a ''pack of lies.'' He responded that advertising is nonmanipulative, honorable, and efficient. He conceded, however, that there is ''one category of advertising which is totally uncontrolled and flagrantly dishonest: the television commercials for candidates in presidential elections.'' They are now ''often the decisive factor in deciding who shall be the next president of the United States,'' and thus ''dishonest advertising is as evil as stuffing the ballot box.'' (We explore political advertising in Chapters 4 and 5.)

Perhaps Ogilvy begged the question in shifting blame from commercial advertising to political advertising. In any case, Ogilvy contended that advertising is but the expression of values held by the larger society. He quoted writer Wilfrid Sheed that ''the sound of selling is the dirge of our times,'' especially with heavy users of television.[26] Certainly the masters of advertising have created one of the ''great realities'' of the present, to use P. T. Barnum's phrase, but to what kind of reality they have guided us remains in dispute.

MICHAEL DEAVER: THE VICAR OF VISUALS

David Ogilvy may have had contempt for political advertising, but he probably would not dispute its efficacy as part of the new propaganda. The great practitioners of the political arts of propagandizing—in campaigns, most notably—share with commercial advertisers the attitudes and techniques that make for the dirge of political selling. In any case, contemporary politics is characterized by people skilled in the propaganda arts, creating ''great realities'' that serve their clients well. Whether political advertising is but the expression of values held by the larger society is a question that has not been fully answered.

In any case, practitioners of the political flack arts often point with as much pride to the fruits of their professions as do commercial propagandists. Certainly this was true of one of the more remarkable recent political operatives, Michael Deaver.

When an assassin's bullet severely wounded newly elected president Ronald Reagan in 1981, concerns were expressed that the 70-year-old president might not be able to continue in office after such a wound and major surgery. In the wake of the uncertainty, White House aide Michael Deaver led a contingent of Reagan intimates to see the stricken president. Deaver had more than an expression of sympathy in mind. He and others wished to alert the world that Reagan was recovering rapidly, and, even in infirmity, was still very much in command of the presidency. Deaver brought with him a minor bill to be signed. Wrote Deaver (along with ghostwriter Mickey Herskowitz):

> It was not really a matter of any urgency, but all of us felt a pressure to demonstrate that the government—meaning Ronald Reagan—was able to function. The system had not lost or sacrificed its continuity. The gesture was symbolic. The president meant it to show that he was on the job.[27]

But was it the president or Deaver's media-conscious staff who meant to show he was "on the job"? As a former movie actor, Reagan clearly knew the virtues of positive news coverage. He gathered around him experts savvy in the trade. Deaver and his team instinctively knew that they had to send the world a message of Reagan's physical recovery and control of the executive branch. Simply releasing the story of Reagan signing the bill was a reassuring symbol of presidential fitness. Whether it was an accurate message is questionable. According to some accounts Reagan was in a much more grave condition than Deaver would admit; it took the president longer to recover than the official version of the assassination attempt portrayed.[28] In any event, Deaver's ploy worked. For example, Washington reporters on PBS's "Washington Week in Review" shortly thereafter, in the wake of White House propaganda, labeled Reagan a virtual "superpatient" with remarkable recovery powers and a capacity for work far beyond those of mortal men.

Deaver become a Reagan aide-de-camp early in the actor-turned-politician's career in California. Deaver shared Reagan's belief that "one could project what kind of person one was on film and, of course, on television. I learned from him in this respect and built some of my own public-relations theories around the things that came so naturally to Reagan."[29] The combination of Reagan's seasoned portrayal of "naturalness" and Deaver's style of public relations made for a winning formula:

> He (Reagan) came to office at a time when the perception of what was done often mattered as much as what was actually done. These may be harsh thoughts. . . . But in the television age, image sometimes is as useful as substance. Not as important, but as useful.[30]

Deaver was convinced of the necessity of his work in the White House: "You have to inspire support for the president if you are going to rally support for his policies. This is basic. This is the essence of good PR. This is politics." Deaver took pride in his achievements. When the economy began to improve, Deaver arranged for the president not simply to announce it, but to do it in striking fashion. Deaver arranged for the president to fly to Fort Worth (the city with the highest rate of housing starts) and congregate with hardhats in a housing development. Why? Here's Deaver's rationale:

> You only get forty to eighty seconds on any given night on the network news, and unless you can find a visual that explains your message you can't make it stick. . . . [I]n the Television Age, it hasn't happened, or at least it hasn't really registered, if people can't see what you see.

Compelling TV visuals, Deaver thought, were "the creative side of my work . . . You had the sense of sweep and panorama that any director must feel. And it is in this kind of environment that Ronald Reagan did more than star. He glowed."[31]

Deaver recalls with pride the television "ceremonies I orchestrated" and admits my "preoccupation with television": "There is simply no way to exaggerate the influence of that medium in the political life of this and other nations." TV coverage can affect, for instance, military strategy: "We will never again fight a major ground war." The strafing of Libya and the Grenada invasion are arresting visuals, but because of television "you can't do it day after day, and you can't send in the troops." We "got away with" Grenada, "the only successful ground action this country has taken since World War II" (unlike Korea and Vietnam), "by establishing special ground rules, by not letting the press in and justifying it later." World War II we had seen in the largely sanitized war movies; but television news, said Deaver, means that war will be in our living rooms; thus policy will have to bend to the requirements of television, suggesting that Grenada was a good visual reminiscent of such movies, but without the drawn out agony of nightly combat news from major military commitments.[32] (It might be noted that Deaver wrote this before the Gulf War of 1991. However, his propaganda rules obtained there: the press was severely censored, the president and the military controlled the visuals, public and press opinion was courted and pressured into compliance, and the Grenada model had been expanded into a major conflict. It was a major triumph for Deaver's propaganda values.)

Deaver was dubbed "the vicar of visuals," but notes that if he qualified "as an expert on anything, it was said to be the staging of a media event; blending the gifts of Ronald Reagan with the proper pageantry," or more prosaically, "selling the sizzle"[33] (not the steak!). As a professional, Deaver analyzed what went wrong with Reagan's visit to a German military graveyard in Bitburg where Nazi SS officers were interred. Because of the controversy surrounding a U.S. president's participation in such ceremonies, Deaver undertook "damage control" to minimize the criticism. (However, Deaver rejected a proposal for Reagan to visit the Shrine of Fatima in Portugal, a place sacred to Roman Catholics, because to Deaver's trained eye "the shrine would not work as a photo site.")[34] Notice that for Deaver the pro considerations of the president's public appearances did not involve a moral or prejudicial judgment (e.g., being pro-Nazi or anti-Catholic or whatever), but rather what constituted effective propaganda.

The so-called vicar's attention to detail was in the professional tradition of modern image management. Perhaps most revealing of how he manipulated his employer in Reagan's own best interest was the "quiet, early dinner" he planned for Reagan before his decisive debate with Jimmy Carter in 1980: "I let Reagan have one glass of wine before the debate . . . a little color for his cheeks.''[35] Michael Deaver told Bill Moyers (in the latter's PBS series "The Public Mind") that the White House team charged with presidential image management knew that they, and the news organizations and reporters they tried to influence, were "not in the news business," they were in the "entertainment business." Believing that "power in America today is control of the means of communication," the Reagan strategists decided to make television the "organizing framework" of the presidency. The news, they thought, was the public forum designed for their use as presidential propaganda. Everything communicated was for propaganda value as much, or more so, than informative content. To the extent the team got their "story line" through the press "filter" unchanged, there was elation. One way they did this was to develop foci for the press, such as a designated theme of the day or issue of the week, which helpfully directed media attention to presidential action and mastery on issues that were deemed politically salient at the moment. Once that was communicated—by finding in their polling a rise in concern over something, prompting a planned and staged response with the aim of allaying public concerns—the propaganda team could move on to something else.[36]

In 1983 the management team sent out notices to 10,000 newspapers and radio and television stations, alerting them that the White House would provide electronic press releases and radio tapes of the administration's official version of things. Later, the Reagan White House used satellite channels owned by the U.S. Chamber of Commerce, the Republican party, and a private system to communicate videos of the official White House story or staged presidential appearance. Such videos could be picked up by local television stations without the intermediary of hostile network producers and reporters who might provide interpretation or commentary deemed not in harmony with the White House hymnal.[37]

In the competition between eye and ear, Michael Deaver believed, "the eye wins every time." Armed with the conviction that in a television-saturated culture the public finds images compelling and words boring, the Reagan media managers sought foremost to propagate those images that were pleasing to the eye. "What are you going to believe," a Reagan official told reporter Hedrick Smith, "the facts or your eyes?" Leslie Stahl told Smith (and Bill Moyers) of a critical piece she did on the "CBS Evening News" about the Reagan media operation. For four-and-a-half minutes she talked about the essential deceptiveness of a president who, she said, "highlights the images and hides from the issues." In today's TV world, however, a critical analysis is not aired solely by a "talking head"; it is accompanied by a montage of images over which the correspondent narrates as voiceover. Stahl regarded the segment as the most critical piece she had ever filed on Reagan. After it aired she was called by a "senior" White House official. Stahl expected to be harangued for being so hard on Reagan. On the contrary, the official praised the story as a "great piece." Why? Because, he told Stahl, there were great visuals! "The public," she was told, "sees those pictures and they block your message. They didn't even hear what you said. So, in our minds, it was a four-and-a-half-minute free ad for the Ronald Reagan campaign for reelection." (Deaver told Moyers that often after a successful manipulation of the national press by getting the desired visuals on the air, his team would conclude, "Ha, ha, we did it again.")[38]

The indefatigable Deaver spared no expense to showcase Reagan as a leader, and nothing was so minor as to ignore planning it in minute detail. Deaver designed the structure of the stage and podium at the 1984 Republican convention to remove sharp corners and bright colors. Thus the spotlighted Reagan appeared as a peaceful and restful center in a world (inside and outside the convention) that was noisy and boisterous. How, Deaver provoked viewers to ask themselves, could such a man *really* be hawkish and aggressive in his policies? "The podium backdrop conveyed a subliminal message of peacefulness."[39]

If Reagan's pollsters detected potential image problems with the public, Deaver responded with a "visual press release" or a series of pseudoevents designed to change negative opinions into positive ones. For example, when public worry about the poor quality of American education mounted, Deaver sent Reagan on the road with an orchestrated campaign featuring Reagan in classrooms, lunching with teachers, and generally expressing "concern" over education—but without proposing any new substantial programs or reversing massive cuts in federal spending on education. Public opinion was swayed, and for Reagan and media master Deaver that "solved" the problem. Deaver told NBC's Chris Wallace, "You can say whatever you want, but the viewer sees Ronald Reagan out there in a classroom talking to teachers and kids, and what he takes from that is the impression that Ronald Reagan is concerned about education."[40]

In Chapter 4 we will explore how presidential propaganda has become not only a substitute for presidential initiatives in policy areas but an imperative that defines the very social problems presidents are willing to tackle. For now, however, consider Deaver's contributions to the new propaganda to be, as the words of one observer suggest, that the contemporary presidential propagandist succeeds by choreographing the leader as someone who occupies a world "where never is heard a discouraging word, and the skies are not cloudy all day."[41]

IS THERE A SUCKER BORN EVERY MINUTE?

A biographer of P. T. Barnum entitled his work *The Fabulous Showman*. In many ways, the disparate figures we have talked about here were all fabulous showmen. They all had in common a commitment to the mastery of communication and media to propagate their message. They were impressed by the ability of previous or contemporary masters to ply their trade, learned from them, and felt confident that they could use propaganda for widespread and even lasting effect. They were comfortable with spreading a propagated truth, and had few ethical qualms about what they did. All of them took the scientific study of public opinion and the psychology of the masses seriously, and believed, whatever their purpose, that people were creatures for suasion and persuasion. These masters were in a sense unwitting popular dramatists, staging Barnumian "great realities" for the benefit of audiences whose attention and allegiance they wished to gain and hold. They understood propaganda as the business of mastering the hearts and minds of large numbers of people regardless of their purpose. Each had his own values and commitments, but their overall contribution was to our understanding of the major uses of propaganda in modern times.

In public at least, none of them probably would admit that they agreed with the most infamous line associated with P. T. Barnum: "There's a sucker born every minute." Were they nothing more than masters of manipulation? That is a question certainly worthy of extended debate. But it suffices to say here that they all viewed the modern world as a place in which "great realities" could be created, like castles in the air. For them, reality is an existential creation, a product of shared belief, rather than something that just *is*, independent of communication.

The propagandists discussed here, as we said at the outset, were not the only ones who mastered their craft but were those who reflected upon its art and science and wrote about it. Their combined writing, lectures, and other pronouncements constitute what appear as the tenets of a creed espoused by a new priesthood. It is a creed whose various principles possess a Machiavellian ring. The masters, for example, all assented to a key tenet in that creed, namely, the *principle of credulity*. That is the basic assumption that everyone may not be a sucker, but there are sufficient numbers of people willing, even eager, to heed a message on the basis of meager or uncertain evidence to make the propagandist's craft not only possible but profitable and replicable.

The representative masters here also adhered to the *principle of expediency*: communication is not for them a matter of the transmission of illuminating truth or unfettered information; rather it is a task of using truth and information as weapons or shields. The definition of truth, however, varies widely—straight facts, arranged facts, half-truths, pseudotruths, staged and orchestrated events, and lies and fabrications. And, frequently, which definition applies depends on the client served, be it corporate, private, personal, or public interest.

These masters agreed as well that propaganda is indispensable and exists in the modern world out of a *principle of necessity*. They were not reformers or moralists, nor did they regard themselves or their craft as evil. Convinced that they were undertaking work that had to be done, none of them appear to have lost much sleep fretting over the ethics of their profession. If they felt their performance required justification, they would simply respond that propaganda was necessary to achieve results in any endeavor, that indeed these results might be undesirable if propaganda were not used well.

Finally, they all adhered to a *principle of beauty*. (Machiavelli too was dramatist and poet as well as politician and thinker.) Propaganda in both form and influence is an artistic creation, the result of aesthetic sensitivity. Based on scientific data or principles, yes, but in execution propaganda is an art, perhaps one of the most notable forms of modern art. These masters took considerable pride in their art and their profession, even in the face of criticism that propaganda is not respectable. Perhaps this criticism is one of the reasons that impelled such figures to think and write about their work, adding to the literature, lore, and knowledge of propaganda that informs its logic as a means of communication. That logic is the concern of the next chapter.

This chapter examined the "working thought" of key practitioners of propaganda. Our aim here was to make you aware of the presence of people, and in particular a few remarkable people, in the long historical process of the creation of the new propaganda. We found that they had both pragmatic and aesthetic concerns, and were not without political and social conviction. Nevertheless, they are memorable for their strategic thought, in reflection upon the principles of propaganda as social communication in action. Now we must turn to academic thought on the new propaganda, turning to the ideas of those thinkers who have most successfully discerned what the growth and practice of propaganda mean for the conduct of our lives in modern society.

NOTES

1. Daniel J. Boorstin, *The Image: A Guide to Pseudo-events in America* (New York: Atheneum, 1973), p. 210; see also Irving Wallace, *The Fabulous Showman* (New York: Knopf, 1959).
2. Except noted otherwise the following discussion of Lee draws on Ray Eldon Hiebert, *Courtier to the Crowd: The Story of Ivy Lee and the Development of Public Relations* (Ames: Iowa State University Press, 1966), *passim*.
3. Ibid., p. 317.
4. Foster Rhea Dulles, quoted in Hiebert, ibid., p. 316.
5. Hiebert, *Courtier to the Crowd,* p. 118.
6. Ibid., p. 118.
7. Edward L. Bernays, quoted in Hiebert, ibid., p. 92.
8. Edward L. Bernays, *Crystallizing Public Opinion* (New York: Boni & Liveright, 1923), pp. 11–33.
9. Ibid, pp. 11–33.
10. Ibid, pp. 11–33.
11. Edward L. Bernays, *Propaganda* (New York: H. Liveright, 1928).
12. Bernays, *Crystallizing Public Opinion,* pp. 11–33.
13. Ibid, pp. 11–33.
14. Bernays, *Crystallizing Public Opinion,* pp. 171–173; Bernays, *Propaganda,* pp. 25–27, 30–31.
15. Bernays, *Propaganda,* pp. 25–27, 30–31.
16. Bernays, *Propaganda,* pp. 48–53.
17. Ibid., p. 61.
18. Ibid., p. 102.
19. Except noted otherwise the following discussion draws on Ibid., pp. 92–94, 97, 100–102, 104–109, 112–114.
20. Interview with Bill Moyers, "A Walk through the 20th Century: The Image Makers," PBS series, 1984.
21. Except noted otherwise the following discussion draws on Louis Lochner, ed., *The Goebbels Diaries* (Westport, CT: Greenwood, 1970); Alan Wykes, *The Nuremberg Rallies* (New York: Ballantine Books, 1970); Alan Wykes, *Goebbels* (New York: Ballantine Books, 1973); Vikto Reimann, *Goebbels* (Garden City, NY: Doubleday, 1976), *passim*: R. C. Raack, "Nazi Film Propaganda and the Horrors of War," *Historical Journal of Film, Radio, and Television* 6(2)(1986): 189–195.
22. David Welch, "Propaganda and Indoctrination in the Third Reich: Success or Failure?" *European History Quarterly* 17 (1987): 419.
23. See the profile in Stephen Fox, *The Mirror Makers: A History of American Advertising and Its Creators* (New York: Vintage, 1985), pp. 225–239.
24. Doyle Dane Bernbach, quoted in David Ogilvy, *Ogilvy on Advertising* (New York: Crown, 1983), p. 205.
25. See David Ogilvy, *Confessions of an Advertising Man* (New York: Atheneum, 1966), p. 90; *Ogilvy on Advertising,* pp. 12, 14–16, 18–20.
26. Ogilvy, *Ogilvy on Advertising,* pp. 208–213.
27. Michael K. Deaver, with Mickey Herskowitz, *Behind the Scenes* (New York: William Morrow, 1987), pp. 23–24.
28. Bob Woodward, *Veil: The Secret Wars of the CIA* (New York: Simon and Schuster, 1987).
29. Deaver, *Behind the Scenes,* p. 43.
30. Ibid., p. 73.
31. Ibid., pp. 140–141.

32. Ibid., p. 147.
33. Ibid., p. 177.
34. Ibid., p. 191–192.
35. Ibid., p. 98.
36. Hedrick Smith, *The Power Game* (New York: Ballantine Books, 1988), pp. 404–405.
37. Ibid, pp. 404–405.
38. Ibid., pp. 407–409.
39. Ibid., p. 411.
40. Ibid., p. 414.
41. Bill Moyers, "Illusions of News," PBS series *The Public Mind* (WNET, Boston), broadcast 1989.

CHAPTER **3**

The Logic of the New Propaganda
The Palaver of Technique
and the Technique of Palaver

In the previous chapters we have attempted to place propaganda in its modern historical setting, dealing with both the processes and people that made propaganda the powerful social force it is today. Now we want to ponder the logic of propaganda, using the thought of French scholar Jacques Ellul. Our focus here is on propaganda as a manifestation of the modern emphasis on technique. Indeed, we will build on Ellul's thought by differentiating types of propaganda that we all encounter. And we will rely upon another important observer of modernity, George Orwell, whose conception of "newspeak" will be discussed as useful to understanding contemporary propaganda. You should take away from this chapter an enhanced vision of the socio-logic of propaganda.

Think back on the energetic and intelligent people we met in the previous chapter. Each possessed a markedly *technocratic* orientation to his craft as propagandist. By technocratic we mean that each focused on ways and means, rather than values and ends. The interest of each was in how to do something well (promote, mobilize, sell, popularize, etc.), sometimes more so than in the product, person, or cause touted. All were interested in results, and the best way to realize those results was through the adroit use of technological devices. In that sense they were "crafty" in their work, thoroughly focused on the techniques of the propaganda craft; thus, they were technocrats. Not only were they important in building a body of professional theorizing about their craft, they also point up the extent to which the technocratic class of propagandists in the modern world are associated with the conduct of rule.

Our technocrats of propaganda worked for a wide variety of clients, people who hired them to ply the arts and sciences of communication to propagate messages on behalf of corporate, government, and other interests. Serving those clients they studied, mastered, and applied the techniques of propaganda to produce efficient results, and worried little about the niceties of what they did. This is not to say that the professional propagandists had no standards for or limits on what they were willing to do, only that they viewed their vocation as involving the skilled use of technical tools, not making moral judgments. Today those same tools, along with others, are available to anyone who wants to try a hand at preparing the soil, sowing the seeds of ideas, and propagating them throughout society. Propaganda pervades public discourse. The palaver of technique, the expertise of guile and charm, has become a form of influence talk not merely on a par with informative, evaluative, and expressive utterance, but frequently overpowering each. Therefore, those who are highly skilled in the technique of palaver are crucial to the exercise of power in modern settings. Certainly the propagandists we have just met typified mastery of the palaver of technique, and achieved power through that mastery. Will the seeds of the new propaganda those masters sowed be the spreading crabgrass of the future, covering all other forms of communication in its dense growth? There is at least sufficient prospect of that happening that we need to examine closely the logic behind the technology of the new propaganda.

THE PROPAGATION OF TECHNIQUE, AND THE TECHNIQUE OF PROPAGATION

One of the most influential French scholars of recent decades, a professor at the University of Bordeaux, has been Jacques Ellul. He led a varied life, fighting in the Resistance in World War II, serving as deputy mayor of Bordeaux, active as a leading Hugenot involved in modern Christianity as a key figure in the French Reformed Church and the World Council of Churches, and a major force in French political and intellectual life. His work as a scholar attracted attention in 1960 when renowned author Aldous Huxley recommended Ellul to the director of the prestigious Center for the Study of Democratic Institutions, noting that Ellul's writing had "really made the case" Huxley had attempted in his novel *Brave New World* (a work we return to in the concluding chapter of this book). With the publication of his core trilogy—*The Technological Society, Propaganda,* and *The Political Illusion*—Ellul's intellectual reputation and influence was established worldwide.[1]

Ellul tried to uncover the underlying logic of modernity and, in particular, the logic of propaganda. His perspective centers on what he thinks is the distinctive feature of modern society, what he calls *la technique*. Technique is not just machinery, it is the "organized ensemble of all individual techniques which have been used to secure any end whatsoever." Put differently, technique consists of "the totality of methods . . . having absolute efficiency in every field of human knowledge." The driving force of modern society, says Ellul, is the logic of technique, impelling us to seek and find ever more efficient means to achieve ever more controlled and complete results. In a sense, argues Ellul, we have made means, the power and might of technique, into an end in themselves, by making technique itself autonomous. What does this mean?

In modern societies technological innovation is irresistible. Each innovation spawns demands for another: we have the automobile so we must have better roads; better roads require efficient means to build them; efficient means require efficient machines; efficient machines require efficient ways to manufacture them, operate them, fuel them; and so on. Instead of technique serving the pursuit of human goals, human goals serve technique ("We'll never keep pace with the traffic problem unless we build more freeways."). In that sense technique is autonomous, a driving force with a life and imperative of its own. This techno-logic becomes an endless cycle: technological innovation requires better technique in order to cope with what has been innovated, but that in itself makes for more innovation and better technique, and so on endlessly. We may think all this is "progress," while traffic worsens, roads proliferate everywhere, and pollution from car engines makes urban life unlivable!

Let us take another example: the development of the atomic bomb and then the strategic means to deliver nuclear capacity (airplanes, submarines, missiles, artillery) involved an irresistible technical urge. The logic of the "national security state" founded on nuclear weaponry (in both the United States and Soviet Union) took on a life of its own. In neither of the two combatants in the cold war was there serious public examination of the ends to be sought through nuclear armaments, only the quest for more efficient means of destruction and defense. The Bomb and delivery systems were just so technically feasible that developing them was irresistible. Technique, argues Ellul, drives individuals and nations toward technical solutions to problems, even to a technical definition of *the* problems, to the exclusion of moral or political resolutions.[2] Given the premise of technique, Ellul argues, all other choices (such as moral appeals or political settlements, primarily disarmament) were excluded as inferior to a technical solution—more and better arms, better defenses, better intelligence, and so on, to the point by the end of the cold war that both sides were virtually bankrupt from the ever-expanding technical demands of the arms race!

Technique, then, has become for Ellul the presiding and determining assumption of organized activity in our modern civilization. But technique, expressed in the ever-widening organizational power of states and corporations, is totalistic. Ellul fears that even as the old totalitarianisms of terror (as in Nazi Germany or Stalinist Eastern Europe) disappeared, they could be replaced by a totalitarianism of technique: "This totalitarianism resembles Huxley's *Brave New World* much more than Orwell's *1984*, since its ultimate technical accomplishment is to manipulate people into believing that they want to do what the state demands of them."[3] Technique has an intrusive and expansionary logic to its use, necessarily thrusting people toward perfecting technologies of power over things and also over one another. Driven by the worship of technique, humans create, perfect, and exercise techniques of power not only to manipulate and control machinery, money, and nature, but also to manipulate and control organizations of people, even masses of people. In countries with traditions of privacy, for example, the technology of computer record keeping is hard to keep private, as the interorganizational techniques of accessing records (credit, bank, job, police, military, sexual) become more feasible; as this happens, one's privacy is threatened. One's privacy—not to mention peace of mind—is also threatened by telephone solicitors who call you constantly, trying to sell something.

For Ellul, the force of technique in the modern world has meant a relentless quest for more efficient forms of rule. The logic of technical rationality goads elites to master how to do things (new practices), how to command people what to do (new authority), and how and what to say in order to get them to do it (new communication). Moved by the logic of technique, rulers are interested in the language of science only to the extent that science can be used to command more efficiently. They are interested in the language of argument only when deemed necessary to arouse or calm the masses more efficiently, or to persuade other elites. But it is propaganda that is primarily the modern language of technique. The power of propaganda lies not in its appeal to the logic of scientific proof, nor the logic of rhetorical argument, but rather—as we stressed in our introductory chapter—in the logic of credulity. Modern communicators imbued with the logic of technique seek the most efficient and expedient means of communication that is available and feasible.

"Knowledge of a fact," says Ellul, "comes down to a question of faith."[4] In contemporary technological society, propaganda is not only ubiquitous, it is for practical purposes not even distinguishable from information. Since technocratic elites control the means of mass communication, what they communicate derives primarily from technique, not moral and/or political constraints. To believe technique-inspired messages requires a leap of faith, or, if you will, a suspension of disbelief. Once the leap of faith has been made, both source and message of propaganda acquire the status of authority. We know something is true not because it is demonstrably so via scientific or rhetorical proof, but because it has the *status* of truth. What we are not aware of is that it is a *propaganda truth,* a truth whose truth value lies in its ability to convince through suasion rather than any real investigation or critical analysis we might undertake. Propaganda thereby is not only a form of communication, it is also a form of knowledge. As Ellul asks, "where exactly is the boundary between propaganda, a massive affirmation of simplified facts, and information made up of general formulas, elementary themes, over which the reader has not the slightest control or power?"[5] When we read through, say, the Sunday newspaper, propaganda abounds, not only in ads and inserts, but also in features with a point of view, editorials, news articles that take official propaganda at face value, columns that purport to be independent but are in fact partisan, pictures of the president taken by photographers that are in fact a "photo op" for propaganda purposes, news stories that are derived from public relations releases, and so on. The boundary between propaganda and news, information, and rhetorical opinion blends, and propaganda becomes a legitimate and familiar source of knowledge. Propaganda so constituted as part of our daily lives becomes not only a way of communicating but also a way of knowing, the form of knowledge most characteristic of advanced modernity. As a habitual form of knowledge, we accord it the status of truth, even if we are dimly aware it is a propaganda truth.

As one observer has noted, Ellul's thesis that propaganda has become the preeminent form of communication in the modern world means that it has subverted "a whole family of epistemic and para-epistemic values and practices." Epistemic values, involving what it is we can and do know, include "information and knowledge; truth and facts; certainty and objectivity"; para-epistemic values include "thoughtfulness and reflection," indeed all those things that "give a total impression of fair play and reasonableness in persuasive discourse." Those values subverted "give propaganda the appearance of genuine knowledge and understanding," weaving a "network of epistemic and para-epistemic values that work the magic of their influence upon readers."[6] We are not aware of the extent to which propaganda is interwoven in common communication.

The word *magic* is key. For Ellul, the essence of propaganda is in a kind of primitive and archaic appeal it has for people. Science appeals to the power of inquiry, rhetoric at its best to the power of argumentation. But propaganda appeals to the power of myth and magic. Propaganda, says Ellul, creates a new realm of "the sacred." This is an "abstract universe representing a complete reconstruction of reality. . . . Men fashion images of things, events, and people which may not reflect reality but which are truer than reality."

However, it is a "sham universe," the "disappearance of reality in a world of hallucinations." To be sure, "man will be led to act from real motives that are scientifically directed and increasingly irresistible. . . . But he acts in a dream," seeking ends that "the incantational magic of propaganda proposes for him." Ellul also speaks of "fictitious universe" and "illusory universe," arguing that "because we live in a universe of images, affecting the masses can be reduced to manipulating symbols."[7] Thus propaganda is magical communication rather than scientific or rhetorical communication; it evokes a world with its own mysterious logic, wherein spurious correlations and fanciful tales abound. It is the magic of created "great realities."

In Ellul's view, then, the logic of propaganda stems not only from the conditioned reflex ("Buy this NOW") but also from myth ("Buy this now and live happily ever after the way the fable says"). In modern society, the individual acquires the habits of responding to propaganda, even though he or she has "sales resistance." Propaganda is so pervasive, and our way of life so imbued with it by necessity, that we habitually respond to it thoughtlessly. Agents of social suasion prepare us (often quite unwittingly) for propaganda by conditioning us (and them) to view it as normal and necessary, so therefore our habitual responses should be seen as quite normal and necessary. But our reflexive response to propaganda is not merely a matter of Pavlovian responses, but more an interest in the mythic tales that propagandistic communication tell.

Using propaganda to make choices when we buy, vote, contribute, attend, celebrate, fight, or just acquiesce is partly reflexive in the technological society. But more than reflex comes into play. For Ellul, modern myths are the key to understanding propaganda. A myth is not only a powerful and captivating ancient story, but more "an all-encompassing, activating image" which "expresses the deep inclinations of a society." In a country like the United States, for example, propaganda that challenged rather than reinforced the pervasive societal myths that work is good, happiness is attainable, and progress is inevitable would, in Ellul's view, not succeed.

A myth is a story truer than reality, and much of the logic of modern propaganda is to perpetuate myths, then capitalize on them. Goebbels propagated the Nazi mythology of race, Lee and Bernays helped shore up the myth of elite benevolence, Ogilvy associated products with nostalgic or sophisticated myths, and Deaver helped create the myth of a peerless president in command of America and the Free World. Goebbels's Adolf Hitler, Lee's New York subway, Bernays's Calvin Coolidge, Ogilvy's Hathaway Man, and Deaver's Ronald Reagan were all portrayed through propaganda as mythical figures. "The facts of their life, translated, 'illuminated,' 'managed,' escaped the categories of true and false, and the illusory man became more real than the closest reality."[8]

Propaganda appeals to more than reflexive responses in another way. Says Ellul, nothing could be achieved if propaganda did not fulfill deep-seated needs in modern humankind: "Propaganda fills a need of modern man, a need that creates in him an unconscious desire for propaganda. He is in the position of needing outside help to be able to face his condition." Ellul thinks that we suffer from "symbolic poverty," a desire for a frame of reference, for things to make sense in a world of seeming chaos: "Man cannot stand this; he cannot live in an absurd and incoherent world. . . . Nor can he accept the idea that the problems which sprout all around him cannot be solved, or that he himself has no value as an individual and is subject to the turn of events." Our need for propaganda is therefore existential: modern man is "a victim of emptiness," "devoid of meaning,'' needing something to ''fill his inner void.'' Ellul seems to agree with G. K. Chesterton that since the decline of religion, modern man's problem *is not that he believes nothing, but rather that he will believe anything* (or, perhaps, suspend disbelief in anything!). Since we feel alone in the large and anonymous crowd, we seek communication from some source that connects us with an authority, community, and explanatory power:

> Propaganda is the true remedy for loneliness. It also corresponds to deep and constant needs, more developed today, perhaps, than ever before: the need to believe and obey, to create and hear fables, to communicate in the language of myths. It also responds to man's intellectual sloth and need for security. . . . All this turns man against information, which cannot satisfy any of these needs, and leads him to crave propaganda, which can satisfy them.[9]

Ellul's critique of modern society and the role of propaganda in it (one we return to in following chapters) is one that should give us all pause. He thinks that democracy and freedom, which we might regard as spreading and taking root like a field of flowers since the collapse of Communist dictatorships in Eastern Europe, are actually undermined by propaganda. The power of technique that resides in large organizations and mass communication is making for an illusion of free choice. Ellul's argument that the logic of propaganda leads to a future when its power will be overwhelming is obviously pessimistic, but it is an argument that must be faced squarely. Ellul is not a lone Jeremiah crying in the wilderness: a trio of scholars recently and chillingly concluded, after a survey of the propaganda literature, that ''in the nation-state of late capitalism information management is inherently totalitarian.''[10] Ellul, however, more than anyone else has tried to delineate the logic of propaganda as a force in modern society. Hence, let us explore further how that logic informs propaganda today.

TECHNIQUE IN THE CREATION OF GREAT REALITIES

We have examined the thoughts of several diverse analysts—for example, a Florentine thinker, two PR consultants, a Nazi minister, an advertising executive, a presidential assistant, a world renowned scholar, even a circus tycoon—regarding the growth, practice, and logic of propaganda. A thread runs through from Machiavelli to Ellul: reality is no longer simply a matter between the individual and those with whom he or she comes in immediate contact but is even more an imagined set of affairs shaped through a host of mediating modes of personal, group, and mass communication. Moreover, the techniques of that mediation may govern reality as much as or more than demonstrable fact. From the point of view of the propagandist, the question has become, how do I translate the logic of imagination, and the logic of communication, into the logic of propaganda?

As a reader of this book, put yourself in the role of the propagandist. Your job is to propagate a message that overcomes inertia, resistance, and competing messages, to spread your message to whom you want to reach, and to achieve a client's desired effect. Not an easy task. If you have talent and have taken seriously the various analysts you have read, especially Ellul, you sense that to do your job well you must concentrate on the techniques of attracting widespread interest in what you, or your client, have to say. You are not a scientist, nor even strictly a rhetorician; you are a propagandist. So what works? You have some idea, since even if you have no experience as a professional propagandist, you do have experience as a consumer of propaganda. You realize that you are now in the position of a glorified carnival barker, trying to lure people to come into your tent and witness wondrous sights and daring feats. You must titillate, intrigue, and fascinate as much as implore. In short, with P. T. Barnum, you create ''great realities.''

You also sense from what you have experienced, read, seen, and heard that all of us live in a small reality, a world of immediate experience and everyday activities. We extend ourselves and our worlds through imagination. As a propagandist, your task is to take people above and beyond mere life by inviting them to suspend disbelief and share with you a great reality. The creative talents of mass communicators working in any medium invent great realities for people's lives; the creative talents of propagandists do so through the arts of suasion. Now, as Ellul understood, propaganda is so often found because it is so often sought. Successful enterprises increasingly must put techniques of creating great realities to the task of meeting the demands of people living in a mythical and magical universe. The logic of propaganda is a *mytho-logic* that uses familiar cultural stories to enhance an appeal put not as a plea but as a tale, proverb, fable, or other enactment. Too, the logic suspends the constraints of ordinary reality by saying, in effect, magic works. The logic and lure of the propagandist is: let us work our magic for you.

Continuing with your task as a propagandist, imagine that you are an advertising executive. Heeding Bill Bernbach's advice from Chapter 2, you decide the best way to sell your client's product is to appeal not only to ''changing'' mankind but to *unchanging* mankind—the deep-seated desire for satisfying stories and magical experiences. Your potential consumers are changing, wanting new things and new experiences, but you frame the desire to be, say, fashionable with the deeper desire to be accepted, outstanding, and self-confident. Consider your marketing task to be selling fashions and beauty aids to people under the age of eighteen. You must use technique (as Ellul views it) to understand not only the demographics and attitudes of teenagers, but also the basic human desires of this latest generation of teens, desires manifested in new, yet old, ways. If we are to believe professional advertisers, the unchanging root desire underlying demands to consume fashionable clothes and beauty aids is human vanity. Young people in particular have anxieties about their own self-worth, so clothes, makeup, and so on help them deal with such doubts. Assuming all that, you develop a campaign to sell a line of goods to a youth market, using all of the sophisticated techniques of advertising and marketing. Your ads run on youth-oriented programs (such as TV dance shows), are featured at rock concerts by teenage heartthrob bands, and appear in teen magazines (such as *Seventeen*). The ads emphasize the myth of happy and carefree (not to mention beautiful and sexy) youth at play, wearing the clothes and using the beauty aids (e.g., pimple controls) that guarantee carefree social acceptance.

The hypothetical task you have been charged with is, of course, not hypothetical at all. Advertisers accept it frequently. Their archetypal myth is that of Narcissus. Narcissus, a youth in Greek mythology, pined away in love for his own image reflected in a pool of water, so much that he was transformed into a flower that bears his name. If advertisers once frowned upon appeals to self-absorption and self-indulgence, they do so no more. Ads now convey the message that not only is narcissism acceptable, it is "in." One *must* wear the "right" clothes, cosmetics, and jewelry (men and women) to enjoy flaunting "me. Me. ME!" I can enjoy myself as a magical being.

A product such as cologne or lipstick is no mere cosmetic, however; it possesses magical properties. In ads the application of the magic potion ensures beauty, attractiveness, and eternal youth. The ad for youth beauty products evokes a world of myth and magic, satisfying basic human vanity, at least temporarily, by offering a myth of self now blessed with newfound magical powers. If such ads are convincing, teenagers act upon them not out of conscious self-indulgence but rather out of self-worth (they hope). The logic of propaganda thus employs a propagated and suasive myth to create a great reality for anxious teens.

Studies of teenage consumption patterns—and those of preteens as well—indicate that targeted advertising achieves success. In part that success stems from the message aimed directly at youth, in part from similar appeals directed at their parents as parents and as former teenagers. A 1990 *Redbook* magazine national poll found that by age 12, about half of American girls are wearing lipstick, blush, eyeshadow, and mascara; by age 6, many children are expressing an interest in designer apparel. American children aged 4–12 have over $8 billion a year in disposable money, especially the upscale "yuppie puppies," to spend on such items as snacks and sweets ($2.2 billion); toys and games ($2.1 billion); movies and sports ($665 million); arcades ($535 million); and gifts and other things ($280 million). By ages 13 to 15, typical American middle-class girls spend nearly $170 a year on adult cosmetics; by ages 12 to 13, 79 percent of boys are using deodorant and 46 percent are using cologne.

Attempting to "act like an adult" and "growing up fast" has its consequences: one out of two junior high school girls report that they've dieted at some time; one out of three fourth graders report pressure to try wine coolers; by age 17, nearly half of all boys are sexually active, and by age 19, 63 percent of girls; and each year, more than one million teenage girls become pregnant. Although there are many factors involved in creating such patterns of behavior, we cannot reject out of hand the importance of propaganda that urges using adult products and looking like adults and extols sensuality, sexual play, and in general having a good time. But even if such propaganda had *no* such social impact, the behavior patterns themselves offer a richly nourished seedbed for product advertising.[11] Obviously ads directed at young people cannot be altogether blamed for these social trends, but on the other hand they may have subtle and long-term impact largely unintended by the propagators.

Move to another hypothetical situation. Suppose that you are a promoter of, say, a rock concert or even an inaugural gala for the president of the United States—in short, any elaborate spectacle designed to display talent, people, or ideas and to be widely covered by the press. Looking for guidance you might consider showman P. T. Barnum; the career of early fight promoter Tex Rickard; and Don King, the contemporary flamboyant fight promoter. King hypes boxing matches far beyond the import of the fights themselves. Or consider David Wolper, the impresario of various public spectacles, most notably the 1986 "Centennial Week-End" commemorating rededication of the Statue of Liberty; for this extravaganza Wolper hired 200 Elvis Presley impersonators, clearly a mark of Barnum's style! It takes a large dose of propaganda "brass" to successfully promote such events (as Edward Bernays did with the opening of Greenfield Village in 1929). Perhaps all such Barnumian characters should agree with the brassy greeting that 1920s nightclub impresario Texas Guinan used to greet the customers her promotional gifts had lured there: "Hello suckers!"

Your task is to promote wrestling matches. It could just as easily be a beauty pageant, the "real, or reel, life" wedding of a Hollywood star and starlet, a daredevil shot from a cannon across the English Channel, even a presidential debate. None of these events is spontaneous; all take place for their publicity value. But let us stay with professional wrestling. A moment's reflection will tell you that the match alone will not draw interest and sell tickets. Wrestling promotions typify the operation of propaganda logic: promoted "rasslin'" is a colorful and amusing "contest" replete with dazzling characters representing good and evil, using outlandish costumes and gimmicks ("death holds"), pitted in a match whose outcome is never in doubt. That hardly constitutes sport or athletics but is certainly attention-getting melodrama. We do not exaggerate: the high hype of championship wrestling matches between professionals Hulk Hogan and Andre the Giant, followed by Hogan versus Ultimate Warrior, provides evidence. For example, in a poll Hulk Hogan ranked first among teenagers as the athlete they admired the most; the Hogan–Andre the Giant match in Detroit's Silverdome brought the largest crowd ever gathered there. Promotion has elevated professional wrestling into a mythic universe in which popular gods contend endlessly over the triumph of good.

The logic of promotion is evident: a pseudoevent is staged as a megaevent with all of the hoopla and glitz of previous "greatest shows on earth"; the principals are cast as bigger than life (a North Carolina schoolboy wrestler named Sylvester Ritter performs as "Junk Yard Dog," and bogus "Russians" as Ivan and Nikita Kolhov, along with their cohort, the "Iranian Iron Sheik"); the event panders to audiences demanding a "Battle of Titans" between good and evil, heroes and villains. The logic of propaganda produces a ritual spectacle conforming to predictable canons of dramaturgy rather than to the rulebook constraints of, say, collegiate wrestling.

Now fantasize yourself in another role, namely, a public relations specialist hired by a major oil company to sustain, and if need be, refurbish the corporate image. You know the awful truth: your company cares not one whit about any environmental damage it does; your job is to convince policy makers and members of the citizenry otherwise. Overcoming any ethical qualms, you set about selling a skeptical press and suspicious public the myth of corporate benevolence, that Clean Oil Corporation is a leader in environmental protection. Your client fully grasps that propaganda is a more efficient and cheaper technique to use in refurbishing the corporate image than measures taken to minimize environmental damage that would be costly risks to the firm's profits and to stockholders' dividends.

Add to this mix a major oil spill with massive coastal damage resulting from a leak in a Clean Oil tanker. The spill provokes headlines, TV filmed reports, outcries from environmentalists. Your PR damage control must assure everyone that the risk to the coast and to water and shore life is minimal, the spill is contained, and Clean Oil's record is as clean as its name. Corporate press releases bemoan the "unfortunate accident," guarantee "the cause" will be uncovered and "corrected," in any event the commanding officer of the tanker will be fired, and, in the meantime, "everything that can be done is being done." A corporate-produced videotape—available to news media and private groups around the land—depicts the magical success of Clean Oil's vigorous cleanup operations. Finally you convince Clean Oil to commission an opinion poll. The question, "Do you agree or disagree that since the likelihood of another oil shortage is imminent—meaning long lines at the gas pump and higher prices—publicity given to oil spills, such as the recent one of a Clean Oil tanker, is far out of proportion to the relatively miminal damage?" The results are heartening: three of every five of those polled agree!

One final scenario. You are campaign manager for a presidential candidate. One adviser speaks up at a planning meeting: "Let the Boss go out on his own, say what he thinks, and provoke a candid and thorough airing of the issues." Another aide responds: "That sounds good in principle, after all that is ideally what running for office is supposed to be all about in a democracy. But, let's face it. The Boss is a lousy, dull, boring speaker. He'll die out there. Let's use newspaper, radio, and TV ads that highlight the differences between how our Boss stands on the issues versus the incumbent. That will fairly contrast the positions of our candidate compared to our opponent." As the seasoned campaign professional you are, you smile, lean back, and give your thoughts: "Boys, that's fine. The Boss is sure proud of where he stands on issues. Loves to talk about them. But, let's be logical. You know something? Nobody cares. What the voters want to know is not what the Boss wants to do, but about him. Is he decisive, strong, hungry; does he have fire in the belly? That's what we must convey. Now I know he's a nice, laid-back, mellow sort of guy, almost wimpish. But that doesn't matter. It's not how he *is* but how he *looks*. There is an old rule of campaign propaganda about gilding the lily. We do three things: attack. Attack. ATTACK."

Granted this is a caricature of what you might find, say, and do were you a campaign propagandist. (Perhaps, however, as we see in Chapters 4 and 5, not that much of a caricature.) But it makes Ellul's point even if by exaggeration. That point is, again: in an age of technique the how of propaganda (means) drives and shapes the what of public communication (content)—including the definition of problems and situations, choices, and courses of action. With propaganda the very language of technique, in the modern society of technique propaganda then is *the* communication means to define and achieve social or group ends. The logic of propaganda as it unfolds in the technique of palaver—guile and charm—bears further scrutiny.

THE GUILE AND CHARM OF AGITATION, INTEGRATION, AND DISPOSITION TECHNIQUE

Review what we, and Ellul, have argued to this point. People have always been ruled; there has always been technique used in ruling; today propaganda is *the* technique, the language, of ruling. In the modern world, because of its effectiveness, legitimacy, and reliability, propaganda has acquired the status of authority. The specialists who advertise products, promote spectacles, fashion corporate images, or manage political campaigns, because they have an aura of expertise and authority, are the technocrats of propaganda. Those technocrats design credulous appeals, the credulity (via suspension of disbelief) yields belief, and the believed is authoritative. Thereby propaganda technique is deemed legitimate, reliable, and increasingly effective in the long term and perhaps in the short.

Propaganda has become like an old friend, one who "would do anything for you."

The friend is reliable. So what if she or he tells a tall tale now and then, exaggerates, gets hyper? So what if our old friend gets his or her way with us by being beguiling and charming? We forgive palaver in a reliable old friend. The reliability overcomes resistance both to the technique of palaver ("That's a person I enjoy and trust") and to the palaver of technique ("It was such a charming story, I knew it was true"). As a habitual, taken-for-granted friend we can envision no other or better one than propaganda. We are not only capable of believing (or disbelieving) literal truth, we are also capable of believing (or disbelieving) propaganda truth. Even when propaganda has an unfriendly premise (drugs fry your brain, the enemy is a threatening demon, the capital is full of political crooks and idiots), the answer is usually friendly (stay drug free and you'll be OK, support the war and we'll kill the demon, vote for me and we'll clean house).

Propaganda Rituals

When palaver achieves this authoritative status, thereby becoming both taken for granted and taken seriously, it can become ritual-like in its practice and reception. Much of the propaganda we encounter in everyday life is a communication ritual, a predictable and rule-governed dramaturgy propagated to mass audiences. A ritual exploits symbols to dramatize vague, abstract beliefs and feelings and evoke them in meaningful ways.[12] Think of television and magazine ads. Many are for "personal" products—household goods, beauty and health aids, clothing and accessories. Take a glance at these familiar ads. Many are clearly ritualized through relating repeatable, familiar little minidramas that usually offer a "slice of life" appealing to our ordinary concerns and anxieties, evoking the product as a panacea for our troubles, and claiming to be an authoritative voice of sweet reason. The TV or magazine ad "talks" to us, nay, converses *with* us, urging that we take part in the ritualized drama, sway ourselves to buy the product, and experience the reliable solution to the problem posed by the enactment. The appeal of ritualized ads is not so much that they are reasonable (in strict logic, they often are not) but that they are comfortable and habitual—user friendly—in a context we are used to and that matches our expectations. So maybe the kids don't eat the sandwiches after we buy Jif peanut butter. Still, "choosy mothers choose Jif" and, being choosy, we buy it anyway. Like the old friend's charming story, it gave pleasure at the time—as always—and who cares if it stretched the truth just a little?

A magazine ad (for Tide) shows two panels, the first of a forlorn little girl in a lovely pink party dress smudged with chocolate pudding (caption: "It was her favorite party dress"); the second of the little girl now smiling in her cleansed party dress ("It still is"). At the bottom, the pitch: "If it's got to be clean it's got to be Tide." Familiar, unremarkable, mundane. Yet the ad illustrates the essentials of propaganda logic. There is no scientific analysis of how Tide gets out a tough stain, nor rhetorical persuasion like, say, the medicine shows of old. This is rather a logic interwoven with unspoken core values, the myth of familial happiness as expressed in a pert little girl's smile, and the magic potion of Tide that efficiently cleaned the dress and joyously resolved a crisis. The logic is both explicit (Tide = completely clean) and implicit (Tide = family happiness). Tide, the reliable ol' friend, beguiles and charms its way into our lives, teaching us of its friendly uses.

We can both use and take for granted such propaganda as something that makes sense as part of our world. Think, in this regard, of the ritual incantation in advertising of "new and improved.'' It seems straightforward enough. But the logic is more complex. The mytho-logic implicit in ''new and improved'' is deeply imbedded in American culture. If Ellul is correct, Progress is one of the ''master myths'' of Western civilization along with Work and Happiness; work achieves technical and social progress that ensures happiness.[13] Now a myth is not a false belief, or even a true one, but a credible one that remains so because its truth or falsity cannot be tested, just taken for granted. A myth is a cultural common denominator in story and symbol representing transcendent human aspirations and anxieties. To assert that work is not ennobling, or progress inevitable, or people destined to be happy runs counter to deep-seated, credible beliefs.

Thus propagandists frame pitches in the context of mythic ideas and images—nostalgia for rural simplicity and ''natural'' things, warm family ties across the generations, holiday settings with patriotic and communal values displayed, or sometimes just cute children or striking young women and men epitomizing the promise of beauty. In TV advertising, ''new and improved'' (even in old products: new Tide, new Ivory, new Wheaties, and more disastrously, new Coke) is mythopoetic palaver that adheres to propaganda logic. The adjectives tell us that we are living better by buying the latest thing; that the old should be abandoned for the new; and that the lure of the new is irresistible since improvement is in the nature of things.[14]

Kinds of Propaganda

As propaganda grew more refined in advanced modern societies it acquired multiple forms and functions. Ellul, for example, writes of *agitation propaganda,* especially of political agitation: ''Propaganda of agitation addresses itself . . . to internal elements in each of us, but it is always translated into reality by physical involvement in a tense and overexcited activity.''[15] The idea is to move people to action, to inflame them to do things they might not otherwise have done. (The Bolsheviks who founded the Soviet Union called this ''agitprop''; we might term it the ''Demosthenes ploy'': after hearing, we say, ''Let us march.'') Ellul distinguishes another kind of propaganda; it aims for more than moving people to act. *Integration propaganda,* he says, is ''a propaganda of conformity'' that tries to get people to relate to each other in acceptable ways. It brings together, promotes cohesion and consensus, and unites. It is ''much more subtle and complex than agitation propaganda . . . seeks not a temporary excitement but a total molding of the person in depth.''[16]

A useful way to think of the difference between the propaganda of agitation and of integration is as follows. Rather than simply asking people to join the march (agitation), integration propaganda structures an emotional background or context for the march itself. For example, in his study of advertising, Roland Marchand has noted that ''in the process of selling specific products, advertisers also communicated broader assumptions about social values. Implicit value statements, passed along unconsciously as givens, usually carried an ideological bias toward 'system reinforcement.' ''[17] (Recall Bernays's ploy of not trying to sell people pianos, rather to sell them on the idea of a music room with a piano, a place that furthers social and familial integration.)

It is common to think of familiar propaganda such as commercial advertising as primarily agitation propaganda, but that isn't necessarily so. Commercial advertising propaganda is highly adaptable, and often combines the effort to agitate potential consumers with integrative messages that flatter both producer and consumer. Advertising bends the desire for social integration—acceptance, fashionability, group happiness or achievement, sociability, and so on—in marketable ways for either short-term or long-term effects. A classic ad built on both agitation and integration appeals was Coca-Cola's 1970 TV commercial featuring young people of different cultures and races gathered on a hillside singing "I'd like to teach the world to sing in perfect harmony." The ad not only promoted Coke but also identified the soft drink with world peace and mutual understanding at a time, during the upheaval over Vietnam, of great discord. Two decades later, when peace seemed to be breaking out with the end of the cold war, Coca-Cola recut the ad, this time not only identifying the product with world peace but providing a subtle hint that drinking the cola might have had something to do with the world's achieving it. The "subtext" of the ad seemed to suggest that the magical incantations of a cross section of the world's hopeful and innocent youth brings peace, and that Coke is an agent of, and elixir of, peace.

Integration propaganda oftentimes follows a ritual format in promoting official or organizational adherence to social values. The adherence may be only lip service or quite sincere. Let us take as examples two new holidays in the American calendar—King Day (Martin Luther King, Jr.'s birthday) and Earth Day (the informal springtime celebration of environmental concerns). King Day was intended as a celebration not only of a significant figure, but also of the values he represented. Since its inception, however, King Day has become an occasion not only for publicized activities to promote interracial harmony and empathy, but also for civil rights interest groups to focus attention on their social agenda, and for politicians and organizations who believe in nothing that King stood for to "go on record" ritually as doing so anyway because voters expect it. In that instance, integration propaganda becomes a dodge, attempting to forestall agitation propaganda advocating real change and not symbolic gestures.

Similarly, Earth Day by the 1990s (it began in 1970) became a ritual occasion for everyone with a propaganda voice to assert support for the environment. Yet many claims sounded suspiciously promotional. With environmental protection a "motherhood issue," Earth Day served as the opportunity for all interests to place themselves on the side of the gods. President George Bush, who billed himself the "environmental president," pledged to spearhead the effort to plant five billion trees in the United States over the next five years (while at precisely the same time he proposed to cut from existing Forest Service tree-planting programs the amount of $32 million for the next fiscal year!). The corporate members of the Chemical Manufacturers Association announced in ads a Responsible Care initiative, a "commitment to continuously improve our performance in health, safety, and protecting the environment," but some critics recalled that some of the association's member companies had created toxic waste dumps that the taxpayers are now paying to clean up. The paper-products association chimed in with similar ads ("For us, every day is Earth Day"), as did the nuclear power industry ("Every day is Earth Day with nuclear energy"). Propaganda thus offers ritual exoneration. Earth Day, like King Day, is the occasion for a flurry of ritual activity, substituted for policy activity.

Clearly the propaganda that integrates at one time may not do so at another. Propagandistic campaigns, like anything else, must keep up with the times and, in so doing, they often shape the times as well. Advertisements, argues Marchand, "contributed to the shaping of a 'community of discourse,' an integrative common language shared by an

otherwise diverse audience.''[18] But in the modern world, communities are always changing, so agencies of propaganda constantly adapt new discourses to meet changing circumstances and activities. Human needs may be unchanging, but the human aspiration to
adapt to changing times is a basic need also.

Glance through magazine ads targeted at women over the decades of this century.
Much of the discourse in those ads targets specific clienteles and their desires for successful social adjustment in a particular social era. For instance, women's desires to be desirable to men, and also to be accepted by their women peers, is a basic need that takes on
new discursive form in propaganda as time goes by. The Listerine ads of the 1920s (see
Chapter 1) spoke to what was deemed the primary desire of women then, namely to marry
before the dreaded ''Big Three Oh''; later Maidenform bra ads helped women entertain
the possibilities of entry into public roles; the Virginia Slim cigarette ads that began in the
early 1970s (''You've come a long way, baby'') associated the brand with independent
modern women pursuing feminist values and lifestyles. By the 1990s, ads targeted at
women extolled a kind of postfeminist eroticism, but also a new aggressiveness (in, for
example, myriad magazine ads showing elegant and independent women shooting pool,
drinking Scotch, traveling for business, and slapping men on the rear). In all cases the
product is important, but the appeal is to associate that product with women's changing
integrative values: what do women want, and how can the product appear as a magical tal-
isman of gender integration?

Integration propaganda, then, targets and shapes changing social relationships. But it
is not confined just to the business of selling people things, and hoping they are buying the
relationship along with the product. Integration propaganda begins for many children at
least in kindergarten, where a representative of social order—the teacher—leads the flag
salute, reciting the Pledge of Allegiance. As they grow older these children find a wide variety of other social authorities telling them don't get into cars with strangers, don't take
drugs or start smoking, fasten safety belts, abstain from sex, use a condom to prevent the
spread of AIDS, don't use handguns, get annual checkups, lower cholesterol, exercise,
''Thank you for not smoking,'' and get an attorney to make out a will.

Integration propaganda targets specific groups to promote ideas in other ways. In the
late 1980s and in the 1990s, a popular form of rock music called ''rap'' became a forum
for integration propaganda directed at blacks, urging them through rap lyrics to stop de-
structive behavior and support community solidarity. In 1989, rap music's biggest stars
produced a record titled *Self-Destruction* (with royalties donated to the National Urban
League) aimed at urban black youth tempted by the lure of sex, quick money, drugs, and
gang violence. The effectiveness of such blatant, intrusive efforts is debatable. Teenagers
since World War II have been swamped with propaganda urging them to abstain from sex,
but for many of them no amount of official condemnation can prevent the urgency of
passion.

Often propaganda messages have ''disintegrative'' consequences, rather than the integrative or agitative ones intended. For instance, ads touting women's products were
made by people who had no identifiable intention of starting a sexual revolution. But if social analysts are right, those ads alleging that products make women alluring also legitimized female eroticism, and the integrative myth of the ''girl next door'' disintegrated in
advertising's wake. Likewise, a steady exposure to advertising extolling the virtues of
having fun through leisure activities (theme parks, outdoor games, travel, and so on) may

have, as some social critics say, led to the disintegration of the "puritan" values of seriousness, thrift and frugality, dedication and diligence; a "fun morality" was born.[19]

Social analysts and critics are not, of course, beyond using propaganda techniques of their own. Hence, whether advertising killed "the girl next door" and/or puritan America is problematic. But social commentators, along with others, engage in what we can identify as a third form of propaganda. If agitation propaganda encourages action (let us march), and integration propaganda encourages relationships (let us cohere), then *disposition propaganda* encourages social knowledge (let us believe). The first involves the propensity to act; the second the propensity to relate; and the third, the propensity to believe. The first two are in many cases relatively easy to spot as modes of propagation; they may stand alone in messages or be combined, and either or both can join dispositional propaganda. But it is dispositional propaganda that speaks to what we assume to be real and true, to what we take for granted as the way the world is. Therein lies its guile and charm.

As Stuart Ewen has remarked of advertising in modern culture, ruling through propaganda did not only involve simply inducing people to buy: "In the broader context of a burgeoning commercial culture, the foremost political imperative was *what to dream*."[20] Those who rule modern societies wish to control and communicate not only proper actions and relationships, but also basic myths. We learn how we should be disposed to act, relate, and believe, based on a worldview that is deemed "of course" to be true and real. Recall that Ellul thought that in modern society what we basically think is "information" (news, government documents, education, even entertainment) is actually propaganda, since it is framed in the social context of the world-taken-for-granted by those who rule. There is nothing necessarily sinister or conspiratorial about this; it simply flows from the logic of rule in our time. Ewen calls such rulers "the captains of consciousness."

Disposition propaganda is the most subtle and imbedded, that is, buried, in normal routines of talk, the common form of suasive communication. It is so deeply ingrained that as communicators we often, perhaps usually, are unaware of it. Theater audiences watching the first movies were delighted by the strange and compelling new spectacle. But they were more than entertained; they learned. Movies taught people raised in other environments (in rural areas, in immigrant communities, etc.) a disposition for life in the new urban order, what they could imagine cities to be like economically, culturally, and politically. Moreover, early movies propagated a lifestyle: how the stars lived on and off screen became a model of the new American dream. In their developing forms movies helped people to learn to abandon old assumptions for new ones without excessive agony; for instance, the old disposition to save before one bought something changed and movies left an impression that it was proper, even expected, to borrow money to enjoy rather than delay pleasures. This change in basic temperament was not so much intentionally communicated as it was the product of both movie producers and audiences exploring ways to imagine a new way of living.

Certainly, however, ad people, PR personnel, promoters, political experts, and others manipulate disposition propaganda. Some social critics argue ruling elites exercise either partial or complete "cultural hegemony" (control) over societies and thereby determine our conception of and conduct in the world.[21] If they are correct, and that is not certain, disposition propaganda is essential to that cultural domination by disposing people voluntarily through suasion to ways of life ruling elites deem appropriate. But those governing elites themselves change through disposition propaganda and accept, say, an art form such as popular music, once regarded as "crass," as the epitome of "class." As part of the flow of social discourse, disposition propaganda may have eventual influence on everyone, including those who are part of the ruling hegemonic force. It can be argued that the powers-that-be undercut the cultural revolution of the 1960s by co-opting aspects of it, selling psychedelic clothes, rock music, and books calling for revolution. On the other hand, sixties advertising propaganda also helped sell some of the dispositional changes under way to social elites, and pretty soon modified forms of change appeared in the attitudes and behavior of the powerful (longer hair, street language, mod clothes, drugs, and sex were only the most obvious things that the older generation adopted from the young, at least temporarily; more fundamental was a degree of toleration of deviant behavior— e.g., living together, homosexuality, racial intermarriage—that had not been acceptable before).

Especially in trying times, rulers may bend over backward to extol the merits of practices they forbade earlier. The United States during World War II offers instructive examples. Before the upheaval of wartime there were widely shared reservations about, and widely imposed restrictions on, women working, especially at tasks deemed "man's work." But with males departing for the armed services during war, women had to fill the void in wartime industries as well as what were formerly peacetime occupations. Wartime propaganda (posters, ads, movies, romance magazines, radio serials, speeches, etc.) urged women to "aid the war effort, get a job." Images of women donning work clothes, toting lunch pails, and riveting bolts in aircraft factories propagated and disposed a new work role. Rosie was no longer sitting around reading love stories, listening to radio soap operas, and eating candies; she was Rosie the Riveter. However, when the war started to wind down, soldiers began to return, and jobs for males were scarce. There was a subtle shift in media imagery. The new reality dictated a change in disposition. Women were now to return to home and hearth, enjoy the fruits of peace, reunite with their men, and make babies so the postwar world of domestic bliss would blossom. Although many women did just that, not every Rosie did. It would be decades before the nation would again be so disposed to accept females in the work force (in many instances it still has not on an equal pay for equal work basis); but once again a message had been propagated that was difficult to undo. What the official propaganda of the U.S. government had been able to propose and dispose in wartime could be but proposed in a postwar world.[22]

Disposition propaganda is also evident in the conduct of "the politics of the obvious." Like the propagation of new economic dispositions (spending beyond your means), or new cultural dispositions (urging women first into work roles, then into domestic roles), disposition propaganda puts a premium on the message "Well, of course! That's just the way things are." From World War I, through World War II, and the hot and cold wars thereafter, it was obvious to rulers and ruled that The Enemy was demonic, and comic as well. The "Hun" or "Kraut" was evil and bumbling; the "Jap" very sinister and cunning, yet a "yellowbelly"; the "Ruski" a tool of the "communist menace" and not too bright all the while. Given the obvious character of the enemy, it was equally obvious the United States must wage a "war without mercy" (as in the title of the wartime song "We're Gonna Have to Slap The Dirty Little Jap," and "There'll Be No Adolf Hitler nor Yellow Japs to Fear"). So obvious, truly, was the enemy's nature that cartoon characters Bugs Bunny and Donald Duck outsmarted moronic little Japanese with buck teeth and glasses on the silver screen. Some observers argue that such propaganda techniques were so effective that at the close of World War II few gave a second thought to the destruction of Hiroshima and Nagasaki with the "A-Bomb."[23]

After World War II the cold war propaganda of both the United States and the USSR demonized one another as The Enemy. In the United States fears of internal subversion were cultivated through such seedlings as TV series; "I Led Three Lives," for example, related tales of an FBI informer, Herbert A. Philbrick, who had infiltrated American communism and thus led the three lives of communist, patriot, and family man. A popular NBC series, "Victory at Sea," (broadcast first in 1952 to widespread interest and critical acclaim) was ostensibly a documentary about the U.S. Navy in World War II; in fact, it was subtle disposition propaganda on behalf of the righteous American anti-Soviet and anticommunist crusade. Viewed today such series seem strangely out of keeping with the times. No cold war, no enemies. Right? Scarcely. Today, depending on the propaganda presented, the Japanese seek to dominate world trade, the Germans Europe, the Iraqis the Middle East, and the South American drug cartel our children.[24] The enemies fashioned by disposition propaganda come and go, but The Enemy is seemingly with us always. Even though George Bush was able to arouse opinion about Saddam Hussein by claiming he was "worse than Hitler," after the Gulf War there was an "enemy gap," especially after word of allied carnage in the war against Iraq sank in, and more importantly with the demise of communism in Eastern Europe. War propaganda taught us who to hate, disposing us to feel good about "Us," and derivatively to believe integration ("We stand united in wartime") and agitation ("Kill the enemy") propaganda. Whether now it will be directed at new foreign (economic competitors, drug cartels) or domestic (the urban poor, the superrich) enemies remains to be seen. It is also unclear whether propaganda can dispose us toward attacking the common enemies of humankind, impersonal dangers such as widespread disease, poverty, pollution, and overpopulation.

A FINAL THOUGHT: PROPAGANDA AS NEWSPEAK

In this and preceding chapters we have employed *logic* loosely to denote different aspects that distinguish propaganda from other means of discourse. We spoke first of propaganda's historical logic, the demographic, social, economic, and political forces that combined to make propaganda an integral and necessary part of ruling in the modern world. We then discussed professional logic, the impulse toward professionalization in the modern world, and the early professionals who contributed to the development of propaganda's unique discourse built on the principles of credulity, necessity, expediency, and beauty. We also considered the logic of technique, Ellul's idea that modern societies exist through the mastery of technique, and the technique of palaver as a distinguishing aspect of the new propaganda. Finally, we examined the typo-logic of propaganda, the logic of agitation, integration, and disposition palaver.

What remains for our consideration is what we shall call the *discursive logic* of propaganda. So pervasive in our lives is propaganda, and so much do we unwittingly take it for granted, that the very rules, the grammar, of palaver become second nature to us. Put it this way: if Ellul is correct and propaganda is a language (with its own unique logic), then in the contemporary world we are not only influenced by propaganda, we *think* propaganda. We think not in scientific ways (using critical logic) nor in rhetorical ways (seriously evaluating arguments), but in propagandistic ways (palaver). Just as a mathematician might "speak" mathematics—by viewing, defining, and solving problems in technical, formulaic ways—or a football coach might speak a language of "quarterback draws," "wide outs," and "nickel defenses," we grow increasingly accustomed to parlaying in and through the guile and charm of palaver.

Many of us are more or less familiar with formal logic, that is, the rules distinguishing sound (logical) reasoning from unsound (illogical) reasoning. Regarded from the viewpoint of formal logic, propaganda is frequently associated with fallacious reasoning or faulty logic based on unwarranted assumptions. (As we shall see in Chapter 7, there is a rich tradition of efforts to analyze propaganda using formal logic.) In carrying out their daily routines, however, people practice informal logic. Such reasoning habits may or may not be faulty, but "it works for me." For instance, we often act on instinct and on intuition. Moreover, there is "the reason of dreams," a kind of irrational and subrational thought triggered by remnants of our archaic past (e.g., the fear of snakes) and childish fantasies (e.g., fear of falling). The logics of magic and myth are, in part, manifestations of dream reasoning.[25] Such spurious correlations employed in advertising when associating products with magical properties (perfume creates beauty and allure) and mythic states of power (immortality through oat bran, purity through soap) also reflect the practice of informal logic.

What we call propaganda's discursive logic is a derivative of the informal logic of everyday life. Appeals to instinct, intuition, suspended disbelief, the reason of dreams, magic, myth, and so forth are all techniques of propaganda. And they are discursive. By that we mean precisely what any dictionary definition says: covering a wide field of subjects; rambling; digressive; from the Latin *discursus,* "a running back and forth." From the many examples cited in this and the three preceding chapters (and those yet to be examined), there is no question that propaganda covers a wide field of subjects in promoting, merchandising, campaigning, warfare, and so on. Moreover, as we have seen, a distinguishing feature of the new propaganda is its use of an influence talk that is frequently vague (i.e., digressive) and verbose (i.e., rambling). In short, *discursus* is another way of characterizing the "running back and forth" of palaver, the technique of guile and charm.

As propaganda has become more pervasive in our daily lives, and as the new propaganda has featured the technique of palaver, discursive logic abounds—rambling, digressive claims covering many persons, ideas, causes, and products cloaked in appealing, ritualistic, beguiling, and charming ways. It abounds on TV ads, entertainment programs, newscasts, talk shows, "color commentary," analysis, and so forth, both in sounds and pictures. It abounds in newspapers and newsmagazines—features, editorials, "Ann Landers," "Dear Abby," syndicated columns, "lifestyle" sections, in print, pictures, and glitzy graphics. It abounds at the barbershop and the beauty parlor; the automobile showroom and the repair shop; the boutique, department store, or shoe store; at Ed's Hamburgers or "doing lunch at the Ritz"; in hospital rooms, classrooms, boardrooms, and bedrooms; among politicians, businessmen and businessmwomen, blue-collar workers, work "temps," service personnel, military officers and enlisted personnel, scientists, preachers, students, and, most certainly, teachers.

We have seen that propaganda frequently employs The Enemy in appeals. To paraphrase Walt Kelly's comic strip "Pogo," perhaps we have met the enemy and it is our palaver. George Orwell hinted as much five decades ago, although he called it something else. Orwell was an English writer, author of the widely read and interpreted novel *Nineteen Eighty-four* (sometimes simply designated *1984*). The work envisions a dark, foreboding world of the future where rulers have perfected the logic and practice of the totalitarian state in Oceania. Orwell prophesied through his novel that if ever such a perfected rule should develop it would initially do so through the exercise of brutal oppression, but in the long run armed force would be unnecessary for the state would have another technique to oppress, namely, its monopoly of all means of communication.

The totalitarian rulers of Oceania fully understood that words are not merely neutral designations for persons, objects, places, and events, but are really *attitudes*. Words define what we see and feel about people, relationships, and all other matters. (Is that 6′2″ muscular 17-year-old a ''boy'' or a ''man''; do we call the instructor in this course ''Miss,'' ''Ms,'' ''Ma'am,'' ''Professor,'' ''Doctor,'' or ''Barbara''?) The rulers constructed a language that would permit only approved attitudes to be *thought* and *spoken* (or written, pictured, and so forth). Orwell called this language Newspeak. Restricting language to Newspeak permitted rulers to engineer and control imaginations, manipulate mass thoughts, emotions, and actions—indeed create or destroy them by coining and discarding words. As language became more and more restricted (fewer words meant fewer options for thoughts), it could increasingly exclude from consciousness heretical or dangerous thoughts, that is, ''thoughtcrime.'' Orwell foresaw a future where the ruling class would sustain itself through an ''artificial universe'' (P. T. Barnum's ''great realities'') perpetuated by thought control through language control.

In the future, Orwell thought, Newspeak could be so pervasive that no other language could exist—not that of science or of rhetoric, nor the formal logic both scientists and rhetoricians employ. The only logic would be the logic of Newspeak. There would be no need for rulers to deceive followers, for followers through Newspeak would have at their disposal only the technique of their own self-deception. Newspeak would be the means of not only information management but mind management. Newspeak would not only ''provide a medium of expression for the world-view and mental habits proper'' to this new order of the future, but also ''make all other modes of thought impossible.'' By excluding all logical processes except the logic of propaganda, thoughtcrime would be rendered ''literally unthinkable.'' In such a world, the rule of propaganda is the accepted, only way of life.

A key feature of Oceania's Newspeak involved restricting the number of words available for use. Syme, a character in Orwell's novel, is an official helping edit a revised edition of the Newspeak dictionary. ''The Eleventh Edition is the definitive edition,'' he says. He goes on, ''You think, I dare say, that our chief job is inventing new words. But not a bit of it! We're destroying words—scores of them, hundreds of them, every day. We're cutting the language down to the bone.'' Why? ''Don't you see that the whole aim of Newspeak is to narrow the range of thought?''[26]

Now it might seem that destroying words so that, as Syme insists, every concept need be expressed ''by exactly *one* word'' would make language cover fewer subjects; would make it less rambling, less diffuse, less digressive, in short, less discursive. That was intended to be the perfected ideal. But as is so often the case with propaganda, intent does not always equal consequence. For yet another aspect of Newspeak increased discursiveness and ''a running back and forth.'' That involved the effort to combine words to remove opposites. What justification, asks Syme, is there for a word that is simply the opposite of some other words. Why have *good* and *bad* when one could simply have *good* and *ungood*? Why have *excellent* instead of *plusgood*?''[27] In principle that makes sense. But combining words does not make them more specific, more concrete, but less. So much so, that ''running back and forth,'' Newspeak contradicts itself. Take the slogans of Oceania's ruling party:

WAR IS PEACE

FREEDOM IS SLAVERY

IGNORANCE IS STRENGTH

Compare examples of contemporary palaver: an ad for a cigarette says, ''Flavor Happens''; a promo for a TV series claims ''Elvis Lives!''; a noted jurist says, ''If you can't say anything good about a dead person, don't say anything, so I won't say anything about George Bush''; and a friend says ''you look perfectly awful,'' another ''you look awfully pretty.'' Neither the Newspeak of Oceania's party nor the palaver of everyday life is specific, concrete, restricted in usage. All the utterances are open to individual interpretation, that is, to suasion. But it is suasion within the confines of the Newspeak/palaver itself, not from without by scientific or rhetorical analysis.

Jacques Ellul worried that the rule of propaganda might lead to an ''Orwellian'' world. Even though we are now past the year 1984, many observers think Orwell's prediction may well still come true, partially if not totally. A recent scholarly article argues that there are firm reasons to doubt Orwell's theories with respect to Newspeak's influence over individuals in even a totalitarian society. Yet, it notes:

> Even if the arguments in this paper are sound, they do not provide grounds for smugness. Unsuccessful as totalitarian regimes have been in achieving their totalitarian aims, their capacity to cause a great deal of misery cannot be denied. Moreover, despite the kinds of limits to the manipulative use of language discussed in this article, the extent to which some of the people can be effectively manipulated through language all of the time and all of the people some of the time is ample ground for sobriety regarding such matters.[28]

In writing his novel Orwell certainly had partly in mind the totalitarian experiences of Nazi Germany and of Soviet Russia and its Eastern European satellites. Rapid political changes in the 1990s indicate that such regimes are history. Nevertheless the seeds of totalitarian rule remain, even in Western countries with traditions of freedom. When we all learn and ''know'' Newspeak, predicted Orwell, the habits of Oldspeak—such as the habits of inquiry inherent in scientific investigation and rhetorical dialogue—will disappear. If language then becomes solely the technique of palaver, the powers of the future can truly be said to have created and embalmed our imaginations. We can speculate better whether that is happening after looking closely at the cultures where the seeds of the new propaganda thrive. We turn to those in Part II.

The chapter you have just read is the most theoretical you will encounter. It also raises some serious concerns about the consequences of propaganda, something that should interest those who worry about an unfree and thought-controlled future. Even with the demise of totalitarian states, it still might be the case that the power of propaganda could create a world of Newspeak to which we have become habitually conditioned to respond. In any case, now you know more about the logic of propaganda, and how such suasive communication can be used to agitate, integrate, and dispose. With these large ideas in mind, let us now turn to the plural cultures of the new propaganda, the ways in which we encounter and use propaganda in everyday life.

NOTES

1. Jacques Ellul, *The Technological Society* (New York: Vintage Books, 1964); *Propaganda: The Formation of Men's Attitudes* (New York: Vintage Books, 1965); *The Political Illusion* (New York: Vintage Books, 1967).

2. Ellul, *Technological Society*.

3. C. George Benello, "Technology and Power: Technique as a Mode of Understanding Modernity," in Clifford G. Christians and Jay M. Van Hook, eds., *Jacques Ellul: Interpretive Essays* (Champaign: University of Illinois Press, 1981); see also Clifford G. Christians and Michael R. Real, "Jacques Ellul's Contribution to Critical Media Theory," *Journal of Communication* 29(1) (1979): 83–93.

4. Jacques Ellul, *Political Illusion*, p. 110.

5. Jacques Ellul, "Information and Propaganda," *Diogenes* 18 (1957): 64.

6. Stanley B. Cunningham, "Smoke and Mirrors: A Confirmation of Jacques Ellul's Theory of Information Use in Propaganda," in Ted J. Smith III, ed., *Propaganda* (New York: Praeger, 1989).

7. Ellul, *Technological Society*, pp. 370–372.

8. Ellul, *Political Illusion*, pp. 116.

9. Ellul, *Propaganda*, pp. 138, 146–148.

10. Kevin Robins, Frank Webster, and Michael Pickering, "Propaganda, Information and Social Control," in Jeremy Hawthorn, ed., *Propaganda, Persuasion, and Polemic* (Baltimore: Edward Arnold, 1987), p. 16.

11. "Are Kids Growing Up Too Fast?" *Redbook* (March 1990): 91–100.

12. David I. Kertzer, *Ritual, Politics, and Power* (New Haven: Yale University Press, 1988).

13. Jacques Ellul, "Modern Myths," *Diogenes* 23 (Fall 1958): 23–40.

14. Caution: Is reference to the "new" propaganda itself a propaganda device?

15. Ellul, *Propaganda*, p. 72.

16. Ellul, *Propaganda*, pp. 75–76.

17. Roland Marchand, *Advertising the American Dream: Making Way for Modernity, 1920–1940* (Berkeley: University of California Press, 1985), p. xxvii.

18. Ibid., p. xx.

19. Martha Wolfenstein, "The Emergence of Fun Morality," *Journal of Social Issues* 7 (1951): 10–15.

20. Stuart Ewen, *Captains of Consciousness* (New York: McGraw-Hill, 1976), p. 109.

21. T. J. Jackson Lears, "The Concept of Cultural Hegemony: Problems and Possibilities," *American Historical Review* 90(3) (June 1985): 567–593.

22. Maureen Honey, *Creating Rosie the Riveter: Class, Gender, and Propaganda during World War II* (Boston: University of Massachusetts Press, 1984).

23. See John W. Dower, *War without Mercy: Race and Power in the Pacific War* (New York: Pantheon Books, 1986); Anthony Rhodes, *Propaganda, the Art of Persuasion: World War II* (New York: Chelsea House, 1976); see also the documentary film *Faces of the Enemy* (Quest Productions).

24. J. Fred McDonald, ''The Cold War as Entertainment in 'Fifties Television,'' *Journal of Popular Film and Television* 7(1) (1978): 3–31; Peter C. Rollins, ''Victory at Sea: Cold War Epic,'' *Journal of Popular Culture* 6(3) (Summer 1973): 463–482.

25. A popularized summary of such research is Carl Sagan's *Broca's Brain* (New York: Random House, 1974).

26. George Orwell, *1984* (New York: Signet, 1949), pp. 45–46.

27. Ibid., p. 47.

28. Fred Eidlin, ''The Breakdown of Newspeak,'' *Political Communication and Persuasion* 5 (1988): 225–236.

The Plural Cultures of the New Propaganda

CHAPTER 4

Palaver in Political Cultures
Electoral, Bureaucratic, Diplomatic, and War Propaganda

Part II deals with the plural cultures of the new propaganda. Some of these will be more familiar than others, but all are important areas of social action in which propaganda plays a large role. In this chapter, we shall see how propaganda has become the conventional political palaver of the powerful, and examine the ways in which we see propaganda used in electoral, bureaucratic, diplomatic, and military settings. The reader should learn from the chapter the variety of ways that propaganda can be used to communicate political power, or to clothe power in the symbols of authority. Power in this sense is a relationship, and propaganda is the communicative means to convey the relationship of the rulers and the ruled. We will even speculate on whether propaganda itself has become the political message, with power and propaganda becoming abilities that are united.

Almost four decades ago a young political scientist, David Easton, made a lasting reputation for himself when he coined a definition of his scholarly discipline. "Political science," he wrote, is the study of the "authoritative allocation of values as it is influenced by the distribution and use of power."[1] Thereafter, generations of American scholars spoke of politics itself as the "authoritative allocation of values," that is, the means people employ to make binding decisions regarding who among them get what they want while others do not. Relatively few of those same scholars took to heart Easton's other key phrase, "as it is influenced by the distribution and use of power." One reason, perhaps, was that Easton himself regarded power as not "the central phenomenon of political life," only a "secondary if crucial aspect." Even if of only derivative interest, "an understanding of who has power and how it is used helps us to understand how social policy is formed and executed."[2] Easton's famous definition may well reflect an American ambivalence about power not shared in other political orders. But it also points up the extent to which political cultures, however varied, do share the feature of the powerful having decisive, and usually authoritative, influence over the allocation of what is considered valuable. In all cases, this requires the pragmatic use of political palaver, language that conveys the political learning that the powerful wish to allocate at the moment. As we have stressed, this does not always work out, since intentions are vague and changing, and what is conveyed may be garbled or reinterpreted; but this does not lessen the necessity of communicating one's own authority, and the power to allocate values. This leads the powerful and the authoritative to study and use propaganda, since in the modern world it has proven to be the most effective, and perhaps the most authoritative, form of public communication available for widespread communication.

This chapter deals with "who has power and how it is used," more specifically with how the use and distribution of *power*, which Easton defined as "the extent to which one person controls by sanction the decisions and actions of another,"[3] resides in contemporary politics through the ever-increasing exploitation of the resources of the new propaganda. If political cultures constitute seedbeds for nurturing the propagation of ideas, power is a key nutrient of those seedbeds. We focus on three areas: first, how propaganda influences the winning of power, primarily in election campaigns, or *campaign propaganda*; second, the role propaganda plays in the exercise of power, what we designate *bureaucratic propaganda*; and third, how propaganda enters into the relationships of national powers with one another, or *diplomatic and war propaganda*. In all of these areas of political life, the control of what we have called the ideoculture is crucial. Propaganda is the discursive form that is most used to influence and, it is hoped, control the ideoculture, whether it is in campaigning for office, enforcing a policy, conducting negotiations, or mobilizing for warfare. In such endeavors, the power to propagate messages throughout the political ideoculture goes a long way in exercising influence over opinions, perceptions, and situations.

These are familiar areas of the exercise of power. What we want to show here is that the new propaganda is essential to exercising power in order to win elections, expedite administrative decisions, and conduct diplomacy. Propaganda furthers the interests of power in all aspects of politics, including not only the controlling of decisions and actions of people through sanctions, but also through agenda setting (defining the parameters and priorities of policy) and even the boundaries of political knowledge (what can permissibly be thought and what cannot even be thought of). These goals clearly involve the powerful who control institutions in the use of all kinds of propaganda—agitation (getting people to vote, support a policy, fight a war), integration (getting people enthused over party solidarity, national unity, and so on), and disposition (excluding the unthinkable, liking the thinkable, disposed in the long run to support what is generally acceptable and predictable, such as war if necessary—Goebbels's *Haltung*). Our aim is to show how propaganda has become an integral component of modern power.

CONVENTIONAL PROPAGANDA AND POLITICAL POWER

Before examining the operation of the new propaganda in campaign, bureaucratic, and diplomatic circles of contemporary politics, it is useful to consider three modern, albeit nineteenth-century, events. Each illustrates one of the forms of propaganda indicated. This permits us to draw specific parallels and contrasts indicating how the new propaganda differs, yet borrows, from the conventional.

Winning Power with Ol' Tippecanoe

Our first case is the 1840 campaign for president of the United States. Although it had changed in character since its first presidential victory in 1800, the Democratic party in one form or another dominated presidential politics for four decades. The incumbent president, Martin Van Buren, was a close ally of former president Andrew Jackson, who forged a new coalition of Democrats in a triumph over John Quincy Adams in 1828. President Adams succeeded a line of Democratic-Republican presidents dating back to Thomas Jefferson. The election of 1840 broke the chain of Democratic victories. The Whig party, formed in the early 1830s to challenge the Jacksonians, elected William Henry Harrison as president. The Whigs did it with campaign propaganda.

During the 1830s many states abolished property and taxpaying requirements for voting. As a result the size of the electorate qualified to vote in 1840 was considerably larger than in past contests. In 1840 more Americans voted than in earlier presidential elections. The Whigs sought to mobilize longtime Whig loyalists and capture the new voters. So, as Mattel would do more than a century later to merchandise the Barbie doll (recall our discussion in the Introduction), the Whigs *created* a candidate to appeal to a newly expanded electorate. First, recognizing the attractiveness of military heroes (both presidents Washington and Jackson had won military fame), the Whigs selected William Henry Harrison. Harrison's actual military accomplishments had, at best, been modest. Harrison served as governor of the Indiana territory and as military commander of the Northwest in the War of 1812. In a battle at Tippecanoe, a river that meanders through Indiana, Harrison led an army defeating the forces of Tecumseh, the Shawnee chief, on November 7, 1811. Although victorious, Harrison's 1,000-man army had heavy losses; the battle proved indecisive, since the frontier was as defenseless after the battle as before. Decisive or not, Whig propaganda recalled Tippecanoe as a great conquest that saved Americans (generals being one type of savior offered voters) from countless Indian atrocities. Whig propaganda labeled Harrison the Hero of Tippecanoe, Ol' Tippecanoe, or Old Tip. A favorite campaign song was "The Soldier of Tippecanoe." To add to and to market the legend, Tippecanoe products were plentiful—shaving cream, handkerchiefs, badges, and buttons.[4]

But that was not all. The seductive appeal of military heroism is but one element in the political culture of presidential elections that nourishes propaganda. Another is the appeal of the man, born of impoverished or modest means, reared in obscurity, who rises to claim the highest office of the land. This is the "log cabin myth."[5] Harrison was scarcely of modest origins or background. In fact, he came from an ancestry of excellent social standing, grew up on a large plantation tended by a cadre of slaves and servants, was college educated, and resided in comfortable Ohio surroundings. Whigs ignored all this, not so much because they intended to at the outset, but because of the fortuitous propagation of ideas from another source. The *Baltimore Republican* reported what it hoped would be a damning characterization of Ol' Tip: "Give him a barrel of hard cider and a pension of two thousand a year and, my word for it, he will sit the remainder of his days in a log cabin, by the side of the 'sea-coal' fire and study moral philosophy."[6] The Whigs, however, capitalized on the derogatory remark, presenting Harrison to voters as a "good old boy." Drawing contemptuous comparisons with the stuffy and proper Martin Van Buren, the Whigs launched the "log cabin and hard cider" campaign.

As with the Tippecanoe theme, the log cabin and hard cider appeal took many forms:

songs (''The Log Cabin Song''); newspapers (the weekly *The Log Cabin*); slogans (The Farmer's President); cartoons (one with Harrison saying ''I have no champagne but can give you a mug of good cider''); products (Old Cabin Whiskey marketed in small bottles shaped like log cabins, manufactured by the E. Z. Booze Co.); log cabins decorated with coonskin hats everywhere; an array of books, songbooks, pamphlets, leaflets, and other paraphernalia; and rally gimmicks, such as rolling a large mud ball from town to town to attract a crowd, urging them to ''keep the ball rolling.'' To interest, charm, and beguile newly eligible voters there were entertaining events: rallies and songfests lasting as long as five hours; free barbecues; and parades ten miles long. Hard cider flowed like water, enhancing voter enthusiasm.

And what of Harrison? What did he do? No previous presidential candidate had campaigned by making public speeches. Political etiquette called for candidates to let others campaign while the standard bearer remained hidden from public view. Harrison broke the code (and was criticized by Democrats but cheered by voters): he addressed crowds with platitudes about his being an ''old soldier and farmer.'' Harrison's public appearances reinforced the carefully contrived image of war hero and self-made man. In the end the 68-year-old Harrison triumphed, only to die of pneumonia one month after his inauguration! But the 1840 campaign was memorable not for the triumph of a man or a party, but more broadly for the legitimate use of campaign propaganda as a way to agitate, integrate, and dispose voters in the new democratic order.

Nicholas Biddle's Propaganda Campaign to Exercise Power

Not all of William Henry Harrison's campaign advisers were happy to see him take to the stump in 1840. They shared a view expressed by an astute propagandist in 1836, namely, that a candidate should ''say not one single word about his principles or creed.'' In fact, he should ''say nothing—promise nothing.'' Moreover, ''let no Committee, no Convention, no town meeting ever extract from him a single word about what he thinks now or will do hereafter. Let the use of pen and ink be wholly forbidden as if he were a mad poet in Bedlam.''[7]

The propagandist was Nicholas Biddle. Biddle earlier had waged his own propaganda campaign not to win power but to hold it. And he lost. In 1823 young (36-years-old), intelligent, monied, and socially prominent Nicholas Biddle assumed the presidency of the Bank of the United States. Congress chartered the bank in 1816 for 20 years. It was successor to the First Bank of the United States founded in 1791, a child of Secretary of the Treasury Alexander Hamilton's financial program. The First Bank's policies in regulating currency provoked a political controversy that led to a defeat of its rechartering in 1811. After five years of uncontrolled currency expansion Congress called for a central regulator of the nation's credit and currency operations—the Second Bank of the United States. The bank served as depository of government funds, issued financial notes, and exercised authority over state banks. The profits earned by the bank flowed to private investors and the federal government.

Critics of the bank regarded it as a powerful political force serving the interests of the privileged few; supporters viewed the bank as essential for the nation's economic stability. When Biddle became president of the bank in 1823 he recognized the institution's tenuous, albeit powerful, position. The economic depression in 1819 and its aftermath threatened the bank's existence; yet the institution had survived to prosper. Biddle wished to keep it that way. Throughout the presidency of John Quincy Adams he did so. But with the election of Andrew Jackson in 1828, Biddle knew trouble was coming. Jackson thought the bank a "monster" that discriminated against the have-nots by protecting and enhancing the privileged few. He was not alone in this view. Americans seeking economic advantage but denied the bank's favors, state bankers resentful of the profits and power of the bank, farmers viewing the bank as a corrupting influence, urban wage earners suspicious of the bank as a monopoly, and lawyers, professionals, merchants, and manufacturers threatened by the bank's influence supported Jackson's position.

Biddle knew that to protect his bank, he required political support. He courted key political leaders from all political parties, including Daniel Webster and Henry Clay, putting the former on a healthy retainer paid by the bank; and he recruited help from within Jackson's own circle of friends by promising financial favors. A variety of propaganda devices were crucial to his efforts. In a bold propaganda gesture, he publicly proposed to pay off the national debt by January 8, 1833—the eighteenth anniversary of Jackson's defeat of the British at the Battle of New Orleans. Four years before the bank's charter was due for renewal, Biddle without warning requested a recharter. The year was 1832 and Biddle fully recognized the propaganda value of seeking a recharter in the very year Jackson would be seeking reelection. Biddle reasoned, first, his maneuver would silence Jackson's criticisms of the bank, since he assumed Old Hickory would never make the bank an issue in the campaign. Second, Biddle was confident that the political and oratorical skills of friendly politicians Henry Clay and Daniel Webster would be effective counterpropaganda in the debate with antibank forces over rechartering. Finally, Biddle poured his own money and propaganda behind congressional candidates sympathetic to the bank, thus helping to elect congressmen who would veto to override any presidential veto of the rechartering.

The conflict over the Second Bank's rechartering was a war of words fought through newspaper editorials, congressional debate, presidential rhetoric, bank counterrhetoric, and campaign hoopla (parades, barbecues, songs, illuminations, hickory pole railings, etc.). Pro-Jackson newspapers charged the bank with having violated its charter. Probank forces in Congress made fearful claims that sound currency would disappear and the country would be ruined without the bank. In Congress the supporters of the bank won recharter on July 3, 1832. On July 10 Jackson vetoed the recharter. His veto message charged that "rich and powerful interests" too often bend government to "their selfish purposes." This should not be. Governments should provide equal protection to all and, "as Heaven does its rains, shower its favors alike on the high and the low, the rich and the poor" and thus be "an unqualified blessing." He concluded, "In the act before me there seems to be a wide and unnecessary departure from these just principles."[8]

Biddle countered that Jackson's veto was "the fury of a chained panther biting the bars of its cage," a "manifesto of anarchy."[9] In the ensuing presidential campaign Jackson's opponent, Henry Clay, exploited the bank issue. Clay's forces, financed in large measure by Biddle, branded Jackson a "Tyrant" and "Usurper." The rhetoric of Jackson's campaigners fulminated against the "Moneyed Monopoly." Although Jackson was the electoral victor, the bank issue took its toll: his popular vote declined markedly from that he had received earlier; he became the only president in history reelected to a second term who registered a decline in his percentage of popular votes.

In the end, however, Jackson defeated "the monster." In 1833 Biddle, saying that if Jackson thought that "if he is to have his way with the Bank," then "he is mistaken," sought to use bank policies to produce an economic panic. It proved to be Biddle's folly: thinking Jackson would yield to pressure and recharter the bank, Biddle encountered an unrelenting Jackson. Approached by business interests seeking aid to avoid bankruptcy, Jackson retorted:

> Insolvent do you say? What do you come to me for then? Go to Nicholas Biddle. We have no money here, gentlemen. Biddle has all the money. He has millions of specie in his vaults this very moment, lying idle, and yet you come to *me* to save you from breaking. I tell you gentlemen, it's all politics.[10]

Politics it was, and in the propaganda talk over the bank Jackson had the last word.

The Monroe Doctrine: Diplomatic Propaganda

When Andrew Jackson won the presidency in 1828, threatening the status of Nicholas Biddle and his bank, he defeated incumbent John Quincy Adams. Years earlier Adams figured prominently in a final case of propaganda we use as a basis for comparing earlier forms of political propaganda with the new.

In 1823 the Russian government declared it would exclude all but its own nation's vessels from the Northwest coast of America north of 51 degrees latitude. Russia was also one of several European governments threatening reconquest of republics in the New World that had declared independence from Spain. Adams, who was President James Monroe's secretary of state, formulated a diplomatic position for the United States. He stated that henceforth European nations could establish no new colonies in the New World, since every portion had already been occupied. President James Monroe's message of December 2, 1823, incorporated Adam's dictum, now known as the Monroe Doctrine.

The Monroe Doctrine occupies an important place in American political mythology. Political mythifiers assert that the doctrine has protected the Western Hemisphere from the encroachments of European powers since its inception. Historian Wayne S. Cole argues otherwise: the "doctrine was not a treaty, not an executive agreement, not an act of Congress, not a multilateral inter-American policy, and not international law."[11] If anything, it was a propagandistic statement intended for an audience of both Americans and Europeans. It appealed to American fancy by announcing, in effect, that this nation could secure not only its own isolation from tugs-of-war between European powers, but also the isolation of all of both continents in the hemisphere. Actually America could have done no such thing. The United States made no efforts to form alliances with its neighboring states immediately after 1823; in fact, many of the new states in the hemisphere became financially, economically, and politically dependent on Great Britain, not on the United States. Moreover, the doctrine had little practical influence on European audiences. European nations ignored the doctrine or received it with irritation, contempt, and ridicule. There were direct violations of the doctrine. A case in point was Great Britain's acquisition of the Falkland Islands (Islas Malvinas) in 1833, a decade after the announcement of the Monroe Doctrine. Both Great Britain and Argentina have claimed sovereignty over the islands ever since, producing the outbreak of shooting war in 1982 that cost several hundred lives, a British destroyer, and an Argentine cruiser.

Hence the words of the Monroe Doctrine, words that seemed to announce a diplomatic policy, have been superseded by the words *Monroe Doctrine* themselves. Policy was superseded by propaganda or, more precisely, *propaganda became policy*. As we shall see, such is still the case in winning, exercising, and negotiating power relations, but in ways that differ from an earlier era. The immediate need for propaganda to support action brought the unintended consequence of creating a political myth, one that has endured to the present in justification of various American interventions (such as the blockade of Cuba in 1962 and the intervention in Panama in 1989). Propaganda necessity is often the mother of political invention, and even political tradition, conjuring a myth on which policy makers can act, since by now the myth has dispositional status, evoking through renewed propaganda support for an American "right to act" in Latin America (a view not shared by Latin Americans, all of whom opposed, for example, Bush sending troops to Panama).

PROPAGANDA IN CONTEMPORARY CAMPAIGN CULTURES: WINNING AND HOLDING POWER

The presidential election campaign of 1840 and President Andrew Jackson's rhetorical attack on the Second National Bank in 1832 illustrate how politicians have used propaganda to win and hold power. We now examine contemporary presidential campaigning and presidential rhetoric to see how much things have changed, how much they remain the same in today's propaganda presidency.

The Permanent Campaign: New Propaganda in the 1988 Presidential Election

Jacques Ellul (see Chapter 3) observed in *Propaganda* that after an election, analysts frequently discount the effectiveness of campaign propaganda in influencing voters. They find, he observed, that propaganda's "gross methods," such as "inscriptions on walls" (i.e., political posters and ads) "can convince nobody" and "opposing arguments neutralize each other." Moreover, "the population is often indifferent to election propaganda." Such conclusions are scarcely startling; "it is not surprising that such propaganda has little effect: none of the great techniques of propaganda can be effective in two weeks."[12] Ellul cautioned against such analyses:

> In fact, one cannot really talk about propaganda in connection with an election campaign. A campaign is the simplest, most imperfect form of modern propaganda; the objective is insufficient, the methods are incomplete, the duration is brief, pre-propaganda is absent, and the campaign propagandist never has all the media at his disposal.[13]

Ellul was writing about propaganda in election campaigns in the first half of this century. At that time campaigners did have "insufficient" objectives, limited as they were to turning out party loyalists and courting the relatively few waverers who possessed no standing party commitments. Propaganda methods were "incomplete" because appeals to various voting segments were only partially coordinated. Campaigns were "brief" with no "pre-propaganda"; presidential campaigns scarcely began in earnest until each major party had selected its nominees; elections at other levels were limited to a few months. Finally, campaigners rarely had all the media at their disposal as campaigns did not dominate news reports, paid advertising, or conversation.

Today the new propaganda operates in a different environment. Campaigns are no longer of short duration. Candidates make electoral plans not merely months before election day but years in advance. Jimmy Carter, elected president of the United States in 1976, announced his candidacy in early 1974 and had formulated a campaign plan months before his declaration. Today seekers of the presidency begin their campaigns four, even six years in advance of election. "Pre-propaganda" is no longer the exception but the norm as aspiring officeseekers posture for visual and sound bites on TV news programs, seek out writers to feature them in articles in prestigious magazines, appear on late night talk shows, and exploit attention-grabbing public appearances—bagging groceries, bicycling across the state, or canoeing the white water rapids. They are but responding to a lesson offered by sociologists Kurt and Gladys Engel Lang over three decades ago:

> All news that bears on political activity and beliefs—and not only campaign speeches and campaign propaganda—is somehow relevant to the vote. Not only during the campaign but also in the periods between, the mass media provide perspectives, shape images of candidates and parties, help highlight issues around which a campaign will develop, and define the unique atmosphere and areas of sensitivity which mark any particular campaign.[14]

Today's propaganda defines the campaign's "unique atmosphere and areas of sensitivity" by being unlike what Ellul viewed earlier. It is carefully coordinated, comprehensive rather than partial, complete rather than incomplete, and responsive to the unexpected rather than inflexible. Finally, no longer is the campaign objective "insufficient" as Ellul regarded it. Once officeseekers and officeholders campaigned for the opportunity to govern; today they *govern for the opportunity to campaign*—seeking election again, again, and again. The period an incumbent is in office is as much a part of the ongoing effort to retain that office as are the final weeks leading up to election day. Propaganda campaigns in elections are no longer periodic, occasional, sporadic, and brief; they are permanent. It is an era of the permanent campaign.[15]

Reflect on selected aspects of the case of George Herbert Walker Bush III, elected president of the United States on November 6, 1988. Bush first became a candidate for the presidency in 1980 when he sought to wrest the Republican nomination from Ronald Reagan. Reagan initially sought his party's nomination even earlier, in 1968; in 1976 came within 117 convention votes of winning it; and, upon entering the 1980 election season he was the Republican front-runner. So confident were the Reagan forces in 1980 that he did not campaign in the first major test for the nomination, the local caucuses in Iowa. Through a carefully orchestrated campaign of media events, paid advertising, and local efforts George Bush won a surprise victory in Iowa. He immediately claimed the "Big Mo" (momentum) he believed would carry him to the nomination. Reagan responded, campaigned hard, and defeated Bush in the New Hampshire Republican primary a week later. Bush remained in the race and performed well in numerous primaries, so well that when nominee Ronald Reagan was casting about for a vice presidential running mate he selected Bush.

Bush's two terms as vice president were devoted to what vice presidents do, namely, supporting the president, making public appearances, attending ceremonial gatherings, and so on. What he also did was use the vice presidential office to prepare to seek the presidency again once Reagan's second term was coming to an end. First, Bush gradually shifted his policy views to be more acceptable to those Reagan supporters he deemed essential for his nomination. Having campaigned in 1980 as a moderate to liberal alternative to Reagan, Bush now voiced Reagan's views—including opposition to abortion, increased spending for the military, and Reagan's economic program, which Bush had in 1980 labeled "voodoo economics." Well before 1988 Bush put together a management team to conduct campaign research, raise money, craft propaganda themes and messages, and fashion an efficient campaign organization. A year before the election Bush led his nearest potential rival for the 1988 Republican nomination by a margin of 2–1 in polls.[16]

As the election year approached the Reagan administration suffered setbacks—the U.S. Senate rejection of a Reagan appointee to the Supreme Court, a widely publicized scandal involving secret efforts to trade military arms for hostages that compromised administration policies in the Middle East and Central America, even embarrassing rumors that Reagan consulted astrologers for advice. With administration prestige declining, the prospects for a Democratic victory in 1988 increased. Bush suffered from this in two respects. First, as a part of the troubled Reagan administration Bush felt the fallout of the decline in GOP fortunes. Second, as Democratic hopes brightened, Republicans began to talk of selecting a nominee not burdened with close connections to the current White House. Moreover, Bush's terms as vice president had been a mixed blessing. It gave him publicity but all too often Bush's public persona came across in news accounts as wimpy, preppy, without substance on issues, prone to put his foot in his mouth, and a mere Reagan lapdog.

These and other factors worked to Bush's detriment early in 1988. He performed poorly in the Iowa caucuses. "CBS Evening News" anchor Dan Rather reported Bush as "desperate" after his "meltdown in Iowa" and his prospects for the next contest in the New Hampshire primary as "dropping like a rock in the Granite State." The Bush campaign in the aftermath of Iowa reflects the responsive, flexible quality of the new propaganda. The former practice in planning campaign propaganda in presidential elections was to probe voters' perceptions and concerns in public opinion polls, build a campaign emphasizing key themes derived from poll findings, and adhere to the overall campaign strategy with few modifications. The practice in today's new campaign propaganda is, by contrast, more reactive and flexible. Polling goes on around the clock (called "tracking polls" in the trade), staged appearances by candidates in newsworthy settings can be quickly arranged, and video recordings form a basis for TV ads rapidly taped, edited, and aired. Taking advantage of these capabilities within the one-week period between the February 8 Iowa caucuses and February 16 New Hampshire primary, the Bush propagandists fashioned a new image for their candidate. A macho, aggressive George Bush attired in work shirt, billed cap, and jacket appeared in news clips driving an 18-wheeler, drinking coffee at a truck stop, and talking it up with the plain folk. To fend off the Iowa victor, Senator Robert Dole, the Bush campaign aired a "straddle ad" depicting Dole as straddling the major issue that New Hampshirites cared about, taxes. Bush made direct appeals telling voters that if nominated and elected he would return to say "Thank you, New Hampshire!"

Bush recovered in New Hampshire and went on to win the nomination and the election. That he was able to return and say "Thank you, New Hampshire" owes much to his propaganda. Consider another illustration. Bush first met with his campaign manager, Lee Atwater, on December 19, 1984, in the vice presidential office to plan the 1988 campaign. By April of 1988, it was apparent that Bush would be the nominee and that the likely Democratic candidate would be Massachusetts governor Michael Dukakis. Atwater called the research director of the Bush campaign, James Pinkerton, and said, ''Look, I want you to get the nerd patrol'' (the research division of the Bush management team consisting of ''35 excellent nerds''). ''We need five or six issues and we need them by the mid-May.''[17] Pinkerton got to work. Reading the transcript of a debate between Democratic candidates he came across a question asked of Dukakis about a Massachusetts program that permitted convicted felons, including murderers serving life sentences without parole, to be released from prison on weekend passes. ''It just dropped into our lap,'' said Pinkerton.[18]

What had dropped into the Bush camp's lap was the furlough issue. But first it had to be tested. Bush's pollster, Robert Teeter, arranged two focus groups—small groups of people who discuss and provide reactions to campaign issues, ideas, proposed ads, and so forth. Each group consisted of 15 Dukakis Democrats who had voted for Ronald Reagan in 1984. They reacted to the furlough question and to other issues, including the pollution of Boston Harbor and Dukakis's veto of a bill requiring schoolteachers to lead their students in the Pledge of Allegiance. At the end of focus sessions one-half of the 30 Dukakis supporters had switched to Bush. Armed with that finding the Bush propagandists emphasized the furlough, Boston Harbor, and Pledge issues as centerpieces of the campaign against Dukakis.

Seeking to make the furlough issue concrete, personal, and easily grasped, propagandists fashioned a TV ad telling the story of Willie Horton. Horton, a convicted murderer, had raped a Maryland woman and terrorized her husband while on a weekend pass from prison. (We will discuss other examples of political advertising as propaganda in Chapter 5.) The ad, however, was produced not by the Bush campaign staff but by a separate and independent group, Americans for Bush. Thus, when the ad became controversial (a major news story questioned whether there was a racial bias to Bush's campaign), the Bush management team was able to distance itself from the Willie Horton ad by claiming Americans for Bush, not Bush's media people, had prepared it. Democratic consultant Robert Beckel cried foul:

> Willie Horton's black face was on the air for 10 weeks. It was paid for by a committee called Americans for Bush, funded by not just right-wingers but by a lot of people that were contributing to the RNC [Republican National Committee] and Ronald Reagan and George Bush for years. So you can assume when they look at this thing that some people will conclude there was a lot of Republican money behind this.

In reply Bush's media consultant, Roger Ailes, said to Beckel, ''That's a lot different from saying the Bush campaign did it. Anyone in here can do it. This is America.''[19]

Regardless of the controversy sparked by the Willie Horton ad, it does illustrate how new propaganda relies upon early planning, continuously updated research, the tailoring of messages to shifting conditions. It marks but one example that a permanent campaign of continuous duration implies differing circumstances than those addressed by Jacques Ellul in his judgment of propaganda's limited role in electoral outcomes.

Presidents Making Propaganda Spectacles of Themselves

In recent years students of presidential communication have argued that a transformation has taken place in the American presidency. They are not agreed on the precise character of that transformation but there is consensus that many of the changes in the presidency parallel those described in our introductory chapter contrasting the old and new propaganda.[20]

For approximately the first century and one-quarter of the American presidency, the office was primarily institutional in character. Several features defined the *institutional presidency* during that period. First, the methods for nominating and electing the president started out as closed and limited to a relatively few influential citizens. George Washington, the first president, was selected by an electoral college composed of leading citizens in each of the states. Procedures for nominating presidential candidates gradually broadened over the decades prior to the Civil War: key congressional leaders meeting in caucus (later dubbed "King Caucus" by detractors) nominated the first candidates after Washington; Jeffersonian Democrats gave state party leaders a role to play and, later, state legislatures began to nominate candidates; and, in 1832, the first national convention of a political party that still survives, the Democrats, met in Baltimore to concur in the nomination for reelection of Andrew Jackson. The gradual expansion of the scope of the nominating process and of the franchise in the first half of the nineteenth century was impressive. Yet the overall means of presidential selection remained restricted to party and legislative institutions.

Second, neither when seeking office nor upon entering it did nineteenth-century presidents appear before large crowds of people. Even after Ol' Tippecanoe dismayed his advisers by going to the hustings in 1840, it was a long time before candidates spoke to massive rallies. For their part, elected presidents spoke before small enclaves of congressional leaders if, indeed, they chose to speak at all rather than to supply written inaugural speeches, proclamations, veto messages, State of the Union addresses, or other remarks (Washington delivered his inaugural address to a select group of congressional leaders). The institutional presidency featured propaganda intended to influence political elites by means of communication to small groups.

Third, the content of that communication made the institutional presidency an information presidency. Questions of principle (the nature of republican government, the proper scope of constitutional power, etc.) and policy (witness Jackson's message vetoing the Second Bank recharter) composed the substance of presidential utterances. Appeals to reason, facts, loyalties, "enlightened" self-interest, and artful bargaining—convincing politicians that presidential action would promote, or at least not delay, their ambitions—constituted the means of persuading political elites to support presidential initiatives.

Finally, the presidential office was at the core of the institutional presidency. By office we refer not to the Oval Office in the White House where the president conducts daily business but to the constitutional grant of authority to the presidency and how presidents exercise that grant. To be sure, presidential election campaigns in the nineteenth century witnessed charges and countercharges about the fitness, moral repute, intelligence, and personal habits of contenders. Few presidents departed office without being reviled in some public manner; the grandson of Benjamin Franklin opened a newspaper attack on George Washington: "If ever a nation was debauched by a man, the American nation has been debauched by Washington.''[21] (Editorial writers repeat the same phrase today, but they refer to the nation's capital, not the first president!) Personalities aside, the essentials in public debate over the president and the presidency pertained not to the person holding the office but to the scope and limits of the office itself. Did the Washington administration have authority to quell the Whiskey Rebellion in 1794? Did the Jefferson administration have authority to purchase the Louisiana Territory in 1803? Did Andrew Jackson usurp authority in vetoing the recharter of the Second Bank in 1832? Or did Abraham Lincoln exceed his constitutional grant in acting against secession, authorizing arrests, and emancipating the slaves during the Civil War?

The institutional presidency thus was based upon relatively closed selection processes, small group communication with political elites, information and argumentation in appealing for support, and the authorities of the office rather than the personality of the incumbent occupying it. These features have not been totally supplanted from the contemporary presidency, but there is a strikingly different emphasis. The presidency that the American public encounters via the new propaganda is not primarily institutional in character. It is a public display, a continuing dramatic production involving the nation and world as a stage, the president in the role of lead character, and the citizenry as both audience and key players of the political theater in the round. This is the *presidency as spectacle*.

How has this transformation in emphasis occurred and what is its character? Consider again the presidential selection process. Toward the close of the nineteenth century there were demands to expand the role of the populace in the selection of public officials. The Populist party became a force in presidential politics in 1892 (Populist leader William Jennings Bryan became the Democratic presidential nominee in 1896); among other items on the Populist program were a call for direct election of U.S. senators, the use of primary elections to nominate candidates for office, and direct popular involvement in policy making via initiative, referenda, and recall elections. It was not long until such reforms entered presidential politics in a modest fashion. When former president Theodore Roosevelt unsuccessfully challenged President William Howard Taft for the Republican nomination in 1912, he was able to claim that he was the rightful party nominee on grounds that he had won nine statewide presidential primaries to Taft's one. However, it was not until the 1960s that presidential primaries and local caucus elections among the party rank and file would be the focal point of the presidential nominating process. Reforms in electoral politics and the steady expansion of the franchise to women, the young, and racial and ethnic groups formerly denied it gradually eroded the closed presidential election politics that had characterized the institutional presidency.

In the process the presidency shifted from an elitist to a populist base. Presidential candidates appeared openly before the masses—in large auditoria and open-air gatherings, on platforms of campaign trains moving from town to town, and—of course—on radio and television as each of these means of communication became available in the twentieth century. Presidents in office—beginning with Theodore Roosevelt for Republicans, Woodrow Wilson for Democrats—demonstrated their awareness that appealing to party and congressional elites via small group communication was not sufficient to hold and exercise power. Instead they went public. From what he labeled the ''bully pulpit'' Roosevelt urged citizens to rally around his New Nationalism and bring pressure on reluctant legislative leaders in support of presidential aims. In clear, concise, lucid, and passionate speeches Wilson spoke of his New Freedom; he too sought popular support for presidential policies, culminating in his national tour following World War I on behalf of approval of his beloved Treaty of Versailles and League of Nations.

As the orientation of presidential propaganda became more populist than elite, a slow, subtle shift in the content took place. Matters of principle and policy, the hallmarks of messages in the institutional presidency, did not vanish; nor did messages appealing to reason and self-interest. But in going public Teddy Roosevelt and Woodrow Wilson hinted at what was to come—shifting the content of presidential messages away from the informative and argumentative to dramatic gesture. At first simply the opportunity for people to see a president in person was enough to stir the imagination. But once the populace grew accustomed to reading in mass circulation newspapers about presidential appearances, hearing him on radio, later seeing him on television and, perhaps, in person, presidents could no longer merely stir people's imaginations, they had to live up to them. They had to adopt presidential personae and act them out; they had to appear in times and settings as people expected them to appear. For a plain, simple, and fun-loving man such as President Warren G. Harding—who engaged in extramarital affairs, played poker, chewed tobacco, and drank whiskey when the law prevented the manufacture, sale, and consumption of alcohol—the adopted persona was of a good ol' boy seeking the peace and serenity of olden days. Witness him living up to the persona: "America's present need is not heroics but healing; not nostrums but normalcy; not revolution but restoration . . . not surgery but serenity."[22]

Many of Harding's public addresses as candidate and as president were packaged by ghostwriters rather than his own creations. But upon occasion he departed from the script and offered his own nostrums and homilies, often based upon his personal experiences. Saying he liked to go out from time to time, commune with nature, and "glovulate" (there is no such word), he would reminisce by telling stories. All presidents have told stories in both informal and public settings—Abraham Lincoln was a master storyteller. But in the spectacular presidency evolving from Roosevelt (Teddy), Wilson, and Harding through Franklin Roosevelt, Harry Truman, and others, the purpose of the storytelling has changed. Presidents no longer tell stories to illustrate or make a point (as did Lincoln). Instead the story they tell (as with Harding) is the point. The content of presidential propaganda is less information and reason than storytelling. If the institutional presidency was an informational presidency, the spectacular presidency is a storytelling presidency. They appeal to popular "narrative reasoning" to tell their presidential story, and ideocultural stories for political purposes. This is a *storied propaganda*.

The role of the president as national storyteller was most clearly demonstrated in the presidency of Ronald Reagan. Rare was the appearance of President Reagan, whether in a public gathering or mediated through radio or television, without a story, homily, or anecdote—of questionable authenticity but an enjoyable, entertaining fable or parable. Sometimes such apocrypha (i.e., stories of dubious authenticity) were intended to make a larger point: the story of America as a "shining city on the hill" related how "God's chosen people" would survive and prosper in adversity; the story of "the Gipper" (a romantic recounting of a football player Reagan had played in a movie) taught the virtues of commitment and dedication (although Gipp's life was in fact anything but admirable); and the story of Lisa Zanatta Henn, who promised her father before he died that she would return to the site of his 1944 D-day experiences to "feel all the things you made me feel through your stories and your eyes,'' stressed that patriotism and self-sacrifice are the highest of callings. Thus did Reagan request audiences to *feel, not act*, and feel as he, Reagan, would feel through *his* stories and *his* eyes.

Three points require elaboration. First, a penchant for homilies, proverbs, and apocrypha has not been unique to Ronald Reagan as a twentieth-century president. Others before him and George Bush afterward relied upon similar storytelling. Bush, in a major televised address in 1989 announcing his administration's renewed war on drugs, produced a bag of crack cocaine he said had been confiscated from a pusher in a park across the street from the White House, thus noting how close the drug problem is to all Americans. What he did not say in the story was that federal Drug Enforcement Administration officers had coaxed the drug dealer from another, far-removed location to Lafayette Park. In short, the drug bust was prepackaged to embellish the story. Later, asked by reporters about such stagecraft, Bush responded: ''I think it was great. I think it sent a message that even across from the White House it's possible to sell drugs.'' No matter that the drug-busting incident itself was fabricated. As Lee Atwater, chair of the Republican National Committee reported: ''George Bush talking from the bully pulpit on drugs is good for us; every time he uses the bully pulpit it's a winner.''[23]

Second, stories that perhaps are conceived to make a point can take on a life of their own. The imperative of the story takes over and guides events rather than illustrates them. Staging a drug bust to embellish a story to make a point does more than make the point: it drives law enforcement. One is reminded of Shakespeare's *Hamlet* (act 2, scene 2): ''the play's the thing wherein I'll catch the conscience of the king.'' Increasingly, to catch the conscience of presidents we must examine closely the playful stories they tell.

Third, the spectacle presidency in contrast with the institutional presidency does not revolve about the presidential office but about the presidential persona. Political scientist Bruce Miroff has examined this idea of presidential leadership as spectacle.[24] For Miroff a spectacle is a symbolic event where particular details stand for broader and deeper meanings. Such symbolic events are dramas that feature the centrality of characters (actors) and what they do (acts). Through their dramatic acts actors establish public identities, or what we have called personae. Spectacles are not designed for mass participation, yet mass audiences have key roles to play. Although audiences do not perform in the drama, they are *absorbed* by it. As in Reagan's tale of Lisa Zanata Henn, they feel what the spectacle's characters feel, see what they see. Audience members are not goaded to action, but to enjoyment and acceptance.

In spectacles, persuasion takes place not through the verbal content of messages but through *gestures*. Gestures like presidential stories are not important for what they accomplish directly (e.g., for the point they illustrate); they convey meanings often quite apart from their apparent ones. Persuasion is less information oriented than persona and performance oriented. Actors may offer facts, but the purpose of the facts is to confirm the plausibility of the spectacle or story, not to prove an argument; the purpose of the spectacle, or story, is to override disconfirming facts.

To illustrate the point Miroff uses an analogy—professional boxing versus professional wrestling. Boxing is a sporting contest; it involves competition between boxers, and the outcome of the contest is uncertain. Precisely because it is a contest with an uncertain outcome, the outcome itself is all important. People wager on who will win. Professional wrestling is another thing. Regardless of the apparent pain and torment of body slams, death grips, spine breakers, kicks, gouges, and other contrivances, the outcome of a professional wrestling match is preordained. People don't bet on who will win. Posturing, grimacing, intimidating, costuming, grandiose names (Hulk Hogan or Killer Karl)—all are gestures conveying moral significance. The oft-repeated scenario: good guy vs. evil guy; evil gets the upper hand with deceit and cheating (which takes place before an unseeing referee); goodness bounces back and triumphs in the end. Miroff grants that "much of what presidents do is analogous to what boxers do—they engage in contests of power and policy with other political actors, contests in which the outcomes are uncertain." But that is not all they do, indeed what they predominantly do: "The contemporary presidency is presented by the White House (with collaboration of the media) as a series of spectacles in which a larger-than-life main character, along with his supporting team, engages in emblematic bouts with immoral or dangerous adversaries."[25]

Miroff traces the application of spectacle as propaganda through the administrations of recent presidents, most notably John F. Kennedy, Jimmy Carter, and Ronald Reagan. In each case the accumulated result of countless gestures, all widely publicized, is to place a certain gloss on the presidency, that is, a surface shininess or luster, a superficial appearance that fixes each on the public mind. Thus, there is the "grace and charm" of Kennedy's New Frontier and the "comfortable amiability" of Reagan's New Beginning, but the "failed presidency" of Carter's promise to provide "Americans a government as good as its people" (not all dramatic performances play to positive reviews!).

Miroff finds several reasons for the shift from a boxing to a wrestling White House: the growing centrality of the presidency in the citizen's grasp of politics, the mass media focus—especially of television—on the presidency, and the association of the presidency with heroic successes (landing men on the moon) and failures (inability to deal with international terrorism). We add another factor. We think it pertains both to the shift from an institutional to a spectacle presidency and to the emergence of a new propaganda out of older variants. Psychologist William Stephenson has drawn a distinction (noted in the Introduction) between two forms of communication.[26] People engage in *communication-pain* as a means to accomplish calculated, intended ends. Like work, it is something we do to achieve something else; we do not undertake work (unless we are workaholics) for the joy of it. In Stephenson's terms, most readers of this book, assuming they are enrolled for college credit, are reading, we are sorry to say, for other than the pure enjoyment of it; they are preparing for an exam, writing a paper, seeking credit in a course, or even trying to find something "useful" or "interesting" to talk about. That is communication-pain. *Communication-pleasure* is akin to play, activities people engage in and consume for the sheer joy of doing it. Many people attend movies, read novels, watch television just for the fun of it, not to learn anything to be used later or in pursuit of some more distant goal (as in Just for the Taste of It, Diet Coke!).

In the era of the institutional presidency, incumbents dealt on a daily basis with politicians advocating principles and policies, seeking favors, pursuing ambitions. Presidents required the support of such politicians and communicated to mobilize it. They recognized that those politicians would attend to presidential utterances as a means of achieving their own goals, be they in the public or self-serving interest. But the principles, policy preferences, private and public interests of millions of Americans—in contrast with a relatively few involved partisans, followers, and adversaries—are difficult to discern, often ambiguous, overlapping, contradictory, ephemeral, and shifting. Spectacles provide a means of transcending diverse public perceptions and preferences. Presented for their own sake as pleasurable communication experiences, they offer a president the opportunity to accomplish two things: first, a pleased citizenry may or may not be supportive, but at least it is pleased; second, to the degree that a pleased citizenry appears to influential policy makers to back a president, the president has a valuable tool in the permanent campaign to hold and exercise power. In this sense spectacle propaganda provides the modern presidency with the resources to govern *through* campaigning as much as it does to campaign to govern.[27]

GUILE AND CHARM IN BUREAUCRATIC CULTURES: EXERCISING POWER THROUGH BUREAUCRATIC PROPAGANDA

In his struggle to exercise control over the nation's fiscal affairs through the Second Bank of the United States, Nicholas Biddle manipulated various means to combat the threat posed by President Andrew Jackson's veto of the bank's rechartering in 1832. He lobbied congressmen, even putting Daniel Webster on retainer, made speeches and public statements, and issued reports describing how the bank's existence strengthened the national economy. In so doing he foreshadowed the practice that sociologists David Altheide and John Johnson call "bureaucratic propaganda," that is, "any report produced by an organization for evaluation and other practical purposes that is targeted for individuals, committees, or publics who are unaware of its promotive character and the editing processes used to shape it."[28]

Smokey Bear and the Magnitude of Bureaucratic Propaganda

The targets of Biddle's efforts were well aware that he was locked in combat with Jackson to save the National Bank. Today, however, bureaucratic propaganda is so routine and pervasive that the nature and consequences of its promotional character are not always apparent either to its targets or the organization engaging in it. As Altheide and Johnson suggest in their definition, bureaucratic propaganda can derive from any public or private organization—economic, religious, ethnic, professional, educational, and so on. Economic, social, and cultural propaganda of political import we shall discuss in Chapters 5 and 6. Here we are primarily concerned with governing organizations employing propaganda in the exercise of power.

The reasons they employ bureaucratic propaganda are clear enough—to build and mobilize support while limiting or restricting opposition. Federal government organizations such as executive departments, agencies, and commissions use bureaucratic propaganda to win sympathy among congressional officials and among citizens when approaching Congress for adequate operating budgets, and in responding to congressional oversight of their activities. To achieve policy goals, governing organizations require public and private support. Since governing bodies compete with one another for funds and in making policies, they engage in wars of bureaucratic propaganda to get an edge on one another. In these conflicts the target audiences lie both inside and outside the agency. Outside the agency are Congress, competing agencies, and the public; inside are the agency's own underlings who receive information and the agency "line" from propaganda. Some agencies have little effective authority to perform their tasks other than through propaganda. The Federal Trade Commission, for example, publicizes cases of misleading advertising of products and services to goad advertisers and their clients into conforming to federal regulations because the power of publicity is virtually the only enforcement power the agency possesses.

It is unclear precisely how much governments spend on bureaucratic propaganda in exercising power. As Dean Yarwood and Ben Enis discovered in their examination of advertising and publicity programs in the administrative branch of the U.S. government, no single figure reflects the total cost of all such programs.[29] Estimates on amounts spent, they found, differ from agency to agency, but range from $17 million to $25 million per year in the Department of Health and Human Services, the Department of Agriculture, or the Department of Defense. In any event, the sums are substantial, with the total governmental outlay for federal advertising and publicity exceeding the total combined budgets of the wire services, three TV networks, and major U.S. daily newspapers.

Although the dollar amounts spent on bureaucratic propaganda are difficult to specify, the types of "reports . . . targeted to individuals, committees, or publics" (to use Altheide and Johnson's expression) are easy to list: press releases; newspaper, magazine, and broadcast stories prepared with agency cooperation; radio and TV programs, both informational and for entertainment; films, documentaries, lectures, civic education programs, traveling exhibits, and junkets for politicos the agencies are trying to impress— this is but a partial listing of the variety. Of particular importance are public service announcements (PSAs), television and radio commercials on behalf of agency programs. PSAs are either fully funded in their conception, production, and distribution by government agencies or are produced in cooperation with the National Advertising Council. The Ad Council receives numerous requests from public and private agencies, sorts through them, and cooperates in support of a select few by producing and distributing ads at costs below what agencies would pay privately for the same services. In 1980 the Ad Council solicited the voluntary efforts of a major advertising agency in a campaign on behalf of the U.S. Bureau of the Census 1980 Census of Population. What would have cost the Census Bureau $40 million cost less than three-quarters of a million dollars. Smokey Bear, Woodsy Owl, and Johnny Owl are all creatures of the Ad Council in cooperation with governing organizations.

J. Edgar Hoover, the FBI, and the Perfection of Administrative Rhetoric

Writing of persuasion and propaganda, literary critic and theorist Kenneth Burke offers a viewpoint that parallels our understanding of the new propaganda:

> All told, persuasion ranges from the bluntest quest of advantage, as in sales promotion or propaganda, through courtship, social etiquette, education, and the sermon, to a "pure" form that delights in the process of appeal for itself alone, and without ulterior purpose. And identification ranges from the politician who, addressing an audience of farmers says, "I was a farm boy myself," through the mysteries of social status, to the mystic's devout identification with the source of all being.[30]

If earlier forms of propaganda reflected the "bluntest quest of advantage," new propaganda is closer to the "pure" form that "delights in the process of appeal for itself alone." Thus spectacle and storytelling invoke communication-pleasure, not pain. So too does another variety of Burke's "pure" form, a variety he labels "administrative rhetoric."[31] Administrative rhetoric, says Burke, is the "rhetoric of bureaucracy"; it is thus key to bureaucratic propaganda. Administrative rhetoric consists mainly of nonverbal *acts* directed in part toward fulfilling the bureaucratic organization's task or mission, but in larger measure toward *appealing* to the eye and to the imagination.

To illustrate the nature of administrative rhetoric and its appeals let us turn to the case of J. Edgar Hoover. For almost half a century, from 1924 to 1972, Hoover was director of the chief law enforcement arm of the nation, the Federal Bureau of Investigation (FBI). He took a fledgling agency struggling for funds and survival and built it into a well-financed empire occupying a palatial fortresslike office building constructed to his design. For decades he set the nation's law enforcement agenda as his agency waged "wars" and "crusades" against racketeering, internal subversion, the Red (communist) menace—in short, all enemies of the United States, foreign and domestic. He possessed considerable influence over Congress, the federal bureaucracy, and a succession of presidents of the United States. All this Hoover accomplished not only through clever administrative practices, intrigues, and bargaining, but in large measure through administrative rhetoric.[32]

J. Edgar Hoover became acting director of the FBI (then simply the Bureau of Investigation) on May 10, 1924. At the time the bureau had as many, if not more, detractors than supporters. Prior to the founding of the bureau in 1908 the various attorneys general of the United States (the cabinet level law officer of the nation) had usually hired private detectives for investigative work. The Department of Justice over which the attorney general presided had no investigative arm, in part because many Americans inside and outside of government feared creation of a federal "secret police." Fears notwithstanding, in 1908 President Theodore Roosevelt created a Bureau of Investigation in the Justice Department by executive order, much to the anger of members of Congress. To mollify congressmen the Justice Department assured that the bureau would confine itself to violations of antitrust and interstate commerce laws. Only a year later Congress passed the Mann Act, or White Slave Traffic Act, making it a crime to transport any woman across state lines for "immoral purposes," a measure aimed at organized prostitution, and the Bureau of Investigation received enforcement responsibility. This mission resulted in placing bureau agents outside the nation's capital for the first time and in collecting information and keeping files on individual citizens, that is, prostitutes and their clientele. Congressional action outlawing interstate transportation of prize fight films, then of stolen motor vehicles, yielded even broader investigative authority to the bureau. With the advent of World War I the Bureau of Investigation began ferreting out "German spies," with an equally active campaign to combat potential internal subversion by a host of alleged communists in the postwar Red Scare.

The ever-widening authority of the Bureau of Investigation did not set well with critics who argued that such a force was a threat to civil liberties and to state prerogatives, and could act as a partisan secret police, since bureau personnel owed their jobs to the incumbent U.S. president, not to the U.S. Civil Service. Upon assuming the acting directorship of the bureau in 1924, J. Edgar Hoover set about to improve the bureau's image. Employing an "innate feel for publicity amounting to genius,"[33] he began with conventional means of propaganda, then displayed a flair for more innovative forms. He employed the FBI's Crime Records Division as a propaganda machine churning out reports and press releases embellishing bureau accomplishments. Hoover made himself readily available for interviews with the press, especially for interviews with admiring reporters. So admiring were some reporters that they acted as unpaid publicity agents for Hoover; by 1929 when he was appointed permanent director, glowing color features in newspapers and magazines extolled how Hoover was building a "world famous detective agency." Thereafter Hoover had a cozy relationship with the press. In the 1930s one magazine alone, *American Magazine*, ran a series of two dozen color stories on Hoover and the FBI, all written by a journalist so close to Hoover that he eventually became a ghostwriter for Hoover's speeches.

Hoover delivered speeches often. He spoke before business groups, veterans' groups, patriotic groups, anywhere he could find a sympathetic audience that applauded his efforts with such enthusiasm that Hoover was guaranteed a positive account of his remarks in the next day's newspapers. Although they could not be labeled speeches, Hoover's appearances before congressional committees to give testimony on behalf of his agency were with an eye both to pleasing Congress and to attracting headlines. Always fortified with statistics, graphs, charts, and other paraphernalia, the nation's head G-man gave impressive performances before friend and foe alike.

The glorified and romanticized G-man image that Hoover assumed for himself and his FBI agents was carefully contrived. A reporter who had published a laudatory article about Hoover in *Forum* magazine (later hired to handle press relations for the Department of Justice and for Hoover's operation) introduced the director to leading radio and movie producers. Out of these encounters emerged over the years numerous half-hour radio dramas and continuing soap operas based upon "true to life" stories about the bureau and its agents. These included "K-7," "The FBI in Peace and War," and "This Is Your FBI" (which was on radio for nine years). In 1935 Hollywood produced *G-Men*, starring Jimmy Cagney, the first in what would become a long line of movie propaganda coups for Hoover. So successful was the film that Hoover adopted Cagney's image for all FBI agents; he issued directives that agents would lose weight, wear short hair, dress sharply, and appear clean-cut! The G-man myth would reappear in later movies, most notably *The House on 92nd Street* (1945) and *The FBI Story* (1959). With the advent of television Hoover promoted his agency on that medium as well. "The FBI," starring Efrem Zimbalist, Jr., as competent, fearless, and dauntless Inspector Lew Erskine, premiered in 1965 and gradually developed an audience of 40 million viewers. Hoover, mindful of the show's popularity, commented on scripts and placed an agent in Hollywood to monitor filming. Finally, the FBI image was continuously refurbished in mass marketed books favorable to the agency's cause. The first, *Ten Thousand Public Enemies*, appeared the same year as the movie *G-Men*. It painted a picture of a nation set upon by villains and defended by courageous FBI agents using high-tech (for the time) weapons and obedient to "the most feared man the underworld has ever known—J. Edgar Hoover."[34] *The FBI Story* (1956), the FBI's authorized history, was written by journalist Don Whitehead, with close bureau editing; it was a best-seller. In *Masters of Deceit*, a 1958 best-seller, Hoover himself told the story of the FBI's successful war against communists in the United States who constituted a gigantic "pyramid of treason."

Newspaper interviews, features in magazines, speeches, press releases, radio, movies, television, books, documentaries, statistics—all constituted the "reports" that coincide with the Altheide and Johnson definition of bureaucratic propaganda cited earlier. But J. Edgar Hoover's administrative rhetoric consisted of appealing acts and not just reports. Consider each of these examples. Hoover's job as FBI director was threatened in 1933 when Franklin Roosevelt assumed the presidency. Just as Nicholas Biddle had prospered during the presidency of John Quincy Adams but had to worry when Andrew Jackson became president, so too had Hoover grown in stature in the Republican administrations of Calvin Coolidge and Herbert Hoover, but had concerns about what Democrat Franklin Roosevelt would do. A new attorney general, Thomas Walsh, announced he would bring new personnel to the Justice Department. This presumably would include a new FBI director. That would mean double trouble for Hoover. Hoover's successor would inherit not only his job but also the FBI files. In those files was one on Thomas Walsh, compiled 11 years earlier without Walsh's knowledge; the file allegedly, and for partisan reasons, documented Walsh's alleged radical activities and shady business dealings. Fortune, however, smiled on Hoover. Two days before Roosevelt's inauguration Walsh died of a heart attack in North Carolina. Hoover immediately dispatched senior FBI officials to accompany Mrs. Walsh and her husband's body back to Washington, then personally met the train and consoled the widow upon her arrival. The totally uncalled for *beau geste* impressed the newly appointed attorney general, one who did not share Walsh's concern over Hoover's FBI. Although such administrative rhetoric alone may not have saved Hoover's position, it certainly created a different climate of opinion in which he was judged by the new administration.

Consider also Machine Gun Kelly. Upon taking office in 1933, Homer Cummings, Roosevelt's new attorney general, launched a "crusade against crime." The crusade fit Hoover's administrative rhetorical plans perfectly, as the case of Machine Gun Kelly demonstrates. George Kelly had kidnapped a wealthy Oklahoma oilman, ultimately releasing him. But Kelly remained a fugitive and was on the Justice Department's widely publicized Public Enemies list. Using informants, working around the clock, Hoover's agents tracked down Kelly on his in-laws' farm in Texas. When Kelly surrendered, shouting "Don't shoot, G-men," the act was widely publicized as a triumph for Hoover's stalwart force; news accounts made Hoover a public hero.

But critics of the FBI remained unimpressed. Summoned before a congressional committee to defend budget requests for his bureau, he found his statistical sleights of hand impeached and his heroism questioned: after all, said critics, Hoover, the nation's chief detective, had never even made an arrest! Shortly thereafter when Alvin ("Old Creepy") Karpis, who had robbed and marauded in midwestern states with his co–gang leader Kate ("Ma") Barker, was traced to New Orleans, Hoover flew in to make the arrest personally. The event was widely and favorably publicized. In the same month Hoover made personal arrests in two other cases and again benefited from banner newspaper headlines and photos. Hoover's bravado even extended to setting up mobsters for arrest. In 1938 Hoover recruited the aid of Walter Winchell, a popular newspaper gossip columnist and network radio personality. Winchell approached Louis "Lepke" Buchalter, of the notorious Murder Incorporated, and told Lepke that he could promise, as Hoover's representative, that the gangster would avoid capital punishment if he would surrender to Hoover. Winchell arranged a meeting of himself, Hoover, and Lepke in an automobile in New York City. Hoover got what he wanted: he made the arrest, promptly publicized by

Winchell in what he wanted, a scoop. Lepke, however, did not get what he wanted. He was tried for murder and executed.

Kenneth Burke has theorized that people strive to "perfect" ideas, principles, practices, ways of life, even themselves. In an ironic fashion, however, there is a certain rotten core at the center of such perfection. Perfection takes its toll; hence, people are "rotten with perfection." In many respects J. Edgar Hoover perfected his administrative rhetoric as a means of propagandizing on behalf of himself and his organization. Perhaps his beguiling and charming promise to Lepke, transmitted through the palaver of Winchell and never honored in the end, suggests the rotten quality of Hoover's perfection.

THE PALAVER OF NATIONAL CULTURES: NEW PROPAGANDA IN PEACE, WAR, AND PEACEFUL WAR

We have seen how political leaders exercise the palaver of new propaganda in winning, holding, and exercising power. In what is now a world of global politics, leaders of the world's nations employ propaganda to retain power in their respective nations; moreover, propaganda figures prominently in their dealings with one another as world leaders. This, of course, has been somewhat the case before the advent of modern propaganda. Julius Caesar, a half century before the birth of Christ, managed to subdue and hold sway over provincial rulers and war lords not only by military force but also through propaganda devices. Many were akin to the new propaganda devices in vogue today. He employed spectacles in the form of parades, pomp, and ceremony. Although he was not chief storyteller he encouraged the myth that he descended from the goddess Venus. He employed catch slogans ("Veni, vidi, vici," or "I came, I saw, I conquered"). And his image on coins that circulated throughout his far-flung empire reminded allies and rivals alike that *he* was Rome.

Here we examine three areas where contemporary propaganda comes into play in the relationships between national cultures. Propaganda's historical role in each—in peaceful international relations, in war, and in the relations of nations in tense times—is the subject of numerous book-length studies. Our discussion, therefore, emphasizes propaganda's current role in each area.

Propaganda in Contemporary Diplomatic Cultures

Scholarly treatises on warfare date back several centuries. One of the earliest and most provocative appeared approximately four centuries before the birth of Christ, *The Art of War*, by a Chinese scholar, Sun Tzu. In it he writes that "to win one hundred victories in one hundred battles is not the acme of skill." No, "to subdue the enemy without fighting is the acme of skill."[35] The enemy, thought Sun Tzu, is deceived by creating "shapes," or what another Chinese student and practitioner of war who led a successful communist revolution in China in the 1940s, Mao Tse-Tung, called "illusions."[36] Sun Tzu's shapes and Mao's illusions propagandists know as images. Although diplomacy—the art and practice of conducting international relations—involves the exchange of information, preferences, and views in negotiating treaties, alliances, and agreements, it involves the exchange of shapes, illusions, or images. Think back to the Monroe Doctrine. Here was a presidential pronouncement that had precious little force to back it up, yet was reaffirmed for more than a century. It was less fact than shape, less policy than image.

A great portion of contemporary diplomacy takes full advantage of Sun Tzu's advice, seeking to treat with enemies, potential enemies, and allies with "shapes." This is not to deny the vast number of material exchanges between nations in financial assistance, military hardware, technical expertise, and so forth, nor to deny the hard bargaining that enters into negotiating disarmament agreements, human rights treaties, and trade protocols. But in all of this, and often instead of it, there is ample room for diplomatic palaver.

Today diplomatic spectacles abound to the point of becoming obligatory rituals. Every year the heads of government of the leading capitalist nations meet at an economic summit. Ostensibly these are occasions for frank exchange, tough-minded bargaining, and the hammering out of "bullet-biting" solutions to difficult economic problems facing the United States, Canada, Great Britain, France, West Germany, Italy, and Japan. More accurately, however, they are exercises in spectacle and administrative rhetoric. Each nation takes turns serving as summit host, and in outdoing the other nations in providing lavish banquets, tours, ceremonial events, and photo opportunities. Each nation's press (more than 3,500 journalists from around the globe attended the 1990 summit in Houston, Texas) covers the ritual performances and utterances of its respective president, prime minister, or premier, filling the front pages of newspapers, feature space of newsmagazines, and radio and TV broadcast hours. Leaders' images are refurbished, national pride provoked, and major cities of the world showcased. In the end the leaders hold a joint press conference revealing "frank" discussions and "progress," issue a joint statement, and the news media report that the "story coming out of this economic summit is that there is no story." The palaver message: yes, there are problems, but the capitalist leaders of the world *are* leaders (that, after all, is what the metaphor of "economic summit" implies), hence, all is basically right with the world. Such meetings are transmitted throughout the world ideoculture to communicate that collective image of control and coming prosperity.

Or consider state visits. The U.S. president goes to London, Paris, Bonn, Rome, Prague, Tokyo, Beijing, Moscow, and numerous other points north, east, south, and west. (Presumably, a tolerance for air travel, jet lag, foreign dining, and versatility with Gerntz, Prosit, A Votre Sante, Salud, and all manner of other national toasts, are prime requirements for seeking the presidency.) Once more the talk is "tough," the atmosphere "friendly," the TV pictures "stunning," the popular reception "warm," the receptions "formal but intimate," and the progress in negotiations "heartening." Turnabout being fair play, leaders of foreign nations pay state visits to the United States—Washington, D.C., New York City, and for the rustic touch, a farm in Iowa, a ranch in Montana, but not an unheated tenement, a home for the aged, a closed shopping center, a strip mine, or a toxic waste dump.

Recent U.S. secretaries of state, in concert with ministers of foreign affairs in various nations, have perfected another form of diplomatic palaver, shuttle diplomacy. In shuttle diplomacy high-ranking diplomatic envoys hurry back and forth between national capitals in jet planes, leaving the impression of face-to-face negotiations between high-ranking diplomats on virtually a daily basis. More often than not the precise nature of the "negotiations" is unclear, although the general aim is publicized—to work out an accord between nations in conflict, free hostages, forge a disarmament accord, and so forth. What is clear is the depiction of the shuttler, that is, the envoy, "on the fly." George Shutlz, secretary of state in the presidency of Ronald Reagan, etched himself into the American consciousness as an active, hardworking public servant in large measure by constantly being pictured in nightly newscasts and in newspapers bareheaded, in overcoat, boarding or debarking from a jetliner, leaving or returning, or simply on his way from place to place to "work out an arms deal," "find a solution to the terrorist problem," or "restore confidence in American intentions."

Summitry, state visits, shuttle diplomacy, and related forms of diplomatic propaganda are made possible, or certainly aided and abetted, by the continent-hopping possibilities afforded by jet travel and the instant publicity afforded the dramatic personae of world leaders via satellite communications. When President Woodrow Wilson went to Paris in 1919 to negotiate the Treaty of Versailles at the close of World War I, his summitry involved negotiations, spectacle, and administrative rhetoric. But Wilson traveled by sea, taking a long time to reach Paris and return; moreover, newspaper accounts communicated by wire services could scarcely capture Wilson's enthusiastic reception by Parisians in as vivid a manner as today is permitted by television. In part, the diplomatic palaver of the new propaganda owes much to technological change.

Political scientists Jarol Manheim and Robert Albritton take note of another contemporary form of diplomatic propaganda that derives not so much from shifts in technology as shifts in techniques.[37] Nations have long recognized that one way to influence one another is to impress each other's citizenries, win a favorable reception from them, and rely on that popular support to help them in making appeals to the citizenries' leaders. A recently favored tactic for doing that has been for nations to hire public relations firms to shape favorable images for themselves in another country's press. Manheim and Albritton examined the efforts of nations that contracted with public relations consultants in the United States to improve national images in the American press between 1974 and 1978—Republic of Korea, Philippines, Yugoslavia, Argentina, Indonesia, Rhodesia. The research contrasted the efforts of those six nations with a seventh, Mexico, that expressly declined to use public relations consultants under similar circumstances in 1975. Using the *New York Times* to examine news coverage, the two researchers examined whether coverage increased or decreased as a consequence of public relations efforts and whether coverage grew more positive or negative. Findings suggest that such *diplomacy by public relations* can improve a nation's image, at least in news coverage (although it remains uncertain whether improved news coverage translates into an improved image of the nation among news consumers). As a means of influencing what Sun Tzu called "shapes," international public relations thus serves as a means of "subduing" one's enemies "without fighting." That, along with diplomatic spectacles and administrative rhetoric, constitutes the "acme of skill" in modern diplomacy.

Propaganda in War Cultures

Another student of warfare, lifelong soldier and scholar Carl von Clausewitz, wrote in his *On War*, first published in 1832, that "war is a mere continuation of policy by other means."[38] It is also a continuation of diplomatic and other propaganda by conventional and other means. We have repeated often that propaganda in some form has always been with us. But it has been war propaganda, especially in World Wars I and II, that has made propaganda a topic of serious concern and systematic analysis. Let us briefly examine propaganda in those wars, then turn to the current phenomena of propaganda in "peaceful wars."

There have been many accounts of the conduct of propaganda in this century's two global wars.[39] Running through them is a focus upon the development of propaganda techniques that have become staples for old and new propaganda campaigns since. A few examples will highlight the shifting techniques across World Wars I and II.

In the Great War of 1914–1918 certain techniques were used by all combatants—leaflets, pamphlets, posters, speeches, news releases, and so on. In the United States 75,000 orators toured the country making more than three-quarter of a million four-minute speeches. In the brief period that the United States was in the war, 1917–1918, the total audience for these lectures was over 300 million, approximately three times the entire population of the United States. The orators were designated four minute men, harkening back to the minute men of the Revolutionary War, of course, with the clever modification to indicate the length of each address. The four minute men consisted of a mixture of ethnic groups, men and women, and there were even 200,000 young persons as junior four minute men. With the exception of German, orators spoke in a wide variety of languages suitable to the ethnic mix of their audiences. The program also included *Four Minute Men Bulletins* and the *Four Minute Men News*—both designed to reinforce the succinctly defined, concise propaganda line set forth in the four-minute lectures.[40]

The propaganda of the principal adversaries in World War I was most notable for the technique of hate propaganda, or the atrocity story. As Garth Jowett and Victoria O'Donnell have summarized, atrocity stories came in three varieties—massacre tales about the needless mass murder of the enemy or innocent bystanders; mutilation stories involving the hacking off of body parts or gouging out of eyes; and accounts of mistreatment of soldiers and civilians through torture, starvation, and punishments.[41] One of many instances of hate propaganda illustrates how a seeded propaganda story can take root and, in so doing, draw persons into the role of propagandists who did not originally set out to be so. When the Germans swept through Belgium as many as 5,000 civilians died at their hands—shot as guerrillas, hostages, or unfortunate victims. France and Britain capitalized on the carnage. The tightly controlled French press published so many stories on the atrocity that it stopped headlining stories; instead it ran a "news" section, "*Les Atrocities Allemandes*" ("The German Atrocities"). The British press editorialized against the German Kaiser, claiming he had personally ordered torture of three-year-old Belgians, even detailing the type of torture for each case. In Britain, a blue-ribbon committee investigating the authenticity of such atrocity accounts concluded that "murder, lust, and pillage prevailed over parts of Belgium on a scale unparalleled in any war between civilized nations during the last three centuries."[42]

Two items are noteworthy about that report. First, as revealed by a Belgian commission of inquiry in 1922 (well after the war's end), no allegation in the original committee's report could be documented. In fact, several things cast doubt on the accuracy of the original report: no witnesses were interviewed, hearsay evidence was taken at face value, and the 1,200 depositions taken from Belgian refugees (by lawyers in Britain), which formed the basis of the report and came from persons neither placed under oath nor identified by name, mysteriously disappeared and have never been found. Second, the blue-ribbon committee's chair was Lord [James] Bryce, former ambassador to the United States and a highly respected political scientist who was author of a classic text on American politics and government, *The American Commonwealth*. Bryce did not *intend* to write a report investigating propaganda that would itself be propaganda; yet, his signature made his committee's report credible even in the face of its numerous flaws.

In World War I two fledgling industries, broadcasting and the movies, were first exploited for their propaganda potential. The United States used radio propaganda to court the sympathies of neutral nations: signals broadcast from the United States to the Eiffel Tower in France were relayed across Europe. By World War II radio warfare was an accepted propaganda device, one that along with TV warfare is today a worldwide phenomenon,[43] practiced by the United States Information Agency's Voice of America, the Soviet Union's Radio Moscow, the People's Republic of China's Radio Beijing, or the shortwave broadcasts of other nations including Radio South Africa, Radio Israel, or even Vatican Radio. The 1990 crisis in the Persian Gulf reminded the world once more of radio's availability as a propaganda tool. Iraqi Radio broadcast messages "to the American soldier in Saudi Arabia" aimed at undermining morale. Broadcasts reminded Americans of the brutal desert heat and that they were away from their families: "Your children are waiting for you, so why are you here?" The United States relied on satellite radio to advise U.S. citizens "detained" by Iraq in Kuwait.

The relatively young movie industry appealed to war propagandists, as it still does today in its maturity, because whether films are made to inform (newsreels, documentaries, etc.) or to entertain (war films, westerns, comedies, historical epics, adventure films, spy movies, or other genres), they can also be propaganda vehicles. Newsreels, short films about current events, covered the Spanish-American War; thereafter, the propaganda potential of newsreels grew. One reason is that they gave audiences a sense of visual immediacy about actual events, that is, "the camera does not lie." Another, however, was that the camera could indeed lie for propaganda purposes. As Raymond Fielding found, "Apparently there was not a single major producer in the period 1894 to 1900 that did not fake newsfilm as a matter of practice."[44] In both World Wars I and II, newsreels, faked and unfaked but always edited to supply a version of the war effort favorable to the nation wherein the film was produced, played to intrigued audiences in movie houses throughout the world. Numerous entertainment films, whether directly dealing with war subjects or not, carried propaganda messages in both wars. So common were war themes in entertainment motion pictures that one movie, *All Quiet on the Western Front*, a 1930 film about brutality in World War I, achieved notoriety precisely because of its antiwar propaganda theme. In all of the principal combatant nations in World War II thousands of propaganda films per se were produced and shown in theaters. Many are still in general circulation, most notably Hollywood director Frank Capra's *Why We Fight* series produced for the U.S. Department of the Army, Information and Education Division.

Propaganda in Peaceful Warring Cultures

The English philosopher Thomas Hobbes (1588–1679) wrote that "during the time men live without a common power to keep them all in awe, they are in that condition which is called *war*; and such a war is of every man against every man."[45] If Hobbes was correct, then the nations of the world even when not engaged in armed conflict, so long as they "live without a common power to keep them all in awe," are in a sense at war. In this paradoxical state of "peaceful war" national powers, borrowing and building on the practices of diplomatic propaganda and war propaganda, engage in a form of propaganda warfare in which the new propaganda is the chief weapon. There are several examples: the propaganda of the cold war that marked US-USSR relations for most of the twentieth century following the close of World War II; the civil disobedience campaign of Mahatma Gandhi that contributed so much to India's gaining independence from the British Empire following World War II; the war of words and deeds in the Middle East for the past half century. In closing this chapter on the propagandistic palaver of national cultures we focus upon a final example of peaceful propaganda warfare, disinformation.

Although *disinformation*, a technique based on forgeries and staged events circulated in the news media as fact, is a translation of a Soviet term *(desinformatsiya)* describing the responsibilities of a department of the KGB, the Soviet secret service, the practice has not been limited to the Soviet Union, nor is it purely modern. As L. John Martin notes, an unperfected form of disinformation existed in biblical times where, in Matthew 26:59, one reads "the chief priests, and elders, and all the council, sought false witness against Jesus." The fabrications of the "false witnesses" were a forerunner of disinformation. In Martin's view propaganda has two elements: "an event, act, or characteristic—a focus" and "persuasive communication centering on this focus—a message." And, he goes on, "disinformation, therefore, is a form of propaganda in which either the focus is based on some unlawful act or the message is a misrepresentation of a lawful act or true situation."[46] In disinformation a propagandist stages or fakes an event, conceals the clandestine action of doing so, and employs clandestine means to "plant" stories, interpretations, and judgments about the faked event in the news media. Since news reports appear authentic, the event—which may not have ever happened—appears authentic as well. Hence, two parties join forces: a news source whose intentions *are* propagandistic and who fakes the event and its initial report, and a news reporter whose intentions *are not* propagandistic and who circulates the phony report as fact.

There are many instances of disinformation. In 1983 a forged document from the U.S. Embassy in Lagos, Nigeria, falsely claimed that the U.S. ambassador ordered the assassination of a principal Nigerian presidential candidate in what was reported in the news media as Operation Headache. Forged letters written to African nations, allegedly by the Ku Klux Klan but actually by the KGB, warned them to keep athletes out of the 1984 Olympics or they would be gunned down. In 1986 the U.S. effort to undermine Libyan leader Colonel Muammar al-Qaddafi included plans to fake radio messages to make it appear that American ships and planes had crossed his "line of death," thus opening the possibility of Libyan armed action against which the United States could retaliate, even in the face of denials by Secretary of State George Shultz to reporters that such plans existed.

Disinformation is not limited to the culture of international politics. Altheide and Johnson discuss a form of disinformation that occurs in bureaucratic politics, that is, "gundecking," the falsification of official reports and their circulation to make it appear that a bureaucratic agency has carried out required laws and procedures when it has not.[47] Colonel Oliver North's testimony in 1987 in hearings inquiring into the Iran-Contra controversy (trading hostages for arms and covertly supplying arms to those opposed to the ruling elements in Nicaragua) revealed instances of gundecking. Even in the practice of new propaganda in electoral campaigns disinformation tactics also appear in the form of dirty tricks. In 1972 Senator Edmund Muskie was a victim of disinformation in his efforts to win the Democratic nomination for president. Before the voting in the New Hampshire primary a faked letter made headlines, a letter allegedly describing how Muskie demeaned French Canadians (''Canucks'') as New Hampshire blacks. Muskie's emotional effort to rebut the story (variously reported as crying, sobbing, tearful, or choking) left an impression of weakness, thus making him an unwitting propagandist against himself, serving the intent of the source of the faked letter.

The Gulf War

The Gulf War of 1990–1991 included all forms of war propaganda—using disinformation, demonizing the enemy, accusing them of atrocities, attempting to harm the morale or resolve of the enemy through broadcasts and leaflets, drumming up support and condemning dissent at home, branding inquiring reporters and doubtful politicians as traitors, in general attempting to mobilize public opinion into a mood of acceptance that no other alternative was possible, and even appealing to bloodthirsty and irrational hatreds and fears, building up a popular ''war fever.''

The language of military briefings included the usual euphemistic language: *delivery of ordnance, airborne sanitation, collateral damage, incontinent ordnance,* and *human remains pouches* are representative terms that obscure visions of the actual and horrible impact of war, in which both soldiers and civilians are maimed and killed. But perhaps most innovative in terms of propaganda was the largely successful effort on the part of the Pentagon to set strict media rules that in effect enlisted the news media in the war effort by transforming them largely into a propaganda conduit that dutifully reported the military version of events. These events (with a few exceptions, such as CNN's reporting from Baghdad) became a function of military briefing, which incorporated the conduct of the war into a coherent story told largely by the verbal and visual imagery provided by official spokespersons. In some measure, the war was transformed into a spectacle that excluded upsetting imagery, such as American dead (the media were not allowed to photograph corpses, body bags, or even coffins returning to the United States). By so doing, the military effectively made the American media into a reluctant but virtually compliant mode of war propaganda that learned to stop worrying and love the war.

THE PALAVER IS THE MESSAGE?

In a series of works published in 1964, Marshall McLuhan, a widely read student of mass communication, made an observation that became as much a popular catch phrase as a scholarly utterance: ''the medium is the message.'' He spelled out what he meant by that: '' 'medium is the message' because it is the medium that shapes and controls the scale and form of human association and action'' not the content or meaning of that content carried by print, radio, television, or other media.[48] McLuhan's view provoked controversy. It would be just as controversial to claim that in contemporary politics the new propaganda, that is, palaver, is the political message. Yet, from what we have seen of the new propaganda's role in winning, holding, exercising, and jousting for power, it is clear that palaver is so vital and pervasive that a major portion of politics as it is normally understood is palaver, that vast numbers of political messages are palaver. Is this also the case in segments of life that on the surface appear marginal to politics—economic, social, and cultural matters? Let us turn to each in succeeding chapters and explore the possibilities.

This chapter dealt with the major plural ways in which propaganda has become the key communicative resource of the modern political ideoculture. Even though most readers are not privy to the inner workings of politics, they are familiar enough with it to recognize how much of it is now propaganda. Like more familiar areas of life, we take for granted that politics will involve propaganda, much of it directed at us. When we watch a major electoral campaign from afar—largely through television—we are now aware that much of what we are seeing is propaganda. Thus this chapter should let you recognize political propaganda that emanates from a variety of sources, and beware the possibility that the message is palaver directed at you by the powerful in order to gain your compliance for the values they wish to allocate at the moment. Now we will turn to the ideocultures of advertising and public relations, areas of social communication also much given to the use of propaganda.

NOTES

1. David Easton, *The Political System* (New York: Knopf, 1953), p. 146.
2. Ibid., p. 143.
3. Ibid., p. 144.
4. Paul F. Boller, Jr., *Presidential Campaigns* (New York: Oxford University Press, 1984).
5. Edward Pessen, *The Log Cabin Myth* (New Haven: Yale University Press, 1984), p. 20.
6. Boller, *Presidential Campaigns*, p. 66.
7. Quoted in Boller, *Presidential Campaigns*, p. 70.
8. Quoted in Robert V. Remini, *Andrew Jackson* (New York: Harper and Row, 1966), pp. 150–151.
9. Quoted in Remini, ibid., p. 152.
10. Quoted in Remini, ibid., 161; emphasis in original.
11. Wayne S. Cole, *An Interpretive History of American Foreign Relations* (Homewood, IL: Dorsey, 1968), p. 134.
12. Jacques Ellul, *Propaganda* (New York: Vintage Books, 1965), p. 19.
13. Ibid., p. 261.
14. Kurt Lang and Gladys Engel Lang, "The Mass Media and Voting," in Eugene Burdick and Arthur L. Brodbeck, eds., *American Voting Behavior* (Glencoe, IL: Free Press, 1959), p. 226.
15. Sidney Blumenthal, *The Permanent Campaign* (New York: Touchstone Books, 1982).
16. CBS News/*New York Times* poll, October 27, 1987.
17. From transcript appearing in David R. Runkel, ed., *Campaign for President: The Managers Look at '88* (Dover, MA: Auburn House, 1989), p. 110.
18. Quoted in Victoria Loe, "Bush Won by Making Change Look Like Risk," *Dallas Morning News*, November 10, 1988, p. 1.
19. The Beckel-Ailes exchange is reported in the transcripts appearing in Runkel, *Campaign for President*, p. 122.
20. Among the scholars considering this transformation, albeit from different perspectives, see Roderick P. Hart, *Verbal Style and the Presidency* (New York: Academic Press, 1984) and *The*

Sound of Leadership (Chicago: University of Chicago Press, 1987); Kathleen Hall Jamieson, *Eloquence in an Electronic Age* (New York: Oxford University Press, 1988); and Jeffrey K. Tulis, *The Rhetorical Presidency* (Princeton, NJ: Princeton University Press, 1987).

21. Quoted in Boller, *Presidential Campaigns*, p. 7.
22. Quoted in ibid., p. 213.
23. Quoted in Elizabeth Drew, "Letter from Washington," *The New Yorker* 65(33) (October 2, 1989): 104.
24. Bruce Miroff, "The Presidency and the Public: Leadership as Spectacle," in Michael Nelson, ed., *The Presidency and the Political System* (Washington, DC: Congressional Quarterly Press, 1988), pp. 271–291. See also Murray Edelman, *Constructing the Political Spectacle* (Chicago: University of Chicago Press, 1988).
25. Miroff, "The Presidency and the Public," p. 275.
26. William Stephenson, *The Play Theory of Mass Communication* (Chicago: University of Chicago Press, 1967).
27. Compare the views of philosopher Niccolò Machiavelli, who argued that the great majority of people are satisfied with appearances. Hence it *might* be possible for leaders to use the logic of political reason in dealing with one another (although leaders too are often given to believing in appearances), but most certainly leaders should rely on *fantasia*, fantasy or spectacle, to engineer and appeal to the play of imagination among the populace. See K. R. Minogue, "Theatricality and Politics: Machiavelli's Concept of Fantasia," in B. Pareth and R. N. Benk, eds., *The Morality of Politics* (London: George Allen and Unwin, 1972), pp. 148–162.
28. David L. Altheide and John M. Johnson, *Bureaucratic Propaganda* (Boston: Allyn and Bacon, 1980), p. 5.
29. Dean L. Yarwood and Ben M. Enis, "Advertising and Publicity Programs in the Executive Branch of the National Government: Hustling or Helping the People," *Public Administration Review* 42 (January/February 1982): 37–46.
30. Kenneth Burke, *A Rhetoric of Motives* (Berkeley: University of California Press, 1969), p. xiv.
31. See Burke's discussion in " 'Administrative' Rhetoric in Machiavelli" in Burke, *A Rhetoric of Motives*, pp. 158–166.
32. There are several excellent discussions of the propaganda devices used by J. Edgar Hoover. The material in this section is compiled from Eugene Powers, *Public Entrepreneurship* (Bloomington: Indiana University Press, 1980), pp. 94–155; Hank Messick, *John Edgar Hoover* (New York: David McKay, 1972); Richard Gid Powers, *G-Men: Hoover's FBI in American Popular Culture* (Carbondale: Southern Illinois University Press, 1983) and *Secrecy and Power* (New York: Free Press, 1987); and Athan G. Theoharis and John Stuart Cox, *The Boss* (Philadelphia: Temple University Press, 1988).
33. Theoharis and Cox, *The Boss*, p. 100.
34. Quoted in ibid., p. 131.
35. Sun Tzu, *The Art of War*, Samuel B. Griffith, trans. (London: Oxford University Press, 1963), p. 76.
36. See Mao Tse-Tung, *Quotations from Chairman Mao Tse-Tung* (Peking: Foreign Language Press, 1966).
37. Jarol B. Manheim and Robert B. Albritton, "Changing National Images: International Public Relations and Media Agenda Setting," *American Political Science Review* 78 (September 1984): 641–657; Robert B. Albritton and Jarol B. Manheim, "News of Rhodesia: The Impact of a Public Relations Campaign," *Journalism Quarterly* 60 (Winter 1983): 622–628.
38. Carl von Clauswitz, *On War* (New York: Penguin Books, 1968), p. 119.
39. See Harold Lasswell, *Propaganda Techniques in the World War* (New York: Knopf, 1927); P. M. A. Linebarger, *Psychological Warfare* (New York: Duell, Sloan, and Pearce, 1954); and Harold Childs, *Public Opinion* (Princeton, NJ: Van Nostrand, 1965), pp. 325–334.

40. Alfred E. Cornebise, *War as Advertised: The Four Minute Men and America's Crusade, 1917–1918* (Philadelphia: American Philosophical Society, 1984).
41. Garth S. Jowett and Victoria O'Donnell, *Propaganda and Persuasion* (Newbury Park, CA: Sage, 1986), p. 130.
42. Quoted in Phillip Knightley, *The First Casualty* (New York: Harcourt Brace Jovanovich, 1975), p. 83.
43. Lawrence C. Soley, *Radio Warfare* (New York: Praeger, 1989).
44. Raymond Fielding, *The American Newsreel* (Norman: University of Oklahoma Press, 1972).
45. Thomas Hobbes, *Leviathan* (Chicago: Encyclopedia Britannica, 1952), p. 85.
46. L. John Martin, "Disinformation as a Form of Propaganda: An Instrumentality in the Propaganda Arsenal," *Political Communication and Persuasion* 2 (1982): 57–58.
47. Altheide and Johnson, *Bureaucratic Propaganda*, p. 184.
48. Marshall McLuhan, *Understanding Media* (New York: Signet, 1964), p. 24.

CHAPTER 5

Propagated Consumers Consume Propaganda

Mass Advertising, Public Relations, and New Propaganda

The previous chapter dealt with political ideocultures. Here we deal with areas of social propaganda more associated with economics, although as we shall see, that is not entirely true. Too, mass advertising and public relations are propaganda practices that have become common in political and governmental life. Advertising has clear entrepreneurial uses, to sell not only products but also politicians, schools, and just about anything else. Public relations firms and offices "relate to the public" for the benefit of corporations, but also government agencies, universities, and so on. You should gain from this chapter some knowledge of how "propagated consumers" are created, and how trust is marketed. It should also stimulate thought as to the extent to which such manipulative activities can continue to perpetuate belief among a public with alternative sources of information, or the evidence of their own eyes.

At this point in our inquiry you may have begun to notice that we attempt to incorporate aspects of modern propaganda that are not on their face strictly political. We do so not only because such propaganda is inherently important to understand, but also because we cannot explain the processes of modern political propaganda without including the larger process of the creation of the new propaganda, such as mass advertising and public relations. For all these phenomena are of a piece: indeed, by now in the history of propaganda many of the people who work in commercial and political advertising and public relations move easily through the "revolving door" in and out of jobs in economic, cultural, and political propaganda. The world of propaganda must be understood as including but larger than its political manifestation, a form of communication and knowledge central to the modern ideoculture. With that in mind, let us turn to mass advertising and public relations.

SMOKE GETS IN YOUR EYES:
PROPAGATING A HABIT

The caption at the bottom of the ad reads, "SURGEON GENERAL'S WARNING: Smoking By Pregnant Women May Result in Fetal Injury, Premature Birth, and Low Birth Weight." Another reads, "SURGEON GENERAL'S WARNING: Quitting Smoking Now Greatly Reduces Serious Risks to Your Health." A third says, "SURGEON GENERAL'S WARNING: Smoking Causes Lung Cancer, Heart Disease, Emphysema, and May Complicate Pregnancy." Yet, occupying far more space and in glitzy colors, each ad provides a picture that belies these dire forebodings of the surgeon general. The first displays two cigarette packs bathed in the antiseptic light of a futuristic scene and promises "Good Smoke. Great Price." The second displays a sun-drenched couple in bathing suits standing on the immaculate, clean sand of a beach, crystal white wake lapping their legs, and clear blue water extending to the horizon. Standing beside the couple are four cigarette packs, each in a different pastel. "Move to Malibu," the message urges. The third ad provides, just below a fresh "soft pack" of cigarettes, the face of an attractive, young, self-assured and successful woman. "The taste that's right for me," she says.

Colorful promises above colorless threats. Or, more aptly, colorful promises to counter what the tobacco industry perceives as all too jaded political threats to its continued economic success. Such is the character of contemporary cigarette advertising. Propaganda made cigarette sales lively and robust in the twentieth century. Can new propaganda provide a life-support system to the waning cigarette in the twenty-first? We cannot answer that question, but a brief examination of the evolution of cigarette advertising provides us with insights into how propaganda has, and will, serve economic interests in changing political environments.

In 1913 R. J. Reynolds introduced his Camel cigarette. In so doing he brought his competitors (temporarily) to heel, revolutionized the tobacco industry, and created a "smoking society." Prior to the Camel, each competing cigarette brand had only sectional appeal—one brand popular in the South, another the West, another the Mid-Atlantic states, and so on. To build brand loyalties cigarette manufacturers advertised by giving away free samples of their product. In 1912, for example, a quarter of R. J. Reynolds Company's sales budget was devoted to "gratis goods," that is, giving away samples. But with the introduction of the Camel brand, and an aggressive advertising campaign to sell it, gratis goods fell to 15 percent of the sales budget in 1913, and 12 percent thereafter. Paid ads, not gifts, were the new wave of sales promotion.[1] "Camels Have Won in a National Way" and "Camels Now a Standard Seller" trumpeted in R. J. Reynolds ads a wish that, in fact, became fact.

It was not long before newspaper and magazine ads depicted the increasingly familiar Camel package—a camel standing outside an oasis with "CAMEL" across the top, "Turkish and Domestic Blend Cigarettes" across the bottom. Soon parlor games made the logo even more widely known. "Look closely," parents told their children, "and you can see a face on the camel's side" (allegedly in the art work that was the drawing of the camel). "Look closely," adolescent males said to their less experienced younger brothers, "and you can see a naked woman on the camel's side." And what really made Camels America's national brand was the I'd walk a mile for a Camel campaign. Ads pictured smiling men saying "I'd walk a mile for a Camel," for "the pleasure is worth it, there's no substitute for Camel quality and that mild fragrant, Camel blend." After all, "the fellow who smokes Camels, *wants* Camels." And with a bow to the independence of the American male, ads continued, "Don't let anyone tell you that any other cigarette at any price is so good as Camels. Let your own taste be the judge. A few smooth, refreshing puffs and you'd walk a mile for a Camel, too."

George Washington Hill, president of the American Tobacco Company, a Reynolds competitor, soon responded to the Camel campaign. American too sought to create national brands and, to do so, spent heavily on advertising—although American's advertising budget would lag behind Reynolds's until the 1930s. Hill, however, recognized that there was more to selling cigarettes than advertising. He turned to another propaganda form, public relations (PR). There were millions of women, thought Hill, who would constitute a large market for cigarettes *if* they could be convinced it was acceptable to smoke in public. So Hill employed public relations consultant Edward Bernays (see Chapter 2) to find a way to break the societal taboo on women smoking in public. Bernays, in turn, consulted a psychologist who theorized that the taboo actually reflected a form of man's "inhumanity" to women, that is, men kept women in bondage by not approving of feminine smoking in public. Bernays's campaign proved simple—and highly effective. He went to a group of New York City debutantes and asked if they would be willing to march in New York's Easter Parade lighting "Torches of Freedom" protesting man's inhumanity to women. The "torches" were cigarettes! The debutantes did so and received ample publicity in newsfilms and newspapers. Within five weeks men's smoking lounges in major theaters were opened to women. Women enjoyed their "torches," Bernays his success, and Hill his vastly expanded market for cigarette sales. What, in effect, Bernays's successful PR ploy had done was not only to propagate cigarette smoking but to *propagate consumers* by planting and sowing an abundant harvest of women smoking in public.

R. J. Reynolds was also quick to exploit the new female market. A series of ads in 1928–1929 undertook progressive, step-by-step introduction of Camels to women. Ads went from (1) a woman looking adoringly at a man smoking a Camel; to (2) the placement of the Camel package closer to the woman than the male in a similar ad—but she still did not light up; to (3) a woman sitting on horseback holding an unlit Camel; to (4) a woman at tea actually smoking a cigarette; to (5) men and women pictured smoking together. Thus, the female smokers propagated by Edward Bernays's campaign became *consumers of propaganda*, regardless of the source—R. J. Reynolds, the American Tobacco Company, or another cigarette manufacturer.

Although it was not until 1964 that the U.S. surgeon general issued a report linking cigarette smoking with the incidence of lung cancer, there had long been concern that cigarettes might harm smokers. R. J. Reynolds actually anticipated the threat three decades before the surgeon general officially posed it. In 1934 a headlined Camels ad provided "NEWS! Science reveals important new Facts for Smokers" (notice Science, Facts, and Smokers are capitalized). The ad went on to report that "a famous New York research laboratory" had discovered something "well known to Camel smokers." The discovery? Cigarette smoking has an "energizing effect," namely, smoking provides a "quick restoration of the flow of natural body energy." So, when feeling "down" it is time to "Get a lift with a Camel!" And, "CAMELS NEVER JANGLE YOUR NERVES." So Camel fans can smoke "as often as they like." Two photos accompany this comforting assurance. One shows a young woman turning desolately away from her suitor, who frowns in dismay. But the next photo shows the same young lady smiling, turning toward her absorbed suitor. Caption: "TOO TIRED FOR FUN . . . and then she smoked a Camel!" Camel ads praised the health benefits of the cigarette well into the early 1960s—picturing the brand endorsed by athletes who require "healthy nerves" to be successful; or by actors and actresses protecting their "T-Zone," throat and taste ("I'd walk a mile for a mild, mild Camel; they're so right they suit me to a 'T' "). Other ads suggested that Camels were good for your digestion.

In the remainder of this chapter we examine how propaganda in the form of mass advertising and public relations constitutes an entrepreneurship creating and serving a host of political and other interests, much as propaganda did for the cigarette industry throughout the twentieth century, through the propagation of consumers who consume propaganda. We begin that examination with how propaganda and entrepreneurship intermesh.

"I CAN GET YOU A DISCOUNT":
THE ENTREPRENEURIAL USES OF PROPAGANDA

In any nation competing groups and organizations, each seeking to serve the interests of its leaders and rank and file, originate a virtually inexhaustible supply of propaganda. Through propagandistic appeals, groups mobilize resources and support among their own members and among the populace at large, blunt the appeals of rival groups, and press their claims for advantage on the nation's political authorities. An American social historian, Vernon L. Parrington, likened this intergroup bickering to a "Great Barbecue."[2] In the nineteenth century, wrote Parrington, "A huge barbecue was spread to which all presumably were invited." By barbecue he meant the vast wealth of the land and the profits that could be made from snatching a piece of it. Parrington noted that "not quite all" were invited: "inconspicuous persons . . . were overlooked; a good many indeed out of the total number of the American people." But, "all the important persons, leading bankers and promoters and business men, received invitations." Since "there wasn't room for everybody . . . these were presumed to represent the whole." It was "a splendid feast." So what if the "choicest portions were served to favored guests"? Still the Great Barbecue "proclaimed the fine democratic principle that what belongs to the people should be enjoyed by the people" with "each free citizen using what came to hand for his own private ends, with no questions asked."

As we approach the twenty-first century the barbecue perhaps is no longer as huge as it was in the nineteenth. And dining is no longer limited to "the important persons" who are American: Japanese, Korean, German, British, and other foreign interests fill their plates as well. Yet, just as in the nineteenth (and twentieth) century "each free citizen" pursues "private ends" by joining with like-minded comrades in groups competing with one another for the "choicest portions." Syndicated columnist Donald Kaul, writing soon after the sale of Rockefeller Center in New York City to the Japanese firm of Mitsubishi Estate Company, noted that "the sad truth is that in our acquisitive, market-oriented society, pretty much everything is for sale."[3] Propaganda is key to the marketing of everything, and is itself a discourse that is largely for sale.

Exchanging Things

In pondering how groups organize to achieve political, economic, religious, ethnic, and other interests, political scientist Robert Salisbury has developed "an exchange theory of interest groups."[4] Groups form, he argues, when individuals pursuing private ends take the initiative to organize them. This alone is scarcely startling, but Salisbury's view of how these "entrepreneurs" do this is revealing. Entrepreneurs invest capital (time, money, imagination, etc.) to provide benefits to those who join the organization. These benefits may be "material," such as jobs, goods, or services; they may be "solidary," that is, the pure pleasure of associating with others, being identified with the group, and socializing; or they may be "expressive," for example, providing a means to express a personal stand for "free choice" or "right to life" in the controversy over legalized abortions. In exchange for investing in the capital resources to provide these benefits to potential members, those who join provide the organizer with selected material, solidary, and expressive benefits. The entrepreneur says, in effect, "I can get you a discount" on the price of a tangible good, being socially happy, or sounding off to those who will listen. In exchange, "join up, ante up." If the entrepreneur fulfills her or his side of the bargain, and continues to do so, and members support the entrepreneur, the organization succeeds and has the vitality to compete with groups placing competing claims.

In approaching potential joiners an entrepreneur promises rewards for joining and appeals to people to have faith that those promises will be fulfilled. Thus the entrepreneur endeavors to propagate notions of benefit and trust. As Salisbury notes, "potential members may be considered as a market which may or may not respond to the entrepreneur's efforts with sufficient enthusiasm to create a viable organization."[5] Much will thus depend upon the persuasiveness of the entrepreneur's propaganda and upon the suasiveness of potential members willing to suspend probable disbelief in the entrepreneur's claims, embracing the organizer as credulous, not incredulous. For example, many—but not all—television evangelists ask viewers to join the "television ministry" by pledging regular "good faith offerings" for which the faithful will be rewarded by ready admittance to the heavenly choir. As a case in point the now defrocked and imprisoned Jim Bakker, former head of the PTL ("Praise The Lord") TV ministry raised $129 million in 1986 through such appeals. The lavish lifestyle of the Bakker family hinted that not all good faith offerings were going to Christian charity (in fact less than 3 percent did). But followers suspended disbelief to ante up nonetheless.

The exchange theory of interest group formation borrows considerably from what we know about how economic enterprises begin but is clearly intended to explain the organization of all manner of formal groups whether organizers and members have economic or other pursuits. It certainly implies the key role played by propaganda in forming and sustaining organizational vitality. As we shall see later in this chapter, such propaganda used on behalf of formal organizations is at the heart of what public relations, or PR, is all about. Frequently, however, entrepreneurs are interested not in recruiting consumers of their propaganda into *formal* organizations (with rules, specified roles for leaders and followers, clear-cut goals, etc.) but in organizing them in the short run to purchase a product, support an idea or candidate, or contribute to a cause.

Consider the regularly scheduled fund drives of radio stations affiliated with National Public Radio (NPR) or television stations with the Public Broadcasting Service (PBS).

One or more times per year for a week or longer each station blocks out a significant portion of broadcast time to appeal for public donations to support "continued growth and broadcasting." Listeners and viewers are reminded that NPR and PBS stations are prohibited "from selling advertising" and, hence, must sustain themselves by means of grants (often from private and public foundations) and by soliciting "donations from you, the listener (or viewer)." Such appeals routinely propagate the language of organization, such as "join our KOST family" and receive in exchange an "I'm a KOST Conscious Listener" T-shirt. There is, of course, no family. The organization is limited to station personnel and the institution (usually a college or university) with which it is affiliated.

Converging on Things

Sociologist Herbert Blumer distinguished between behavior that derived from "concerted action" (i.e., joining and working in formal organizations) and from "individual lines of activity" (such as "the selection of a new dentifrice, a book, a play, a party platform, a new fashion, a philosophy, or a gospel"). The latter behaviors, said Blumer, are "in response to the vague impulses and feelings" that form not organizations but "congeries of individual lines of action."[6] Psychologist and communication scholar William Stephenson calls these congeries of individual lines of action "convergent selectivity."[7] Each individual when confronted with a range of options makes a choice among them. In part that choice stems from applying the methods of evidence or argument described in our introductory chapter. But frequently evidence is ambiguous, and/or sound and unsound arguments can be marshaled for each option. Here the method of credulity comes into play. From suasion (self-persuasion) come individual choices (self-selection). Some individuals will select Option A (and, say, purchase Crest toothpaste), others Option B (and converge on, say, Colgate), and others Options C, D, or E. Convergent selectivity, then, is the convergence of individual suasions in response to propagandistic appeals. This type of entrepreneurial effort *seeks not organized followers but converging consumers*. As public relations is to the propagandist of organized, concerted action, mass advertising is to the propagandist of personalized, convergent action.

MASS ADVERTISING: MARKETING PRODUCTS, PEOPLE, AND EVERYTHING ELSE

William Stephenson summed up the distinctive logic of mass advertising, saying that "in advertising one characteristically wants to sell *one* old piano to *one* person—classified ads in their tens of thousands every day attest to the convergence of one person on one object for sale."[8] Over the years advertisers have gradually shifted their strategies for achieving convergence through sales of *one* object to *one* person. In the process there have been changing emphases on the material, solidary, and expressive benefits promised to potential customers.

The serpent in the Garden of Eden was an entrepreneur with a product to sell. If Eve and Adam would but eat of the apple, they would have knowledge; no matter that the price was to be forever banished from Eden. Perhaps herein lies the origin of the well-worn adage in purchasing goods, caveat emptor, or let the buyer beware. In any event the serpent advertised and sold the product and, as we know, the price is still being paid. In a TV interview Lincoln Diamant, founder of the Diamant Museum, an archive for a vast number of TV ads dating back to the beginning of television, observed that in the 1960s it was estimated that by the time an average child graduated from high school she or he would have viewed 100,000 TV commercials in growing up. By the opening of the 1990s that estimate had risen from a minimum of 250,000 to a more likely 500,000.[9]

Product Advertising

Product advertising is, in any event, the oldest form of advertising. Two advertising professionals, Al Ries and Jack Trout, describe product advertising as focusing on the features of goods to be sold, stressing the benefits customers receive because of unique product qualities. Simply put, the aim was to "build a better mousetrap," then market it by informing consumers what made it *materially* better. Rosser Reeves, a guru of advertising in the 1950s, coined a phrase for such advertising that emphasized the material rewards of the product: Unique Selling Proposition, or USP.[10] Reeves developed USPs for a host of products, for example, selling the pain reliever Anacin on the promise that it would deliver "FAST, FAST, FAST RELIEF." It is a phrase that persons who were exposed to TV ads in the 1950s can recite today almost as a liturgical prayer.

Using USPs, advertisers planted promises of material benefits in the mind of the consumer, benefits unique to the product. With repetition over time USPs, such as "I'd walk a mile for a Camel," built up a following all their own. Through acquired USPs customers grew loyal to the products associated with those USPs. Thus arose *brand loyalties* with Camel smokers as fiercely loyal to their brand as Lucky Strike smokers were to theirs, Ford owners as loyal to their autos as Chevrolet owners were to theirs, and Democrats as loyal to their party as Republicans were to theirs. Advertisers found it hard to break those brand loyalties. Hence, the thrust of product advertising was not to convert consumers from one brand to another but to seek out new markets and build loyalties, much as both the American Tobacco Company and R. J. Reynolds did in the early days of cigarette marketing on a national scale.

Ries and Trout argue that changes began to occur in advertising approaches in the late 1950s. Products for which advertisers could claim unique qualities were increasingly hard to develop. No sooner did a new product appear on the market than one or more "copycats" would pop up, each claiming to be materially better than one another: faster relief, better taste, cheaper on the pocketbook, brighter for the teeth, mintier for the breath, and so on. *New* and *Improved* became favored buzzwords in product advertising, so much so that the claims often offended brand loyalists who liked their usual pain relievers or deodorants just as they were, thank you, so buzz off!

Image Advertising

Searching for more effective ways to market, advertisers developed an alternative to product advertising, namely, *image advertising*. Image advertising did not deemphasize brand loyalties, nor supplant product advertising; rather it reinforced and capitalized on brand and product loyalties. Whereas in product advertising brand loyalties originated as a result of repetition of USPs planting in consumers' minds catchphrases capsulizing material qualities of products, image advertising planted images of solidary benefits associated with a product that, in fact, differed from its competition in no material way. Advertisers gave products personalities with warmth, comfort, emotion, and exciting social appeals. To use a product was not to use a material good but to identify with an attractive social set. For example, Proctor and Gamble, with several brands of soap to market, created a social persona for each brand: Ivory was as pure as the love of mother and daughter pictured in Ivory ads; Camay was *the* soap for women seeking glamor, sophistication, success. Automobile ads stopped selling cars; instead they sold status: Cadillacs were for the responsible, socially mobile, proud; Fords were for the practical, upper lower class, also proud; Mercurys were for the substantial, modern, assertive. Summing up the distinction between product and image advertising was the phrase: "Don't sell the steak, sell the sizzle."

Positioning Advertising

There are, however, only so many ways that steaks sizzle. So too there are only so many social identities to be sold. As the "jeaning" of America and the world took place, attire, soaps, beers, automobiles—each of which varied little materially from its competitors— also began to differ little socially from competitors. The adage "clothes make the man" no longer was appropriate, no more than "designer jeans make the woman." So advertisers explored novel marketing strategies. *Positioning advertising* developed as an alternative to product and image advertising when and where appropriate. Position advertising stresses *expressive* benefits associated with marketed goods, more so than material or solidary differences. Precisely what consumers might wish to express about themselves through the products they buy and use is taken in position advertising as something that must be discovered, not something that can be *planted* in the minds of consumers through USPs or images.

Ries and Trout explain position advertising as follows. That people see what they expect to see, hear what they expect to hear, taste what they expect to taste, feel what they expect to feel, and believe what they expect to believe is a truism of propaganda. Researchers label this selective perception, attention, recall, and acceptance. Now, say Ries and Trout:

> One prime objective of all advertising is to heighten expectations. To create the illusion that the product or service will perform the miracles you expect. And presto, it does. But create the opposite expectation and the product is in trouble.[11]

Position advertising exploits expectations by permitting consumers to express expectations unique to them, not unique to the product. Ries and Trout ask us each to imagine a series of ladders in our minds. Each ladder is a different product (pain reliever ladder, breakfast cereal ladder, auto ladder, soap ladder, etc.); each step on the ladder is a different brand of that product (Bayer, Bufferin, Tylenol, Advil, etc.). Some ladders, they say, have many steps, others have few, for people can recall many brands for some products, but few brands for others. The steps on any ladder reflect rankings of the product. "A competitor that wants to increase its share of the business must either dislodge the brand above (a task that is usually impossible) or somehow relate its brand to the other company's position," say Ries and Trout. And, they go on, "an advertiser who wants to introduce a new product category must carry in a new ladder." But, "this, too, is difficult" for "the mind has no room for what's new and different unless it's related to the old."[12]

Note that whether it be a new brand or product the problem is the same, namely, the new must position itself in consumers' minds with respect to the old. This means finding out what people think of the old, what they expect when they consume it, and how they can express the same expectations or more by consuming the new. For example, in fighting the "cola wars" with Coke and Pepsi, 7-Up positioned itself as the "Uncola." Thus, 7-Up asked consumers to suspend a disbelief (that lemon-lime drinks are *not* colas when they are), express that suspension, and expect 7-Up to taste like an alternative to cola drinks. In the fierce competition of the cola wars the "Uncola" became the third largest of the cola sellers. Describing the Uncola campaign Ries and Trout conclude, "What you must do is look inside the prospect's mind. You won't find an 'uncola' idea inside a 7-Up can. You find it inside the cola drinker's head."[13]

We have been speaking thus far solely of the marketing of products. Advertising also sells people and lifestyles. As we shall see in the next section, the marketing of politicians involves strategic uses of brand loyalties, images, and positioning. So too, as we explore more fully in Chapter 6, does the manufacture and marketing of politically relevant social celebrities: industrialists such as Lee Iacocca or Donald Trump, popular music stars such as Michael Jackson, Bruce Springsteen, and the life and legend of Elvis Presley; movie stars, starlets, and superstars (pick any); sports figures (Bo [Jackson] Knows Baseball, and everything else), news personalities (Diane Sawyer, Sam Donaldson), authorities both scientific and not-so-scientific (Carl Sagan, Joyce Brothers), and all manner of other cultural icons.

Aristotle and Advertising

Whether the strategy be product, image, or position advertising—or a subtle and sophisticated combination of the three as today characterizes mass advertising in the age of new propaganda—there are various media for marketing products, people, and lifestyles. Rhetorical analyst Robert Root has suggested a way to understand how advertisers bend various media to their purposes.[14] With a bow toward Aristotle, Root argues that all advertising employs three means of persuasion. First, an advertiser must fashion a persona, a presence as a credible source of information (*ethos*). What the ad says contributes to such presence but so too do such things as tone, inflection, speed, or volume of a speaker, or style, vocabulary, and syntax in written ads. Second, the advertiser must research the audience (especially audience evaluations and expectations of various products and people), and gauge appeals accordingly—*pathos*. This involves researching, designing ads, and directing appeals to targeted audiences. Finally, ads present arguments designed to appear reasonable, whether by way of evidence or through inviting audiences to suspend disbelief—*logos*. Suppose, for example, the magazine *Sports Illustrated*, as it frequently does, employs a television commercial to sell subscriptions. The ad promises, along with all the alleged benefits of actually reading the magazine each week, a free videocassette of selected sports replays ("Greatest Moments in Sports," "Greatest Slam Dunks," "Funniest Moments in Sports"), a free *SI* calendar, a bonus *SI* swimsuit issue (with photos of attractive models in swimsuits), and a "discount" for ordering "NOW!"

The pitch is clear enough: suspend a disbelief, namely "there's no such thing as a free lunch," and subscribe, thus getting something for nothing!

Advertising Media

All advertising incorporates ethos, pathos, and logos but the relative emphasis on each differs from one advertising medium to another. Consider *print*, namely, ads that appear in newspapers and magazines or that are mailed directly to one's home. Here is a magazine ad: "FREE COFFEE GRINDER when you try the world's freshest coffee beans." Note we have product advertising—these beans are not ordinary coffee beans but the "world's freshest." We find later in the ad that in addition to being the freshest, the beans are the "world's rare and legendary coffees." They consist of the "light and lively flavors of the Costa Rica Tres Rios region . . . the intense heartiness of the mountain highlands of Kenya . . . the tanginess of the lush island fields of Papua New Guinea." Here then are claims for the product, ethos claims identifying credibility with exotic coffee-growing regions. But the greater appeal in this particular ad is a logos appeal. This is not always the case in print advertising where logos appeals are often not developed. But here in larger type and at the beginning of the ad appears the self-interested argument of something for nothing: the free coffee grinder when the purchaser samples four whole bean coffees "for only $18.95 (the grinder alone is worth $20!)." That argument is repeated at the end: "So why not take advantage of this opportunity to sample four of the world's rich and legendary coffees for only $18.95 . . . and get a free Bosch grinder!" Note that the question ends not with a question mark but with an exclamation point, thus reinforcing the appeal to suspend disbelief. Pathos is not explicit in the ad, but clearly the advertiser has researched the emotions of the potential market—the ad appears in the upscale and ever fashion oriented magazine *The New Yorker*.

Audio media are also widely used for mass advertising. Radio is a principal medium but so too is the telephone. In print advertising, as noted above, the relative emphasis is upon the word. The logos appeal may be muted, yet the overall target of print advertising is the consumer's mind with a capacity to weigh and sift through reasons, evidence, and arguments. In audio advertising the emphasis is upon sound; the appeal is to the consumer's ear and the capacity to imagine and feel emotions (pathos). Radio broadcasters, in an effort to increase the amount of advertising on radio in competition with print and with television, formulated an imaginative way to market the medium. The principal ad of that campaign revolved about the theme, "I *saw* it on the radio." The ad consisted of a conversation between A and B. A tells B of a product, idea, or event. B claims already to know about it because "I saw it on the radio." A is struck with disbelief. "What do you mean, you saw it on the radio?" B asks A to play along and imagine all the things that can be "seen" on the radio in response to sounds: an ocean lapping against the shore, a bird in flight, a sun-drenched beach. The promotion appeals more to imagination (pathos) than argument (logos) or credibility (ethos). In fact it overrides argument and tests credulity. Needless to say, however, in the end A suspends disbelief, and finds B's appeal credulous, for B too can "see it on the radio." Thus do audio ads appeal to the "mind's eye," that is, the ear.

The *visual* advertising media are many and varied. They include, among others, pictures, displays, clothes, buildings, and all manner of appearances—not merely television or film media. The appeal is to the eye as well as mind and/or ear; hence, we might assume a balancing of ethical, pathetic, and logical emphases. Such is not the case, at least with respect to televised and filmed visuals. For instance, Root says that "the appeal to pathos in television advertising is likely to be stronger than the appeal to logos."[15] A case in point is that televised ads frequently ask viewers to identify products with family and a love of children (how frequently do we see families, elderly couples, kids, or smitten teenagers pouring in to enjoy the familial love of a McDonald's Big Mac or a Burger King Whopper?) We suspect the appeal to ethos is also greater than to logos. Whether employing product, image, or position advertising, advertisers strive to make the marketed auto tire, oat bran cereal, athletic shoe, or whatever appear incredible, not credible. Incredible in depicting that the product differs in some significant way in a material, solidary, or expressive fashion from its competitors. The credible claim, of course, is that the product does not so differ.

Entrepreneurs thus create and sustain viable markets for products, people, ideas, causes (even lifestyles, as we shall see in Chapter 6) through differing advertising strategies and appeals. In incorporating such strategies and appeals mass advertising joins campaign, bureaucratic, and diplomatic propaganda in shaping the character of the new propaganda of the age. The bond between mass advertising and new propaganda is particularly close in the marketing of political candidates and causes, as we shall now see.

TELEVISED POLITICAL ADVERTISING: MARKETING POLITICS THROUGH NEW PROPAGANDA

As we saw in Chapter 4, propaganda has played a prominent role in election campaigns throughout the history of the republic. We also noted the striking shift from earlier methods of campaign propaganda, as exemplified by our discussion of the Whig campaign in 1840, to the use of new propaganda, as in George Bush's 1988 presidential campaign. Although paying to advertise candidates takes numerous forms—leaflets, newspapers and newsmagazines, posters, song books, buttons, banners, torchlit parades, films in movie houses, radio commercials, and even the log cabin whiskey bottles of 1840—the most prominent medium for political advertising today is television. Therefore, it is televised political advertising that will be our focus in this discussion. Moreover, since the evolution of political advertising has been traced many times, we limit our discussion primarily to the arrival of the new propaganda in televised political advertising.[16]

We restrict our discussion even more. Political scientists and communication scholars have undertaken meticulous research projects, written hundreds of articles, and published myriad weighty tomes since 1952 analyzing the content of televised political ads and how voters respond.[17] Beyond noting (1) that the overall conclusion of such research is that the conditions under which particular ad campaigns succeed or fail vary widely, (2) that the precise effects of TV ads on voters is difficult to measure and to generalize about beyond specific campaigns, (3) that competing ad campaigns frequently cancel one another out, (4) that ads are but one of many intersecting forces that move voters in elections, and (5) that TV ads have other purposes in a campaign than simply to win votes— such as to "show the flag" and thus raise the morale of one's campaign workers—we shall not endeavor to review that vast literature. It suffices to say that televised political advertising is key to contemporary campaigning but not the overriding factor in victory or defeat or even the sole means of propagating candidates and ideas.

Prior to the TV era of politics a chief method of campaigning for public office was for the candidate or a party precinct worker to canvass neighborhoods by going door to door to visit personally with potential voters. Today the candidate and/or candidate's representative is replaced by the TV set. Indeed, candidates now boast that campaigning on television is "like having a precinct worker in every home." Candidates for every possible office, from school boards to the "leader of the free world," take to the video airways each campaign season. Depending on the office sought, locale, numbers of voters contacted, tightness of the race, and a host of related factors, candidates average spending one-half to more than three-fourths of their entire campaign budgets on TV advertising. Such propagation of candidates via TV ads is worldwide, just as commonplace in South America, Australia, various nations in Europe, Asia, and Africa as in the United States or Canada. Moreover, candidates are not alone in being sold through televised ads. Political parties use TV commercials to invite people to join, special interests use television to advertise their positions on all manner of controversial issues, and—as we described in Chapter 4—government bureaucratic agencies use public service announcements (PSAs) and other commercials on behalf of various causes (Only *you* can prevent forest fires), or the agency itself (Be . . . all that you can be, find your future in the Army!). Given the number of candidates, interests, and causes using the marketing propaganda of television, it is only a small exaggeration to say that at any given moment somewhere in the world some TV political ad is being broadcast.

Political Product Advertising

We are now in the fifth decade of televised political advertising. The first election using TV commercials was in a U.S. Senate election in 1950. However, it was in the presidential election of 1952 that TV ads became a prominent feature of campaigning. The Republican candidate, General Dwight ("Ike") Eisenhower, possessed a distinguished World War II military record, indeed was regarded as a war hero. Recall that the 1950s was a period of product advertising and Republican campaign strategists did not think his admirable military background and war heroics alone could sell Ike as a uniquely qualified *political* statesman. Moreover, Ike-the-Product bore the brand label "Republican" in a nation where members of the electorate that identified with either political party thought of themselves as Democrat over Republican by a 57 to 34 percent margin.

In short, Eisenhower as product and brand possessed ethos assets, but noticeable logos deficits as well. Republicans sought the aid of two advertising professionals, Rosser Reeves, partner in the advertising firm of Ted Bates and Company, and Carroll Newton of the ad firm of Batten, Barton, Durstine, and Osborn (BBD&O). As the saying goes, the rest was history. Reeves, the man behind Anacin's "FAST, FAST, FAST RELIEF," developed a series of 20- and 60-second ads around the slogan It's Time for a Change (a change from two decades of Democratic control of the White House). In two series of spots, "The Man from Abilene" and "Eisenhower Answers America," the product-candidate appeared with unique qualities—warmth, conviction, experience, and a "commonsense" grasp of specific issues. Democrats countered with their own ad campaign created by the Joseph Katz agency, but Democrat ads were few in number and emphasized the brand label, Democrat, more than the product, candidate Adlai Stevenson. Typical of Democratic ads was "The Wallet" spot depicting a man asked to go through his wallet to discover why he should vote Democrat; the wallet contained money, a Social Security card, a photo of the house he owned, and his secure family—all belongings that derived from the Democrats having saved the nation from Republican economic depression. The ad made Stevenson an afterthought.

Political Image Advertising

As with commercial advertising, political marketing after the 1950s began to incorporate image ads. Material differences between candidates respecting backgrounds, experience, and issues received less emphasis; the promise of solidary rewards emanating from candidates' personalities became the package in which material promises were wrapped. A popular cigarette of the period, Marlboro, was marketed not by specifying how it differed materially from competitors, but with a jingle about how its tobacco was packaged: "You've got a lot to like with a Marlboro, Filter, Flavor, Flip Top Box." The flip top box had its solidary appeal: it could be flipped open to offer a Marlboro to a friend or a stranger, or to court a fair maiden or handsome man. Packaging thus provided a social image and an ethos appeal, that is, the more attractive the package, the more credible the cigarette.

So too it was with political advertising. Consider, for example, TV ads in John Kennedy's 1960 presidential campaign. Kennedy had ethos problems. One was his wealth. How could a man with so much money care about ordinary people? Another was his religion. He was a Roman Catholic in a nation that had never elected one of his faith to the presidency. If he were president, would his loyalty be to America, or to Rome? To deal with these problems Kennedy's advertising consultants developed a breakthrough in political advertising, namely, they filmed commercials on location and framed Kennedy speaking, greeting, and brushing up to ordinary people. This was a promise of solidary benefits. In one ad the heir to Kennedy family wealth talks about unemployment with coal miners *inside the mine*—in a setting so natural the miners are largely unconcerned about the camera's presence. In another spot, a woman in West Virginia stridently questions Kennedy's religious qualifications; the candidate responds forthrightly and with intense conviction. And catch the solidary sizzle in the Kennedy steak in his campaign song: "Marchin' down to Washington to shake the hand of President Kennedy. Marchin' down to Washington, like we used to do."

Political Position Advertising

Product/brand advertising and image advertising were, as we have seen, joined in commercial marketing by position advertising. So too did position advertising enter politics. Positioning involves creating new markets for products, goods, services, and so on by designing ad campaigns that permit people to express their individual hopes, fears, wants, and needs; such ads stress pathetic, emotional appeals over those of logos or ethos. The textbook case, after which many campaigns are still patterned, came in the 1976 presidential campaign. A virtually unknown former governor of Georgia sought the Democratic nomination for president. Jimmy Carter (dubbed "Jimmy Who?" in the press) announced his bid. His better known competitors all sought to distinguish themselves from one another as being more or less liberal or conservative. Carter's pollster Pat Caddell advised the candidate to avoid the liberal/conservative continuum. Polls indicated voters were disenchanted with all politicians, liberal *and* conservative. On advice of his pollster Carter positioned himself on an entirely different dimension, that of trust/distrust. Advertising that he would "never lie to the American people," would be a "President you can trust," and that he wanted America to have a "government as good as its people," Carter appealed to what was in voters' minds, concerns they expressed through their selection of his candidacy in victorious early statewide primaries that led to the nomination and to the White House.

Types of Political Ads

Whether the strategies be those of product/brand, image, or position advertising, contemporary political ads are of a variety of types. In a nationwide study of TV ads for Republican candidates for the U.S. Senate in 1984, J. Gregory Payne and Robert Baukus found that "attack" ads aimed at discrediting opponents and "argument" ads regarding candidates' stands on issues were predominant, while "ID" ads, that is, ads giving voters a sense of who the candidate is, were less frequent. "Resolution" ads in which the candidate sums up thoughts to the voters are rare.[18] These findings document a trend discovered by other analysts of political advertising, namely that political commercials have grown more negative in recent elections.

Communication analysts Larry David Smith and Anne Johnston Wadsworth offer a typology of political advertising emphasizing the dramatic features characteristic of the new propaganda.[19] Recognizing that commercial and political ads frequently use narratives, that is, they tell stories as entertaining ways to appeal to consumers/voters, the analysts exploit a scheme borrowed from critic Kenneth Burke for classifying dramas, narratives, and stories. The epic, tragedy, and comedy are "positive" story lines. Epics portray candidates in heroic guises, have a panoramic scope, and make the character dominant in any setting. The Marlboro Man in Marlboro Country is such an epic ad. In a random sample of more than 200 of the 806 ads televised in the presidential election campaigns from 1952 to 1984, 59 percent provided an epic rendering of the candidate. Tragedies stress human limits, but emphasize a character's courage and dignity in coping with critical situations in spite of his or her "tragic flaws." A miniscule 1 percent of the Smith and Wadsworth sample involved a tragic story. Comedies point out human frailties and fallabilities, but the "fools" are lovable, their behavior admirable. No presidential ads examined were comic. "Negative" story lines consist of the elegy, satire, and burlesque. Elegies lament existing conditions but do not suggest improvement through heroic, tragic, or comedic effort; there is no promise of a positive resolution to problems. Of the presidential ads 35 percent were elegies. Satires attack and criticize weaknesses, weaknesses that are those of the satirist but that are displaced on those attacked. Attack ads and negative ads in campaigns fit this category; only 2 percent of the sample of presidential ads were satires. Burlesques also attack, but through exaggeration rather than biting subtlety as do satires. A mere 1 percent of the sampled ads were burlesques. By such a count, then, we might expect future political ads either to be largely tales of epic heroism (thus adapting to the "log cabin" and "rags to riches" myths described in Chapter 5) or elegiac laments, with surprisingly few satiric attacks on, or burlesques of, the opposition.

As noted, the above typology of political commercials takes account of the key role played by dramatization in promoting political candidates, groups, and causes. Dramas, of course, invite audience members to sit back and enjoy the show. But they do more. They provide audiences with opportunities to express and project their own inner desires and concerns through and upon the drama's leading characters. Dramas provide vicarious enjoyment and suffering that *involves* the audience in the show via entertainment. Interviewed by Bill Moyers for the 1986 PBS series "Walk Through the Twentieth Century," ad consultant Tony Schwartz was asked by Moyers if trying to get into audience members' minds in order to discover what might trigger a positive response to TV commercials constituted "manipulation" of the buyer or voter. Schwartz thought not. He preferred to call it "partipulation," that is, people participating in their own manipulation. If Schwartz is correct, the pathos and expressive appeals of position political advertising that constitute "partipulation" thus capitalize on what we have called suasion, the self-persuasion dimension of the new propaganda.

There are other features of contemporary political advertising that capitalize on new propaganda as well. On October 19, 1987, prices in stock markets around the world dropped drastically. Fears of another Great Depression like that of 1929 echoed in the news media. By October 21 a major brokerage firm had conducted telephone surveys of consumers to discover if there were changes in their projected spending. Finding such changes, the firm employed an ad agency to conduct an emergency campaign to bolster consumer confidence. Research plus advertising constitutes *reactive advertising*, a technique of new propaganda. Reactive advertising is now common in both commercial and political advertising. In election campaigns media consultants routinely create ads, conduct tracking polls (surveys of people's responses) on a nightly or weekly basis, assess the impact of their candidate's and the opposition's ads, and react accordingly by creating and airing new ads within days, even hours.

In her study of political advertising in the "new mass media elections" of the 1980s, Montague Kern specifies ways televised ads in the past decade differed from those in the previous decade of the seventies. The differences parallel those between traditional and newer forms of propaganda. Kern notes that political ads in the 1980s were "freighted with entertainment values and what are described as emotional appeals"; moreover, "the relevant metaphor for today's mass media campaign is the commercial message—that of 'touching someone.'" Emotional, pathetic, appeals in the 1980s used "ever more elegiac techniques to create a misty-eyed effect." Regardless of type of appeal, there was, says Kern, "referential advertising, which seeks to transfer affect-laden meaning to the candidate from a symbol that already has meaning to the viewer." What we have called brand appeals, such as party or special interest group labels, according to Kern have given way to "individually oriented" ads, the basis of convergent selectivity. Finally, and again very much in keeping with the new propaganda, Kern notes that the use of the "media blitz concept, which combines news and advertising efforts according to advertising principles" (not news principles) "is now the prevalent concept."[20]

Political ads—be they propagated on behalf of candidates, groups, governing or opposing institutions, or causes—are ubiquitous. They are planted and sown, or borne on the winds of television's airwaves, in the mental seedbeds of people throughout the globe.

They are an integral part of the political ideoculture of modern nations. No land is sanitized against the presence of the charm and guile that is mass advertising generally or political advertising in particular. Nor are seedbeds less conducive to propagation by another form of palaver, that is, public relations.

PUBLIC RELATIONS: MARKETING TRUST IN PEOPLE AND ORGANIZATIONS

Edward L. Bernays, who developed the Torches of Freedom Easter Day march on behalf of George Washington Hill's desire to expand the market for cigarette sales, was the first to make a full-time career being a public relations consultant. In that sense he was the father of modern public relations. However, attending the birth of the fledgling child of propaganda was someone else, Ivy Ledbetter Lee, whom we first met in Chapter 2 along with Bernays.

It was Lee who developed a public relations campaign to humanize the reputation of John D. Rockefeller, Sr. Until Lee's arrival, the creator of the Rockefeller fortune was depicted in the nation's press as an ogre, a robber baron, and even the "greatest criminal of his age" in some circles. As part of his vast financial empire Rockefeller owned the Colorado Mining Company. In 1913 the United Mine Workers sought to unionize the mines in Ludlow, Colorado, a company town of Colorado Mining. The Rockefeller management refused, and the miners went on strike. They built a tent city outside Ludlow, and 1,300 miners and their families set up house. On April 20, 1914, at the behest of Rockefeller interests, armed soldiers opened fire on the strikers with machine guns. Fifty-three persons died, including 13 children. The nation's press condemned Rockefeller. Here Lee, a newspaperman, enters the picture as a paid consultant bent on refurbishing the Rockefeller name.

Lee acted on several fronts. Two were particularly noteworthy. First, he churned out dozens of "fact sheets" explaining management's side of the strike issue. More importantly, he suggested that John D. Rockefeller, Jr., travel to what the press called "Bloody Ludlow," meet with the miners, get to know them, and show compassion for their families. He did. Photos of a concerned Rockefeller appeared on front pages of newspapers across the land. One newspaper headlined the visit with "Rockefeller Turns Hate to Love." Second, Lee worked on the reputation of Rockefeller, Sr. Rockefeller had always given large amounts of money to philanthropic causes. But he did so privately and anonymously. Lee urged him to make his charitable giving public. He did. Highly publicized was Rockefeller's "habit" of giving away dimes to children. Newspapers, magazines, and newsreels blossomed with favorable Rockefeller publicity. By the time the 97-year-old senior Rockefeller died he was eulogized in the press as a "Great Humanitarian."

Lee defined public relations (PR) as simply "the art of getting believed"; Bernays defined PR in the title of one of his many books on the subject as "the engineering of consent."[21] From "Bloody Ludlow" origins public relations has grown to a worldwide industry. Rare is the hamlet of any size on the globe that does not have one or more PR firms plying the engineering of consent. No government on earth is without its public relations personnel. Colleges and universities offer programs of study for students wishing to become public relations professionals. Such programs bear various titles—training in "public relations," in "persuasion," and the current vogue, in "issue management" (but never, *never* in "propaganda"). The Public Relations Society of America (PRSA) embodies that professional view in its annual conferences, its guidelines for ethical practices, professional journals, and its PR campaigns on behalf of PR. Each year new textbooks vie to capture a piece of the market in public relations training. And, as we shall see in Chapter 6, those same colleges and universities that train people in public relations techniques have their own public relations campaigns—to raise finances, build public support, recruit the Kens and Barbies, market athletic programs, and maintain a sense of a unique identity among faculty and students.

An activity as far-flung as PR is, of course, bound to have practitioners, supporters, and critics who differ over what public relations is *really* about. We saw in Chapter 4 that campaign, bureaucratic, and diplomatic propaganda evolved from earlier forms to those of the new propaganda. As noted above, the propaganda of mass and political advertising developed into newer forms. Such is also the case with public relations. Consider, for example, definitions of what propaganda *really* is. Straightforward definitions such as Lee's art of getting believed or Bernays's engineering of consent no longer suffice. Reflect on the following definition that endeavors to include all the major functions of the modern, new public relations: "Public relations is a communication function of management through which organizations adapt to, alter, or maintain their environment for the purpose of achieving organizational goals."[22] Each term in the definition specifies a key aspect of PR:

- *Communication function* suggests that communication is but one, yet a vital one, of several organization activities: developing, formulating, manufacturing, and selling products, policies, or people (college students, for example); hiring and firing workers; acquiring and holding resources; and so on.

- *Management* designates that specialists working under managerial supervision conduct public communication. A star football player may win the Heisman Trophy, a professor the Nobel Prize, a student a Rhodes scholarship. University PR staffs propagate the good news. Or the football program may be put on probation, a professor arrested for shoplifting, or a student suspended. University PR on behalf of college management repairs the damage to the institution's reputation.

- *Organization* implies that PR operates primarily on behalf of organized activities: American Tobacco Company, the Rockefeller empire, United Way, the Democratic party, and so on. The assumption is that what is good for the organization is good for its members, and what is bad for a member may reflect badly on the organization. Allegations in 1989 that baseball superstar Pete Rose gambled on baseball were poor public relations for the game of baseball; Rose's suspension from the game for life protected the integrity of the game, said typical PR copy.

- *Adaption, Alteration, Maintenance of Environment* emphasize that organizations exist in social, economic, legal, political, technological, and diversified contexts. PR uses ideas and information to assist in adapting to changing contexts (Lee's campaign for the Rockefellers), altering them (Bernays's expanding the cigarette market by his Torches of Freedom), or maintaining things as they are—as when a university solicits its alumni for funds to "continue our mission of excellence."

• *Goals* of an organization and its public relations effort ''are not reciprocally related,'' say some students of public relations; ''public relations goals are the consequence of organizational goals not the reverse.''[23] Simply put, the organization is the dog, the PR the tail, and the tail should not wag the dog. As we shall see momentarily, however, sometimes it does, and with unexpected consequences.

George Does Dallas: PR in U.S. Politics

In 1948 the American Medical Association (AMA) had a problem. Democrats in the White House and in Congress proposed that the federal government adopt a national health insurance system. There were various proposals but the gist was that a federally sponsored program would provide medical, dental, hospital, and nursing care; payroll taxes on employers and employees would raise the necessary funds. The AMA viewed this as a threat: doctors caring for patients would be paid for services by the program, implying to the AMA the dire possibility that physicians would become federal employees collecting fees or salaries from government and unable to charge as they desired. To meet the threat the AMA hired a public relations firm, Whitaker & Baxter Inc., one of the first to involve itself in campaigns for political clients. The PR campaign, dubbed the National Education Campaign, centered on labeling the proposal for federal health insurance as ''Socialized Medicine.'' The AMA's alternative, largely maintenance of the status quo, was ''The Voluntary Way.'' Through a variety of techniques Whitaker & Baxter pitted ''Socialized Medicine'' versus ''The Voluntary Way.'' One of the most celebrated involved an appeal to pathos as the basic theme of the campaign. It consisted of placing in doctor, hospital, and clinic waiting rooms across the nation a poster portraying a kindly doctor leaning over the bedside of a sick child. There was a caption: ''Keep politics out of this picture!'' The message below read, ''When the life or health of a loved one is at stake, hope lies in the devoted service of your Doctor. Would you change this picture?'' Admonishing that ''compulsory health insurance is political medicine,'' the poster advised against placing ''a politician'' between ''you and your Doctor,'' and against binding ''your family's health in red tape.'' Medical care would become ''inferior.'' Yes, ''you have a right to prepaid medical care—of your own choice.'' Patients should consult ''your Doctor'' for ''budget-basis health protection'' as well as for treatment of organic maladies.[24]

The National Education Campaign as a PR strategy contributed to the delay of federally sponsored health insurance of any kind for well over a decade, and there is still no nationwide plan for all citizens. It taught special interest organizations the benefits of a well-orchestrated PR campaign. Elected politicians quickly learned the merits of hiring professional public relations personnel on their own behalf. Today public officials, and those who aspire to public office at all levels of American politics, routinely engage in sophisticated PR campaigns. Few campaigns, however, are as continuous as those orchestrated by the White House to promote the institution and the man that is the U.S. presidency. We alluded to the nature of such presidential PR in Chapter 4 in considering, for example, how presidents use summit meetings with world leaders for propaganda purposes. Let us now examine a case of a full-ranging PR effort typical of every week, every day in the life of the PR president.

On November 10–11, 1989, the seventy-first anniversary of the signing of the Armistice ending World War I (called at the time the Great War), President George Bush was in Dallas, Texas, for a total of 23 hours and 20 minutes. There were three major public appearances: a speech at a fund-raising dinner to pay off the campaign debts of an outgoing Republican governor, a speech before the National Realtors Association convention, and a speech dedicating a newly unveiled Texas Vietnam Veterans Memorial. Each appearance made nationwide and worldwide news. Here was a president starring in three dramatic sketches: as politician, as statesman, and as memorializer. Orchestrating these sketches so as to make them appear spontaneous required the energies of more than 100 federal government employees (not even counting the president's Secret Service protectors or U.S. Air Force personnel detailed to fly the presidential jet *Air Force One*); several hundred local government officials and employees; and volunteers from as far away as Waterloo, Iowa. Costs to the federal taxpayer were $27,757 for *Air Force One*, $13,182 for a cargo plane and backup, $27,000 for 150–200 hotel rooms, per diem expenses of at least $1,830 for 61 aides—not to mention salaries of federal and military employees. The city of Dallas shouldered expenses for police and fire protection.

Such a public relations drama involving a cast of thousands and sparing no expense can scarcely be put into production overnight. And, like the seemingly countless performances of PR presidents, this one was not. A casual remark by candidate Bush in 1988 to Governor Bill Clements that President Bush would come to Texas to assist the governor in retiring his 1986 campaign debts resulted in Clements's request in July 1989 that the president deliver. A month earlier, Bush's advisers, shopping around for a Veterans Day event to showcase the president, received an invitation from the Vietnam Memorial Fund of Texas; the National Realtors Association, which gives a standing invitation to presidents to appear at the national convention, would be meeting in Dallas also on Veterans Day. Thus, everything said "Go!" to the entrepreneurial White House. In October a "preadvance" party of security agents, aides from the White House Communications Agency, and a team of Bush's speech writers traveled to Dallas to scout the scene. The official public announcement of the trip came November 1, the advance team for final arrangements arrived in Dallas on November 3–6, and on November 10 George Bush, his wife Barbara, and the presidential PR entourage touched down at Love Field to "do Dallas."

The production team for the PR drama, "George Does Dallas," left little to chance. Each of the president's moments were minutely choreographed and printed in confidential booklets, along with diagrams. Thus, as the saying goes, each member of the presidential performance team would "have the same hymnal, sing from the same sheet of music." White House stewards arrived to prepare meals. The city of Dallas checked county jails, alerting security agents to anyone who might be up to mischief; detailed a special sniper unit, motorcycle officers, and a K-9 unit for duty; had the fire department ensure that all facilities where the president would be were hazard-free; and took precautions to secure all necessary medical and hospital facilities should anything go awry, as it had when President John F. Kennedy visited Dallas 26 years earlier.

Three presidential speeches (eight pages typed double-spaced, running 14–16 minutes) were drafted, redrafted, and revised. The five-person speech-writing unit carefully researched a Dallas woman, Connie McWright, who had lost two sons in Vietnam, so that the president could personalize his references at the Vietnam Memorial. And on the flight to Dallas an aide added a 3-minute, 10-second portion to the speech intended for National

Realtors—a speech whose chief topic was housing—so that Bush could respond to the dramatic opening of the Berlin Wall that was the chief item in all headlines worldwide. One aide had the responsibility of carrying the presidential speeches, and in three forms— one on four-by-six-inch white cards in capital letters; one on a computer disk; and one on 8 1/2-by-11-inch papers to be read should the TelePrompTer fail.

The presidential visit to Dallas as a public relations spectacular was not unique for Bush who, as we saw in Chapter 4, has employed such travel often. Nor has it been unique to the American presidency for the past three decades. President Dwight Eisenhower was the first to travel by jet but John F. Kennedy ushered in the jet age presidency. After Kennedy, presidential travel has become routine. The White House now has a budget of $100,000 annually for the president's travel and more than six times that amount for the travel of his staff. Add Secret Service and Air Force travel expenses and it is clear that there is a major outlay for presidential PR in travel alone. (A new presidential jetliner provided to the Bush White House cost taxpayers $391 million.)

Whether such presidential PR influences how people perceive the office and its occupant in specific ways is difficult to measure.[25] But the new propaganda of presidential PR is most certainly, as communication scholar Roderick Hart has found, a distinguishing mark of the American presidency in the age of new propaganda. Indeed, he finds that the "sound" of leadership, that is, presidential palaver, has replaced leadership itself.[26] Perhaps, however, the PR sound has not replaced leadership so much as it increasingly drives political policies and outcomes. Such may be the case with another example of presidential PR, Mikhail Gorbachev's *glasnost* in the Soviet Union.

Gorby Does Europe: PR in Falling Bloc Politics

When Mikhail Gorbachev came to power in the Soviet Union in 1985, six Eastern European nations were tightly bound to the USSR economically and militarily; moreover their political lives and fortunes were also linked to events in Moscow. East Germany, Poland, Hungary, Romania, Czechoslovakia, and Bulgaria had been ruled by orthodox Communist governments virtually since the end of World War II. For almost two decades peoples of the Eastern bloc had been inundated with propaganda from two sides. Official Communist propaganda intentionally sought to buttress each regime, propagating calls for active support or at least popular acquiescence. From outside the Eastern bloc, principally via shortwave services of the United States, Great Britain, and elsewhere came another propaganda line—that peace and prosperity reigned in the Free World. Let freedom and reform be the rallying cry for the enslaved behind the iron curtain. There were a few notable uprisings—for example, East Berlin in 1953, Hungary and Poland in 1956, Czechoslovakia in 1968—and anti-Communist propagandists took credit for sparking them. That the revolts were put down by military force, claimed anti-Communists, did not negate the effectiveness of their propaganda. The official Communist line differed, arguing that the "truth" about Western ways and intentions propagated via Communist propaganda made all the difference in keeping Eastern Europe in line.

While the propaganda of the cold war continued, something else was evolving. A genie was born in the Communist bottle, a bottle that Mikhail Gorbachev's PR campaign of *glasnost* would uncork. By 1989 the genie, a new propaganda, would be striding with ease across Eastern Europe, released not so much by the intent of Communist or anti-

Communist propaganda but by the unintended consequences of television's penetration of the Eastern bloc. To understand how a new form of propaganda helped provoke striking reforms in Eastern Europe, including the collapse of the Berlin Wall, we need first to consider *glasnost*.

As political scientist Ellen Mickiewicz has written, "*glasnost*, the new openness and public discussion [in the Soviet Union after Gorbachev's rise to power], is a media phenomenon."[27] Gorbachev recognized that to secure his power base he must expand the scope of the Communist elite that had ruled the Soviet Union since the days of Joseph Stalin and, more recently, Leonid Brezhnev. Older, hardline, orthodox Communists unfriendly to Gorbachev must be replaced by an expanded ruling corps of younger, reform-minded supporters. Gorbachev embarked on a program of reform of economic, political, and social institutions called *perestroika*. To foment institutional change Gorbachev turned to the mass media. *Glasnost* assigned a new role to Soviet mass media, the revolutionary role of building public support for change on behalf of Gorbachev and his regime. *Glasnost* thus became a PR tool with domestic aims of reducing the legitimacy of long-standing Soviet institutions Gorbachev regarded as obstacles to reform and of legitimizing newly created institutions by appeals for public support. *Glasnost*'s foreign policy aim was to fashion a new image of the Soviet Union in the world. Mickiewicz quotes Gorbachev's remarks in *Pravda*, September 25, 1988: "Publish everything. There should be a pluralism of opinions. But the thrust should be such that the line of *perestroika* [and] the cause of socialism are defended and strengthened."[28] Ivy Lee or Edward Bernays could scarcely have said it so well for a client's cause.

Although all Soviet mass media were subject to the openness of *glasnost*, Soviet television became a particularly important vehicle of the new propaganda of Gorbachev's public relations effort. A key Soviet observer of *glasnost* commented, "The TV image is everything."[29] It is the most genuine of "mass" media in the Soviet Union, spanning 11 time zones; with 93 percent of Soviet citizens watching, TV programming reaches as many as 200 million viewers. TV viewing is a primary leisure activity, replacing movies and radio listening in popularity. A popular television program, "12th Floor," became with *glasnost* a centerpiece of debate and offered a forum voicing the dissatisfaction of Soviet youth with older ways of doing things. And it all may have had the desired effect. When the old-line party leaders attempted to oust Gorbachev in 1991, they seized the mass media temporarily; but the promise of *glasnost* had spread and rooted with significant parts of the population, who resisted and disbelieved the propaganda line of the party coup. The coup quickly collapsed, Gorbachev was restored, and *glasnost* continued to propagate far beyond Gorbachev's original and modest seeding of new life in an old and worn land.

Public relations, as with any form of propaganda, may become a force in its own right, soon going far beyond what the original PR campaign may have envisioned. To employ our metaphor of propaganda as the propagation of ideas, a PR campaign can become a strong wind that sweeps everything in front of it aside as it propagates new ideas in seedbeds once not receptive to them. *Glasnost*, especially in its televised aspects, became such an imperative. In the world of suspended belief that is mass advertising, public relations, and the new propaganda, "seeing is believing," even if what one sees is not so and not believable. Throughout all regions of the Soviet Union, bordering states, and the Eastern bloc viewers watched things never seen before: news coverage of natural disasters, a major earthquake in 1985 and another in 1988, and nuclear disaster at Chernobyl in 1986; journalists criticizing government policies; and private citizens expressing their grievances openly. When the 1989 Congress of People's Deputies proceedings were carried live on television, the audience was huge, involved, and enthralled. Television portrayed a spectacle of Communists in open debate, even challenging Gorbachev without hesitation.

Witnessing all of this, citizens of Eastern European nations began to ask, "If there, why not here?" Even without televised *glasnost* to draw them, East Europeans had increasingly been influenced by other telecasts, this time from the West, especially West Germany. News broadcasts, documentaries, entertainment programs—all pictured a people to the west of the iron curtain free, prosperous, and happy. Hearing of such things on broadcasts of the Voice of America was one thing, but actually seeing designer jeans, Reeboks, and Rolex watches worn by Western youths was quite another. Conditioned for decades to disbelieve in such things, they suspended those beliefs and acted. The spores of reform windborne by television found increasingly receptive seedbeds. In a matter of weeks in 1989 Poland, Hungary, East Germany, Czechoslovakia, and Bulgaria moved toward institutional reforms and free elections. By the end of the 1980s *Playboy* and *Penthouse* magazines—formerly symbols behind the iron curtain of the decadence of capitalism—were sold on newsstands in East Berlin and Budapest. The new PR propagation meant that the new ideoculture of these countries could not be forced back into the old habits of harvesting bitter political fruit.

IT SLICES, DICES, GRATES, AND SHREDS!

The above claim is made in an ad for the "Mini Wonder," a kitchen marvel that, we are told, is "a juicer and garnisher, too," and the base "is also a covered refrigerator container." Such "puffery" (exaggerated claims for a product) is so common in contemporary advertising that we should not be surprised to find a U.S. president traveling about the world with a similar message about his administration: "It binds, it heals, it protects, it enlightens" (George Bush proclaiming a Kinder and Gentler America, a War on Drugs, and an Education Presidency). Nor is it any longer startling to find a Soviet president traveling about the world hawking the *glasnost* and *perestroika* of his reign: "It tells all, it reforms, it disarms, it provides a common home." Yet, in spite of the remarkable changes that have occurred in recent years, one cannot help but wonder as the world faces the seemingly intractable problems of the twenty-first century whether the "covered refrigerator containers" of both administrations are indeed being filled by political advertising and public relations, or simply emptied. The coming century may not be a continuing age of propaganda, a theme we will return to in the conclusion.

This chapter showed how propaganda activities usually associated with economic marketing—advertising and public relations—have political, and indeed cultural, uses. In particular, we wished to point out the extent to which politics is now a matter of marketing, defining problems as something to be handled through adroit propaganda. Yet we also noted that there are distinct limits to that kind of approach. As economic advertisers have long noted, if the dogs don't like the dog food, no amount of marketing will sell it if the dogs won't eat it. You take away from this chapter new understanding of what is going on in advertising and public relations, such as the reliance on Aristotelian concepts in order to sell products and the attempt to shore up a presidential image through designed trips and appearances. Now we want to turn to another range of ideocultures, namely the marketing of popular culture.

NOTES

1. N. M. Tilley, *The R. J. Reynolds Tobacco Company* (Chapel Hill: University of North Carolina Press, 1985).
2. Vernon L. Parrington, *Main Currents in American Thought* (New York: Harcourt, Brace, 1930), p. 23.
3. Donald Kaul, "A Nation for Sale," *Kansas City Times*, November 11, 1989, p. A-23.
4. Robert H. Salisbury, "An Exchange Theory of Interest Groups," *Midwest Journal of Political Science* 13 (February 1969): 1–32.
5. Robert H. Salisbury, "Interest Groups," in Fred L. Greenstein and Nelson W. Polsby, eds., *Handbook of Political Science*, vol. 4, *Nongovernmental Politics* (Reading, MA: Addison-Wesley, 1975), p. 193.
6. Herbert Blumer, "The Mass, the Public, and Public Opinion," in Bernard Berelson and Morris Janowitz, eds., *Reader in Public Opinion and Communication* (New York: Free Press, 1966), p. 45. See also Gustave Le Bon, *The Crowd* (New York: Viking, 1960), especially chaps. 3 and 4.
7. William Stephenson, *The Play Theory of Mass Communication* (Chicago: University of Chicago Press, 1967), p. 34.
8. Ibid., p. 35.
9. Bill Moyers, "Consuming Images," PBS series *The Public Mind* (WNET, Boston, broadcast 1989).
10. Al Ries and Jack Trout, *Positioning: The Battle for Your Mind* (New York: McGraw-Hill, 1981), p. 27.
11. Ibid., p. 34.
12. Ibid., p. 37.
13. Ibid., p. 40.
14. Robert L. Root, Jr., *The Rhetorics of Popular Culture: Advertising, Advocacy, and Entertainment* (New York: Greenwood, 1987).
15. Ibid., p. 57.
16. For a brief, concise summary see Kathleen Hall Jamieson, "The Evolution of Political Advertising in America," in Lynda Lee Kaid, Dan Nimmo, and Keith R. Sanders, eds., *New Perspectives on Political Advertising* (Carbondale: Southern Illinois University Press, 1986), pp. 1–20.
17. See, as examples, Frank Biocca, ed., *Television and Political Advertising*, 2 vols. (Hillside, NJ: Lawrence Erlbaum, 1990); Kathleen Hall Jamieson, *Packaging the Presidency* (Oxford: Oxford University Press, 1984); Richard Joslyn, *Mass Media and Elections* (Reading, MA: Addison-Wesley, 1984); Dorothy Davidson Nesbit, *Videostyle* (Knoxville: University of Tennessee Press, 1988); Thomas E. Patterson and Robert D. McClure, *The Unseeing Eye* (New York: Putnam, 1976); Thomas E. Patterson, *The Mass Media Election* (New York: Praeger, 1980).
18. J. Gregory Payne and Robert A. Baukus, "Trend Analysis of the 1984 GOP Senatorial Spots," *Political Communication and Persuasion* 5 (3): 161–178. See also Michael Pfau and Henry C. Kenski, *Attack Politics* (New York: Praeger, 1990).

19. Larry David Smith and Anne Johnston Wadsworth, "Burke's Sociological Criticism Applied to Political Advertising: An Anecdotal Taxonomy of Political Commercials," in Frank Biocca, ed., *Television and Political Advertising*, vol. 2: *Signs, Codes, and Myths* (Hillside, NJ: Lawrence Erlbaum, 1990), 201–222.
20. Montague Kern, *30-Second Politics: Political Advertising in the Eighties* (New York: Praeger, 1989), pp. 207–211.
21. Edward L. Bernays, *The Engineering of Consent* (Norman: University of Oklahoma Press, 1955).
22. Vincent Hazleton, Jr., and Larry W. Long, "Concepts for Public Relations Education, Research, and Practice: A Communication Point of View," *Central States Speech Journal* 39 (Summer 1988): 82.
23. Ibid., p. 83.
24. For a detailed account of the Whitaker & Baxter National Education Campaign consult Stanley Kelley, Jr., *Professional Public Relations and Political Power* (Baltimore: The John Hopkins Press, 1966), chap. 3.
25. Judy Vanslyke Turk and Fred K. Beard, "To Know Us Is to Love Us: Do Public Relations Messages Really Make a Difference?" *Southwestern Mass Communication Journal* (1987): 80–92.
26. See Roderick P. Hart, *The Sound of Leadership* (Chicago: University of Chicago Press, 1987).
27. Ellen Mickiewicz, "Mobilization and Reform: Political Communication Policy under Gorbachev," *PS* 21 (June 1989): 199. On the consequences of *glasnost* see also Richard Stites, "Soviet Popular Culture in the Gorbachev Era," *The Harriman Institute Forum* 2 (March 1989): 1–8; and Alec Nove, *Glasnost in Action* (New York: Longman, 1989).
28. Alexander Yakovlev, quoted in Mickiewicz, ibid., p. 204.
29. Ellen Mickiewicz, *Split Signals: Television and Politics in the Soviet Union* (New York: Oxford University Press, 1988).

CHAPTER 6

The Marketing of Popular Culture
Propagating Personae, News, and Education

This second part of the book relates the dimensions of propaganda as practiced in the contemporary world. In this chapter, we continue that inquiry by ranging over aspects of popular culture, all those forms of popular activity that large numbers of people find amusing or interesting. This may include celebrities, shows, news, and yes, schools. Propaganda brings people together as a "taste culture" that unites in interest of some popular object. Here you should become more aware of the practice of "hype," and how hype-artistry is central to the propagation of popular culture. Indeed, we shall speculate that such widespread popularization is another principle of the new propaganda that threatens to turn such "information services" as news and education into propaganda.

In the previous two chapters of this part of our inquiry, we looked at dimensions of the "plural cultures"—first, different ways in which propaganda palaver manifests itself in various political settings, and second, how propagated consumers (a role created by propaganda) do in fact consume the goods and services that propaganda presents for our delight and instruction. In this chapter, let us complete our look at these modern plural cultures by examining how personae (public celebrities), news (in which propaganda is interwoven), and yes, even education are marketed and indeed penetrated by propaganda values and practices. Once that task is completed, you should possess a firmer grasp of the sweep of propaganda in modern pluralistic cultures and then can move on to the analysis and critique of propaganda, essential for coping with these cultures that we all encounter.

MODERN PYGMALIONS

Joseph C. Rinelli is a name few Americans recognize. So too are Richard Guy and Rex Holt. Yet the three are master propagandists of the TV era. What they propagate is people, or more precisely, personae. *Persona* is a term borrowed from drama and literature. It re-

fers to a character in a dramatic or literary work. If we take seriously William Shakespeare's view (*As You Like It,* act 2, scene 7) that,

> All the world's a stage,
> And all the men and women merely players:
> They have their exits and their entrances;
> And one man in his time plays many parts,

then all of life is drama and each of us plays roles expressing our characters to ourselves
and to others.[1] Opportunities to manufacture and distribute personae are as common as the
manufacture and sale of the Barbie doll.

The personae created and propagated by Joe Rinelli, Richard Guy, and Rex Holt are
beauty pageant contestants and, above all, pageant winners: Miss Texas, Miss USA, and
Miss Universe. Beauty contests are a staple of popular culture throughout the world. One
of the oldest continuing pageants, the Miss America Pageant, has been promoted and ballyhooed for seven decades since the first winner was selected in 1921. The success of the
Miss America extravaganza has sparked many a rival pageant: Mrs. America, Miss Teen
Age America, and so on. In 1951 Miss America, Yolande Betbeze, refused to pose in a
swimsuit. The pageant's sponsor, Catalina Inc., a major swimsuit manufacturer, with-
drew support and helped launch the rival, global Miss Universe pageant. The concept was
simple: winners of national pageants would vie for the title of Miss Universe; in the
United States the national winner, Miss USA, would be selected from a competition
among state winners, in effect, making Miss USA coequal with Miss America as reigning
national beauty.

The Miss USA/Universe Pageant licenses individuals and/or groups within nations
and national subdivisions (the U.S. states in this country) to operate individual pageants
and competitions. In 1975 Richard Guy and Rex Holt formed GuyRex, the licensee of the
Miss Texas USA Pageant. GuyRex has made Miss Texas USA the preeminent statewide
beauty contest, far surpassing Miss Texas America and rivaling even the Miss USA Pageant itself. A chief reason for this has been Joe Rinelli. Rinelli recruits, trains, and promotes many Miss Texas USA candidates. His very first recruit won the state pageant in
1973, two years before GuyRex bought the franchise. Since then Rinelli has worked
closely with the licensees. Through 1988 Rinelli's recruits had won six of the last seven
Miss Texas USA titles; moreover, of five consecutive Miss Texas USA winners who went
on to win the Miss USA crown, four were Rinelli's candidates.

How does Rinelli create the personae of the Miss Texas/USA/Universe dramas? He
works annually with 60 "girls" (the term used by the pageant for contestants). He conducts recruitment sessions at colleges and modeling agencies, organizes local pageants,
and selects the most promising contestants. Rinelli supervises every detail of each contestant's performance: the selection of evening gowns and swimsuits; how to walk in high
heels without looking down; how to twist frontward and sideways simultaneously (try it!)
so as to model swimsuits to full advantage; the amount of water each contestant drinks; the
amount of sleep required for each; and how to become a convincing talker in interviews.
In the end, to be a "Rinelli Girl" is to be a precisely trained and propagated persona,
a perfected vision of loveliness and grace that Barbie herself would envy. (This modern

profession of "body management" is not confined just to female beauty contests: male muscle competitors often employ managers who train them in the art of self-presentation, and indeed, a whole industry exists to advise businesspersons, politicians, and people testifying in public as to how best to dress, speak, move, and act—all the histrionic skills necessary for "impression management.") In all cases, such figures are in a sense propagandists of performance art, creating and advising such personae as Miss Texas, movie stars, and Oliver North in his dramatic appearance before Congress and the country. Like Pygmalion and Professor Henry Higgins, experts like Joe Rinelli create new personae to present at modern courts wherein we may gaze upon and admire their performances.

What Rinelli does with beauty pageant contestants other specialists in new propaganda do in countless areas and ways of contemporary social and cultural life. In this chapter we examine a few of the areas and ways. We begin by examining the relationship between propaganda and popular culture; then we consider the role new propaganda plays in the marketing of people, information, and learning.

MARKETING THE SKIN: PROPAGANDA AND POPULAR CULTURE

"The Sun King," Louis XIV (1638–1715), had visions of making France superior to all other nations in every way. His financial advisor, Jean Baptiste Colbert, had responsibility for making the French economy self-sufficient. What did the French have, he thought, that no other nation had and that could be marketed at a profit to other nations? His answer was culture, or taste: "With our taste let us make war on Europe, and through fashion conquer the world."[2] Stuart Ewen, a student of popular culture, notes that Colbert's strategy was to "construct and communicate an aristocratic veneer."[3] That French culture was not necessarily superior to other cultures (Colbert thought it was) was not the point. What the French must do is market the illusion, the veneer, of superiority. That for four centuries they have been successful in propagating that veneer is summed up in the term *haute couture*, "high culture," a refined Gallic taste for fine art, music, fashion, and food and wine allegedly transcending lesser, more crass, desires and lusts. (On the other hand, the French greatly admire the comedy of Jerry Lewis.)

The reputed superiority of *haute couture*, a reputation achieved through propaganda, has been so taken for granted that only in recent years have scholars seriously regarded the tastes of the populace and masses worthy of investigation.[4] As recently as the 1960s an influential social critic was able to accept the superiority of *haute couture* without question, indeed even enhance the propagation of "high culture's" superiority. Writing in 1962 Dwight Macdonald argued that for the past two centuries Western culture consisted of two cultures, "High Culture," and a "novel kind that is manufactured for the market" (apparently ignoring Colbert's manufacturing and marketing of *haute couture*): "The latter may be called Mass Culture, or better Masscult, since it really isn't culture at all. Masscult is a parody of High Culture."[5]

High Culture, according to Macdonald, challenges audiences by informing, instructing, and enlightening them. High Culture respects standards in judging whether a cultural work is good or bad. These standards are applied by informed, sophisticated circles—composers judge the worth of musical compositions, artists the worth of paintings, sculptors of sculptures, fashion designers of fashion, writers of the written word, or, in sum, the intelligentsia evaluate the creations of the intelligentsia. Today we call this peer review. (For example, scholars, not the undergraduate students who actually read it, decide a textbook's worth.) By contrast, Masscult, wrote Macdonald, asks nothing of its audience and gives nothing; standards are those of the marketplace (does it sell?); and consumers decide a cultural product's worth. Somewhere between High Culture and Masscult Macdonald found room for a third culture, "Midcult." Midcult, like Masscult, derives from a standardized manufacturing formula (say a Barbara Cartland romance or a Robert Ludlum thriller) and has no standard of worth other than popularity. Unlike Masscult, however, Midcult proclaims to have the standards of High Culture when, in fact, "it waters them down and vulgarizes them."[6] Following Macdonald's categories, then, Shakespeare's *Hamlet* is High Culture, TV's "Knots Landing" is Masscult, and TV's "Lonesome Dove" is Midcult. Or, *The Federalist Papers* are High Culture; the *National Inquirer*, Masscult; and "60 Minutes," Midcult.

What Macdonald's distinctions teach is that culture, like beauty, is in the eye of the beholder. But, like beauty pageants, culture is also in the eye of the promoter. Reflect on Jacques Louis David (1748–1825), a *haute couture* artist famous for his paintings *Liberty Leading the People*, *The Death of Marat*, and others. What standards made David's paintings "art" when he produced them? Were they superior artistic standards? Perhaps. More than that, however, it was the standard of popularity that measured David's work. For David was a propagandist whose works provoked protests and revolt against the *ancien régime* prior to the French Revolution in 1789. After the Revolution the Emperor Napoleon exploited David's talents to create for the dictator a majestic, imperial, respected image—with the populace.

David was not the first or the last artist of High Culture whose initial success owed as much or more to popular approbation as to peer review. Shakespeare's audiences were made up of the Great Unwashed as well as the Rich and Famous. The point is twofold. First, multiple standards, peer and popular, enter into the evaluation of cultural creations. In this sense *all* culture is popular to some degree. Such distinctions as High, Mass, and Mid culture are notions propagated for their own sake, or the sake of those who draw them, not because culture as such is high, mass, or low. Second, since all culture has a popular base to it and since artists creating that culture rely on some degree of popular success to survive, there is a strong impetus for cultural entrepreneurs to create not only artistic objects but audiences to consume them.

Taste Cultures

We saw in Chapter 5 that entrepreneurs employ propaganda, promising benefits to potential followers/consumers in exchange for support. Cultural entrepreneurs do the same and use propaganda to create "taste cultures." A *taste culture* is a collection of individuals formed by the process of convergent selectivity described in Chapter 5. Its members share the same preferences, are frequently well informed on matters involving their expression of those preferences, believe their preferences to be superior to others, seek reinforcement of those preferences, yet are tolerant of the preferences of others in matters they don't really care about.[7] *Popular culture* consists of a multiplicity of overlapping, compatible, and competing taste cultures created, sustained, and eroded by cultural persuasion and suasion. David's paintings, Richard Wagner's operas, MTV (Music Television), the movie *Batman* (plus the paraphernalia huckstered in connection with it), Vanna White of television's "Wheel of Fortune," or Ted Koppel of ABC's "Nightline" all exemplify the continuous rise, persistence, and demise of taste cultures.

The taste cultures of propagated popular culture ("pop culture") need not derive from the marketing of cultural products that are demonstrably superior in any material, tangible ways. Rather, akin to what we discussed in Chapter 5 with respect to mass advertising, it is an illusion, image, style, or veneer that is propagated. Stuart Ewen calls this "skinning."[8] Ewen summarizes an essay written in 1859 by Oliver Wendell Holmes. Holmes was praising what was for its time a major invention, photography. Photography, wrote Holmes, represented a "conquest over matter." Before photography the qualities of a person, object, or place were inseparable from their material substance. A painting of an object might try to provide a facsimile, but it could not do so because the rendering inevitably depends upon the view and skills of the artist. A photo, however, is something else. A photo can capture something as it actually appears without picking up the thing itself. Holmes thought this a major breakthrough: form could be divorced from matter, "image would become more important than the object itself, and would in fact make the object disposable." The possibilities would be endless: "Every conceivable object of nature and art will soon scale off its surface for us. Men will hunt all curious, beautiful, grand objects, as they hunt cattle in South America, for their skins and leave the carcasses of little worth."[9]

Pop culture, and the taste cultures composing it, consists of skins, not carcasses. In politics campaign propaganda, war propaganda, and diplomacy transmit ideas, ideas frequently disembodied from the material consequences of their acceptance or rejection (see Chapter 4). In entrepreneurial propaganda the promise of benefits often replaces the receipt of material benefits themselves; in mass advertising brands, images, and positions substitute for the pluses and minuses of the material product sold; and in public relations reputation is everything (see Chapter 5). So too in the popular culture of beauty pageantry, Joe Rinelli markets skin as *the* material substance. Witness what he had to say about his favorite "girl"-candidate during the 1989 Miss Texas USA Pageant. First, as she stands on stage during a TV commercial break: "Yay! Come on Margaret! I'm really pleased with her. She's doing just what she should do, standing proud and tall, hand on her hip." What pleases Rinelli in this instance is that Margaret's standing makes her *appear* to dominate the other contestants. She is, in his words, taking "a big piece of the stage." Then, as she responds to an interviewer's question about how everything is in "Big D" (Margaret was Miss Dallas USA): "Everything in Big D is fabulous." The emcee asks her hobby. "I love letter-writing. I'm a model and a lot of my friends are models. . . ." Once more Rinelli is approving: "She's doing it." *It* in this instance is what Rinelli coached her to do, namely, turn her answers to any questions to her career accomplishments: "I'm currently a full-time fashion model and a part-time student. . . ." Rinelli exudes, "I feel great. I feel great about this." In the end, however, it was not to be. Margaret's "piece of the stage," and the title of Miss Texas USA, was captured by the stagecraft of Miss Houston USA. Was it a matter of substance over skin? No, not if one accepts Rinelli's judgment. Instead it was a matter of packaging, namely, Miss Houston's revealing evening gown: "Houston's got the outfit. . . . Look at how clever she is."[10]

MARKETING PERSONAE BY HYPE: AGENTS AS PROPAGANDA'S FACILITATORS

Propagating personae is Joe Rinelli's avocation. He is a stockbroker by trade and compares himself with a United Way volunteer who makes time for his hobby. Other marketers of personae, however, make it their full-time occupation. "Hype" is their trade, "agent" their designation.

Hype, according to cultural critic Steven M. L. Aronson, is either a verb or a noun, "a word aggressively in tune with the times." As a verb it means "the merchandising of a product—be it object, person, or an idea—in an artificially engendered atmosphere of hysteria, in order to create a demand for it or to inflate such demand as already exists." As a noun it is akin to "hyperbole," that is, excess or exaggeration. In either usage "its very sound—sharp, shrieky, cheap, belligerent, predatory—alerts us: A hard sell is in the works." Aronson notes that "since we're buying the hype when we buy the product," since advertising is as much a contest between hypes as material goods, "hype is a product, too."[11] What Aronson says of products applies also to people or ideas. In spite of all the "intimate profiles" of a movie star, rock musician, politician, or other celebrity appearing in publications as diverse as *People* magazine or *The New Yorker*, what we learn about the individual in question is minimal, and carefully edited to restrict our acquaintance to what the celebrity wants us to learn, namely, the hype. Consider a politician with a new idea labeled, for instance, a Program for New Understanding. At best what we get are the broad outlines, the form of the outline, not the tangible details, particularly as they apply to how the New Understanding will be financed.

In this respect, then, hype is but another variant on skinning. The product, person, or idea promoted is the hype or skin—the tailored and crafted *expressions* about what is promoted that influence the *impressions* we receive.[12] In 1961, faced with growing numbers of citizens leaving the nation by crossing freely into West Berlin, officials in the German Democratic Republic (East Germany) erected a fortified wall around West Berlin to prevent further emigration. The Berlin Wall stood for 28 years, not only symbolizing the cold war between the United States and the USSR, but effectively prohibiting access between parts of a divided Berlin—separating friends, families, economies, and so forth. Then as a result of mass protests leading to reforms in East Germany, the Berlin Wall was opened in 1989 and ultimately dismantled. The people who had lived with a partitioned city for almost three decades knew well the tangible economic, political, and social consequences of what they had lived through and of what they might anticipate in the future.

Here hype enters the picture—economic, political, and social. First, an enterprising radio station in the United States, ever mindful of the benefits of building its audience, secured portions of the Berlin Wall, then held a contest to award those pieces to the winners. Other entrepreneurs saw the possibilities of reaping more direct economic profit by selling pieces of the wall. Neiman-Marcus of Dallas announced that its prestigious department store would stock pieces of wall suitable for purchasing as Christmas gifts. Other entrepreneurs popped up on TV news and interview programs promoting the legitimacy of an irony, that is, a capitalist system making a profit by selling portions of a Communist edifice that capitalists had bemoaned the existence of for years. Uppermost was the effort to promote Wall sales "tastefully." A typical TV interview would go thus:

QUESTION: Isn't it crass marketing a prison that meant deprivation, misery, even death, for so many? Isn't that like selling pieces of the ovens at Dachau or Buchenwald?

ANSWER: Not at all. Purchasers will own a continuous reminder that the yearning for freedom will never die.

And what tangible reminder did the purchasers receive? One example will suffice, in this case a certificate. Mounted on the certificate were a few grains of the pulverized wall and a gold seal reading "Berlin Wall Authenticated Piece." Inscribed on the certificate: "THE BERLIN WALL." Below, and on either side of the grains of the wall were quotations. On the left, John Kennedy's 1963, "Ich bin ein Berliner"; Ronald Reagan's 1987, "The wall cannot withstand freedom"; and George Bush's 1989," . . . it must come down." On the right, Nikita Khrushchev's 1959, "We will bury you"; Erich Honecker's promise in 1987 that the wall would stand "50 or even 100 years," and Mikhail Gorbachev's 1989, "Nothing is eternal in this world." Below the wall grains were inscribed words hyping the purchasers' status: "In the spirit of individual initiative and freedom, [Name of Purchaser] owns a piece of the Berlin Wall." Finally, all of the tangible detail one would apparently ever need, inscribed next to the authenticating seal:

In 1961, what had been known as the Iron Curtain became a stone wall. It was called the Death Strip. Those who attempted to scale its eastern face were shot on sight. It neither protected nor secured. It split a nation, then the world. Until 1989, when shaken by chants of "Freedom! Freedom!" The Wall came tumbling down.

The effort to market the Berlin Wall "tastefully" illustrates a major feature of hype. Hype endeavors to render legitimate, acceptable, and desirable behaviors that, upon concrete reflection, are questionable. Granted, for example, one might want to consume a diet high in fiber to combat cancer and heart disease, but the hyping of oat bran, whole grains, and lentil beans grows to excess when it promotes such staples as coveted, gourmet fare. In his book *Hype*, Steven Aronson provides notable examples of activities made acceptable, then desirable, then routine by hyperbolic promotion: lavishly expensive visits to hairdressers in search of a New Me, repeated plastic surgery to restore self-image and self-confidence, payment of high prices for bad food and bad service just to be seen with the "in crowd," and the easy acceptance of gossip as the principal source of information about people, places, and things.

Status Theater

What has this to do with politics? Hype not only legitimizes behavior, it legitimizes hype itself. As we discussed in Chapter 5, the cosmetic (concern with appearances) side of electoral, presidential, and diplomatic politics is now commonplace. Simplified solutions to intractable political problems are as faddish as the latest health diet to reduce cholesterol—witness the rise and fall of such proposals as the "Star Wars" missile defense system, federal subsidies to bail out troubled financial savings and loan institutions, catastrophic health insurance for the elderly, or restrictions on imports to alleviate the nation's trade imbalance. Moreover, *status theater*, being seen with the "right people" in the "right places," is as crucial in politics as it is in corporate, entertainment, or other forms of endeavor. And gossip, the skinning of political discourse, is the fare of news and public affairs reporting and programming, whether it be in the *National Inquirer* or on PBS's "Washington Week in Review."[13]

Status theater also involves staged political hobnobbing. Recent presidents, for instance, arrange scheduled and mass-mediated encounters with celebrities. Presidential status theater works to the advantage of both politician and invited celebrity guest: the association of political and nonpolitical "stardom" makes both glitter a little more. George Bush was fond of inviting movie stars, athletes, and so forth to golf, dine, and otherwise be reported and photographed in the mutual presence of celebrated greatness. Hype artistry is truly bilateral, since the pseudoevent of Bush playing golf with Kevin Costner or dining with Michael Jackson propagates a great reality of political celebrity hobnobbing with the equally celebrated that suggests the president is as exceptional as the celebrities he allows into his presence.

Hype involves professional skills and know-how. Hype is the specialized vocation of agents—press agents, booking agents, employment agents, and so on. An agent is a paid promoter hired by an individual, company, or other entity to hype people, places, and things in every possible manner. An agent is a go-between who communicates on behalf of clients, a facilitator of clients' claims for money, power, and status. For example, Major League Baseball has a rule that allows any player in the major leagues, after having been with a team for a designated number of years, to file for free agency. This means the player is free to negotiate with any major league team for the sale of his services. The freedom, however, comes at a price. For it is not the player who negotiates, but the player's agent, an individual or firm hired by the player to contact major league teams, negotiate lucrative contract offers, and work out the financial and other details of any contract the player ultimately signs. In exchange for hyping the player the agent receives a lucrative fee.

Agents are most frequently identified with the Hollywood film industry; yet they operate in all areas of politics, business, sports, entertainment, and so forth. This includes an area familiar to many readers of this book, namely, American colleges and universities. There was a time when American institutions of higher education wishing to hire a high administrative official—a president, chancellor, provost, dean—simply made the fact known, received applications, and on the basis of tangible standards, scholarly and otherwise, selected the new official. Now agents enter into that process. Colleges and universities hire "headhunters," that is, professional agents or firms that for a fee recruit promising candidates for administrative openings. Many of the candidates themselves hire agents to act as go-betweens in negotiations with headhunters and the colleges or universities they represent. Whether the standards applied in such negotiations are scholarly or entrepreneurial varies widely from agent to agent.

Because they play a crucial role in facilitating the palaver between clients, employers, and audiences, agents are also influential in shaping lives, careers, and policies. For example, Michael Ovitz, a talent agent, has been described as "the most powerful individual in Hollywood today.''[14] His agency, Creative Artists Agency (CAA), consists of 65 talent agents with 600 clients that include such stars as Sylvester Stallone, Tom Cruise, Kevin Costner, Glenn Close, Robert Redford, Paul Newman, and Jessica Lange. CAA represents the stars' talents and marketability to the degree that, ''in a nutshell, the person who controls creative talent controls the movie business, and where once that talent was contracted to the Hollywood studios, today it is the province of the agent.''[15]

Once more the question, has this to do with politics and with political propaganda? Again, it does. An example: In 1976 Sylvester Stallone reached star status in *Rocky*, as an underdog boxer, symbolic of the ''weakened, dispirited America of the Ford-Carter years fighting its way to victory.''[16] After two box office failures, Stallone returned with box office successes in *Rocky II*, *Rocky III*, and *Rocky IV*. Latent political themes repeated the story of America's redemption in the face of enemies foreign and domestic. Stallone also appeared in another hit during this period, *First Blood*. It too carried a political theme, this time not so masked: the agonies of a returning Vietnam War veteran. Stallone and his agent had learned from the success of *Rocky* followed by two flops that ''Rocky,'' not Stallone, was the movie star. That is, the skin, not the material actor, could be marketed. So too could ''Rambo,'' the character of *First Blood*, achieve stardom. So, *Rambo: First Blood Part II*, another box office success, appeared, followed by the more modestly successful *Rambo III*. ''Rambo'' became ''the blustery, self-confident America of Ronald Reagan, cooly stomping its funny-accented enemies into the ground.'' Now Reagan's America has gone and:

> The first icon of the Bush era may have already emerged, in the tweedy English teacher played by Robin Williams in the Ivy League fantasy *Dead Poets Society*—a charismatic figure who incites his followers to ''be all they can be,'' not by nuking Russia but by reading Vachel Lindsay in a cave.[17]

Thus do hype, the palaver of cultural propaganda, and its purveying agents have political implications. These implications become even more apparent when we move from the entertainment media to those of public information.

PROPAGATING REAL-FICTIONS: NEWS AS INFOTAINING PROPAGANDA

TV Guide is a triple-hyper. First, it hypes itself and its sales (it outsells every weekly magazine in the nation). Second, it hypes the far-flung publishing empire of Rupert Murdoch, who paid $3 billion for the magazine in 1988. And, third, it hypes information about television and the industry itself, by publishing program guides, profiles of TV stars, program reviews, articles on TV trends, and insider gossip. In a sense it is a newsmagazine, but in another sense a form of entertainment in itself. It falls into a hybrid and hyped form we might call *infotainment*, news as entertainment. Infotainment approximates what Walter Fisher, a discerning student of rhetoric, calls ''real-fictions.'' Real-fictions are accounts of actual people, places, or events—hence, ''real''—but the accounts cannot be verified empirically as true or false.[18]

Sometimes in the hyped hybrid of the real-fictional world of infotainment, it is difficult to discern what is information and what is entertainment. On the cover of the August 26, 1989, issue of *TV Guide* there appeared a photo of popular TV talk show hostess Oprah Winfrey. Winfrey, who had reached TV stardom as plump and matronly, had undertaken a widely ballyhooed weight reduction diet. The magazine cover pictured the results. Winfrey posed in a gauzy dress, seated on a large mound of cash. The photo conveyed information about her success, both financial and physical, and hyped the feature article on Winfrey inside the magazine. Or so it appeared. But whereas the face on the cover was Winfrey's, alas, the svelte figure was not. Instead, the face was imposed on the figure of actress Ann-Margret, noted for her seductive, sexy roles.

The retouching of photographs, either stills or motion pictures, has always served marketers of personae well. Marlene Dietrich, a legendary movie actress, reminisced about the image contrived for her and propagated by the 1930 film that made her a star, *The Blue Angel*:

> I [now] look at my face on the television screen and remember how every tooth was capped, how every hair in that head was dyed and shaped, and in spite of knowing all of that, I sit back and say to myself, "That is *still* the most beautiful thing I've ever seen in my life."[19]

Does editing of visual reality extend to politics and political news as well? It does, as political infotainment. For example, in the 1988 presidential campaign (see Chapters 4 and 5), backers of Republican George Bush fashioned several TV ads calling attention to Democrat Michael Dukakis's alleged failings as governor of Massachusetts. One charged that Boston Harbor was polluted and filthy, that Dukakis's policies had failed to correct the mess. A picture provided viewers with visual evidence of the harbor's sorry condition. Only after the election did people learn that the picture was not of Boston Harbor at all but of polluted waters in another state entirely. With respect to a picture being worth a thousand words in TV news, consider what a major TV news network did in depicting the disastrous nuclear explosions that tore open a reactor at the Chernobyl plant in the Soviet Union in 1986. NBC secured film of what was thought to be the destroyed plant: it turned out to be a damaged cement manufacturing plant in Milan, Italy.

The era of new propaganda has brought an added dimension to the retouching of the skins that are the visual presentations of real-fictions. Newspapers, newsmagazines, and TV newscasts now incorporate computer-enhanced pictures of "the way it is."[20] In a photo appearing on the cover of *National Geographic*, computer retouching slightly moved one of the Great Pyramids of Giza; the *St. Louis Post-Dispatch* electronically removed a can of Diet Coke from a published photo; in its coverage of the 1984 Olympics the *Orange County Register* used computers to make the color of the sky in all outdoor photos smog-free blue. But electronic tinkering does not stop with editing, retouching, and enhancing news photographs of what happened; it extends to providing visual depictions of events that were never photographed, or never happened. TV news producers can use computers to construct composite photographs of, say, a space shuttle's journey, the recreation of news events never captured on camera. It is also possible to use computer technology to fabricate an entire TV story.

Whether such skinning and reskinning possibilities are endless we do not know. But they are sobering. A photographic specialist notes that in World War II the Nazis touched up photo stills and films for propaganda purposes, "though some of the results were a bit of a joke.'' But, ''nowadays you wouldn't be able to see the joins'' (i.e., editing splices). Hence, ''the potential for political manipulation is quite worrying. . . . You could easily turn a crowd scene into a riot scene.''[21]

Hype and skinning to produce infotaining real-fictions occurs in other journalistic ways, including simulations such as reenactments or dramatizations. Such portrayals are scarcely new, simply more pervasive. For example, prior to television's arrival as a medium of information and entertainment, newsreels screened in movie theaters were a principal means of picturing for people what ''really happened'' at a newsworthy event. Simulating events was common. At the 1948 Republican National Convention one day prior to the delivery of the keynote address, newsreel cameras filmed the keynoter delivering his speech to an empty convention hall. The films were developed, edited, enhanced with appropriate cheering and crowd noises and cuts of file footage of cheering Republicans, reproduced in multiple prints, packed in film canisters, and shipped to movie houses across the nation. At precisely the moment the keynoter actually addressed the convention the movie houses screened the newsreels, leaving an impression of live coverage of a breaking news event.[22]

The Great Simulator

In today's new propaganda the great simulator is TV news. Syndicated shows such as ''The Reporters'' or ''America's Most Wanted'' routinely use reenactments. Since they are entertainment programming rather than bona fide news, they purposely seek a suspension of disbelief. But when in 1989 NBC premiered two hourly newsmagazines, ''Yesterday, Today, and Tomorrow'' and ''Saturday Night with Connie Chung,'' the network made clear that it would incorporate simulations into news programming, assuring audiences simulated details would be documented as actually having happened and recreations would be identified as such. Whether viewers make such a distinction, between ''reel'' and ''real,'' is problematic. In 1984 when ABC News' ''Nightline'' aired a reenactment of D day on its fortieth anniversary (reminding viewers that it was indeed a reenactment), the network still received dozens of phone calls asking if France was being invaded! In 1989 the same network was not so cautious. ABC's ''World News Tonight'' presented, without initially labeling it as such, a reenactment of an incident in which a U.S. spy, portrayed by an actor, gave a Soviet agent, another actor, a make-believe briefcase containing sensitive and classified material.

Sophisticated retouching and reenactments derive in part from the technological wizardry available. They stem as well from an activity that is as old as journalism, indeed inherent in the craft—the editing of reality. Newspapers, newsmagazines, newscasts—all have editors and the purpose of editors is to edit. Editing involves many things. One is skinning. A good example appeared in the earliest days of the television news documentary, in what many refer to with nostalgia as the ''Golden Age of Television.'' U.S. senator Joseph McCarthy built a career and reputation in the early days of the cold war on his investigation and exposure of what he called ''communists in high places.'' In the process he raised fears and charges that he was smearing the characters and ruining the reputations and livelihoods of innocent individuals against whom he was making groundless accusations. So controversial did he become that he gave a name to the period, that is, the ''McCarthy Era.''

On March 9, 1954, CBS aired one in a series of half-hour TV documentaries produced and edited by Edward R. Murrow and Fred W. Friendly, "See It Now," namely, "See It Now: Report on Senator McCarthy." The documentary consisted primarily of film clips of McCarthy making public statements and speeches, in interviews, and congressional investigations. The film covered approximately two years of McCarthy's career. The precisely edited clips were framed by correspondent Murrow's introductions and leads. Murrow's closing statement briefly discussed citizens' responsibilities, quoting Shakespeare's *Julius Caesar* to the effect that "the fault [McCarthy's methods], dear Brutus, is not in our stars, but in ourselves."

Responses to the documentary varied and included claims that it was a partisan attack on the senator, a flawed and biased presentation, an objective and impartial account, and a dangerous precedent for TV news. Rhetorical critic Thomas Rosteck has analyzed the "Report" from a different perspective, one that highlights how editing can serve as a process of selective skinning. Rosteck treats the "Report," both in its verbal and visual aspects, as an example of ironic discourse[23] or what we might call ironic propaganda. Irony is a form of indirect expression whereby verbal and nonverbal means convey the opposite of their literal meaning. We need search no further for an example than to return to Shakespeare's *Julius Caesar* and Mark Anthony's soliloquy honoring Caesar and indirectly attacking his enemies, especially Brutus (act 3, scene 2):

> The noble Brutus hath told you Caesar
> was ambitious: If it were so, it was
> a grievous fault,
> And grievously has Caesar answer'd it.
> Here, under leave of Brutus and the rest—
> For Brutus is an honorable man;
> So are they all, all honorable men.

Here Anthony asserts repeatedly that Brutus is "an honorable man," indicating by manner and tone he means otherwise. Something more is also at work in ironic discourse. Audiences must recognize it as ironic, that is, they must have sufficient understanding of the context and phrasing of the message to detect that the opposite is meant by utterance and manner. Thus does irony serve as a potent propagandistic tool: "because irony cloaks what it means and requires reconstruction [on the part of the audience], the ironic text invites a kind of self-persuasion." Irony adjusts to the suasive dimension of palaver. In his analysis of the "Report" Rosteck provides ample demonstration of Murrow's use of irony. On the surface Murrow offered a straightforward recounting of McCarthy's actual behavior when, by contrast, the irony skinned McCarthy's acts to suggest a different point of view: "Though each audience member who 'gets' the irony cannot fail to reconstruct the message in a *form* that tells against McCarthy, each will reconstruct to his or her own estimate of the Senator." Thus, "while this *See It Now* is built from the raw material of McCarthy's own words and actions, the text ironically redirects the connotations in the McCarthy footage" such that an "ironic layering of another sense over the 'objective' footage partly depends upon our assent to the 'actuality' of what we see."[24] Irony, then, like retouching and reenactment, requires some suspension of disbelief.

Infotainment raises important questions about what is sound journalism, objective journalism, and ethical journalism. Intriguing though those questions are, the question we pose is why do news organizations engage in faking, fabricating, and ironic reporting?

The answer is that news seldom consists of information reported about a person, problem, or event. To repeat, in Ewen's term, *all* news is the "skinning" of newsworthy matters, the lifting of the form from the material of events. In infotainment the form skinned off the complex political, economic, and social materials is entertaining and dramatic. That form is *hyped as news*, marketed in competition with forms propagated by rival news organizations. Journalist Walter Lippmann wrote in 1922 in his classic work on the nature of news, *Public Opinion*, that "journalism is not a first hand report of raw material," but "a report of that material after it has been stylized."[25] To the degree that news helps people adjust to their everyday lives and world, the adjustment "takes place through the medium of fictions." However, wrote Lippmann, "I do not mean lies. I mean a representation of the environment which is in lesser or greater degree made by" people and "as a work of fiction may have almost any degree of fidelity." Concluded Lippmann, "so long as the degree of fidelity can be taken into account, fiction is not misleading."[26]

Certainly Lippmann's key phrase is "so long as the degree of fidelity can be taken into account." We have seen repeatedly that the pervasiveness, persuasiveness, and suasiveness of new propaganda derives from the propagation of fictions. If Walter Lippmann is correct in his assessment of fiction, and if Walter Fisher is correct in his assessment of real-fictions, the news as infotainment is propaganda. Whether that propaganda is misleading depends upon its degree of fidelity. Our capacity to measure that fidelity, in turn, depends upon the tools we have (the topic of Chapters 7 and 8), and means provided to teach us those tools, that is, education.

HYPING KNOWLEDGE: PROPAGANDISTIC DIMENSIONS OF EDUCATION

The American philosopher and founder of pragmatism, Charles S. Peirce, in 1877 wrote a brief article entitled "The Fixation of Belief." The title, he wrote, "refers to the ways of arriving at ideas that settle down in the minds of a people as habits, customs, traditions, 'folkways' of thought. . . ."[27] When people find themselves in perplexing or puzzling situations, when they don't understand what is going on, or when they are just plain curious, they experience what Peirce called an "irritation of doubt." Sooner or later such doubt produces tension, making people uncomfortable. In effect, they can only suspend disbelief so long. Then they want to reduce the tension, confront the doubt, and "arrive at ideas that settle" the matter. Peirce described the means people use to fix beliefs: (1) they may apply beliefs they have learned earlier in other situations, beliefs they cherish, do not question, and have faith in—the method of tenacity; (2) they may go to someone or a group they respect, admire, or have faith in and accept advice—the method of authority; or (3) they may acquire beliefs based on experience and reason, checking and modifying their fixations against changes in what they observe—the scientific method. Readers of the introductory chapter to this book will quickly recognize the similarity of Peirce's methods of fixing beliefs with the three "habits" of suasion, respectively, credulity, argument, and science.

Appropriately conducted, the method or habit of science has no ax to grind, no point to prove, no faith to satisfy, no person or group to please. As a means of reducing the irritation of doubt it is, so to speak, disinterested. We normally associate education with such disinterest. That is, through education people learn the skills to undertake dispassionate inquiry and/or they learn what beliefs have been fixed and modified via the scientific method. (Remember, we speak here of science broadly, with a small *s*, as the observation, identification, empirical investigation, description, explanation, and modification of explanations of phenomena; we do not speak of "Science" as restricted to any specific mode of investigation, say, a laboratory experiment, or set of phenomena, for instance, viruses, genes, or asteroids.) We also normally associate schools, colleges, universities, and other places where education occurs with the disinterested sharing of inquiry's skills and conclusions.

Propagating Educational Self-interest

After all, educational institutions are social entities. They involve people dealing with people, groups dealing with groups, and organizations dealing with organizations. Educational entrepreneurs compete for coveted money to carry on their work, prestige for their institutions, and power and recognition for themselves. So, even though ideally education involves the disinterested search for belief in the face of irritating doubt, Education (capital *E*) and the enterprises identified with it have their self-interests to promote. Education is thus political and in no way immune to the use and consequences of palaver, the new propaganda, in promoting those interests.

The number of institutions of "higher education" in the United States is considerable and varies depending upon whether we take into account two- or four-year institutions, private or public colleges and universities, and other factors. To fulfill their respective missions (usually couched in the palaver of "teaching," "research," and "public service") they require funds. They generate those funds from a variety of sources—public tax monies, private donations from benefactors and alumni, research grants, student fees, and so forth. The stronger the image of any college or university the better it is positioned to compete with other institutions for precious funds, prestige, and social influence. So like political entrepreneurs seeking votes, corporate entrepreneurs seeking consumers, and all enterprises seeking good will, institutions of higher education advertise, use public relations, and propagate their accomplishments. In the process they skin and hype themselves.

Consider the "teaching mission." The better an institution's student body—as measured by numbers of National Merit Scholars, average scores on Scholastic Aptitude Tests (SAT) and/or American College Tests (ACT), record of nationally and internationally recognized scholars, number and renown of graduates, and other factors—the greater the likelihood of raising needed dollars. To strengthen the student body, colleges and universities routinely recruit promising high school graduates, just as Joe Rinelli routinely recruits Miss Texas USA contestants. Letters, brochures, personal contacts, tours of high schools, invited visits to campuses, mailed videotapes, precommitment "orientations," phone calls, advertisements in college guides and professional programs, and scores of other measures tout brand names (Harvard, Yale), product images and associations (Ivy League, Big Ten), and distinct positionings ("Stephens is the place to study fashion design"). Promises of an "outstanding faculty," "low student-teacher ratios," "intimate, caring contact with teachers," "unlimited access to computer labs," and "rewarding, life-preparing experiences" abound. Look at the brochures they mail out to prospective students: typically, they hype educational paradise, a place of eternally green trees (no winter), much fun and games, dynamic teachers, beautiful and smiling female students and handsome and upright male students, an atmosphere of community and individuality, learning and ease, devoid of the problems that beset the outside world and even, it would appear, much hard work to do well.

The promotion of the institution's teaching mission is not limited to prospective consumers, that is, students. In a manner very similar to how new propaganda via PR (recall Chapter 5) creates issues and issue agendas through "issue management," educational PR does the same. The audience for the PR is both external (potential students) and internal (the faculty). Here is a typical example. A small, Midwestern, liberal arts university with relatively high tuition recently sought to enhance its image for excellence in teaching. To that end it obtained funds from a private foundation subsidized by one of the nation's largest and oldest chains of retail department stores. The foundation sponsored a national Teaching Excellence and Campus Leadership Award Program. Under the program faculty members, according to an internal memorandum from the Vice President for Academic Affairs, were to be awarded stipends for "campus activities aimed at promoting excellence in teaching." "Excellence," the memo read, would have a special meaning, that is, "the main emphasis will be on leadership in innovative teaching." "Innovative" would also have a special meaning. The "receptacle" model of teaching would be skinned (that is, the "teacher-fills-empty-student" via assignments, lectures, discussion). The form that would emerge, and would be rewarded, would be "involvement." Through "participatory learning" students and faculty together would be "actively involved in curriculum, course, and syllabus design"; "helping students help one another"; "varying normal pedagogical rhythms"; "examining basic beliefs"; "opening channels for fuller feedback"; helping "find and manage time"; "treating students (convincingly) as persons"; "respectfully challenging . . . stereotypes"; "risking new things"; and more than a dozen other activities specified in the memo. Candidates would be nominated by faculty-student committees and a winner selected, an appropriate award ceremony convened, presumably with a public recital of all "new things" risked and "pedagogical rhythms" varied.[28]

The purpose here is not to demean efforts to improve learning. Rather, it is to call attention to a process that hypes a form, in this case "involvement," and promotes it. Granted that college teachers, students, administrators, and funding sources might have doubts about the effectiveness of a "receptacle model" or stereotype of teaching. To promote a single alternative as superior or rewardable is to ask audiences to suspend disbeliefs about the alternative, thus substitute one model legitimized by the habit of credulity for another heretofore legitimized by the same habit. Propaganda, not a disinterested search for beliefs, reigns. It is possible that such hype artistry is performance, an effort to convince all interested parties that both thought and innovation are taking place, and that somehow, through the magic of educationist palaver, student involvement, not to mention faculty involvement, will be transformed and redeemed.

Research Palavering

The imperative to use the palaver of new propaganda to charm and beguile funding sources, prospective students, faculties, alumni, and others extends to all institutions of higher education but it is particularly pronounced in the "multiversity." Communication scholar James Carey notes that the multiversity developed after World War II when universities concentrated on two activities, neither "undertaken for purely scholarly and moral motives."[29] One consisted of the federal government and corporate establishment turning over to a particular class of universities research for technical- and defense-oriented developments in the natural and social sciences. The second extended benefits of higher education to an unrestricted class of students to fill the need for college-trained workers in a variety of skilled professions and occupations. Formidable though these twin research and teaching missions are, they were never fully funded. Hence, within the multiversities research and teaching assistants, employed at far lower salaries than full-time faculty, performed them (How many of your undergraduate classes are or were taught by "TAs," how many labs by "RAs"?).

Carey stresses that two unintended consequences came from the rise of the multiversity. The first was that the model of the research university trickled down and "soon every college acted like a research university irrespective of its resources, talent, and mission." The small but expensive liberal arts college described above illustrates Carey's point. Second, the discipline of physics, by tradition a field best adapted to the mission of the multiversity, became the "model for every department and activity on every campus." Both consequences, regardless of the palaver of "excellence in teaching" that flows from college and university PR facilitators, elevated research over teaching in higher education. Even promotional efforts on behalf of "excellence in teaching" often mask research aims. For example, the memo cited above on "involvement" teaching includes as a criterion in innovation "involving students in meaningful research." Teaching excellence is the skin institutions use to promote themselves to prospective scholar-consumers; research prestige is the skin faculties and administrators use to promote themselves to funding sources:

> It is not that people are deserting teaching for research, not that people are uncompensated for teaching. It is simply that faculty are drawn increasingly to the *culture of research*—grants, travel, conferences, graduate students, royalties, book contracts, newspaper and magazine articles—into the *culture of visibility and celebrity*.[30]

Remember from our introductory discussion of the nature of propaganda that ideas propagate in cultures, that is, among people who constitute the seedbeds of ideas. The cultures of research, visibility, and celebrity are such cultures. Like campaign, presidential, war, and diplomatic cultures (Chapter 4); entrepreneurial, consumer, and organizational cultures (Chapter 5); and the popular cultures of entertainment and news discussed above, they both nourish and thrive upon propaganda.

What typifies the educational cultural propaganda of research, visibility, and celebrity? Reviewing three recent book-length studies in urban anthropology, Marc Ambroise-Rendu provides an insightful look at the cultural overlap. All three books focus upon the lifestyles of the *haute societe* and *couture* of the French aristocracy in Paris. Here are members of a closed, upper class who are suspicious of media exposure, be it by journalists or sociologists. Hence, the researchers, who used personal interviews with the aristocrats in their investigations, were forced to adjust their inquiries to the wishes of their subjects. First, to obtain interviews they had to negotiate with several tiers of advisers, friends of the family, and confidants before actually reaching the aristocrats who were the targets of their research. Penetrating the membership of the exclusive social clubs the aristocrats belonged to was essential, yet exceedingly difficult. The anthropologists endured long waits after being granted audiences, cancellations, and other frustrations. Then, to prepare for entry into the ancestral manor or château where interviews took place, they had to purchase expensive wardrobes suitable to the surroundings and consult etiquette manuals on proper forms of address and deportment. Interviewees prescribed a largely unchanging ritual: interviews took place in drawing rooms, not in dining rooms, studies, libraries, or other places off limits to researchers; interviewees acted with polite condescension, discretion, and secretiveness ("I'm telling you all this, but please don't put it in your book" was often repeated); the invariable sign that the interviewee was ready to cease was the proffering of a "drink"; finally, at the end the subject in obligatory manner expressed enjoyment at the time spent with the researchers.

Did the researchers produce an accurate portrayal of aristocratic life? Perhaps, but Ambroise-Rendu suggests that the three books serve, first, the privileged interests of the aristocrats and, importantly, visibility and celebrity of the sociologists more than scholarship. He notes that the researchers were "forced to censor themselves," promising interviewees complete anonymity and scrupulously avoiding any discussion of money, politics, and sex. The results show the aristocracy "in the most favorable light" while "masking its imperfections." And as for the researchers' visibility and celebrity, "it is surely significant that some of the exclusive clubs which so dreaded indiscretions on the part of the researchers actually urged their members to read the resulting book. Who would ever have suspected that urban anthropologists could be used as a flattering mirror by the upper classes?"[31]

As carried out, then, the method of science, or science as a habit of suasion, does not necessarily produce disinterested results. Scientific research may have propagandistic import. Robert L. Root, Jr., has suggested that this is especially so with what he calls "popular science," that is, science exploited precisely for the ends of visibility and celebrity that are hallmarks of contemporary popular culture. Root distinguishes popular science from "academic" science. Academic science addresses an audience of scholars conversant with technical details, jargon, formulae, and procedures. Reports of research appear in a style that "restricts the development of ethos and pathos as it facilitates the development of the logos" (see Chapter 5).[32] The audience for popular science differs; it is less knowledgeable, less technically competent, less interested in intricacies and details. The presentation style of popular science is less restrained, more informal, and more likely to highlight the credibility (ethos) of the author and may appeal to emotion (pathos).

Clearly popular science, as envisioned by Root, offers more propagandistic possibilities than does academic science. A microbiologist reporting the results of a highly technical study of gene splicing to a small group of specialists is more restricted in her claims for what she did or did not learn than, say, a noted science writer describing the marvels, benefits, and ominous possibilities of gene splicing for the future of the human race. This is not, however, to say that academic scientists do not engage in palaver in promoting their own research, visibility, and celebrity among their scientific peers. For example, "pure" mathematics develops mathematical theory; "it is what mathematicians do to please themselves, or each other." The use of theories to predict weather, plot the trajectory of a rocket to Mars, or accomplish "the tasks set by the rest of society" is "applied" mathematics. Both involve academic science. In contrast stands a "rhetorical" mathematics akin to popular science. It is neither pure nor applied: "Not pure, because nothing of mathematical interest is done, no new mathematical ideas are brought forward, no mathematical difficulties are overcome; and not applied because no real world consequences are produced—except publications, reports, and grant proposals.''[33] The consequences of rhetorical mathematics are persuasion and/or suasion.

Neal Koblitz, a mathematician, in the article ''Mathematics as Propaganda,'' about the use of mathematical ''formulae'' to prove theorems about politics, provides an illustration of precisely why the article bears such a title. The theorems in question appeared in a 1968 study entitled *Political Order in Changing Societies* by a widely celebrated political scientist, Samuel Huntington. In the study Huntington formulates three ''equations'' relating (a) social mobilization, (b) economic development, (c) social frustration, (d) mobility opportunities, (e) political participation, (f) political institutionalization, and (g) political instability. Here are the equations:

$$\frac{\text{social mobilization}}{\text{economic development}} = \text{social frustration } (a/b = c)$$

$$\frac{\text{social frustration}}{\text{mobility opportunities}} = \text{political participation } (c/d = e)$$

$$\frac{\text{political participation}}{\text{political institutionalization}} = \text{political instability } (e/f = g)$$

If these are indeed equations, then the techniques of ''ninth grade algebra,'' according to Koblitz, produce the following:

$$a = b \times c = b \times d \times e = b \times d \times f \times g$$

such that ''social mobilization is equal to economic development times mobility opportunities times political institutionalization times political instability!'' This Koblitz concludes is ''mystification, intimidation, an impression of precision and profundity,'' but scarcely the disinterested search set apart from propaganda.[34]

Koblitz does not single out Huntington for unwittingly using mathematics as propaganda. Indeed he cites other examples—students of demography, slavery, and intelligence. Other scholars have suggested that academic science, like popular science, has its propagandistic side in the science of economics[35] and in marketing the personae of scholars themselves.[36] The thrust is the same, namely, that educational cultures of research, visibility, and celebrity are susceptible to the growth of propaganda despite seemingly disinterested scholarly intentions. The marketing of scholarship as mystification, among scholarly audiences and from scholars to lay audiences, can have propagandistic consequences no less than do palaver, skinning, and hype in other areas of communication.

CHARM, GUILE, AND REASON IN POPULAR, DEMOCRATIC CULTURES

In this book's introduction we quoted Harold Lasswell's observation that ''democracy has proclaimed the dictatorship of palaver,'' the rule of charm and guile. Elsewhere Lasswell wrote that ''propaganda is a concession to the rationality of the modern world.'' He then continued:

A literate world, a reading world, a schooled world prefers to thrive on argument and news. It is sophisticated. . . . All the apparatus of diffused erudition popularizes the symbols and forms of pseudo-rational appeal; the wolf of propaganda does not hesitate to masquerade in sheepskin. All the voluble men of the day—writers, reporters, editors, preachers, lecturers, teachers, politicians—are drawn into the service of propaganda to amplify a master voice.

Mixing his metaphors, Lasswell ended the passage with ''All is conducted with the decorum and the trappery of intelligence, for this is a rational epoch, and demands its raw meat cooked and garnished by adroit and skillful chefs.''[37]

The literate, reading (and viewing), schooled, sophisticated world of today ''popularizes the symbols and forms'' (we have called them skins) of ''pseudo-rational appeal'' throughout popular culture: in beauty pageants, celebrity personae, infotainment, the multiversity's teaching veneer and research for visibility, and the latter-day Ph.D. wolf that ''masquerades in the sheepskin.'' But surely, you say, it is not all cooked meat and garnish; something of the raw meat and material remains; it is not all ''symbols and forms.'' And, you insist, Dan Rather of the ''CBS Evening News'' is not just another chef like Johnny Carson of NBC's ''Tonight Show''; a Nobel laureate is not a Hollywood star; this book offers more than the Miss USA Pageant. If not all is propaganda, how then do we know propaganda when we see it? To approach that question we turn to the analysis of propaganda.

This chapter completes our survey of the variety of ideocultures in which propaganda is seeded and spread. A glance backward at the plural cultures of the new propaganda should alert you to the virtual ubiquity of propaganda regardless of what kind of social enterprise is being undertaken. From presidential selection to movie reviews, propaganda serves a universal range of organized and vested interests seeking to sway opinion and action, whether it be the choice they make in the voting booth or at the movie box office. But we are complicit in the propaganda activities of these ideocultures too, for propaganda guides many of us in our choices. Few of us are immune to the guile, charm, and ''pseudo-rational appeal'' of propaganda. For that reason, the student of propaganda should be familiar with how to analyze and critique propaganda, becoming knowledgeable not only about what propaganda is but also how to deal with it in a rational and mature way. It is to that task that we now turn.

NOTES

1. See, for example, James E. Combs, *Dimensions of Political Drama* (Santa Monica, CA: Goodyear, 1980); Ferdinand Mount, *The Theater of Politics* (New York: Schocken Books, 1973); Kenneth Burke, *A Grammar of Motives* (New York: Prentice-Hall, 1950); Hugh Dalziel Duncan, *Communication and Social Order* (New York: Bedminster Press, 1962); James E. Combs and Michael W. Mansfield, eds., *Drama in Life* (New York: Hastings House, 1976); Dennis Brisset and Charles Egley, eds., *Life as Theater* (Chicago: Aldine, 1976); and Erving Goffman, *The Presentation of Self in Everyday Life* (Garden City, NY: Doubleday/Anchor, 1959).
2. Ingrid Brenninkmeyer, ''The Sociology of Fashion,'' Ph.D. dissertation, Frieburg, 1962.

3. Stuart Ewen, *All Consuming Images* (New York: Basic Books, 1988), p. 30.
4. Among contemporary views on how popular culture should be evaluated, which vary widely, see James W. Carey, *Communication as Culture* (Boston: Unwin Hyman, 1989); John Fiske, *Reading the Popular* (Boston: Unwin Hyman, 1989); John Fiske, *Understanding Popular Culture* (Boston: Unwin Hyman, 1989); and Robert L. Savage and Dan Nimmo, eds., *Politics in Familiar Contexts* (Norwood, NJ: Ablex, 1990).
5. Dwight Macdonald, ''Masscult & Midcult,'' in Macdonald, *Against the American Grain* (New York: Random House, 1962), p. 3.
6. Ibid., p. 37.
7. H. L. Nieburg, *Public Opinion: Tracking and Targeting* (New York: Praeger, 1984), pp. 29–34.
8. Ewen, *All Consuming Images*, pp. 24–25.
9. Quoted in Ewen, ibid., p. 25, with emphasis removed. The original statement is in Oliver Wendell Holmes, ''The Stereoscope and the Stereograph,'' *The Atlantic Monthly* 3 (June 1859).
10. Quoted in Mike Steere, ''Joe Rinelli's Favorite Girl,'' *Dallas Life Magazine* 8 (August 13, 1989): 22.
11. Steven M. L. Aronson, *Hype* (New York: William Morrow, 1983), p. 15.
12. Goffman, *The Presentation of Self in Everyday Life*.
13. On the gossip bases of such programming see Dan Nimmo and James E. Combs, *Mediated Political Realities* (New York: Longman, 1990), chap. 7.
14. Michael Cieply and Lisa Gubernick, ''The Agent,'' *Gannett Center Journal* 3 (Summer 1989): 59.
15. Ibid., pp. 59–60.
16. David Kehr, ''The Star,'' *Gannett Center Journal* 3 (Summer 1989): 53.
17. Ibid., pp. 53–54.
18. Walter R. Fisher, ''A Motive View of Communication,'' *Quarterly Journal of Speech* 56 (May 1970): 132–139.
19. Quoted in Aronson, *Hype*, p. 69 (emphasis in original).
20. During his reign as anchor of ''CBS Evening News,'' Walter Cronkite made famous his signature line signing off each telecast, ''And that's the way it is.'' On computer enhancement of photos and film see J. D. Lasica, ''Photographs That Lie,'' *Washington Journalism Review* 7 (June 1989): 22–25.
21. Quoted by Mike Gerrard, ''Computers Make a Clean Breast . . . or Do They,'' *Manchester Guardian Weekly* 141 (July 9, 1989): 5.
22. Joseph C. Goulden, ed., *Mencken's Last Campaign* (Washington, DC: The New Republic Book Co., 1976), pp. 32–33.
23. Thomas Rosteck, ''Irony, Argument, and Reportage in Television Documentary: *See It Now* versus Senator McCarthy,'' *Quarterly Journal of Speech* 9 (August 1989): 277–298.
24. Ibid., pp. 287–288.
25. Walter Lippmann, *Public Opinion* (New York: Macmillan, 1922), p. 347.
26. Ibid., pp. 15–16.
27. Charles S. Peirce, ''The Fixation of Belief,'' *Popular Science Monthly* 12 (November 1877): 1.
28. The quoted items in this section were drawn by the authors from a compendium of typical memoranda sent to faculty members at a variety of institutions at which the authors have taught over the years. The memos should remain anonymous. They are used not to embarrass or demean the authors or the institutions but to illustrate a larger point about educationist talk.
29. James W. Carey, ''Review of *ProfScam: Professors and the Demise of Higher Education*,'' *Journalism Educator* 44 (August 1989): 48–53.
30. Ibid., p. 58 (emphasis added).

31. Marc Ambroise-Rendu, ''Snobbery Is Alive and Well and Living in Paris,'' *Manchester Guardian Weekly* 141 (December 10, 1989): 14.
32. Robert L. Root, Jr., *The Rhetoric of Popular Culture* (New York: Greenwood, 1987), p. 74.
33. Philip J. Davis and Reuben Hersh, ''Rhetoric and Mathematics,'' in John S. Nelson, Allan Megill, and Donald N. McCloskey, eds., *The Rhetoric of the Human Sciences* (Madison: University of Wisconsin Press, 1987), pp. 58–59.
34. Neal Koblitz, ''Mathematics as Propaganda,'' in Lynne Arthur Steen, ed., *Mathematics Tomorrow* (New York: Springer-Verlag, 1981), p. 113.
35. Donald N. McCloskey, *The Rhetoric of Economics* (Madison: University of Wisconsin Press, 1985).
36. Michele Lamont, ''How to Become a Dominant French Philosopher: The Case of Jacques Derrida,'' *American Journal of Sociology* 3 (November 1987): 584–622.
37. Harold D. Lasswell, ''The Wartime Propaganda Front,'' in Dwaine Marvick, ed., *Harold Lasswell on Political Sociology* (Chicago: University of Chicago Press, 1977), p. 227.

The Analysis and Critique of Political Propaganda

CHAPTER 7

Scraping the Surface
The Tradition of Propaganda Analysis

Part III is devoted to the analysis and critique of propaganda. We undertake this section of the book in the conviction that just knowing about propaganda is not enough. The enlightened citizen also needs the ability to critically analyze propaganda. In some measure, having such an ability breaks the spell of propaganda, freeing oneself from one major form of social seduction. To that end, this chapter introduces the now knowledgeable student of propaganda to the tradition of propaganda analysis, that body of social scientific inquiry that still serves us well in the critical analysis of propaganda, past and present. As we shall see, the tools of thinking well about propaganda date from Aristotle, but also from those modern inquirers who began to examine the sources, message, and influence of propaganda after World War I. If you heed their analysis, you will have gone a long way in breaking that spell of which we spoke.

The interested reader will have by this point learned a great deal about the history, development, and contemporary use of propaganda. We hope that you will agree with us that propaganda is a much more powerful force than is usually admitted. For that if no other reason, you should be concerned about the effects of propaganda on yourself and society in general. This section promises that if you take it seriously it will give you some useful tools in understanding the palaver of propaganda, demystifying that palaver, and thereby in some measure freeing you from any insidious effects and letting you choose intelligently which propagandas you think are most helpful to you. In so doing, you will have achieved a level of awareness in which you use propaganda rather than let propaganda use you. But that requires a bit of learning about propaganda so you can limit or select what you learn from propaganda.

PROPAGANDA TREKKIES

Stardate is 2534.0. Far, far out in the heavens travels the U.S.S. *Enterprise* on its mission: "to explore strange new worlds, to seek out new life and new civilizations—to boldly go where no man has gone before . . ." Approaching the planet Ekos, the *Enterprise* encounters attack by atomic missiles. Ekos has no technology that sophisticated. How can this be? Captain James T. Kirk and his faithful sidekick, Mr. Spock, beam down to the planet to find out what is happening and why. They find a society seemingly ripped from the fabric of an ancient, uncivilized past: Nazi Germany on the planet Earth in the 1930s. Storm troopers march in goose step, beat, flog, and persecute—all under the command of John Gill, Kirk's former teacher at Starfleet Academy.

Gill earlier had traveled to Ekos as a cultural observer from the United Federation of Planets' Earth, then remained to impose coordination and order upon Ekos's fragmented political structure. Gill's actions violated the federation's prime directive never to interfere with alien life forms. Gill's imposition of a businesslike, Nazi-like bureaucracy, undertaken with humane intentions, has been converted by Melakon, an aide, into a crucible of brutality. Melakon drugs Gill and assumes dictatorial powers in Gill's name, displays Gill's portrait on posters, props a sedated Gill up before TV cameras, and stages Gill's public appearances. In the interests of justice, humanity, and federation law Kirk, Spock, and other officers of the *Enterprise* must restore democracy to Ekos. To do so they infiltrate Melakon's headquarters, bringing Gill to his senses in the nick of time just as he is about to deliver a TV address calling for extinction of all enemies of Ekos. Gill denounces Melakon to a planetwide audience only to perish at Melakon's hands. Gill's death notwithstanding, Melakon's plot is foiled and the *Enterprise* continues its mission at warp speed.

This story line is but one of many of the TV adventure series "Star Trek" that ran for three seasons in the 1960s. The series spawned more than 450 fan clubs, 600 fan publications, "Trekkie" conventions across the nation, syndicated reruns that still air throughout the world, an animated TV version also in syndication, *Star Trek* feature films produced in the 1970s and 1980s, and an updated TV series, "Star Trek: The Next Generation" in the 1980s and 1990s. "Star Trek" was the first TV series to be released in its entirety on videocassettes; hence episodes still line the shelves of shopping mall bookstores and videostores and the racks of convenience stores.[1] Persons not even born when the first show aired in 1966 have had their "Trekkie" years, and along with other fans travel the country attending Trekkie conferences held each year. If all that were not enough to immortalize "Star Trek," the New York City Opera announced plans to commission a music drama to commemorate the twenty-fifth anniversary of the series in 1991.

The popular success of "Star Trek," spanning a quarter of a century and counting, derives from its entertaining formula, the appeal of its characters, and its clever production techniques. The popularity also owed much to the series' propaganda message. That message exalted the rights and responsibilities of Americans to counter all threats to peace and justice not only on this planet, but on all planets. The message of "Star Trek" was to "boldly go" and achieve America's manifest destiny, spread the American Way throughout "space . . . the final frontier," and bring to all "strange new worlds . . . new life and new civilizations" everywhere the promise of technological redemption and salvation.[2] Even though the crew was international on the old "Star Trek" (Lt. Uhuru, for instance) and interstellar on the new (Counselor Deanna Troi from the planet Betazed), the propaganda "subtext" of the shows was one of righteous empire, the right of an American-led coalition to make the universe safe for democracy. By portraying such a just and benevolent mission, the "Star Trek" series propagated the message of legitimate and rational American intervention in strange lands that need—often whether they want it or not—our guidance and even alliance.

"Star Trek," however, was not only propaganda about America's lordly spacewide role, it was propaganda about propaganda. "Patterns of Force," the tale of deliverance from Nazism recounted above that aired on February 16, 1968, was typical of many "Star Trek" episodes. In it Ekos's rulers combine terror, symbolism, and deception to retain unbridled power. Viewers see jackbooted troopers pummeling victims with nightsticks; young maidens forced to serve the wishes of tyrants; armbands, banners, and flags with Nazi-like insignia; and a sedated John Gill fronting for a malevolent Melakon. "Star Trek" portrays propaganda as manifest, flagrant, blatant assaults to persuade; there is no subtlety, guile, or charm. The message about propaganda: it lies on the surface and anyone with but minimal instruction can detect, analyze, and combat it.

The "Star Trek" message about propaganda and its analysis is not unique. The tradition of propaganda analysis is a long one, dating back well before the term itself came into politicoreligious use with the convening by Pope Gregory XV of the Congregatio de Propaganda Fide in 1622 (see the opening chapter to this volume). That tradition has frequently emphasized techniques readily acquired and applied to analyzing manifest propaganda. In this chapter we explore that tradition; then, in Chapter 8 we review contemporary ways of thinking critically about the palaver of new propaganda.

GREEK ARGUMENT: PRECURSORS
OF PROPAGANDA ANALYSIS

Our contention in this work can be succinctly summarized: It is useful to view political propaganda as the propagation of ideas regardless of whether the intent of those ideas is to persuade or not, the propagation planned or fortuitous, and the source governmental or nongovernmental. Viewed in this manner the analysis of propagandistic communication extends to the analysis of the content of all messages of political consequence that have potential for taking root, maturing, and spreading. In this respect the tradition of propaganda analysis has a long and honored legacy dating back several centuries, to times when we encounter the teachings of Confucius (551–479 B.C.)., Buddha (563–483 B.C.), Socrates (469–399 B.C.), and Jesus Christ (5 B.C.–A.D. 30).

The emphasis of these precursors of propaganda analysis was on the soundness of ideas in seeking truth and/or moral goodness. The logic of communication was a central concern. Among such precursors of the Western tradition of propaganda analysis were the Athenian teacher Socrates, his pupil Plato (427–347 B.C.), and Plato's student, Aristotle (384–322 B.C.). Given to walking the streets, countryside, and school grounds, they questioned, argued, reasoned, and cajoled. Of the three it was Aristotle who systematized his teachings in works we consult centuries later as book-length treatises on politics, rhetoric, ethics, and poetics. Contained in them we find lasting insights on how ideas originate, propagate, flourish, and perish. This is not the place for extended consideration of Aristotle's analytical method. However, a brief review of his thinking helps us place the overall tradition of propaganda analysis in historical perspective.[3]

Aristotle's chief contributions to what would later become propaganda analysis lie in his teachings in the art of rhetoric. Athenian culture both nurtured and thrived on the spoken word. Educated male Athenians enjoyed arguing about the nature of truth. They delighted in exposing contradictions in one another's arguments, hoping thereby to discover truth. This art of argument was the *dialectic*. Athenians also enjoyed drama, performances acting out everyday foibles and triumphs. Here was the art of the *poetic*. And they sought to persuade one another to courses of action, the art of *rhetoric*. Of course, dialectic, poetic, and rhetoric often overlapped in spoken discourse. (They do today, as TV viewers addicted to Phil Donahue, Geraldo Rivera, Sally Jessy Raphael, or Oprah Winfrey readily recognize.) Aristotle realized this, yet was intrigued with each in its own right, especially with rhetoric. He regarded rhetoric, the art of persuasion (specifically, discovering in any given case the available means of persuasion), as the counterpart of dialectic, the art of reasoned discourse. If dialectic reveals truth, rhetoric helps truth prevail through persuasion. Rhetoric provides speakers with a means of affirming truth, conveying it to an audience, analyzing all sides of questions, and defending truth (and speakers) against attacks.

Aristotle's *Rhetoric*, apparently a compilation of lecture notes, is open to a variety of interpretations.[4] Our interest here, however, is in the *Rhetoric* as a very early guidebook in propaganda analysis. If defined as rhetoric, that is, as the art of persuasion, what would one look for in analyzing propaganda? Aristotle provides a lengthy, and he thought definitive, list of categories, subcategories, and items. Begin with *proof*. To persuade people to act in a recommended way, a speaker must prove the recommendation worthy. One way to do this is to offer evidence at hand, documentation, or other existing proof. A U.S. president says, "I am the Education president," then lists a detailed accounting of his administration's budgetary recommendations and expenditures for education programs, "K through College." Assuming the president's statistics can be verified, whether they do or do not convince the president's detractors, this proof Aristotle called "nonartistic," that is, readily available for citation. In contrast "artistic" proof the speaker creates for persuasive purposes. We have already encountered in Chapter 6 the three forms of Aristotle's category of artistic proof: logos, which demonstrates something is or is not so by logic; ethos, which relies on the credibility of the propaganda source; and pathos, an appeal to audience emotions as a source of credulity.

Certainly propaganda employs artistic proof. What would we look for in analyzing such artistry? In the case of pathetic proof Aristotle taught that speakers must understand their audiences, especially their emotional makeup and inclinations. The "Willie Horton" commercial used in the presidential campaign of 1988 (described in Chapter 4) employed pathetic proof. On the basis of focus group interviews, supporters of George Bush discovered fears of released criminals, indignation at the release of convicted murderers, and so on. Following Aristotle, propaganda analysis would identify the emotions the Horton ad appealed to, inquire how and why these emotions were targeted, and to what end. Aristotle's *Rhetoric* provides a long list of possible emotions (and their opposites) along with the types of persons (young/old, rich/poor, etc.) inclined to act upon them. In this respect Aristotle foreshadowed the elaborate and systematic study of audiences' attitudes so much at the heart of current mass advertising.

Ethical proof we recognize today as proof based upon a candidate's or a product's *image*. Analysis directs us to examine, for example, a politician's reputation for being politically experienced. Composing this image as politician are both background as an officeholder or aspiring officeholder and as a seasoned partisan with loyalties to political party, special interest groups, and so forth. Also, following Aristotle, we would look closely at the personal dimension as well as the political side of the image—intelligence, trustworthiness, character—and the candidate's characteristic style in addressing audiences—appearance, delivery, diction, pitch, volume, rhythm of speaking, and identification with the audience. Contemporary analyses of the images of political candidates and officeholders that focus upon these political and personal sides of ethos derive much from Aristotle.[5]

With respect to logical proof Aristotle regarded the *enthymeme* as fundamental. An enthymeme is a rhetorical syllogism. We are all familiar with the classic example of a syllogism, or mode of reasoning, from a universal truth to a conclusion. Critics of TV advertising on behalf of George Bush in 1988 would probably have no problem with the following syllogism: All men are mortal (major premise); Willie Horton is a man (minor premise); therefore, Willie Horton is mortal (conclusion). That, however, was not the message of the ad. Rephrased from the critics' perspective the syllogism appears more slippery: To furlough convicted felons is to be soft on crime; Michael Dukakis furloughed Willie Horton; Michael Dukakis is soft on crime. In the typical syllogism the major premise (All men are mortal) brooks no exceptions. In the rhetorical syllogism, or enthymeme, the major premise is problematic, that is, it deals with what is known not with certainty but with degrees of likelihood. To furlough convicted felons means being soft on crime is a likely truth to some, not to others. It states a premise true or false within limits of probability.

As vital to logical proof the enthymeme has another characteristic, namely, in achieving persuasive success enthymemes rely on the stock of beliefs, values, and expectations already in the minds of audience members. An enthymeme is seldom a complete syllogism that precisely announces the major premise, minor premise, and conclusion. More frequently the enthymeme leaves something out, prompting audience members to fill in the gap on the basis of their everyday experiences. The enthymeme thus permits audiences to make explicit what the rhetorical syllogism states only implicitly. When in 1988 George Bush visited a firm that manufactures U.S. flags, appearing on TV news holding a large rendering of the Stars and Stripes, the visual enthymeme left viewers to complete the message: "I am patriotic whether my opponent is, or is not." One lesson to be drawn from Aristotle for purposes of propaganda analysis is thus twofold. Enthymemes are key to propaganda but beware the enthymeme that (1) gives the improbable the certainty of a major premise and/or (2) suppresses portions of the syllogism (e.g., Willie Horton was a murderer, rapist, and black; blacks are all like Willie Horton).

The Art of *Dispositio*

In addition to proof and the analysis of its forms, Aristotle's *Rhetoric* discusses the importance of the arrangement or organization of messages to adapt them to various occasions and audiences. This is the art of *dispositio*. For Aristotle there were three kinds of speaking adjusted to three audiences. Deliberative speaking addresses policy-making audiences, such as legislative bodies, and argues the advantages and disadvantages, benefits and costs, of various courses of action. Forensic speaking is for judicial bodies, arguing the facts of events and demonstrating guilt or innocence, accountability, rewards and punishments. Epideictic speaking praises and blames, amplifies the good and bad qualities of politicians, institutions, and ideas. The dollar costs of supporting furlough programs for convicts involves deliberative talk; the guilt or innocence of felons alleged to have committed crimes while on furlough involves forensic talk; whether politicians supporting furlough programs are ''soft on crime'' is a matter of epideictic debate.

The organization of a message for Aristotle involves the arrangement, in order, of a ''poem'' (stating the purpose of the message); statement revealing necessary facts; argument proving, refuting, or questioning ideas; and epilogue recapitulating the main points. Poem and epilogue might not always be necessary, depending on the occasion. The statement and argument emphasize logical proof; the epilogue introduces ethical and pathetic appeals. The skilled speaker adjusts each portion of the message to the deliberative, forensic, or epideictic discourse and audience addressed. Aristotle's *Rhetoric* provides detailed guidelines regarding the appropriate subject matter to be included in deliberative, forensic, and epideictic speaking, respectively, and in organizing persuasive appeals accordingly. We need only point out here that for purposes of propaganda analysis Aristotle's detailed guidelines emphasize repeatedly the importance of analyzing proofs (logical, ethical, and pathetic) and organization (both the types of discourse and the dispositio) with an eye toward detecting the *latent* aims of speakers and messages in their surface or *manifest* linkages of proofs, discourses, audiences, and styles. To accept a candidate's pledge not to raise taxes if elected when the candidate's opponent remains silent on the matter is to accept the candidate's enthymeme of logical proof (''My opponent will raise taxes and should admit it''), ethical and pathetic proof (i.e., ''My pledge is my bond'' and ''You hate taxes'), dispositio (''Competent governance with restricted income is the key issue in this campaign''), and forensic, but veiled epideictic, discourse (''My opponent is guilty of Tax, Tax, Tax; Spend, Spend, Spend''). To assume that the pledge and its proofs, priority, and mode of discourse will prevail before an audience of policy makers once elected, however, is quite another thing, as demonstrated in 1990 when President George Bush retracted candidate George Bush's 1988 boast, ''Read my lips. No new taxes!''

In sum, the earliest precursors of propaganda analysis, as reflected in Aristotle's teachings, alert us to examine the content of appeals for the misuse of spoken argument for persuasive intent. Aristotle's *Rhetoric* offers guidance for distinguishing between valid and invalid proofs, ways of talking, and priorities in persuasion. Although he recognized that all speakers use both dialectic and rhetoric, the arts of reasoned versus persuasive discourse respectively, he viewed each in the service of the other—dialectic to discover reasoned truth, rhetoric to propagate it. Faulty rhetoric (for example, sham enthymemes) were inimical to reasoned truth. In this teaching Aristotle influenced thinkers for centuries to follow. As we saw in our introductory chapter, it is a distinction still very much in vogue, one that remains central to the analysis of rhetoric, and which by extension restricts propaganda analysis to the examination of efforts of *intended* persuasion—as evidenced in current teaching and research on the subject.

For example, one of the most widely used textbooks that introduces students to logic is *Logic and Contemporary Rhetoric: The Use of Reason in Everyday Life*.[6] First published in 1971, the text has been updated in several editions. In each the author, Howard Kahane, states his continuing mission: ''to help students improve their ability to reason about everyday political and social issues, and thus to help raise the level of political discussion in America.''[7] Reason, he goes on, is essential to problem solving and can be viewed as argument. Reasoning is not easy, not automatic, and the trick is to do it "*well*" (Kahane's emphasis). Doing it well involves distinguishing valid from invalid arguments. The book proceeds to describe "good" and "fallacious" reasoning.

Given this emphasis on reasoning and argument, validity and fallacy, one might think that *Logic and Contemporary Rhetoric* is more concerned with logic, that is, dialectic, than with rhetoric. Moreover, since the author makes only passing reference to Aristotle, it might also be assumed that the influence of toga teaching is now minimal. This, however, is not the case. The text does not define rhetoric or persuasion per se but the bulk of the text is not about reasoned discourse in the sense of the discovery of truth, but about persuasive discourse in the service of untruth. In chapters dealing with fallacies perpetuated through statistical arguments, speeches, editorials, political columns, mass advertising, the news media, and textbooks, the vision of Aristotle reigns. Readers learn to "read between the lines" (Aristotle urged the analysis of enthymemes), that "ads play much more to emotion than to reason" (pathos over logos), and that news stories can be "played up or down," "misleading or unfair headlines can be used," or "information can be buried well within a story" (all matters of dispositio).

That Kahane incorporates lessons passed down from the precursors of propaganda analysis in constructing a textbook argument for what is *not* sound reasoning via argument is itself not surprising. Nor is it surprising that the teacher who first formulated many of the guidelines, Aristotle, is scarcely recognized. That he is not is, of course, precisely the point. So influential have Aristotle's teachings continued to be over 23 centuries after his death that, unlike his principles regarding the natural sciences that have long since been discarded, his views on rhetoric remain givens—so much so that they are routinely, often unwittingly or with scant acknowledgment, incorporated into leading textbooks. One influential text, for example, introduces students to the analysis of mass media content by employing Aristotle's definition of rhetoric and his notion of enthymeme to analyze mass advertising.[8] Another critiques methods of historical analysis,[9] compiling a list of a dozen "fallacies" historians are guilty of in their studies. A reader of Aristotle's *Rhetoric* will find that the fallacies derive from that work. Thus, the Aristotelian notion that the key to the analysis of persuasion is sensitivity to the difference between "good" and "fallacious" reasoning, which preceded conventional propaganda analysis by many centuries, remains an influential element of it.

Think, in this regard, how much conceptual power Aristotle gives you in the daily exposure to propaganda that we all experience. The myriad spot ads you hear and see can be more easily seen as involving fallacious proofs that your newly learned habit of logical analysis helps you notice. In a day's time, observe how many ads involve the use of enthymeme: something is left out of the logical procession of assertions. Armed with these and the other tools dating from Aristotle, you too can use reason in everyday life.

WAR TALK: CONVENTIONS OF PROPAGANDA ANALYSIS

The tradition of propaganda analysis was born in a preliterate era when the spoken work reigned and toga talk dominated. Yet it was not until the twentieth century that propaganda became a sufficiently visible phenomenon to warrant continuing and systematic investigation by a class of scholars and critics that we can refer to as propaganda analysts.

As one such analyst put it, "If propaganda analysis is ever to transcend the realm of *belles lettres*, systematization is indispensable."[10] World War I and its aftermath, World War II, and the protracted cold war that followed provided the stimulus for systematic study. With propaganda thought to be a powerful and threatening weapon, right-thinking people everywhere rallied to urge steps to detect and to counter it. If the toga talk era had focused primarily upon sorting sound from fallacious logic in spoken persuasive appeals, the war talk era centered on the detection of deceptive emotional appeals in all manner of persuasive messages—spoken, written, filmed, and so on. In the context of recurring warfare, and the propaganda it provoked, several conventions developed for how to think about and analyze propaganda. In the remainder of this chapter we examine those conventions. Many were generated specifically for propaganda analysis. Others were peripheral to that task, yet became part of the analytical apparatus. These conventions, some borrowed from the precursors just described, form the tradition of propaganda analysis.

Analyzing Claims: The Seven Deadly Signals of Propaganda (Or Is It Thirteen, Six, Five, or Four?)

During the 1960s, as recounted earlier, the TV series "Star Trek" gave birth to a generation of "trekkies," and subsequent reruns and remakes of the series have continued to do so in the 1990s. But in spite of its popularity "Star Trek" never had the broad appeal to TV audiences of some of its competitors in the 1960s. One such competitor was "Bonanza," a western that revolved about the adventures of Ben Cartwright and his three sons Adam, "Hoss," and "Little Joe." The series propagated myths about the values of manliness, honesty, responsibility, courage, and straight shooting, virtues allegedly vital for carving out an empire in the Old West. In 1966 "Bonanza" had such a commanding lead in TV viewer ratings that producers of competing shows regarded it as invincible. As with any TV series, however, its charm finally faded and it left the air. "Bonanza" is today born again on cable television in reruns.

Our interest in "Bonanza" is not in its popularity or its propagation of mythical values. Rather it is in the star of the series, Lorne Greene, who played Ben Cartwright, scion of the family. Greene was more than an actor. He was also a student of propaganda. In 1966 when "Bonanza" was at its zenith, Greene in collaboration with Robert Allen published "The Propaganda Game." In the booklet accompanying their board game, Allen and Greene state that propaganda is both a "nefarious" and "noble art." It can "whip up racial hatred among groups" as well as move people to "warmth and kindness." In the give-and-take of nefarious and noble intent it is "imperative" that people "be able to analyze and distinguish between the emotional aura" surrounding ideas and "the actual content" of ideas. The aims of "The Propaganda Game," therefore, were to introduce players to "the techniques used to distort the thinking process," especially making them "*aware* of the emotional overtones in all arguments and suggestions" (authors' emphasis).[11]

The game thus falls squarely in the tradition of propaganda analysis as war talk, that is, emotional appeals directed at stirring people to action as much via pathos as logos or ethos. The equipment and rules of the game we need not consider except for one item, the "Technique Card." Each player received a card divided into six sections. Each section consisted of a listing of specific propagandistic techniques within a given category, techniques of "self-deception," "language," "irrelevance," "exploitation," "form," and "maneuver." In all, cards listed 55 specific techniques in the six categories. In their game booklet the authors explain each technique and give examples of its use. If players through the game could but master the capacity to spot these techniques in messages they encounter in their everyday lives, they would develop greater control over their responses to problems and situations.

Many of the techniques identified in "The Propaganda Game" can be traced to Aristotle. But many others derive from the concerns and efforts of scholars and social reformers after World War I who sought to expose what they regarded as the powerful appeal of propaganda's emotion-laden logic. One such scholar, political scientist Harold Lasswell, analyzed how the use of emotionally appealing symbols had aroused people to action during World War I.[12] Journalist Walter Lippmann, who during World War I had been instrumental in the drafting of President Woodrow Wilson's "Fourteen Points," alerted citizens to the role of "stereotypes" and how emotional appeals in propaganda could both create and exploit the "pictures" people have in their heads of the "world outside."[13]

Detailing the Fine Art of Propaganda.   These and other threads of scholarly and reformist thought in propaganda analysis converged in 1937 with the founding of the Institute for Propaganda Analysis (IPA). The institute coordinated and published the works of leading historians, political scientists, sociologists, and journalists conducting propaganda analysis. Those publications included a monthly bulletin, *Propaganda Analysis*, that had a subscription of over 10,000. Each bulletin analyzed a current propaganda campaign, such as efforts to win support for the foreign policy of the administration of President Franklin Roosevelt. The institute also organized courses for secondary schools and provided study guides with bibliographies and suggestions on how to analyze propaganda. In addition a speakers' bureau gave lectures to adult groups on the detection of propaganda. Finally, the institute published a vastly influential book, *The Fine Art of Propaganda*.[14]

The Fine Art of Propaganda described the "ABCs of Propaganda Analysis" consisting of seven propaganda devices contained in messages with persuasive intent. Although the Institute for Propaganda Analysis ceased to exist just prior to the entry of the United States into World War II, these seven devices have been repeated so frequently in lectures, articles, and textbooks ever since that they have become virtually synonymous with the practice and analysis of propaganda in all its aspects. With rare exception, guidebooks instructing readers in how to think more clearly, reason properly, or argue well repeat the seven devices. Howard Kahane's *Logic and Contemporary Rhetoric* mentioned earlier incorporates them; so too they appear as "techniques" in "The Propaganda Game"; and they reappear in books on propaganda per se.[15] *The Fine Art of Propaganda* not only defines each device and demonstrates how to detect it in claims made for ideas, arguments, and points of view, but also offers a visual symbol for each device so that readers can associate device and picture. This association was to simplify memorization of the seven devices. Here, then, are IPA guidelines for what to look for in reading any text or listening to any appeal (including the text you are now reading), along with a defining example:

Name Calling, or condemning an idea on its face by giving it a bad label regardless of the evidence: "A tax increase is garbage."

Glittering Generality, or using a positive or "virtue" word to recommend an idea: "Only our positive outlook can win the day."

Transfer, that is, attaching the authority, sanction, and prestige—or the authority, sanction, and disrespect—of one idea to another: "Ivory Soap, 99 and 44/100 percent *pure*."

Testimonial, or having an admired or hated person endorse an idea or product: "Willie Nelson wears Wrangler Jeans."

Plain Folks, or associating ideas with common, ordinary ways and customs: "Ed and I thank you for your support" (for Bartles & Jaymes wine coolers).

Card Stacking, namely, the *dispositio* effort to arrange arguments and evidence to serve one's purposes: "You've seen the rest, now buy the best."

Band Wagon Appeal, or since everyone else is doing it, so should we: "Only limited quantities are available, so don't miss out, place your order *now*!"

These seven deadly danger signals of propaganda have not survived without criticism. Leonard Doob, one of the IPA's members, notes several problems with the ABCs: (1) classifying an appeal or portion thereof in one or another of the seven categories is arbitrary and subjective; (2) simply identifying the presence of the devices offers no more guidance than would a chemist who specifies the elements of a liquid without measuring the quantities of each; (3) it is not clear whether the power of the "devices" arises from the propagandist's clever intent in employing them or from the propagandees' susceptibility to them regardless of intent; (4) the ethos or credibility of the propagandist is not included in the analysis of the message. In sum, the seven devices oversimplify the total propaganda process. For Doob this "need to oversimplify also gave rise to the elimination of crucial problems or to an informal treatment of them which depended upon the ability and bias" of people doing the detecting and analyzing. He pointed out that the IPA had a laudable purpose, that is, instructing people in the detection of propaganda, but:

> This laudable purpose required that the analysis be simple and easily comprehended by high school students or, as some members of the Institute's Board used to say to one another, by taxicab drivers. The analysis had to be based upon a limited number of "devices" which could be understood and memorized with no great difficulty.[16]

Criticisms aside, as already noted, the effort to analyze claims by searching for the symbols and themes that reflect propagandistic intent continued, albeit, as we shall see, not as the whole of the tradition of content analysis. In the process the list of the IPA's Seven Devices expanded and contracted. Thus, for example, in a series of books an influential post–World War II social critic, Stuart Chase, turned to propaganda analysis. His *Guides To Straight Thinking* succinctly summarizes the state of the art in the mid 1950s. In it he identifies 13 "fallacies in ordinary thinking and discussion to which all of us are prone." They have a noticeable resemblance to the IPA's seven and, given Chase's readily grasped descriptions, deserve repeating to provide a tidy photograph of popularized propaganda analysis of the era:[17]

1. *Over-generalizing.* Jumping to conclusions from one or two cases.
2. *"Thin entering wedge."* A special type of over-generalizing involving prediction, e.g., if A is done, then B—usually dire—will follow.

3. *Getting personal*. Forsaking the issue to attack the character of its defender.
4. *"You're another."* My point may be bad, but yours is just as bad, so that makes it quits.
5. *Cause and effect*. If event B comes *after* event A, then it is assumed to be the result of A.
6. *False analogies*. A, it is argued, is exactly like B—but it isn't.
7. *Wise men can't be wrong*. Clinching an argument by an appeal to authority.
8. *"Figures prove."* A subclass of the above, especially popular in America today.
9. *Appeal to the crowd*. Distorting an issue with mass prejudices.
10. *Arguing in circles*. Using a conclusion to prove itself.
11. *"Self-evident truths."* Trying to win an argument by saying "everybody knows" it must be true.
12. *Black or white*. Forcing an issue with many aspects into just two sides, and so neglecting important shades of gray.
13. *Guilt by association*. Making a spurious identification between two dissimilar persons or events.

Chase noted that propagandists utilize all of these fallacies, plus variations, but especially favor the first four. It is not possible to estimate how widely Chase's views of propaganda reached. However, given that portions of *Guides To Straight Thinking* were published in the *Reader's Digest*, the magazine with the largest mass circulation of the period, and that Chase repeated his guidelines in several other popularly selling volumes, he was clearly the heir to the heritage established by the Institute for Propaganda Analysis.

Ranking Message Claims.   Today that legacy continues in one of the most comprehensive and systematic of schemes for the analysis of message claims, one developed by communication scholar Hugh Rank. In two books, *The Pitch*, dealing with how to analyze advertising,[18] and *The Pep Talk*, concerning the analysis of political language,[19] he provides guidelines for analyzing propaganda. Rank regards propaganda advertising as involving five stages, each stage incorporating specific techniques. More than 42,000 TV ads alone—not counting newspaper, magazine, direct mail, and other vehicles of advertising—appear in the United States each year. Given the clutter of ads, admakers employ devices to make their commercials stand out from the crowd. These devices are what Rank calls *attention-getting* techniques; they appeal to the senses (motions, colors, graphics, music, etc.), emotions (associations with fun, family, etc.), and thoughts (claims, demonstrations, stories, etc.). A second series of techniques, *confidence-building*, strive for ethos, that is, to establish the credibility of the source of the advertising message—testimonials, authority figures, brand names, packaging, and so forth. Third, ads employ *desire-stimulating* techniques. These techniques form the main part of the ad. They appeal to people's efforts to obtain or keep what they want (to get a "good" or to keep a "good," according to Rank) and to desires to avoid a "bad" or to get rid of a "bad." To aid people in detecting desire-stimulating techniques, Rank provides an extensive categorization and listing of key words employed in ads that make claims for products. The fourth stage of advertising employs *urgency-stressing* techniques, which are similar to bandwagon appeals identified by the Institute for Propaganda Analysis. Finally, ads employ *response-seeking* techniques telling people precisely what to do to obtain the pleasures and avoid the pains claimed in the ad—buy, sell, join, act, drink, taste, call the toll free number, or whatever.

Following stride for stride in the footsteps of the IPA in simplifying the complexities of advertising appeals, Rank presents a formula to assist in memorizing the five techniques:

HI!: Attention-getting techniques.
TRUST ME!: Confidence-building techniques.
YOU NEED!: Desire-stimulating techniques.
HURRY!: Urgency-stressing techniques.
BUY!: Response-seeking techniques.

Rank's recommendations for the analysis of political language derive from and parallel those he makes for the analysis of advertising. Political appeals in oratory, conversations, TV appearances, news conferences, and advertising also promise acquisition (getting a good), protection (keeping a good), prevention (avoiding a bad), and relief (getting rid of a bad). Political claims endeavor to intensify the claimed "goods" of those making them while downplaying the "bads" asserted by opponents; and they try to intensify the "bads" charged against opponents while downplaying the "goods" opponents claim to possess. The generic pattern for making such claims is "the pep talk." Typically such talk, according to Rank, has four stages with specific propaganda techniques associated with each. Again, Rank offers a formula for memorization: (1) LOOK OUT! asserts "The Threat" that obtains people's attention by warning that something bad is in the offing; (2) GET TOGETHER! appeals to audiences to rally in unity, loyalty, and supreme effort to combat the threat, that is, "The Bonding"; (3) DO GOOD! spells out the cause, the vision, the sacrifices that must be made, and the benefits that will be won by rallying around the politician making the appeal, what Rank labels "The Cause"; and (4) LET'S! or "The Response" sought by the political claimant—vote, march, protest, and so on. As with his analysis of ads, that is, "the pitch," Rank pens a detailed listing of key words, phrases, and symbols common to each of the four techniques that compose "the pep talk."

As we did with Aristotle, think what keeping these ideas in mind can do for you when you're confronted with big talk and great realities. Everything from an ad to a public relations tape to a political speech takes on a new aspect: what are they saying here, and does it make any logical sense? If you hear from a candidate name calling and self-description as a "country boy," appeal to dubious statistics and trends, stressing the urgency that you vote for him or her, and so on, you now have the conceptual tools to notice and take heed. After hearing a great deal of suspicious political talk, you now can say with Spock of "Star Trek," "It is not logical!"

Content Analysis: Quantifying Political Discourse

We noted above that one of the members of the Institute for Propaganda Analysis, Leonard Doob, was critical of the IPA's approach to propaganda analysis, in part because it merely listed without measurement the propaganda techniques in the manifest content of messages, a listing largely produced by subjective appraisals. What such critics as Doob said of the IPA's seven devices might also be said of its precursor, Aristotle's analysis of rhetoric, and its heirs—Kahane's analysis of reasoning, the six categories of propaganda techniques, in ''The Propaganda Game'' or Rank's five- and four-stage analyses of advertising and political language.

One of the earliest to raise such criticisms was a scholar who pioneered in propaganda analysis after World War I, Harold Lasswell. Lasswell's first major work, *Propaganda Techniques in the World War*,[20] published in 1927, identified the common themes running through the propaganda of all the combatant nations in World War I. It listed but did not count them. By 1949, however, Lasswell was critical of his earlier procedures and called for qualitative analysis (lists of themes, symbols, techniques, etc.) to become quantitative.[21] One means for achieving this Lasswell identified as ''content analysis.''

Whereas the Institute for Propaganda Analysis, Kahane's textbook, ''The Propaganda Game,'' and Rank's analytical schemes aimed at teaching simplified ways of detecting fallacious arguments to schoolchildren, lay persons, and, as Doob noted, ''the taxi driver,'' content analysis is for trained specialists. It is scarcely a convenient method for the average high school graduate, for example, to use in comparing the competing claims made by colleges recruiting students, or by buyers weighing the hyperbolic pitches of used car salespersons. Instead it is a research technique that measures the manifest content of messages objectively, systematically, and quantitatively. Although we need not delve deeply into the technical aspects of content analysis, a few such technical matters must be addressed. Readers seeking a more detailed accounting of the intricacies and mysteries of content analysis may consult several readily available texts.[22]

The focus of content analysis is the *manifest* content of messages. It assumes a relationship between the surface words, pictures, and other symbols of a message, that is, manifest content, and the intent of the propagandist, and/or the effects on the propagandees. Moreover, it posits that the meaning of a message's content can be derived from the frequency of occurrences of various elements (words, pictures, other symbols) in the message. As a research technique content analysis (1) defines precise categories of content elements, (2) systematically counts those elements in all messages constituting a representative sampling, and (3) draws conclusions about propagandistic content, intent, and effects from the pattern of frequencies derived. Let us consider each of these three steps separately.

Any given oral, written, or visual message (or a message combining oral, written, and visual materials) consists of several elements. These elements may be words, sentences, or assertions (i.e., themes) consisting of combinations of words, sentences, and so on; they may be vocalizations of tone, pitch, volume; they may be pictured facial expressions, bodily postures, movements, or objects. Take as an example one recorded 60-second televised segment of a presidential candidate accepting the party nomination before a national convention. There would be the words, sentences, and themes of what the candidate said; the vocal style of how he or she said it; and the sights and sounds of the auditorium, the audience, and its reactions. All constitute content elements to be categorized, recorded, counted, and analyzed.

Given the multiplicity of possible elements, the analyst must do something that, on the surface, seems contradictory. The analyst must *objectify subjectivity*. The analyst must decide which content to take into account, which should be classified as similar and, thus, fitting into the same category and recorded and counted as such. These are subjective appraisals. They are, in the jargon of referees or umpires officiating at athletic contests, ''judgment calls.'' Hence, it is incumbent on the analyst to define precisely what categories of message content are to be investigated and precisely what elements fit each category.

Moreover, those definitions must be applied consistently without caprice or bias to all messages composing a representative sampling of the body of communication under investigation. Assume one wants to compare pro-Democrat versus pro-Republican discourse on the three nightly network TV newscasts (ABC, CBS, NBC) in a four-year period between presidential elections. Examining all newscasts across the four years is a formidable undertaking. It is more manageable to examine a sample of all newscasts that represents the whole. Suffice to say that there are several techniques for selecting representative samples in content analysis. None are foolproof; all require judgment calls. Again subjectivity must be objectified by precisely defined and stated procedures.

Assume the analyst selects a representative sampling of all messages under investigation (say selecting for each news network 150 nightly newscasts from the total nightly newscasts each network aired in a four-year period, sampling to take into account all days of the week, confounding news events, and other imponderables). A unit of analysis and a unit of enumeration must then be defined. The unit of analysis may be a word, sentence, TV anchor's or correspondent's entire report, an entire news story, even an entire newscast. The enumerated unit refers to what precise unit to count, and how—for example, the number of pro-Democrat or pro-Republican references in each newscast. In defining both units of analysis and enumeration there are, again, judgment calls and requirements to define precisely and apply systematically such definitions.

Of course, someone must listen to, read, or view the content under investigation (perhaps all three) and count each appearance of each defined content element. Such "coders" must be selected, trained, and monitored, as well as provided with an adequate form, or "coding instrument," to record their observations. The aim of all this effort is to assure that all of the precise definitions generated throughout the investigation continue to "ensure that one's findings do not reflect one's whims, tastes, prejudices, or other idiosyncrasies." Yet this is not enough, for "even the most precise definitions may not be used in the same way by different students, indeed, by the same student at different times." For example, "we may be sleepy one day and wide awake the next, upset about a personal matter at one moment and very content about life at another." "These different conditions may lead to variations in our classification of the data into different categories."[23] Content analysts deal with such possibilities by comparing samples of data coded by separate coders through the calculation of a measure called "intercoder reliability." In its most direct form such a calculation consists of dividing the total number of items coded into the number of items the coders have coded in identical ways. If, for example, 1,000 items were coded and coders agree on 900 codings, the intercoder reliability is 90 percent. Here there is yet another judgment call, the "drama of intercoder reliability" enacted when content analysts decide whether an attained level of intercoder reliability is sufficiently high: 75 percent? 85 percent? 95 percent? Finally, the analyst of propagandistic content reaches the stage of drawing conclusions from the revealed pattern of frequencies of content elements. One more time issues of subjectivity arise. If, for example, one finds that the ratio of pro-Democrat references to pro-Republican references in ABC newscasts is 55-45, in CBS newscasts 53-47, and in NBC newscasts 51-49, does that demonstrate that ABC is more pro-Democrat than its rivals? To objectify that judgment call, analysts turn to "tests of statistical significance," measures indicating when frequency differences found in two or more samples are "significant," that is, "real," or are simply a matter of chance. Much like Scrooge conjecturing whether his visit from Jacob Marley reflected the ghostlike but material Jacob or the digestive upsets of underdone roast beef and an over-done potato, content analysts weigh significance tests. When and if they find differences in content statistically significant, there remains one final problem: is a significant statisti-cal difference significant in substance? Does it matter to viewers that TV networks differ in how they treat the two major political parties? Do statistically significant differences in network coverage reflect network intentions (i.e., biases) or, say, differing ways of gath-ering and presenting the news?

During and following World War II, content analysis became the dominant strain in the tradition of propaganda analysis. Moreover, quantitative studies of the content of com-munication other than propaganda also proliferated, accounting for one-third of the studies in mass communication by 1980. The emergence of computer technology stimulated con-tent analysis as a research tool even more. The creation of sophisticated computer pro-grams for content analysis helped reduce reliance on human coders (texts can be machine scanned and automatically coded), produced computerized dictionaries to identify and count content elements, reduced sampling problems by making it possible for analysts to manipulate entire bodies of content rather than portions thereof, made more elaborate analyses of findings possible, and minimized the time required for routine tasks. It did not remove all subjectivity, however, for humans must still determine what words compose computerized dictionaries, what merits analysis, and what constitutes substantively im-portant differences in findings.

Although quantitative analysis of propaganda content does not eliminate subjective judgments, it does provide controls over their free rein. Those controls enable propaganda analysts to chart trends in content over time, compare content output across sources and media, and make inferences more valid, reliable, and systematic than, for instance, the IPA's "ABCs." But those same controls are not purchased cheaply—in time, labor, or money. At least the purchase is not so inexpensive as to be within the reach of most aver-age citizens faced with the inundation of propaganda in their everyday lives. Content anal-ysis, to be sure, has—to return to Doob's metaphor—made propaganda analysts more like chemists, who list *and* measure. As yet, however, most citizens remain alchemists searching for the quick fix or panacea borrowed from experience and residing in intuition to analyze claims and content.

Nevertheless, the principles of content analysis can, like the other concepts we have talked about, aid us in dealing with propaganda encountered every day. Without getting too technical, one can examine documents or images for what kind of textual and sub-textual messages the propagators may be trying to convey. If you are bombarded with campaign literature from one party, say, attacking the incumbent of another, informally analyze the content of their stuff: What messages are most prevalent? What is mentioned less or not at all? What do the pictures "say" over and over? You can tape campaign ads during the preelection blitz and look at them carefully: Are there subtle messages, like ap-peal to racism or patriotism "hidden" in the imagery? Do they appeal to attacks on the op-ponent's character or other negative themes? And so on. One does not have to be a social scientist to use content analysis. If you develop the habit of critically reading or viewing everything, it becomes easy enough to keep a running count of what they're trying to pitch to you. And you don't have to be Commander Data to figure it out.

MORE HELPFUL TALK: RELATED TRADITIONS OF SEMANTIC, ETHICAL, RITUAL, AND EFFECTS ANALYSES

The mainstream of traditional propaganda analysis, then, pours from the confluence of two wide tributaries, both flowing during the period when war propaganda was a dominant concern of this century. Qualitative claims analysis is the older stream, quantitative content analysis the younger. Also flowing into the mainstream from creeks filled by occasional rains prompted by war concerns, albeit different kinds of wars, have been other, lesser contributors to the tradition of content analysis. Three are worthy of special focus, both in their own right and because they offer transitions to the more recent critical ways of thinking about propaganda considered in Chapter 8.

Semantic Analysis

Stuart Chase, the popularizer of propaganda analysis discussed earlier in this chapter, contrasted fallacious appeals and reasoning with scientific methods. Among the techniques he listed as "chief mental tools of modern science" was "the tool of semantics," or "the systematic study of meaning."[24] Students of semantics analyze not only what people say but what they mean when they say it. The question posed is not "Did I say what I mean?" but "What do I mean when I say?"

In large measure semantic analysis derives from a broader intellectual movement called general semantics. That movement's leader, Alfred Korzybski (1879–1950), taught that many ills of the world, war included, sprang from fallacies not so much in reasoning but in meaning, especially the meaning of words and phrases. Korzybski likened language to a map: "If we reflect upon our languages, we find at best they must be considered *only as maps*." But "a word *is not* the object it represents" and "a map *is not* the territory it represents" (Korzybski's emphasis).[25] Like early propaganda analysts, semantic analysts founded a center for study, The Institute of General Semantics, published informative materials, and offered courses of instruction. Although scarcely having the impact of other intellectual movements, say the Enlightenment or Marxism, the general semantic movement left its mark, and the basic dictum, "the map is not the territory," is a given for many students of language.

With respect to propaganda analysis that basic dictum has several implications. One is that since words in and of themselves can mean nothing literally—that is, they no more say anything intrinsic about persons, objects, or events than maps depict actual territories—words and phrases can be manipulated by propagandists to mean anything they wish. "The cold war is over" is neither true nor false, simply incomplete, without detail. What is "cold" about "war" and what is "war"? When is it over? When the Berlin Wall falls or, as baseball legend Yogi Berra said, "It ain't over 'til it's over"? Without definitive answers, and there are none to be had, propagandists of various persuasions can turn "The cold war is over" to confusing and contradictory special pleadings.

Instead of looking to words for meanings, semantic analysts teach us to look to how people react to them, their "semantic reactions." As a leading scholar of general semantics (and later U.S. senator), S. I. Hayakawa, described in detail, words mean different things depending upon different reactions in different contexts. Frog fishing, a frog in the throat, braided frog adornments, a horse's frog, and a railroad frog are not the same.[26]

Now all of this is obvious and would be scarcely worth noting except for one thing: People develop fixed, knee-jerk semantic reactions to words and other symbols regardless of contexts. Semantic analysis labels these reactions "identification reactions." There is a fixed pattern of response where all occurrences of a symbol provoke the same behavior *and* people identify all cases under the same name and treat them as identical regardless of differences. Thus, all "free spenders" are the same, all "right-to-lifers," all "free choice advocates," and so on.

There are several sources of identification reactions. One lies in language itself, another in the general reluctance of people to search for differences in symbolic meanings. For students of general semantics, propaganda also plays an important part in creating identification reactions. Coke Is It; I'd Walk a Mile for a Camel; That Great Feeling, Toyota; I Like Ike; LBJ All the Way; Nixon's the One—all exemplify what Hayakawa says is "almost entirely a matter of pound, pound, pounding into people word-mindedness to the exclusion of fact-mindedness."[27] Although semantic analysts do not dismiss the merit in exposing fallacies in logic and reasoning, they do not believe that such claims analysis alone will alleviate the pain of such pounding. We must go farther. Namely, in analyzing *all* communication, overtly propagandistic or not, we must be cautious about one particular word: *is*. To say in any form that something "is" too frequently implies an identification that does not exist in reality. *Is* creates fuzzy abstractions; they purport to state precise relations between things—between words and persons, concrete objects, specific events—when they do not. The "tyranny of language" stems from *is*; to relieve the tyranny, the semanticist warns "Beware the *is*."

Before we close this discussion of semantic analysis, consider one final point. If general semantics is correct that words and other symbols do not represent people, objects, and events faithfully, but only "map" them, the semantic dictum has particular relevance for politics. Politics involves many activities—arguing, cajoling, complaining, marching, lobbying, bargaining, commanding, and a host of others that only hint at politics' many facets. One activity central to politics involves quarreling over the meanings of symbols and the reactions to them.[28] Semantic arguments join semantic reactions in politics: What is democracy? What is equality? What is freedom? Disputes provoked in response to these questions are not "merely semantic" but involve the shedding of blood. Meanings are not taken for granted but contested. Politics, and political propaganda, create meanings and identification reactions as well, as we shall see in Chapter 8.

Ethical Analysis

If semantic analysts explore the surface of propaganda ever mindful of *is*, ethical analysts scratch message surfaces pondering the *should*, that is, the moral implications of communication. In 1622 when the Congregatio de Propaganda Fide came into existence to spread the faith, propaganda was considered a moral endeavor. The era of World Wars I and II left propaganda in ill repute. Distinctions between "white" (accurate information from a known source), "gray" (uncertain accuracy and source), and "black" (fabricated information, phony source) propaganda existed, but the overall assessment of propaganda was negative. Propaganda was what the enemy did and, by definition, bad. Hence, ethical analysis simply consisted of using the techniques of claims analysis to detect the propaganda devices in messages. To be ethical one has to avoid the devices.

Contemporary analyses of the ethics of propaganda go beyond the identification of propaganda devices. A leading example is the work of Robert Goodin. He regards propaganda as one form of "manipulatory politics." Lying, withholding information, co-opting opponents, and overloading people with too much and/or with irrelevant information are other forms. Manipulatory politics is unethical and consists of any unwelcome interference in the life of another person: "when we manipulate people we cause them to do something they would not otherwise have done—which is to say, manipulation of human agents runs contrary to their putative will."[29] For Goodin, even if a propaganda message is accurate, it is still incomplete. The propagandist selects only information to aid her or his cause. Comparing propaganda along selected dimensions with the other forms of manipulatory politics, Goodin judges propaganda to be "slightly" deceptive and "slightly" contrary to the putative will of persons propagandized, to have only short-term effects because people soon recognize propaganda for what it is and a means of persuasion available to everybody. In Goodin's assessment, propaganda is thereby "marginally" manipulatory, hence, marginally unethical.

This sanguine verdict is not shared by Jacques Ellul. As we described in Chapter 3, Ellul has argued that in contemporary politics propaganda's cumulative impact is to create a world of fantasy, myth, and delusion. No amount of accurate information, sound reasoning, or semantic purity can penetrate that self-enclosed world. In it propaganda elevates power to an ethical imperative, namely, one who exercises power should do so and possesses the ethical right to do so. Moreover, propaganda's focus is on the here and now, for example, getting the newest car models off the dealer's showroom floor *today*, reporting "the next news when it happens," and promoting *today's* hottest single, rock star, or movie. In *today's* world neither historical perspective nor critical judgment counts, only "happiness." Finally, according to Ellul, propaganda isolates people from one another, rhetoric drives out dialectic, and imposed truth supplants the search for truth. By creating people enclosed in their individually self-contained, Saran-wrapped bubbles, propaganda is not simply unethical. No, propaganda wipes out the possibility of ethics at all.[30]

Ritual Analysis

When the symbols composing propaganda and the responses to them are standardized and repetitive, we have rituals. Ceremonies such as flag salutes or presidential inaugurations, summit meetings between world leaders (see Chapter 4), even standardized sign-offs in news programs ("Brenda Starr, PDQ News, Washington") are examples of rituals and of ritual propaganda.[31] The analysis of rituals occupies an important niche in the tradition of propaganda analysis. An example of ritual analysis from 1930s Germany, namely, the analysis of Nazi party rallies, is illustrative. Adolf Hitler, and his minister of propaganda Joseph Goebbels, placed a premium on precisely staged and orchestrated mass rallies to build popular support for the Nazi regime, or at least the image of having that support. Political scientist Thornton Sinclair attended Nazi party rallies in Hitler's Germany over a period of six summers from 1932 to 1937. His observations led to a systematic analysis of the symbolism of the key elements at each rally: the grandiose scale of the buildings and grounds, intended to create a sense of confidence in Germany's future; the use of precise procedures for pageantry at party congresses; special assemblies convened at rallies to appeal to cultural groups; frank emotional appeals in mass demonstrations employing flags, marches, songs, and sham battles, all with elaborate staging; and displays of loyalty by Hitler Youth groups. Central to the ritual was Hitler himself, so central that he was a *ritual figure* symbolizing security, prosperity, and superiority: "Every means of publicity informs one that the great moment for each demonstrator arrives when he looks at the *Führer*, and in fact, the first question the returning visitor is asked is, 'Did you see the *Führer*?' "[32]

Propaganda rituals extend beyond observing how people act in standardized, repeated ways. Depictions of behavior in songs, stories, photographs, films, and so on can be ritualized. Sociologist Erving Goffman, for example, analyzed the ritual-like displays of females in product advertising, what he labeled "gender advertising." His analysis of 500 ads revealed consistent ritualistic portrayals of women, portrayals propagating ideas about their social status compared with males. Gender ads depicted women as smaller in stature; obsessed with touching and caressing products; subordinate in face-to-face situations with men (males are executives, females are not, and the female lowers the head more than does the male); and, when alone, sitting, reclining, and posturing; bonding with daughters in the family while fathers bond with sons; and withdrawn from social situations rather than a part of them.[33] Like Sinclair's analysis of Nazi party rallies, Goffman's rests on the view that close observation of rituals reveals their propagandistic intent.

Effects Analysis

One final tributary to the mainstream tradition of propaganda analysis should be added. During and after World War II there was considerable concern with the pernicious effects propaganda might have upon a people; after the war the same concerns were expressed about mass communication, especially radio, then television. Using a variety of research techniques, principally experiments and surveys of peoples' views, scholars explored the problem. Two sets of studies warrant specific mention. One, the Yale Studies in Attitude Change and Communication, inquired into the effects of specific propagandistic approaches: the credibility of the message source (Aristotle's ethos); the order of presentation in making appeals (Aristotle's *dispositio*); the ordering of pro and con arguments (Aristotle's *poem*); various types of appeals, such as "fear-arousing" (Aristotle's pathos); and whether some people are more susceptible to persuasion than others.[34] The other set of investigations, "the voting studies," asked whether propaganda in election campaigns influences votes.[35]

Both the attitude change and voting studies reached the conclusion in assessing the effects of propaganda messages on people that "it depends" on a host of mediating factors. The Yale attitude change studies tended to detect more overall impact than did the voting studies, a difference due in large part to differing research techniques. The general assessment was that effects of persuasion are "marginal" and "mediated" rather than "direct." Research then turned away from traditional propaganda analysis altogether and, instead, to the discovery and inventory of an ever-growing number of variables producing marginality and mediation in peoples' responses to mass communication generally, but not to propaganda.[36]

As before, these related methods of looking at propaganda can be used by anyone interested in understanding the pitches that are made. For example, ritual analysis helps you to understand what is going on in presidential rituals. When presidents Reagan and Bush arrived at and left the White House, this often was the occasion for an elaborate ritual that communicated presidential majesty through pomp and circumstance, suggesting that the man who occupies the office is majestic, magisterial, a great man deserving of adulation, a colossus that bestrides the world, and so on. Ritual analysis demystifies such pseudo-events as staged to try to shore up the image, and perhaps even the agonizing lack of self-esteem, of the rather ordinary man who occupies the office.

RETHINKING TRADITION: IS WHAT YOU SEE ALL THAT YOU GET?

As the semanticists would say, tradition "is" but a word. The tradition of propaganda analysis described in this chapter is far more diverse and rich than any brief account can suggest. The main features of the tradition, however, are clear: it assumes propaganda to be intentional; if not blatant, or open, still capable of being analyzed from its surface, manifest content; and employing detectable fallacies in reasoning, identification reactions, deception, and emotionally charged situations. Propaganda's direct effects vary, that is, "it depends," and the cumulative impact of propaganda is difficult to measure. Finally, one other point: the "tradition" of propaganda remains unfixed; it, like propaganda, changes as newer ways of propagating ideas incorporate and replace earlier ones. In the process novel ways of thinking critically about propaganda emerge in a time of suspended beliefs. We turn to those in the following chapter.

You now have advanced to the stage of understanding how to critically analyze propaganda. Armed with a conceptual and historical grasp of modern propaganda, you now complement that with critical tools with which to spot and critique propaganda. Now this new knowledge and critical ability must be sharpened by familiarity with recent critical thinking about propaganda. Once you grasp this, you will possess a good working knowledge of the world of propaganda, the varieties of propaganda, and the analysis of propaganda. Let us now turn to that task.

NOTES

1. For a history of "Star Trek," see Allan Asherman, *The Star Trek Compendium* (New York: Pocket Books, 1986).
2. See Robert Jewett and John Shelton Lawrence, *The American Monomyth* (Garden City, NY: Anchor/Doubleday, 1977), Chap. 1.
3. For a readily grasped review of Aristotle's method relevant to propaganda analysis, consult James L. Golden, Goodwin F. Berquist, and William E. Coleman, *The Rhetoric of the Western World* (Dubuque, IA: Kendall/Hunt, 1976), Chap 4.
4. One of many translations is *The Rhetoric of Aristotle: A Translation* (Cambridge: Cambridge University Press, 1909).
5. See, for example, Dan Nimmo and Robert L. Savage, *Candidates and Their Images* (Pacific Palisades, CA: Goodyear, 1976) for a review of the dimensions of political and personal images activated in communication.
6. Howard Kahane, *Logic and Contemporary Rhetoric: The Use of Reason in Everyday Life* (Belmont, CA: Wadsworth, 1971; 3rd ed., 1980).

7. Ibid., p. vii.
8. See, for instance, Kathleen Hall Jamieson and Karlyn Kohrs Campbell, *The Interplay of Influence*, 2nd ed. (Belmont, CA: Wadsworth, 1988).
9. See David Hackett Fischer, *Historians' Fallacies: Toward a Logic of Historical Thought* (New York: Harper Torchbooks, 1970), where the author passingly incorporates Aristotelian techniques of rhetorical analysis to dispute Aristotle's understanding of history!
10. Jerome S. Bruner, "The Dimensions of Propaganda: German Short-Wave Broadcasts to America," *Journal of Abnormal and Social Psychology* 36 (3) (1941): 337.
11. Robert W. Allen and Lorne Greene, "The Propaganda Game" (New Haven, CT: AIM Publishers, 1966), pp. 1–2.
12. Harold Lasswell, *Propaganda Techniques in the World War* (New York: Knopf, 1927).
13. Walter Lippmann, *Public Opinion* (New York: Macmillan, 1922); a contemporary assessment of Lippmann's approach is Ellen Seiter, "Stereotypes and the Media: A Re-evaluation," *Journal of Communication* 36 (Spring 1986): 14–26.
14. Alfred McClung Lee and Elizabeth B. Lee, eds., *The Fine Art of Propaganda* (New York: Harcourt, Brace, 1939).
15. Thus, for example, a leading text in propaganda appearing after World War II, William Hummel and Keith Huntress, *The Analysis of Propaganda* (New York: Holt, Rinehart, and Winston, 1949) incorporates them, as does a more recent text, Garth S. Jowett and Victoria O'Donnell, *Propaganda and Persuasion* (Newbury Park, CA: Sage, 1986).
16. Leonard W. Doob, *Public Opinion and Propaganda* (Hamden, CT: Archon Books, 1966), p. 289.
17. Stuart Chase, *Guides to Straight Thinking* (New York: Harper and Row, 1956), pp. 37–38.
18. Hugh Rank, *The Pitch* (Park Forest, IL: The Counter-Propaganda Press, 1982).
19. Hugh Rank, *The Pep Talk* (Park Forest, IL: The Counter-Propaganda Press, 1984).
20. Lasswell, *Propaganda Techniques in the World War*.
21. Harold D. Lasswell, Nathan Leites, and Associates, *Language of Politics* (New York: George W. Stewart, 1949).
22. Among such texts is the highly readable, although dated in some respects, Bernard Berelson, *Content Analysis in Communication Research* (New York: Free Press, 1952); see also Robert C. North, Ole R. Holsti, M. George Zaninovich, and Dina A. Zinnes, *Content Analysis* (Evanston, IL: Northwestern University Press, 1963); Ole R. Holsti, *Content Analysis for the Social Sciences and Humanities* (Reading, MA: Addison-Wesley, 1969); and Klaus Krippendorff, *Content Analysis* (Beverly Hills, CA: Sage, 1980).
23. James N. Rosenau, *The Dramas of Political Life* (North Scituate, MA: Duxbury Press, 1980), pp. 241–242.
24. Chase, *Guides to Straight Thinking*, p. 29.
25. Alfred Korzybski, *Science and Sanity* (Lakeville, CT: International Non-Aristotelian Library Publishing Co., 1933), p. 58.
26. S. I. Hayakawa, *Symbol, Status, and Personality* (New York: Harcourt, Brace, and World, 1950).
27. Ibid., p. 25.
28. For discussions of how much contests over symbols pervade politics see William E. Connolly, *The Terms of Political Discourse* (Lexington, MA: D.C. Heath, 1974) and Daniel T. Rodgers, *Contested Truths: Keywords in American Politics Since Independence* (New York: Basic Books, 1987).
29. Robert E. Goodin, *Manipulatory Politics* (New Haven: Yale University Press, 1980), p. 13.
30. Jacques Ellul, "The Ethics of Propaganda," *Communication* 6 (2) (1981): 159–177. See Richard L. Johannesen, *Ethics in Human Communication* (Prospect Heights, IL: Waveland Press, 1983) for a more detailed discussion of ethical analysis.

31. David I. Kertzer, *Ritual, Politics, and Power* (New Haven: Yale University Press, 1988).
32. Thornton Sinclair, ''The Nazi Party Rally at Nuremberg,'' *Public Opinion Quarterly* 2 (October 1938): 583.
33. Erving Goffman, *Gender Advertisements* (New York: Harper and Row, 1979).
34. The most relevant of the Yale studies is Carl Hovland, et al., *The Order of Presentation in Persuasion* (New Haven: Yale University Press, 1957).
35. The assumptions and conclusions of the voting studies are reviewed in Dan Nimmo, *Political Communication and Public Opinion in America* (Santa Monica, CA: Goodyear, 1978), pp. 361–393.
36. A review of how attitude change and voting studies, along with other emphases, eclipsed propaganda analysis is J. Michael Sproule, ''Propaganda Studies in American Social Science: The Rise and Fall of the Critical Paradigm,'' *Quarterly Journal of Speech* 73 (February 1987): 60–78.

CHAPTER 8

Digging Beneath the Surface
Contemporary Critical Thinking about Propaganda

By this point you should have acquired some skills useful in the personal analysis and critique of propaganda. This chapter will help you complete those skills by examining some contemporary critical thinking about propaganda. If carried into daily life, these rounded skills should acquit you well in your encounters with propaganda. Here we delve into ideas that are not confined simply to detection, with which much traditional analysis of propaganda was concerned. Rather here we are concerned with what we might term "texts": text, subtext, and context. Whereas traditional inquiry into propaganda derived from the social sciences, this more recent work derives from the humanities, in particular literary criticism. This is why we name this chapter "digging beneath the surface": if we examine propaganda as literature, we can critically evaluate its text; if there are hidden or covert messages there, we may look for such subtexts; and if the propaganda can be identified by cultural, historical, or personal origin and authorship, we may examine it in its ideocultural context. If you grasp the rudiments of such deep inquiry, you will now have a ready ability to understand and criticize propaganda. In a sense, you will now be a literary critic of propaganda.

The "Star Trek" adventures of Captain James T. Kirk and the U.S.S. *Enterprise* are, as we saw in opening Chapter 7, more than simply whimsical tales of fiction and fantasy. They are also propaganda about America and about propaganda itself. To detect the propaganda in "Star Trek," however, one must dig beneath the surface content of the TV series and such successors as the *Star Trek* movies, animated versions, and the plethora of paperback adventures arranged on spinning metal shelves in shopping mall bookstores. We find tools for such digging in separate, distinct forms of analysis that, for the most part, lie outside the tradition described in the preceding chapter. Here we discuss those forms and how they apply to critical thinking about the new propaganda.

"QUE SERA SERA," BUT, "IS THAT ALL THERE IS?": CRITICAL THEORY, RESEARCH, AND THE NEW PROPAGANDA

Alfred Hitchcock's (1899–1980) career as a movie and TV maker of films spanned six decades. He was known as the Master of Suspense for his chilling, spine-tingling, macabre productions that appealed to audiences, he thought, because everybody likes to be frightened occasionally. Pick up the TV remote control and graze across channels; his movies and TV shows remain readily available. His 1956 film *The Man Who Knew Too Much* (a remake of a movie he had made in 1934) is a story of how an innocent Midwest doctor and his wife, vacationing in French Morocco, get caught up in a plot of intrigue, murder, kidnapping, and attempted assassination that moves from North Africa to London. The film features a hit song of the period, "Que Sera Sera." The song figures prominently in the climactic scene, one so skillfully crafted that it still is studied closely by makers of suspense films.

So as not to spoil the plot, we leave it at that and turn to the words of the song: "Que sera sera, what ever will be will be; the future's not ours to see, Que sera sera." The fatalistic message of the popular hit is, upon reflection, sobering: what is, is; what will be, will be; and that's that. If J. Michael Sproule, a communication scholar who has probed the changing emphases in the analysis of propaganda in the twentieth century,[1] is correct, then "Que Sera Sera" might well be the theme song of the main thrust of propaganda studies since the arrival of content and effects analysis. To understand why this might be so we need to look back briefly at the tradition of propaganda analysis discussed in Chapter 7, take note of its change, and contrast those changes with contemporary emphases on critical thinking about propaganda.

Studies of propaganda in the period between World Wars I and II reflected, according to Sproule, the spirit of American progressivism. The progressive movement was one of social, economic, and political reform. It peaked during the first quarter of the twentieth century. Progressives sought to identify powerful selfish and vested interests, then root them out through institutional reforms. One tool for identifying those interests and their deleterious social consequences was propaganda analysis, specifically the analysis of interests' claims using the methods devised by the Institute for Propaganda Analysis. During and after World War II the progressive movement waned. Moreover, as we saw in Chapter 7, propaganda studies turned away from claims analysis to quantitative content and effects analysis. The scientific study of propaganda, that is, of what *is* the content and impact of communication, ceased to be rooted in reform-minded concerns of what *ought* to be. Que sera sera.

No longer motivated by efforts to change the status quo, scholarly analyses of propaganda exemplified what social scientists call *administrative research*. Administrative studies make several assumptions: reigning social, economic, political, and cultural institutions are basically sound despite minor defects; defects can be cured by policies improving the efficiency of institutional processes; the mass media play key roles in promoting such improvement by facilitating communication; research into the uses, content, and short-term effects of the media by empirical, quantitative means will suggest more efficient means of communicating; the result will be socially desirable effects for everyone.

With but minor changes, "if present developments continue, the future will be an improvement over the past."[2] Que sera sera.

Although administrative assumptions, that is, that minor administrative repairs may be called for but not wholesale reform, dominated the study of mass communication in the United States after World War II, not all investigators accepted those assumptions. This was especially the case of social theorists on the European continent and of scholars in the United States influenced by them. So diverse, complex, and sometimes obscure are the views of these theorists that the label generally applied to their efforts, namely, *critical research*, suggests a consensus of outlook, that is, "critical theory," that does not exist. There are, however, selected aspects of critical research and theory that have a bearing on contemporary propaganda analysis. Although not all critical theorists subscribe to each aspect, there is sufficient agreement to make summarization possible.[3]

If "Que Sera Sera" captures much of what administrative research is all about, the song "Is That All There Is?" typifies the critical attitude. "Is That All There Is?" is a bittersweet, melancholy acceptance that the world is not all that it's cracked up to be. If things simply continue as they are and "that's all there is," then indeed we might as well resign ourselves to our fate and make only cosmetic changes. Then, foolishly and as the song says, we "break out the booze and have a ball." Critical theorists, however, are not resigned. Without radical change things will get worse. One place to seek radical change is with the mass media. Critical theory underscores the importance of mass media in creating culture. Changes in media technology bring environmental change, hence, cultural change. Research should identify those long-term changes, make people aware of them, critically evaluate them, and propose basic reforms to improve the lot of everyone throughout society. "Is That All There Is?" "No!" say critical theorists. There can be much more, so much more that we need not resign ourselves to "Que Sera Sera."

The Culture Industry

The mass media are basic to what two critical theorists called the "culture industry."[4] For the critical theorist, the way people lead their daily lives, earn a living, and simply survive constitutes their "material" culture. In contrast with these routines there is also an "intellectual" culture, the life of the mind reflected in science, religion, art, and the humanities.[5] The material goods involved in daily living—refrigerators, automobiles, and smoke detectors; athletic shoes, warm-up outfits, and jeans; fast foods, frozen foods, and microwaved foods—are mass produced. We reside in a world of standardized, packaged, advertised, sold, and consumed products. Tangible differences among a line of products are at best marginal (recall the discussion of advertising in Chapter 5). Claims aside, Miller Lite, Bud Light, and Coors Light are not all that strikingly dissimilar. A Valvoline Motor Oil TV commercial, after depicting the folly in a crotchety old man's insistence that "motor oil's motor oil," proclaimed "not all motor oils are alike." Advertising aside, however, in the world of mass production, "motor oil's motor oil."

Critical theorists hold that what is true of the mass production of material culture holds for intellectual culture—standardization of marginally different products (in this case ideas, artistic "creations," etc.), packaging, advertising, sales, and consumption. One romance novel is very much like another, one soap opera very much like another, one pop tune very much like another, one slasher film very much like another, one CBS "60 Minutes" very much like another ABC "20/20"—yes, "motor oil's motor oil." The success of the culture industry depends in large measure upon the mass media. Openly, of course, the mass media carry the messages of advertising that stimulate the sales and consumption of material and intellectual commodities. Advertising sustains people's frenzy to consume commodities, a frenzy that drives them to work hard to afford their all-consuming addiction to consume. Working to Consume, Consuming to Work serves as the driving motto of the capitalist economy.

But more than advertising is at work in the mass media's crucial contribution to the culture industry. For the critical theorist *all* messages in the mass media, not just mass advertising, must be examined for the role they play in sustaining established social, economic, and political practices. That is, all of the messages propagated by mass media have potential for preserving a distribution of power in society that advantages the few, disadvantages the many. For all messages can shape people's consciousness and the meanings they share and, thus, message manipulation in the mass media is an effective strategy for exerting and maintaining control, that is, for convincing people that "that's all there is" so "Que sera sera."

Since all mass mediated messages have such potential, critical analysis searches for the long-term, not easily detected, meanings and effects in a wide variety of media, particularly the full range of entertainment media. That range includes, for example, romance, spy, or crime novels; TV crime, comedy, or adventure series; cartoons or comic strips; radio call-in shows; motion pictures of all genres; even astrology columns. As an illustration, one of the leading proponents of critical analysis, Theodore Adorno, examined astrological columns in a metropolitan newspaper over a three-month period. He found that beneath the surface of daily advice based on a "reading of the stars" lies an oft-repeated message whose considerable cumulative impact is to justify and sustain the social status quo. Astrology, in effect, instructs a person—at one and the same time—to realize that she or he can *count* for something by coming to terms with the inner and outer life, yet to accept the frustration that things cannot be changed, that what will be will be. A person counts, yet one's fate lies in stars, *not* in one's self.[6] Thus does the consumer of astrological advice receive an affirmative answer to the question "Is That All There Is?"

In arguing that the culture industry working through the mass media propagates ideas that serve vested interests, critical analysts revive that emphasis of traditional propaganda analysis staked out by claims analysts after World War I. But there are differences. Claims analysis, as we saw in Chapter 7, searches directly the overt, manifest content of messages for the presence or absence of propaganda devices. Critical analysis searches for "hidden meanings" that are not directly observable or readily detectable, yet may be there and, if so, leave a lasting, cumulative effect in shaping peoples' tacit, taken-for-granted acceptance that "that's all there is." Moreover, claims analysis assumes a deliberate intent in propaganda, a purpose that can be discovered through the identification of propaganda devices employed. Critical theorists focus as much on *implied* meanings as *intended* ones. Thus it should come as no surprise, as often happens, when a movie intended as an "antiwar" statement carries so many implied messages of heroism, commitment, and quiet acceptance of death that it exalts war instead of decrying it.

Finally, in pointing to the propaganda *potential* in all messages regardless of source, intent, or genre, critical theory moves beyond traditional propaganda analysis and recognizes a world of new propaganda, a world of palaver where guile and charm succeed as much through suasion as persuasion. In this respect critical theory joins another source of critical thinking about propaganda, namely, literary criticism.

"I KNOW NOTHING ABOUT ART, BUT I KNOW WHAT I LIKE": LITERARY CRITICISM AND THE NEW PROPAGANDA

It may appear odd that literary criticism would provide us with any assistance in thinking critically about political propaganda. Literary criticism shares with film criticism, music criticism, architectural criticism, and other forms of criticism the description, explanation, analysis, and evaluation of works of art. Surely a critical essay on Shakespeare's *Romeo and Juliet* has no more bearing on the analysis of politics than does a Siskel and Ebert "thumbs up" or "thumbs down" of *Batman* on "At the Movies." Such a judgment, however, overlooks a key political role that literature and other art forms have played historically. Every society develops means to stabilize itself, to achieve a degree of coordination and control sufficient to permit people to live together rather than split into warring factions. In some cases the concentration of military might in the hands of rulers serves as such a means of social control. For a long period of history religion served this purpose in many nations. Religious images, symbols, habits, rituals, and myths provided meaning to people's lives and loyalty to church and nation became synonymous.

But for a variety of reasons—technological developments, economic changes, population shifts, and others—the hold of religion on people began to wane in the nineteenth century. What then would provide social "cement" in times of upheaval? Terry Eagleton, a scholar in English literature and a student of literary criticism, argues that literature "was in several ways a suitable candidate" to replace religion as a means of social control:

> Since literature, as we know, deals in universal human values rather than in such histori-cal trivia as civil wars, the oppression of women or the dispossession of the English peas-antry, it could serve to place in cosmic perspective the petty demands of working people for decent living conditions or greater control over their own lives, and might even with luck come to render them oblivious of such issues in their high-minded contemplation of eternal truths and beauties.[7]

Moreover, literature possessed other characteristics that made it a useful means of social control: it could transmit a pride in national heritage, language, and myth; instruct citizens in proper, civilized behavior toward one another and their rulers; and "since reading is es-sentially a solitary, contemplative activity, curb . . . any disruptive tendency to collective political action."[8]

Thus, as we saw in Chapter 6, literature was part of that popular culture (along with painting, music, sculpture, and later film, radio, and TV programming) that did more than entertain: it propagated ideas. Early on, students of literature recognized this and, hence, began to scrutinize literary works not only for their surface themes, plots, characteriza-tions, and so forth but also for their "deeper meanings" and ideas. At the center of their search was a key question, namely, ''Where does *meaning* lie?'' Put differently, if we want to know what the hidden message is in a Shakespeare play, a romance novel, an Elvis Presley song, a Michael J. Fox movie, or ABC's ''thirtysomething,'' where should we look? Critics have generated many answers to the question of where meaning lies in a work of art. Several of those answers assist us in thinking critically about the art of the new propaganda.

Try ''Close Reading''

Any work of art, literary or not, propaganda or not, derives from the efforts of one or more artists, in a given time and place, speaking to audiences with a particular style, air, or flourish. This is so for *Moby Dick* or for a ''Bud Light'' TV commercial. What the work ''means'' may lie in the content of the work itself, the context of time and place that have influenced the artist, the artist's intentions, how audiences respond to it, the way the artist presents it, or elsewhere. One tradition of literary criticism tells us that the single place to look for the meaning of an artistic message is in the message itself. Whether examining a poem or political speech, a Beethoven symphony or a national anthem, we should isolate the message, or ''text,'' from its cultural and historical surroundings, the artist's intentions, audience reactions, and anything else that obscures the meaning. *Meaning lies in the text.*

''Close reading'' consists of a detailed, microscopic analysis and interpretation of the words on the page, pictures on the screen, or melodies of the song. The practice of close reading was especially important to a method of literary criticism that flourished in the United States from the 1930s to the 1950s called the *New Criticism*. New Criticism consisted of a cluster of ideas, not all shared by everyone labeled a ''New Critic,'' but practiced widely enough to hold the group together in a loose fashion. One such idea was what has come to be called the ''objective theory of art.'' This theory holds that a literary work is an object in its own right and warrants analysis independent of the author's stated intention, what it purports to represent, its composition, or the effect it produces on an audience. Thus, to grasp the meaning of ''Star Trek,'' ignore what producer Gene Roddenberry had in mind in creating the series (fashioning ''parallel worlds'' where ordinary human beings from Earth could exist thousands of years in the future). Ignore any likenesses between the five-year mission of the *Enterprise* and America's Manifest Destiny. Ignore the standardized composition of the episodes (the crew of the *Enterprise* encounters an alien, hostile planet, beams down, faces and conquers danger, and restores order, peace, and tranquility). And ignore the ''trekkies'' who made ''Star Trek'' survive through four decades in one form or another. Isolate the ''Star Trek'' text, read (or view) closely, and in a disinterested way discover its various ''tensions,'' ''paradoxes,'' and ''ambivalences'' and how these get resolved. How, for example, in a typical episode does the love-hate relationship between the science officer, Mr. Spock, and the chief medical officer, Leonard ''Bones'' McCoy, get resolved? What ideas does that resolution propagate about sibling rivalries, the friendly competition between teammates, or the hustling between two junior executives to catch the boss's eye?

The meaning of a work may thus teach us something about matters external to the work itself (e.g., we might learn something about sibling rivalries by watching Spock and McCoy closely), but that meaning itself does not derive from those external matters. It lies instead in the work as a self-sustaining and self-contained entity. Summarizing the New Critics' approach to poetry, Art Berman captures the nature of such criticism and its difficulties:

> The relationship among the words of the poem construct a linguistic milieu that contains a meaning defined by that milieu. Meaning is not derived by evoking direct factual correspondences between the poem and facts of the matter otherwise ascertainable, although the critics are obliged to ask how the poem relates to the external world. The poem is an object open to an analysis that can be confined (more in theory than in practice) to the poem itself. The procedure of close reading and a working critical vocabulary evolve around this assumption.[9]

Of what, then, does close reading of propaganda consist? First, the work of propaganda, or potential propaganda, must be isolated and studied closely in its own right to reveal tensions, ambiguities, and resolutions. For example, communication scholars Michael Hemphill and Larry David Smith have read closely the lyrics of various songs of popular rock singer Bruce Springsteen. An often repeated theme they find is *the dream*—to pull up stakes and move on, to get a good job and start all over again, to join the circus, always to seek something better. But seldom are the dreams realized. Instead the lyrics reveal "a confusing mixture of optimism and pessimism in that his tales stress the need for dreaming of a world that has been proven not to exist." But close reading of Springsteen suggests a second lesson for thinking critically about propaganda, namely, the resolution of tensions yields ideas for political propagation. The resolution in Springsteen's lyrics is such an ideal: "To Springsteen, even in a world of subjugation, the American Dream of individual prosperity remains an eternal bastion of hope."[10]

Dig for Intent

Close reading of texts offers an overriding lesson for those who want to think critically about the new propaganda. An artist's, author's, or propagandist's intentions, even if we could discern them through close reading, should not be confused with what a text means, that is, whether or not it is propaganda. Such confusion constitutes the "intentional fallacy," a pitfall New Critics admonished against. Not all critics agree. Those who do not say that meaning lies not in the text but in the artist. Such critics adapt a *phenomenological* approach to their analyses. That approach holds that we cannot peer into the "real" or ultimate nature of phenomena (i.e., facts, objects, events, etc., that we encounter). We know those phenomena only as they appear to us through our senses. This does not, however, imply that we cannot know things at all. What we *can* know is how things *appear* to us in our immediate consciousness, even if what we experience is an illusion and not concrete. People, places, events, and so on are not independent of our consciousness; rather, they become "things in themselves" because we "intend" them as such by our senses, our consciousness. These intended things are the things to study and to know.[11]

Thus, should we want to explain the behavior of another person, a classmate for example, what we must do is suspend any biases, preconceptions, and judgments we have of that person ("She's really smart," or "He doesn't need to work his way through school as I do, so he has more time to study"). We ignore, or "put in brackets" as phenomenogists say, anything that is beyond our immediate experiencing of the classmate. Then we examine how our classmate perceives things, say, how she or he senses what the class is about, what the teacher wants, and so forth. The phenomenological approach holds that the influences shaping a person's actions are the phenomena as perceived by that person. Hence, for that person the *meaning* of an object derives from one's *relationship and reaction to it*.

Far from dismissing intentionality as irrelevant to criticism, the phenomenological approach gives priority to, or "privileges," intentions. The world is as a person "intends" it: it is to be known in relation to that person, as flowing from that person's consciousness. The individual's subjective consciousness is, following the phenomenological approach, the source and origin of all meaning. Hence, whereas New Critics privilege the text of a work of art, bracketing out everything else, phenomenological criticism privileges the author's intentionality and brackets out all else: "The text itself is reduced to a pure embodiment of the author's consciousness: all of its stylistic and semantic aspects are grasped as organic parts of a complex totality, of which the unifying essence is the author's mind."[12] This does not, however, extend to examining biographical facts and details of the author's life. Phenomenological critics focus upon the "deep structures" of the author's mind manifested in the text itself by searching for recurring themes, images, allusions, and related hints regarding what it was like for the author to "live" the writing of the text.

Obviously this is no easy task. Phenomenological critics differ over how to perform their craft every bit as much as New Critics differ over how to apply their approach. One key area of difference that, as we shall see, has implications for propaganda analysis concerns the shelf life of an author's intentions. One school of thought holds that the meaning of an artistic work (an opera, TV news special, soap opera, or Harlequin Romance is no less a text than Edgar Allen Poe's *The Raven* for critical purposes) is established once and for all at the time of writing; it is identical with what the author had in mind in "intending" it at the outset. Granted that readers of Adolf Hitler's *Mein Kampf* today might draw vastly different conclusions than did those who read it in the 1920s. Granted also that the film *Gone with the Wind* may appeal to audiences in the 1990s in vastly different ways than it did to those who first saw it in 1939. This, however, does not change the *meaning* Hitler intended or the meaning intended by the script writers of the Hollywood epic. Authors, say this school of phenomenological critics, establish meanings, readers but assign changing significances. Another school of thought, in contrast, argues that the meanings of a work are never exhausted by the intentions of the author. Contexts change—historical, cultural, social, economic, and political. As a result new meanings may be derived from the work that were never intended by the author or inferred by its original audience. As contexts change, audience interpretations of texts change as well, that is, the text they "intend" in their consciousness may be quite apart from the author's intended text.

As an example let us return again to "Star Trek." The phenomenological critic would have us bracket what we know about the author, in this case Gene Roddenberry, who conceived the idea for the TV series, the conditions for producing the show, its success with audiences, and so on. Instead we would privilege recurring themes and patterns of images revealing the "deep structure" of Roddenberry's consciousness. Thus would we dig to reveal the "mental object" Roddenberry had in mind when he intended "Star Trek." This is not the place to engage in such an extended analysis of "Star Trek." However, let us make an assumption (one that phenomenological critics would undoubtedly label as "gross"). Let us *assume* that after digging deeply we unearth precisely the same mental object that Roddenberry himself said he intended when he wrote on March 11, 1964:

> The time is "somewhere in the future." It could be 1995 or maybe even 2995. In other words, close enough to our own time for our continuing characters to be fully identifiable as people like us, but far enough into the future for galaxy travel to be thoroughly established. . . . The "parallel worlds" concept is the key to the . . . format . . . . It tends to keep even the most imaginative stories within the general audience's frame of reference through such recognizable and identifiable casting, sets, and costuming.[13]

Again, assume that critical analysis of the themes and images in "Star Trek" episodes would lead us to concur, that is, that Roddenberry intended what he said he intended, the creation of "parallel worlds" to court audiences. Did ensuing generations of series fans unearth the same set of author's intentions? Did they see the intended parallel worlds? Did they "live" the writing of the same series that Roddenberry lived? Perhaps. But it is more likely that as an object of consciousness for each "Trekkie" the intended series differed considerably. Some may have relived each week an old-style Western "shoot 'em up" brought to life in the galactic future. Others may have lived the closely knit life of the "Star Trek" family, not much different from "Leave It to Beaver," with Captain James T. Kirk as father, nurse Christine Chapel as mother, Spock as the more galactic-wise Wally Cleaver, and "Bones" McCoy as the often naive "Beave."

What the two schools of phenomenological criticism tell us is that it is certainly important in analyzing propaganda to take into account intentions. Close reading alone of the text of a document, film, speech, or other means of propagating ideas will not provide us with the latent persuasive and suasive messages it may contain. But in digging for intent we must excavate not what the propagandist intended but also what readers, listeners, and viewers intended as the mental object of the message. A third critical tradition suggests lessons for doing so.

Read Between the Lines

Close reading of a text, either for its own sake or to discern the intended world of the author, is not enough. Frequently the consequences of a message are foreshadowed not by what the text says, but by what it does not say; not what is written line by line but what can be discerned only by, as the saying goes, reading between the lines. *Reception theory* addresses such reading between the lines, although as in the case of the New Criticism and of phenomenological criticism, there is scarcely universal agreement on what constitutes such theory.

Reception theory assumes that literary texts—whether made up of words, gestures, pictures, or combinations thereof—acquire meaning only in the practice of reading them. Any text "is really no more than a series of 'cues' to the reader, invitations to construct a piece of language into meaning." Thus, "in the terminology of reception theory, the reader 'concretizes' the literary work," which in the case of a written text is "no more than a chain of organized black marks on a page."[14] Moreover, the "black marks on a page'' have gaps between them, not just spatial gaps between the words and sentences but gaps of *meaning*.

Here is the text of an advertisement for an automobile:

> As your family grows, so does your need for a four-door sedan. You need a car with extra elbowroom for all those extra elbows, a car that's comfortable enough to make long trips seem much too short. Quite simply you need a car that makes sense.
>   On the other hand, you want a car that not only makes sense, but can excite your senses.

Although the second sentence of the ad yields a clue regarding why growth in family size demands a four-door sedan, the reader must make the connection. The reader must also make another connection or the phrase ''make long trips seem much too short'' is without meaning. Yet another reader-supplied connection must link ''Quite simply you need a car that makes sense'' with ''you want a car that not only makes sense, but can excite your senses.''

Literary theory regards this as a ''hermeneutical circle,'' that is, the reader moves from part to whole, whole to part, over and over to make meaningful connections between passages. As Eagleton says,

> Reading is not a straightforward linear movement, a merely cumulative affair: our initial speculations generate a frame of reference within which to interpret what comes next, but what comes next may retrospectively transform our original understanding, highlighting some feature of it and backgrounding others. . . . We read backwards and forwards simultaneously, predicting and recollecting.[15]

All of this filling in of gaps, moving backwards and forwards, predicting and recollecting constitutes the ''reading between the lines'' of reception theory. What contribution to critical thinking about propaganda does reception theory offer? Whereas much of literary criticism searches for the meaning of a message in a text, reception analysis gives priority to the participation of the reader/auditor/viewer. ''Trekkies,'' not the content of ''Star Trek,'' are the centerpiece of reception analysis. In this respect reception analysis is much like the efforts described in Chapter 7 to analyze propaganda not by examining its content but by probing the effects a propagandistic message has upon an audience. However, there is a key difference. In effects analysis the meaning of a propaganda message abides in the message itself; whether that meaning changes or reinforces audiences' attitudes and actions is the central question. In reception analysis audiences complete the meaning of propaganda texts by interpreting the significance of gaps in content.

In the 1980s scholars undertook numerous studies using the tools of reception analysis. Many of those studies, such as the reception of soap operas, TV news, or the motion picture *Rocky*, had implications for examining new propaganda via reception analysis.[16] A study undertaken in Finland illustrates both the focus and tools of such efforts.[17] The text under investigation was a war film, *The Unknown Soldier* (1985), based upon a widely discussed novel published in 1954. The theme of the film parallels that in movies available to American viewers in the 1980s such as *Platoon* (1986) and *Full Metal Jacket* (1987). The view of war portrayed in the film is that of the ordinary soldier sent into combat where he never wanted to be in the first place. The soldier must come to grips with combat, war, and the emotions evoked by death and destruction. Researchers asked whether the reception of the film by Finnish audiences was uniform across all viewers or reflected cultural differences among them. To probe that question the researchers selected two Finnish cities where *The Unknown Soldier* premiered. After the performance they interviewed 86 members of the film audience, all within less than two weeks of the film's screening. In 30-minute interviews researchers probed filmgoers' impressions of the film, the message they thought the film conveyed, and their personal feelings about the film. Analysis of the interview data revealed, not surprisingly, that viewers read between the lines of the film in different ways. Spectators agreed on no single, clear theme. Yet different readings had no cultural base but instead were linked more to viewers' own personal experiences, social positions, and gender. Such "different strokes for different folks" imply, once again, that to focus our thinking alone on what propagandists intend is insufficient to grasp the received meaning of propaganda. As we have seen frequently, suasion is a defining aspect of the new propaganda's persuasive capabilities.

Recognize Speaking in Tongues

Although receivers construct the meaning of texts by reading between the lines, these readers, listeners, and viewers are not free to choose just any interpretation. Words, for example, are not neutral. They carry extra baggage in the form of attitudes and stereotypes: thus, *doll*, *dame*, and *babe* carry stereotypes toward women that feminists object to as sexist. Because words are not neutral, receivers frequently are limited in their close reading and filling in of gaps by the very words that compose the text. When Humphrey Bogart playing Rick Blaine in the movie classic *Casablanca* repeats several times during the film, "Here's looking at you, kid," there is some latitude for viewers to interpret the meaning, but far less than if he had said, "Here's looking at you, Miss Lund."

Nor are entire languages any more neutral than the words that compose them. "Language is sermonic," wrote rhetorical critic Richard Weaver:

> We are all of us preachers in private or public capacities. We have no sooner uttered words than we have given impulse to other people to look at the world, or some small part of it, in our own way.[18]

But language is more than a vehicle for simply transmitting our teachings and preachings. Language does more than *say* what we mean; language *produces meaning*. This is the thrust of yet another school, or schools, of literary criticism that provide us with insights regarding how to think about the new propaganda—"structuralism" and "poststructuralism."

Structuralist Thinking: Things Really Are Not Always What They Seem

As with several other potential means for analyzing propaganda that we have discussed thus far, *structuralism* rejects the "obvious" meaning of a message on grounds that things are not always what they seem. Instead the focus is "deep" structures below the surface content. Structuralists argue that the individual elements of a message—words, sounds, pictured objects, movements in film, and so on—have meaning only in relationship to one another. No single symbol has any meaning in and of itself. Thus, for example, in the original "Star Trek" TV series and in the feature films that followed, Mr. Spock's pointed ears were meaningful only in the larger context of his Vulcan origins, almost mystical insights, the intergalactic mission of the *Enterprise*, and Spock's ties to other members of the crew. As structuralists would say, symbols have no "substantial" meanings, only "relational" ones. Hence, meaning resides in the relations of images to one another.[19]

Such a view of meaning brackets *content* and gives priority to the *form* of a message. Let us extend our "Star Trek" example. The TV series depicted stable, predictable relationships between the principal characters of Captain Kirk, Mr. Spock, Dr. "Bones" McCoy, and nurse Chapel. Regardless of the story line in any particular episode, any viewer knew that at the show's end this family structure would remain intact. Story content changed, but since the imposed formula for relationships did not, essentially every story was the *same* story. In short, a *formulaic* (structural) *imperative* drove the series regardless of superficially shifting plots. Now consider one of the many TV series that vied with "Star Trek" for popularity, namely, "Gunsmoke." That series was set not in the intergalactic future of "Stardate 2534.0" but in Dodge City, Kansas, a century ago. There Marshal Matt Dillon maintained a fragile social order weekly threatened by unruly residents or outsiders intent on evil deeds. In his task Dillon enlisted the aid of his deputy, Chester (later Festus), the town's physician, Doc, and the owner and operator of the Long Branch saloon, Miss Kitty. Again, as with "Star Trek," the structured relations between these four characters did not change from week to week even though, on the surface, story lines did. Each character's meaning derived from his or her relation to the other three. (Would there be a Dr. Watson without Sherlock Holmes and vice versa; a Robinson Crusoe without Friday?).

Now dig yet deeper. We find that the structural relations among the crew of the *Enterprise* and the peacekeeping family of Dodge City are so alike that the characters are almost substitutable across TV series. Kirk, on the one hand, relates to Spock, Bones, and Chapel as Dillon, on the other, does to Chester, Doc, and Kitty. The same can be said for each of the other characters in each series. As a result, not only did each series itself tell the same story every week, *both* series told the same story every week. Or at least so structural analysis might argue.

That, however, is not the whole of structuralism. As is the case with critical theorists, New Critics, phenomenologists, reception analysts, and so forth, structuralists differ on many things, but share the view that *language structures produce meaning*, not merely reflect it. The argument is complex but can be simplified as follows: A language is a system of signs. A "sign" consists of a "signifier" (e.g., a red octagonal object bearing *STOP* attached to a pole is a signifier to motorists), and a "signified" (the "meaning" to bring the auto to a halt). The relation between signifier and signified is arbitrary. Take four black marks, *F, L, A, G*. We recognize the word *flag* signifying a piece of cloth or bunting varying in size, color, and design that by historical and cultural convention "stands for" a nation, group, or cause. But in French what signifies such a piece of cloth is the word *drapeau* or, sometimes, *fanion*.

Thus is the meaning of a sign, the relation of signified and signifier, both conventional and arbitrary. Moreover, a sign's meaning is also by virtue of its *difference* from other signs. *Flag* has meaning not for what it *is* but for what it is *not*: not *flak* (bursting artillery shells), not *flam* (a drumbeat), not *flan* (a custard tart), not *flaw* (an imperfection), and so on. In sum, for structuralists meaning isn't inherent in a sign but is a function of its difference from other signs in a system of signs. This leads structuralists, as we have seen, to concentrate less on what is said (content) in actual writing, speech, or pictures than on the structure of signs that makes such writing, speech, or pictures possible and meaningful in the first place.

One other distinction is necessary. Consider any tune—classical music, rock, country/western, and so forth. When the instruments in the band play simultaneously, thus making noises heard in combination with one another, we recognize the *harmony*. By the same token a tune also consists of one note following another in sequence, or *melody*. Although they vary among themselves in how they label it, structuralists make a similar distinction in analyzing signs. One form of analysis (typically given the tongue-twisting label of "paradigmatic" analysis) involves probing messages for the hidden associations among signs in a combined structure, much as when musical instruments play in harmony. Distinguished from that procedure is the effort to mine below the surface of messages for chains, or sequences, of events that form a hidden narrative structure. This is akin to listening for melodies to uncover themes, leitmotifs, and so on. This search also has a jaw-breaking label, namely, "syntagmatic" analysis.

Two examples will illustrate the difference between paradigmatic and syntagmatic analysis as each pertains to thinking about propaganda. We turn first to an election campaign for the governorship of a southern state in 1978. As is characteristic of candidates in the era of new propaganda (see Chapter 4), both the Republican and Democratic candidates spent heavily on televised political advertising. In the spirit of the tradition of propaganda analysis discussed in Chapter 7, it would be possible to submit the surface content of each candidate's ads to examination, perhaps by searching for the presence or absence of the "ABCs of Propaganda," or perhaps using content analysis to quantify the key themes in the manifest content of the ads.

Structuralism, however, suggests a different approach. Following the tenets of paradigmatic analysis, researchers could examine all of both candidates' ads in combination, probing for a hidden pattern of oppositions buried there that produce a meaning to the campaign nowhere apparent on the surface. When researchers did this they found that signifiers in Democratic ads stressed the values of work, efficiency, progress, success, and happiness. In contrast Republican signifiers repeatedly pointed to dirt in government to be removed, stamping out of special interests, pride in people, the state, and the common folk. Grouping these opposing signifiers revealed deeper patterns. The propaganda of the Democrat produced an overall meaning of a campaign appealing to newly rich and successful voters (or those who aspired to be such) with a message of the triumph of progress. Republican propaganda appealed to thrift, not wealth; tradition not progress. The deep structure of campaign propaganda thus pitted two opposing cultures and myths: the Self-made Man versus Mr. Clean.[20]

By contrast, syntagmatic analysis probes propaganda for a logic that unfolds in the sequence of presenting elements in a message. A typical procedure is for an analyst to identify selected sets of "functions" (i.e., signifiers signifying signifieds) that images in a message perform regardless of message content. For example, one function both Captain Kirk and Marshal Dillon perform is to restore peace and tranquility, coordination and order, whether to an alien planet or good ol' Dodge. Fairy tales, heroic epics, comic strips, even TV situation comedies also portray efforts at peace restoration: Prince Charming functions to make the world of the ugly duckling beautiful; the Beastmaster (in the movie *Beastmaster*) functions to return an evil world to benign nature, with a little help from his friends; Charlie Brown functions relentlessly to discipline his baseball team in the comic strip "Peanuts"; and even Lucy in "I Love Lucy" functions to bring order out of chaos in the waning minutes of each episode of the TV series.

Structuralists have identified numerous other such functions—performing difficult tasks, violating rules, struggling against odds, helping others, punishing, and so on. Analysts search texts for the appearance of such functions and the sequence in which they appear. Again, turn to TV advertising for an example. This time take a product commercial, one for a decaffeinated coffee. Two adult females appear in the office of an art gallery. One announces she has just sold a sculpture (function: the initial situation introducing the characters). The other responds, "Wonderful, have some coffee" (function: interdiction directed to the heroine who sold the sculpture). As she pours, the first woman says, "Whoa" (function: violation of the interdiction). "Only half a cup? Don't you like my coffee?" says the second woman (function: she is now a villain attempting reconnaissance, that is, asking why she is a villain). The first woman says, "Mmmm. Love the rich taste. It's the caffeine I could do without" (function: delivery, that is, the now-villain receives information about the now-victim). "You happen to be drinking Brim decaffeinated coffee," the second woman responds (function: the heroine is tested with a magical agent). "This is Brim?" asks the first woman (function: heroine's reaction to the villain, now a "donor"). "This is freeze-dried Brim, and it's decaffeinated. So you don't have to stop at half a cup," says the donor (function: test of the heroine). The first woman urges, "If it tastes this rich, I don't want to stop. Fill it to the rim. . ." (function: the heroine acquires the use of the magical agent). ". . . with Brim," completes the sentence (function: heroine and donor, no longer a villain, collaborate).

The functions and their sequence identified above follow a pattern similar to one in a 1928 book, *Morphology of a Folk Tale*, written by Vladimir Propp after an exhaustive study of numerous folktales.[21] Such functions were always present and in identical sequence. Propp discovered 31 such functions in a patterned sequence. In the case of the Brim commercial we have, so to speak, an abbreviated folktale. Abbreviated or not, the syntagmatic form is typical of thousands of "true to life" TV commercials broadcast since television's debut.

These examples of structural analysis derive from the field of study called *semiotics*, that is, how systems of signs *generate* meaning. Those systems may be anything—traffic lights, movies, statues, jokes, jogging shoes, domed stadia, or the Sears Tower. What structuralist/semiotic analyses taught students of textual analysis was, "reality is not reflected by language but *produced* by it: it was a particular way of carving up the world which was deeply dependent on the sign-systems we had at our command, or more precisely which had us at theirs."[22] And therein lies a difficulty, one that gives rise to poststructural ways of thinking about messages.

Poststructuralist Thinking: Open Relationships

As we have seen, structuralist analysis holds that the meaning of a sign lies in, and is generated by, how it differs from other signs. Again, *flag* is *flag* because it is not *flak* or any other set of marks. Since meaning is not tied to a particular signifier, and thereby not present in the immediate sign but in relation to other signs, can we ever know what a signifier signifies? That is, can we ever know the meaning of a sign? Poststructuralists think not. If, for example, we look up *flag* in the dictionary, we are directed toward other signifiers, that is, "a piece of cloth" or a "banner," or a "bunting," with "design." But what does a "bunting with design" signify? If we turn again to the dictionary we find *bunting* signifies, for example, "a light cotton or woolen cloth used for making flags." (We also find it signifies a bird with a cone-shaped bill, and, as well, a snug-fitted, hooded sleeping bag.) We continue the process endlessly, but no ultimate "signified" for *flag* will turn up; indeed we are like dogs chasing our tails in a circular fashion: *flags* signify "buntings" as signified, *buntings* signify "flags" as signified.

Thus, whereas structuralism stresses that the relation of signifier and signified is arbitrary, poststructuralism points out that the relationship is not only arbitrary but fluid, open-ended, partial. The meaning of every sign is bound up with the meanings of fragments of innumerable other signs with which, at one and the same time, the sign is related yet set apart from by being *not* other signs. Language is not stable but unstable, not productive of clear meanings but productive of ambiguities in meaning. The key to meaning is, as a prestructural student of language wrote long before structuralism or poststructuralism, the "wave motions of . . . linguistic behaviors . . . advancing and receding across the centuries."[23]

What this suggests to poststructuralists is that, in the ebb and flow of signifiers and signified, selected meanings serve as anchors in the wave motions of linguistic behaviors. They are so privileged by social and political interests who, because of their powerful positions, can stabilize those meanings in laws, statutes, customs, practices, history, and the everyday life of people. *Freedom*, for example, has no specific referent; it is a signifier with no specific signified. Yet in our society we place such a premium on freedom that the concept serves as an anchor grounding countless other terms. Why do we fight wars? To preserve freedom. Why did Americans kill native Indians? To expand freedom. Why do we build prisons and imprison people? To protect against "criminals" threatening our freedom—of movement, of accumulating and spending, of life itself. For poststructuralists signs and sign systems derive from power relations and they produce meanings that preserve, protect, and defend such relations.

What this implies is that we are prisoners of our own discourse. Claims that something is "true" or "false," "right" or "wrong" are true, false, right, or wrong only relative to our language. The tasks of the analyst are to dig through surface claims and demonstrate (1) that relativity, (2) how claims are products of a particular system of meaning anchored in privileged concepts, and (3) how such taken-for-granted meanings serve powerful vested interests. One analytical tactic is to examine claims and meanings for what they *exclude* as much as for what they *include*. This "deconstructive" analysis probes the binary oppositions (high/low, light/dark, Self-made/Common Man) in texts; in that sense deconstructionist thinking is akin to structural analysis. But deconstructionists examine how those oppositions serve powerful interests and doctrines. Such interests acting in their own behalf exclude from consideration meanings that undermine their claims. The tactic of deconstructive analysis "is to show how texts come to embarrass their own ruling systems of logic; and deconstruction shows this by fastening on the 'symptomatic' points, the *aporia* or impasses of meaning, where texts get into trouble, come unstuck, come to contradict themselves."[24] The break in a thought, as when a speaker pauses as if unable or unwilling to continue, may say as much about meaning as the thought's surface logic and continuity.

In a search for anchoring meanings and the interests served by them, deconstructionists are fond of exploring figures of speech, particularly metaphors. Metaphors (such as "no man is an island") substitute one set of signs ("island," and all that is not) for another ("man," and all that is not). Metaphors—as we saw in developing a horticultural metaphor to define propaganda—are convenient fictions by which we explain one thing as being, or not being, another. We expect them in novels, poetry, songs, and so forth, and they also pervade philosophical writing, laws, works of political theory, and all propaganda. "A SPECTRE is haunting Europe—the spectre of Communism." So said the *Manifesto of the Communist Party* in 1848. For a century and a half the "communism as spectre" metaphor anchored the meanings of propaganda and policy for powerful advancing and receding interests. As 1989 and 1990 witnessed the dismantling of Communist regimes and parties in Eastern Europe and in the Soviet Union, few statesmen, scholars, and militarists whose lives and careers had been constituted by fighting the communist spectre were able to reconstruct, yet alone deconstruct, their thinking. Although they had fought for years to turn communism into "Casper, the Friendly Ghost," they continued to counsel caution lest the spectre reappear again.

Poststructuralists are suspicious of all authority and of the powerful interests who constitute their entrenchment in that authority through language. "Space . . . the final frontier" seemed in the 1960s like an innocent enough way to grab the viewers' attention at the beginning of every episode of "Star Trek." And perhaps that indeed is all that it was. Yet viewed from a deconstructionist view, the "space" and "frontier" metaphorical linkage of signifier and signified would hint at much, much more. Digging deeper and deeper into the frontier metaphor they might indeed uncover advancing and receding interests. For instance, the advancing interests of federal agencies, private contractors, the scientific-technological elite established during a period of global orbits of the earth, men walking in space and on the moon, space shuttles, and probes to the vast beyond—interests supported by lavish outlays of the taxpayer's money, using discourse to deflect attention away from the impoverished, the destruction of the environment, and other social problems. Or the receding interests of the United States striving to protect a position of international dominance in the "final" days of "America's Century."

Dramatism: The Theater of Propaganda

Where does the meaning of propaganda reside—in authors, texts, audiences, language structures, anchoring figures of speech, where? Each approach to literary criticism we have examined "privileges" a different residence. We now turn to a final approach that gives due weight to a variety of possibilities, namely, *dramatism*, the theater of propaganda.

Critic Kenneth Burke defines dramatism as "a method of analysis and a corresponding critique of terminology designed to show that the most direct route to the study of human relations and human motives is via a methodical inquiry into cycles of terms and their functions."[25] Any message or text can be viewed as a story, a narrative account that contains five elements: Act, Scene, Agent, Agency, and Purpose. For illustrative purposes we return a final time to "Star Trek." In any given episode of the original TV series, the

"Next Generation," the animated version, or in any of the *Star Trek* feature films, people do things: James T. Kirk, for example, commands, "Beam me up, Scotty." Kirk is the agent performing the act of commanding. He gives his command from a locale, most likely an alien planet, that constitutes the scene. Kirk talks to Scotty across space with his "communicator," an instrument, or agency, used to perform the act. Finally, we assume that Kirk does all this so as to return to the *Enterprise*, the purpose.

"Star Trek," of course, is an avowed drama. The identification of the five dramatistic elements is straightforward and simple. That is not always the case. If not, the critic must do a little digging. Consider a color photograph. Two objects are pictured. On the left is an unopened can of Del Monte "Quality" yellow cling, sliced peaches. Next to it is a plate of pancakes covered with syrup and six slices of peach. Across the top of the photo appears "HOTCAKES." In the lower right-hand corner is the message, "It's better with Del Monte Fruit. You'll flip for flapjacks with peaches. Or top your waffle with pears. Quick, easy and delicious year-round. Del Monte Fruit is the top of the morning." Here we have objects pictured in a scene, a suggested act (flip for flapjacks, or top your waffle) to be undertaken by the consuming agent, and Del Monte peaches and pears as agencies that will achieve purposes of preparing a quick, easy, and delicious treat.

The critic's digging task is not arduous with respect to the Del Monte ad, although not as easily accomplished as with "Star Trek." But consider this dry, bureaucratic narrative drawn from the Internal Revenue Service booklet instructing taxpayers on how to file Form 1040 for payment of their income tax:

> If you reported jury duty pay on line 22 and you were required to give your employer any part of that pay because your employer continued to pay your salary while you served on the jury, include the amount you gave your employer in the total on line 30. Write the amount and "Jury pay" on the dotted line next to line 30.

Here are several conditional acts—that is, "if" you reported, and "if" you gave pay to your employer, then you "write," and so on. The principal agency for you, the agent, is line 30 and the dotted line next to it. The scene for this exciting drama is the Form 1040; the purpose of the act, to avoid tax complications in the future.

Individual dramas occur within wider dramas; each story can be part of a larger story. A single inning of a baseball game is a drama unto itself involving acts, agents, agencies, scenes, and purposes that are part of an entire game that is, in turn, part of an entire season that is, in turn, part of the history of baseball, and so on. In short, each effort to identify the elements of a drama is partial and incomplete, specific to that drama. Or, when considering propaganda, the analysis of a particular message is specific to that text, which, in turn, may be extended to related texts. Thus we may identify and analyze the five dramatistic elements in Abraham Lincoln's Gettysburg Address, but in the larger drama of the Civil War the address may be thought of as an agency Lincoln used to achieve broader purposes than simply to make a few remarks at a battlefield site.

Dramatistic analysis goes beyond identifying the elements in a text. It also involves exploring the relationship between elements to uncover if one or more elements are privileged, or dominant, over the others. This constitutes a search for dramatic "ratios." Hugh Duncan, basing his views on the writing of Kenneth Burke, identifies ten ratios that are dominant.[26] Four involve the matching of the setting of action, the scene, with other elements (scene-act, scene-agency, scene-agent, scene-purpose). For example, a politician (agent) says, "I had no choice; I was a prisoner of the situation." This is a scene-agent ratio, that is, the politician excuses acts on grounds that the situation (scene) demanded them, that acts had to be congruent with setting. Or, after 45 years of division the act of German reunification occurs because the "times (scene) demand it." Three other ratios (act-purpose, act-agent, act-agency) give priority to the act. Thus the act of tearing down the Berlin Wall in 1989 contributed to additional acts congruent with the wall's demise— changes in East German leadership (agents), scheduling of free elections (agencies), and a revised sense of what Germany was about (purpose). An eighth dominant ratio, agent-purpose, matches ends with actors: *L'état c'est moi,* "I am the state," said Louis XIV of France, making his purposes his nation's purposes. When an individual selects ways of doing things in conformity with his or her character, this is an agent-agency ratio ("My honor demands satisfaction," proclaimed many a gentleman before slaying another in a duel in a bygone age). Finally, means become ends, agency-purpose ratios, as when during warfare the claim is made that the village had to be destroyed in order to "save it."

A dramatistic analysis of Abraham Lincoln's Second Inaugural Address provides an example of how critiquing the play contributes to thinking about propaganda.[27] On the surface we have Lincoln as agent presenting a speech (agency), in the inaugural setting, drawing parallels (act) between the plight of North and South for the purpose of reunifying the nation at war's end. The act of equating North and South for purposes of binding post-war wounds produces a seemingly dominant act-purpose ratio. However, the most remembered and quoted passage privileges an agent-agency ratio:

> With malice toward none; with charity for all; with firmness in the right, as God gives us to see the right, let us strive on to finish the work we are in; to bind up the nation's wounds; to care for him who shall have borne the battle, and for his widow and his orphan—to do all which may achieve and cherish a just and lasting peace among ourselves, and with all nations.

Here Lincoln is no longer the agent, God is. God's purposes are to be served. But how and by whom? By "us" and "ourselves." These are the agencies of God's will that must be instruments of "malice toward none" and "charity for all." Had Lincoln simply pleaded for people in North and South to act as agents employing charity as an agency for the purpose of binding wounds in a postwar scene, his speech might well have fallen on deaf ears. But by transforming people from agents to agencies of the Divine Agent, Lincoln made them an offer they could not refuse.

Many other aspects of dramatistic analysis have a bearing on how to think critically about propaganda. We will close with two. One is the matter of form. There are various dramatic *forms*: epic, tragedy, comedy, elegy, satire, burlesque, grotesque, didactic, and so forth.[28] (Review our discussion of each in Chapter 5.) All can serve as agencies of propaganda. For example, the epic *Gone with the Wind* (1939), tragic antiwar *All Quiet on the Western Front* (1930), or Charlie Chaplin's comedy *The Great Dictator* (1940) not only are classics in movie history, they were texts of propaganda as well.

Dramatistic analysis also considers *tropes*, or figures of speech employed in texts. One such trope, the metaphor, we have mentioned. It has been the focus of rhetorical analysis at least since Aristotle. For Aristotle the metaphor consisted of "the application of a strange term either transferred from the genus and applied to the species, or from one species to another or else by analogy.''[29] Rhetorical critics Robert Denton and Dan Hahn provide an example of the use of metaphor in propaganda analysis. They examined speeches of President Ronald Reagan and uncovered consistent use of two types of metaphors. Path metaphors (phrases such as ''are we simply going to go down the same path we've gone down before,'' or ''we're not going to go down the dead-end street'') are everyday metaphors that tapped Americans' yearning for a sense of direction. Disease/health metaphors (''crime is an American epidemic,'' or ''federal government today is overgrown and overweight'') ''reverberate positively in a citizenry that is 'into' health—jogging and other forms of exercise, . . . diets, . . . herbs, vitamins, chiropractors, iridologists, psychologists, and health foods.''[30] Such path and disease/health metaphors, argue Denton and Hahn, made Reagan's rhetoric popular and persuasive because they appealed at a subconscious level to Americans' everyday beliefs and values.

Metaphors are persuasive so long as they are suasive. That is, metaphors require people to see the connection between the familiar, say ''overgrown and overweight,'' and the abstract, ''federal government.'' If they make the connection, then audiences are fertile seedbeds for the propagation of appeals. This is also the case with a second major propaganda trope, irony. (Recall our allusion to irony in discussing Edward R. Murrow and Senator Joseph McCarthy in Chapter 6.) Since irony is an indirect way of expressing ideas by saying one thing when the actual meaning is another, irony requires audiences to ''catch the joke.'' That is, people must recognize irony for what it is, irony. They must reconstruct the surface text as a deeper, ironic one. If they do so, the resulting story creates an experience that alters the meanings they would normally assign to the words, movements, and pictures of the text. If they do so, suasion can occur. Failing such recognition and reconstruction, self-persuasion does not occur and the propagated ideas die in a soil that fails to nourish.[31] In 1968 the Republican candidate for vice-president of the United States was Spiro T. Agnew, a heretofore almost obscure governor of Maryland. Democrats attacked Agnew's qualifications in an ironic TV ad prepared by consultant Tony Schwartz. On the TV screen appeared the message ''Agnew for Vice President.'' In the background, however, was the sound of tittering laughter slowly building to a guffaw. It was not hard to grasp the irony.

FROM ''STAR TREK'' TO ILL-STARRED TEXTBOOKS: A CRITICAL INVITATION

In an article entitled ''Suspending Disbelief: The President in Pre-College Textbooks,'' political scientist Harold M. Barger reports the findings of a study he undertook of how middle and senior high school textbooks portray the U.S. president.[32] He found the portrayals glowing: presidents are cut from heroic cloth, are ''take-charge guys,'' possess a great deal of influence as political party and/or legislative leaders, fix up the economy like a mechanic, bestride the world as a ''global Paul Bunyan,'' and are the people's voice. So romanticized and exaggerated are such treatments that Barger concludes they require a ''suspension of doubt or disbelief'' that a president can really be anything more than merely human. As we have seen throughout our discussion, such a suspension of disbelief is a major sustaining condition of the new propaganda. Hence, perhaps textbooks are but agencies of new propaganda.

In this chapter we have summarized several recent thoughts on how to analyze literary texts, defining "text" broadly. This book itself and the chapters that constitute it make up such a text. Is it propaganda? Before concluding our discussion of the new propaganda in the final chapter, we invite you to pause, reread much of what we have written, and think critically about it. How many times have we used the ABCs of propaganda? How many semantic tricks have been played? What can be said of the manifest and of the hidden themes in this book? Is it but another effort to prop up the "culture industry" that critical theorists bemoan? What can be learned by "close reading," digging for intent, reading between the lines, speaking the text's tongue, and critiquing the dramatic performance? In short, has all of this been propaganda about propaganda? You be the judge and beware, lest you have been propagandized! But recall that now you possess an arsenal of critical skills about propaganda, and even this textbook is fair game.

The stalwart reader has completed our survey of the world of propaganda. As we suggested, now you can even turn your talents on us! If you have taken seriously what we have tried to say, you can never go back to the easy acceptance of propaganda as a natural and harmless part of your social universe. This chapter in particular should give you pause about what messages are hidden subtexts in otherwise innocuous-looking texts, what ideo-cultural seedbeds bring forth what kind of propaganda fruit, and what dramas with propaganda value are enacted daily for our edification. It is not wise to conclude that everything is propaganda; but it is smart to be alert to, and able to specify, those communications we encounter that are overtly or covertly propaganda. To be able to do that is no mean ability, and will serve you well as a useful skill the rest of your life. With that in mind, let us now talk about the future of propaganda, as well as your future.

NOTES

1. Michael Sproule, "Propaganda Studies in American Social Science: The Rise and Fall of the Critical Paradigm," *Quarterly Journal of Speech* 73 (February 1987): 60–78; "Progressive Propaganda Critics and the Magic Bullet Myth," *Critical Studies in Mass Communication* 6 (September 1989): 225–246; "Social Responses to Twentieth Century Propaganda," in Ted J. Smith III, ed., *Propaganda: A Pluralist Perspective* (New York: Praeger, 1989), pp. 5–35.
2. Dennis K. Davis and Stanley J. Baran, *Mass Communication and Everyday Life* (Belmont, CA: Wadsworth, 1981), p. 33.
3. A useful and readable guide to the tenets and key thinkers in critical theory is David Held, *Introduction to Critical Theory* (Berkeley: University of California Press, 1980).
4. Max Horkheimer and Theodore Adorno, "The Culture Industry: Enlightenment as Mass Deception," in Horkheimer and Adorno, *Dialectic of Enlightenment*, John Cumming, trans. (New York: Herder and Herder, 1972), pp. 120–167.
5. Herbert Marcuse, *Counterrevolution and Revolt* (Boston: Beacon Press, 1972), p. 83.
6. Theodore Adorno, "The Stars Down to Earth: The *Los Angeles Times* Astrology Column," *Telos* 19 (Spring 1974): 28–41.
7. Terry Eagleton, *Literary Theory* (Minneapolis: University of Minnesota Press, 1983), p. 25. See also W. J. T. Mitchell, ed., *The Politics of Interpretation* (Chicago: University of Chicago Press, 1983).
8. Eagleton, *Literary Theory*, p. 25.
9. Art Berman, *From the New Criticism to Deconstruction* (Urbana: University of Illinois Press, 1988), p. 30.

10. Michael K. Hemphill and Larry David Smith, ''The Working American's Elegy: The Rhetoric of Bruce Springsteen,'' in Robert L. Savage and Dan Nimmo, eds., *Politics in Familiar Contexts* (Norwood, NJ: Ablex, 1990), p. 211.

11. The phenomenological approach has many variations. Key works include Edmund Husserl, *Ideas: General Introduction to Pure Phenomenology*, W. B. Boyce Gibson, trans. (New York: Collier, 1962); Martin Heidegger, *Being and Time*, J. Macquarrie and E. Robinson, trans. (New York: Harper and Row, 1962); and Hans-Georg Gadamer, *Truth and Method* (New York: Continuum, 1975).

12. Eagleton, *Literary Theory*, p. 59.

13. Quoted in Allan Asherman, *The Star Trek Compendium* (New York: Pocket Books, 1986), p. 9.

14. Eagleton, *Literary Theory*, p. 76.

15. Ibid., p. 77.

16. See David Morley, *The Nationwide Audience* (London: British Film Institute, 1980), and David Morley, ''The Construction of Everyday Life: Political Communication and Domestic Media,'' in David Swanson and Dan Nimmo, eds., *New Directions in Political Communication* (Newbury Park, CA: Sage, 1990), pp. 127–143.

17. Maria Linko and Kimmo Jokinen, ''The Reception of a War Film,'' *The Nordicom Review of Nordic Mass Communication Research* (1) (1989).

18. Richard M. Weaver, ''Language Is Sermonic,'' in Richard L. Johannensen, ed., *Contemporary Theories of Rhetoric* (New York: Harper and Row, 1971), p. 179.

19. Useful introductions to structuralism and poststructuralism may be found in Edmund Leach, *Culture and Civilization* (New York: Cambridge University Press, 1976); Arthur Asa Berger, *Media Analysis Techniques* (Beverly Hills, CA: Sage, 1982); Eagleton, *Literary Theory*; Berman, *From the New Criticism to Deconstruction*.

20. See Dan Nimmo and Arthur J. Felsberg, ''Hidden Myths in Television Political Advertising,'' in Lynda Lee Kaid, Dan Nimmo, and Keith R. Sanders, eds., *New Perspectives on Political Advertising* (Carbondale: Southern Illinois University Press, 1986), pp. 248–267.

21. Vladimir Propp, *Morphology of a Folk Tale* (Austin: University of Texas Press, 1973).

22. Eagleton, *Literary Theory*, p. 108.

23. Arthur F. Bentley, ''Epilogue,'' in Richard W. Taylor, ed., *Life, Language, Law: Essays in Honor of Arthur F. Bentley* (Yellow Springs, OH: Antioch Press, 1957), p. 212.

24. Eagleton, *Literary Theory*, p. 132.

25. Kenneth Burke, ''Dramatism,'' in David L. Sills, ed., *The International Encyclopedia of the Social Sciences*, vol. 7 (New York: Macmillan, 1968), p. 445. See also Kenneth Burke, *A Grammar of Motives* (Berkeley: University of California Press, 1969).

26. Hugh Dalziel Duncan, *Communication and Social Order* (New York: Oxford University Press, 1962), pp. 434–436.

27. Dan F. Hahn and Anne Morlando, ''A Burkean Analysis of Lincoln's Second Inaugural Address,'' *Presidential Studies Quarterly* 9 (Fall 1979): 376–379.

28. Kenneth Burke, *Attitudes toward History* (Los Altos, CA: Hermes, 1959).

29. *Poetics*, W. Hamilton Fyfe, trans. (Cambridge, MA: Harvard University Press, 1955), p. 81.

30. Robert E. Denton, Jr., and Dan F. Hahn, *Presidential Communication* (New York: Praeger, 1986), p. 70. For a discussion of how metaphor shapes as well as reflects actions see David Zarefsky, *President Johnson's War on Poverty* (University: University of Alabama Press, 1986).

31. Wayne C. Booth, *The Rhetoric of Irony* (Chicago: University of Chicago Press, 1974).

32. Harold M. Barger, ''Suspending Disbelief: The President in Pre-College Textbooks,'' *Presidential Studies Quarterly* 20 (Winter 1990): 55–70.

Conclusion
Surveying Future Fields of Dreams

The readers of this book who have come this far have now a much firmer grasp of the extent and depth of propaganda. If you will reflect on the intellectual journey you have undertaken, you may be astonished at how much you have learned. But we cannot leave it at that. A book is written in the conviction, and hope, of persuading the reader that what she or he has learned can be put to use. In that sense, the purpose of the book is not simply or merely "academic." Since propaganda is so pervasive, the individual who takes it seriously is well served to possess the kind of knowledge and skills we have tried to outline in this book. If it so succeeds, then its own persuasive purpose will have been served. With that in mind, let us speak of the future.

Most younger readers of this book are likely to live into the twenty-first century. Indeed, those who have children in the years after 2001 will be giving birth to progeny who could still be living in the twenty-second century! What will the world be like in the years, decades, and centuries to come? Will it be richer or poorer, cleaner or dirtier, more peaceful or belligerent, scarcely or densely crowded, a paradise or a nightmare? In the words of the song "Que Sera, Sera" that we recalled in the last chapter, "Will I be happy? Will I be rich? What does the future bring?" What alternative scenarios might we envision for the coming century? Here are a few. Consider them, contemplate their worth, then cultivate your own imaginations of what the future holds.

FROM MODERNITY TO POSTMODERNITY

Throughout this book, we have spoken of our subject, the new propaganda, as a property of modernity. We argued that as the modern age, culminating in the twentieth century, matured, it became increasingly a civilization devoted to the myth of technique, a dream of progress to be achieved by the magic of science. Propaganda evolved as the language of power of that civilization, a form of communication deemed necessary for the operation of a modern society. Propaganda seeded the nurturing fields of commerce, popular culture, and politics, changing and being changed by those seedbeds. By the late twentieth century some observers argued that modernity had reached its apex. Perhaps modernity had, but propaganda was now so essential to the workings of the contemporary world that it was impossible to imagine even the most mundane of daily routines existing without it.

As the last decade of the twentieth century opened, it appeared that the values and practices at the core of modern civilization—democratic politics, capitalist economics, and widespread popular culture—had triumphed not only in the West, but also in the Communist East, and would gradually spread throughout the world. Granted there were setbacks such as the brutal treatment of prodemocratic student protestors in China in 1989. Yet, as Eastern Europe and the Soviet Union joined "the European homeland" and free elections took place in Latin American nations, the world was experiencing what Harold Lasswell, a foremost student of propaganda, had hinted at in 1927:

> Propaganda is a reflex to the immensity, the rationality and willfulness of the modern world. It is the new dynamic of society, for power is subdivided and diffused, and more can be won by illusion than by coercion. . . . The study of propaganda will bring into the open much that is obscure, until, indeed, it may no longer be possible for an Anatole France to observe with truth that 'Democracy (and indeed all society) is run by an unseen engineer.'[1]

As a case in point, Soviet president Mikhail Gorbachev's new breed of official propagandists, "charm campaigns," transformed the Western anticommunist hostility toward what Ronald Reagan had once called "the evil empire." The image of the aggressive and implacable Russian bear yielded to that of the cuddly and trustworthy bear cub. Rather than a Europe ruled through intrigue, force, and warfare, it looked as if a new unified Europe from the Atlantic to the Urals would witness the invasion of propaganda forms long active in capitalist areas. The stagnant economies of the East would be infused with a propagated consumerism. No sooner did East Germans have Deutschmarks in their hands than product advertising urged them to spend them. On the first day that East German television accepted advertising, Mattel, Inc. ran ads for—you guessed it—Barbie dolls! What better representative of the penetration of the new propaganda in newly tilled cultures than Barbie herself, a propaganda triumph. After decades of being denied freedom, the citizens of former iron curtain economies could freely buy *the* toy of modernity.

As the twentieth century drew to a close, conventional wisdom foresaw freedom as the wave of the future; the brutalities and fetters of old authoritarian and totalitarian dictatorship would be thrown on the scrap heap of history. Now humankind would enjoy not only the lessening of superpower tensions and an ensuing extended period of peace, but also expanding world prosperity, an end to poverty and disease, a loosening of old bonds of repression in places like South Africa, Romania, and Chile, and the dawning of an enlightened age of freedom.

Not everyone is so sanguine about the future. As the century moves to a climax there is also an apocalyptic feeling. Scholars, writers of fiction, and artists of all kinds express a sense common to many people, a sense that the world is turning a corner, ending one era and beginning another—but what? For lack of a better term, this sensibility carried the label "postmodernism." What the postmodern world would be like, or what it would keep or abandon from the modern world, or even what it was before ("pre-" what?) was not at all clear.

There are those who imagine a gloomy future. Environmental scientists warn that the expanding world economy could wreak untold havoc on the fragile biosphere of the earth, leading to such phenomena as the greenhouse effect. Coastal cities and developments could vanish under water. (New York City might become another Venice, with the cabbies driving speedboats!) Economists worry that the gap between the rich and the poor will keep on growing wider, making for catastrophic national and class conflicts as the many poor who live in squalor and deprivation grow weary of being governed by the rich few who live in opulence and immense wealth. (New York City will be the "Gotham City" of *Batman*, a dark and foreboding crime-infested metropolis, but without a superhero to save it.) Other cultural critics talk of the postmodern world in even more fundamental ways. We live, they say, in a period without stable values or beliefs in any transcendent truths. Basic spiritual values and practices of modernity no longer make sense. Hence, artists, who try to make sense out of the world, express feelings of confusion, disarray, and hopelessness. (The rock group Talking Heads was, according to critics, a postmodern group attuned to times when the only sense is to "stop making sense.") Finally, there are political critics, many foreshadowed by Jacques Ellul, who simply deny that contemporary historical trends add up to an uninterrupted march toward freedom. For them postmodernity ushers in subtle means of control that enslave in ways people largely accept, even warmly embrace. To be sure, no more will there be iron fists of brute dictatorships, or the greased palms of corrupt officialdom; the velvet glove of soothing propagandists replaces the ways of old modernity.

Ellul's major thesis warrants succinct review. The modern world grew increasingly captivated with technique. Highly skilled, highly specialized technicians and technocrats became the creators and operators of invention, wealth, ideas, discourse—everything and everybody. Their techniques, skills, and specialties (from nuclear engineering to bioengineering, from professional communication to professional commiseration, from the "killing professions" to the "helping professions") made them indispensable. For only *they* could understand the complexities of how ever-increasingly complex things worked. Such is the way of technological society.

Such is also the source of a political illusion, namely, that elected politicians can any longer govern and be held accountable for their actions. For example, locally elected officials could no longer simply decide "Let's build a city airport." They must instead seek the aid of technicians. Environmental impact studies must be commissioned, conducted, and interpreted to gauge the intricate effects of such a move on the population, economy, culture, polity, vegetation, animal life, fish and fowl, air quality, land development, traffic patterns, and countless other areas. Faced with thousands of technical details it is small wonder that the elected official, perhaps a specialist in some area but certainly not in all that demand political attention, asks for the new technician's recommendation, takes a stab at asking pointed questions, then ratifies the technician's proposals. Policy decisions rest more on a faith in the technician's expertise than in the politician's capacity to govern.

But political leaders cannot simply say that technicians, not politicians, make key societal decisions. If that were the case, why in fact have elected politicians at all? So leaders turn to the third element in Ellul's view of modernity, propaganda. In fact, they turn again to technicians—to the masters of the new technique of propaganda. In all the ways we have discussed in previous chapters technicians elect policy officials, make policies, sell policies, heap praise and blame—and all the while propagate myths of self-governance, liberty, equality, progress, and happiness. That is Ellul's triad: (1) technological society, (2) political illusion, and (3) propaganda to provide the illusion that the governed, not technique, govern. Consider what Ellul wrote in the preface to *Propaganda* in 1962:

> When man will be fully adapted to this technological society, when he will end by obeying with enthusiasm, convinced of the excellence of what he is forced to do, the constraint of the organization will no longer be felt by him; the truth is, it will no longer be a constraint, and the police will have nothing to do. The civic and technological good will and the enthusiasm for the right social myths—both created by propaganda—will finally have solved the problem of man.[2]

BUT ARE THERE NO LIMITS?

We saw in Chapter 3 that George Orwell said similar things about the future of the world, but we alluded then to critics who challenged Orwell's assumptions. Many did so on grounds that Orwell's views pertained to totalitarian societies. Their challenges to Orwell's notions about the likelihood of *total* propaganda being the wave of the future emphasized the limits of propaganda in a totalitarian society. There citizens are so accustomed to propaganda that they largely ignore it (as did the "proles" in Orwell's *1984*), or they turn it against their own rulers. As changes in the Soviet Union and revolutions in Eastern Europe in 1989–1990 illustrate, such limits on totalitarian propaganda indeed exist. However, Jacques Ellul's theory pertains to *all* societies where the triad of technique, illusion, and propaganda operates. Are there also, then, limits to propaganda under those conditions? Let us examine areas exemplifying such limitations.

Subliminal Politics

Consider "subliminal seduction." There is a view that advertising contains, below the surface or threshold of conscious awareness, hidden messages not directly or immediately perceived. Wilson Bryan Key claims that a wide variety of product ads contain subliminal messages that surreptitiously arouse desires. Hidden messages in magazine ads, say students of subliminal advertising, include gender appeals to one sex or another (recall our discussion of gender from Chapter 8), even four-letter words embedded in pictured ice cubes![3] However, not everyone is as convinced as Key that covert appeals exist in ads, even though many messages are subtle and speak to hidden and/or forbidden desires. Too, psychological research has failed to detect the widespread presence or any effectiveness of subliminal seduction.[4]

The absence of demonstrated effectiveness does not, of course, deter merchandisers from trying to capitalize on a notion related to subliminal advertising, namely, that people can be induced to do things they would not normally do through seemingly effortless, unconscious appeals. There is, for example, a $50 million self-help industry based upon sales of audio and video tapes to persons looking for shortcuts to success: in giving up smoking, losing weight, building self-esteem, making better grades in school, moving up the corporate ladder, even ending bed-wetting. Many such tapes are musical in content, but transmit messages just below the level of consciousness that people allegedly hear and heed eagerly, painlessly, and successfully. The industry also supplies musical tapes for office sound systems. The tapes overlay inaudible messages motivating employees to overcome procrastination and work harder, for example, "I do it today" and "I take action now." Again, however, there is scant evidence that the higher production wishes of the Ebenezer Scrooge office managers are fulfilled. Even though many studies and prestigious scientific bodies such as the National Academy of Sciences discount the impact on behavior of subliminal messages, both the effort and the potential for suggestive engineering of behavior are there, and it is not beyond the capacity of propagandists in politics or elsewhere to use such communication to advance their purposes.

Consider also the area of popular music. Critics of heavy metal rock 'n' roll claim that musical groups hide subliminal "satanic" or antisocial lyrics beneath the surface sounds. An indication of the lengths to which such concern can go came in 1990 when a Nevada family sued the English rock group Judas Priest. The suit alleged that the album *Stained Class* contained subliminal messages advocating suicide, and that the family's son and a friend had formed a suicide pact after listening to the album. The parents argued that one song on the album, "Better By You, Better Than Me," contains the hidden messages "Do it," "Try suicide," and "Let's be dead." The family attorney and subliminal researcher Wilson Bryan Key (called to testify for the plaintiffs) spoke of *mind control* and *brainwashing*. Both terms derived from the supposedly successful techniques of the Communist Chinese and North Koreans during the Korean War to convert U.S. prisoners of war to the Communist cause. The terms sound ominous, but as is the case with "subliminal seduction" there is little evidence that mind control or brainwashing has lasting effects.[5] Nor, as it turned out, was there evidence that Judas Priest worked subliminal messages into their musical compositions. But again, if it could be demonstrated that such subconscious suggestion could affect behavior, such a way of "behavior modification" could be extremely useful to those who would exercise mind control through communication.

HUXLEY'S BRAVE NEW WORLD OF PROPAGANDA

Recognizing that there are limits to the effectiveness of totalitarian propaganda, subliminal advertising, musical symbolism, mind control, brainwashing, or even the shrieking blasts of the TV automobile pitchman ("I *want* to sell YOU a *car!*") is one thing. A long tradition of social science research has time and time again demonstrated that the *direct* effects of efforts to persuade individuals to change their behavior are marginal; are mediated by a host of factors sometimes bearing on, and at others having nothing to do with, the persuasive appeal; and are more temporary than long lasting.[6] As we have seen throughout this book, however, *persuasion* per se is not the whole of the new propaganda. Propaganda constitutes the environment of the contemporary world; in that environment human suggestibility, credulity, and *suasion* are as key to assessing propaganda's role as are the effects of persuasive efforts. In short, limits to persuasion are not necessarily limits to suasion and, thereby, to the new propaganda envisioned by Ellul, Orwell, and others.

Recall from Chapter 3 that Ellul regarded his thesis as similar to one propounded by novelist Aldous Huxley. The Huxley viewpoint preceded both Orwell's *1984* published in 1949 and Ellul's writings published in the United States in the 1960s. Huxley's provocative novel *Brave New World* first appeared in 1932. When *1984* was published, Huxley wrote Orwell a letter arguing that they both were dealing with "the philosophy of the ultimate revolution." Each foretold a future marked by "the evolution which lies beyond politics and economics, and which aims at the total subversion of the individual's psychology and physiology." Huxley's views complement Orwell's (and Ellul's) vision of a world wherein "the ruling oligarchy will find less arduous and wasteful ways of governing and of satisfying its lust for power." Huxley predicted that "within the next generation . . . the world's rulers will discover that infant conditioning and narco-hypnosis are more efficient" and that the "lust for power can be just as completely satisfied by suggesting people into loving their servitude." In the long run, the "change will be brought about as a result of a felt need for increased efficiency."[7]

Orwell imagined a world in which rulers use propaganda to try to exercise control in the presence of scarcity and deprivation. Futurists since Orwell have built upon this, prophesying a world of controlling techniques, including incessant propaganda, that are essential to the survival of the state. Robert Heilbroner, one of the most eminent among them, has argued that the only government that will be viable in a future world of growing population, diminishing resources, and violent upheaval will be a "survival state," that is, "one that blends a 'religious orientation' with a 'military' discipline. Such a monastic organization may be repugnant to us, but I suspect it offers the greatest promise of making those enormous transformations needed to reach a new stable socio-economic basis."[8]

Huxley envisioned the ultimate triumph of scientific management and behavioral technology applied by an elite that believes itself to be thoroughly benevolent (what governing elite from the most dictatorial to the most democratic does not?), ruling a pacific and healthy population whose members consider themselves blissfully happy. Whereas Orwell's state seemed to rely on agitation and integration propaganda at specific times, such as war (see Chapter 3), Huxley's utilizes disposition propaganda throughout the whole of everyone's life. For example, Winston Smith, the protagonist of Orwell's novel, is "converted"—from hating to loving "Big Brother"—only after considerable resistance, physical pain and coercion, and conditioning. In Huxley's futuristic world such conversions are unnecessary. Disposition propaganda begins at birth, for instance, with "sleep-teaching." Each citizen learns a set of comforting slogans, taught from infancy, such as "Every one works for every one else," and "Everybody's happy now." (Compare that with such contemporary slogans as "Brush three times a day," "Give your fair share," "Buckle up," "Vote your choice, but vote," and "Don't worry, be happy.")

In Huxley's *Brave New World* "controllers" encourage people in ruler-approved pleasures—periods of sexual play, vacations, and tranquilizing narcotics—and in return citizens are grateful and loyal to the regime. (Compare such pleasures with those contained in the current vernacular of "Practice Safe Sex," "Have a Happy and Safe Fourth of July," and "Know When to Say When.") Everyone's disposition is so tranquil in fact that no one entertains a critical thought, antisocial impulse, or independent action. In such a world, every expression is propaganda, from education to play to conversation. Language consists of slogans, and thought (occurring through language) is short-circuited. In

Huxley's future, everyone habitually speaks a form of Orwell's Newspeak, and everyone practices doublethink.

In 1958, Huxley returned to his brave new world in his published work, *Brave New World Revisited*. In it he reflected on the power modern techniques of communication were exerting to bring about the future he had imagined. Modern communicators, he thought, were "concerned in the main neither with the true nor the false, but with the unreal, the more or less totally irrelevant. In a word, [we have] failed to take into account man's almost infinite appetite for distractions." In the future, "non-stop distractions . . . are deliberately used as instruments of policy, for the purpose of preventing people from paying too much attention to the realities of the social and political situation." People in the future will spend a great part of daily life "somewhere else," in the "irrelevant other worlds of sport and soap opera, of mythology and metaphysical fantasy" and therefore "find it hard to resist the encroachments of those who would control them." Huxley considered that before the birth of the era of brave new worlds propagandists had relied on "repetition, suppression and rationalization—the repetition of catchwords which they wish to be accepted as true, the suppression of facts which they wish to be ignored, [and] the arousal and rationalization of passions which may be used in the interests of the Party or State." But "as the art and science of manipulation come to be better understood," the controllers of the future will learn "to combine these techniques with the non-stop distractions" that threaten to "drown [us] in a sea of irrelevance."[9]

The admirers of Huxley have argued that those of us who live in the postmodern West are in danger of drowning in those irrelevant distractions. In this view, closely akin to Ellul's, the mass media have become subtle and unintended instruments of policy distracting us from serious thought or attention, and framing whatever thought or attention we do accord the world. Further, the technology of behavioral science has been exploited by managerial elites—in government, mass media, corporate, educational, and myriad other organizations and institutions—to advance the aims of control, not thought. Choices between candidates for public office or proposals for public law are not debated democratically but dictated by their presumed efficiency, then marketed and sold. Nor are the consequences of action assessed in a democratic forum: when something happens government, corporate, university, or other propaganda technicians work on "damage control," attempting to frame and manipulate perceptions of reality. Increasingly, elites define the problem of control as one that focuses on power over thought rather than power over tangible consequences. As with Orwell's "inner Party" and Huxley's "controllers," reality is subjective and not objective; hence those who control how the masses see things control reality.[10] (Recall, from Chapter 2, how closely Michael Deaver's practices paralleled this view.)

Huxley's adherents note, again like Ellul, that the brave new world we are creating is no conspiracy, but rather the result of our complicity in creating a technological civilization, a world based not on control but self-control, not on deception, but self-deception, not on pain inflicted upon us, but rather on self-inflicted pleasure. Writes Neil Postman:

> What Orwell feared were those who would ban books. What Huxley feared was there would be no reason to ban a book, for there would be no one who wanted to read one. . . . Orwell feared we would become a captive culture. Huxley feared we would become a trivial culture. . . . In *1984*, people are controlled by inflicting pain. In *Brave*

New World, they are controlled by inflicting pleasure. . . . There are two ways by which the spirit of a culture may be shriveled. In the first—the Orwellian—culture becomes a prison. In the second—the Huxleyan—culture becomes a burlesque.[11]

Postman, like other Huxleyans, points to the ubiquity of television as an agent of what we have called disposition propaganda, a signifying mark of new propaganda. "Big Brother is you, watching," argues TV critic Mark Crispin Miller, suggesting that we are both creators and consumers of our own propaganda, living in a condition of "credulous spectatorship."[12] We do not need external controls because television's disposition propaganda has lulled us into a state of banal and passive contentment. Like the subjects of Huxley's fantasy, diversions such as television are our major drug, narcotizing us into happy Smileyfaces, urging, nay commanding, each other to "Have a nice day!" (President George Bush's campaign slogan, Be Happy, Don't Worry, may be prescient and appropriate for the age.)

In Huxley's future, disposition propaganda successfully perfects conformity. His world shares with Orwell's the degradation of public discourse. Like Orwell's duckspeakers, everyone in Huxley's Smileyface future mouths easily the childish array of guiding slogans that make mature thought and action impossible ("Never put off till tomorrow the fun you can have today"; "You can't consume much if you sit still and read books"). Such a world would not be as sinister as it would be puerile. We would be totally propaganda-directed, drawing our cues about what is real and true from a hegemonic source that assures us that we, and the world we live in, are having a nice day.

As Ellul noted, propaganda aims not only at *orthodoxy* (conformity of thought), but also *orthopraxy* (conformity of action). To that we may add *orthopathy* (conformity of emotion). A world dominated by the beguiling and charming new propaganda would invite us to think along lines useful to the palavers of charm and guile but not require it. It is up to us to convince ourselves of the worthiness of such thoughts. The complement of that is the invitation to emote in useful ways as well. To the degree that human thoughts, feelings, and actions are intertwined, the orthodoxy, orthopathy, and orthopraxy invited by the new propaganda goes a long way to resolving what Ellul called "the problem of man": love of our servitude, all the while believing that we are free.

These propaganda-dominated futures are in a sense worst case scenarios. But Ellul, Orwell, and Huxley certainly alert us to the possibilities and pitfalls in a world of all-pervasive palaver. If present trends continue and certain conditions prevail, we might live to see a world with power following not the divine, not the flag, not the sword, not the dollar (or Deutschmark), but the palaver. Then what?

THE FUTURE IS NOW: FENDING OFF
THE PALAVER OF A NOISY WORLD

Football coaches have a cliche they repeat in ritualistic ways when stuck with a team possessing minimal talent. To excuse the losing season they know is before them they intone, "We're building for the future." A legendary coach, recognizing such palaver for what it is, when asked if he were building for the future surprised everyone by coining a new cliche in response: "The future is now!" In many respects the scenarios we have reviewed about the future and propaganda's role in it are not of the future at all. For with respect to palaver, the future is now. Whether trends and forecasts of futurists prevail is not so much at issue as whether we can learn ways to cope with the new propaganda that pervades our daily lives in the present. In a world where palaver reigns, the powerful are the palaverers. To fend off the noise of guile and charm we must understand that world, adopt a critical and independent stance toward it, and learn how to take action in spite of palaver's dictates.

This book has been an effort to help readers understand the nature of propaganda, especially the emergence, content, and techniques of the new propaganda. Harold Lasswell's insight, which we have noted at various times, states that democracy proclaimed propaganda as dictator; and the principal technique of dictating to that dictator, that of practicing propaganda, is palaver. Ellul, Orwell, and Huxley warn us that a *total*itarian regime of palaver, although it might seem beguiling, charming, and pleasurable enough, may be no more acceptable than any other totalitarian form. Indeed, in 1990 a Romanian dissident intellectual who had fled the old totalitarianism of Communist Romania to the West offered a sobering argument, namely, as the old totalitarianism of the Eastern bloc was collapsing, the organizational order of the West was busily creating a new totalitarianism. Andrei Codrescu wrote that "the two former oppositions of East and West will join together in a new electronic globe that is not a good thing for human beings." Like Mark Crispin Miller, Ellul, and others, Codrescu thinks that our multimedia world has created a new reality, one that is a "simulation," or a semblance of reality, not the conventional world of commonsense reality.[13] In a world dominated by mass media, people risk assuming that the contrived semblances of propagated reality have a "truth-value" that is denied their mundane everyday reality that constantly gets checked and cross-checked by daily successes and failures. Propaganda is the ascendant form of communication in civilization; its exalted status lends weight to our lives, but a weight that is actually a lightness of being.

Earlier in this book we suggested that, increasingly, propaganda drives policy in organizational life. The idea here is that every problem is conceived in terms of propaganda, the language of mastery through technique. A political leader and his or her organizational team therefore increasingly conceive a solution to health care or educational problems as one of communicating their concern and effort and pointing to evidence of solutions, but the process is effectively substitutionary: the problem remains, but it is "solved" for the politician through propaganda producing the desired effect on the public. This obviously does not always work, and equally as clearly does not solve the problem. But the point here is that problems are conceptualized as essentially a problem of propaganda. Propaganda is the solution to political or other organizational problems because it creates a "semblance of reality," or what Barnum called "great realities" that offer a postmodern solution.

We also suggested that there is something else insidious about propaganda. Not only does it become a panacea, but we come to expect that every area of life, including those with traditional values of truth-seeking and respect for inquiry, will be pervaded by propaganda values. This was no more evident than in the movement on college campuses in the 1990s dubbed "political correctness." College administrators, faculties, and student groups moved to attempt to control behavior and even thoughts on campuses by reforming language that would be "linguistically inclusive" and also expanding curricula to include minority or excluded voices. On its face, attempting to curb sexist or racist behavior and make curricula more diverse seems a noble academic consideration. But quickly the movement abandoned traditions of free expression and curriculum reform and transformed linguistic inclusiveness and multicultural diversity into "political correctness," wherein both campus language and curriculum would become propaganda for values allegedly higher than free speech and the traditional canon of literature. A number of universities enacted "bad language" codes, and one, the University of Michigan, even tried to make laughing at the wrong kind of jokes grounds for expulsion. Thinking unacceptable "bad thoughts" was condemned, and saying something politically uncorrect—that homosexuality was a disease or morally wrong, that feminists are sometimes offensive and boring, that a work by a great artist with racist views (such as D. W. Griffith's landmark film, *Birth of a Nation*) might still be worth studying—became a punishable offense. An entire language of inclusion was invented that everyone on campus was to learn and use: "people of color," "the vertically constrained," "the optically challenged," "the sexually disinclined," and so on infinitely, in an effort to create an acceptable category for everyone. Curriculum reform became a battleground for new and strange affiliations—the "Eurocentrics," "Afrocentrics," and so on, all of whom seemed to find nothing wrong with using the curriculum for its propaganda value. Indeed, the whole thrust of the movement, arguing that there are higher academic values than free speech, is that the highest value for the academic world is propaganda. If successful, such an academic and campus atmosphere would be patently Huxleyan, with everyone mindlessly mouthing the correct palaver, thinking in the correct categories, suppressing bad thoughts that campus propaganda has condemned, and reading only those books that further the correct line. Long forgotten are older, and modern, values of free thought and canonical standards, subordinated to the higher postmodern value of propaganda. In the twenty-first century, the primary form of academic communication will be propaganda.

What, however, if we deny palaver's dictation and insist that what is real is not what is reduced to the technique of insubstantial guile and charm, that is, not the lightness of being sustained by our palaver, but the weight of thought sustained by our doubts? Contemporary propaganda germinates in a seedbed of suspended disbelief, be the ideas "true" or "false," correct or incorrect, open to test or not. For to suspend disbelief is to say, in effect, "It sounds crazy, but it's OK." A culture of disbelief and doubt, what we shall call skepticism, is not conducive to the weedlike flourishing of palaver. To activate disbelief is to say, in effect, "Things are not always as they seem, so what *is* going on?" Such a posture is difficult for many people to sustain. In fact, skeptics such as the eighteenth-century philosopher David Hume admitted it is impossible to maintain extreme skepticism, since in doing so one would doubt one's own existence. Yet a "healthy skepticism" provides people with a will to doubt in a world all too willing to believe in guile and charm.

A Rose by Any Other Name?: Recognizing It When We See (or Smell) It

There is a postmodernist notion that skepticism will lead nowhere in coping with propaganda. After all, goes the thesis, one "truth" is just as true or false as another; hence, we now live in an age that lies beyond truth and falsity. Such thinking certainly helps explain the importance of the new propaganda that itself goes beyond truth and falsity. The content of palaver may be true or untrue; more frequently it is neither but lies somewhere ambiguously in between. A skeptical stance, if it is to be useful, must recognize palaver for what it is. The new propaganda and its attendant palaver is a constituent part of a range of public utterances that has many labels. Here are a few more common ones: "baloney," "blarney," "buncombe," "conning," "equivocation," "hogwash," "humbug," and "vacillation." The specifics of these practices differ, but all have a tendency toward exaggeration, that is, a certain bending of the accuracy to embellish accounts; double meanings that foster a sense of confusion, even mystery; wandering and wavering so that there is always something the listener "can't quite put a finger on"; figurative language (metaphors, etc.) rather than literal talk; and the guile, even charm, in speaking that marks palaver.

We experience these practices every day, indeed, engage in them. To the degree that propaganda employs them, we are in that sense all propagandists. However, these features of discourse are not "danger signals of the new propaganda" (such as the ABCs of propaganda featured in the traditional analysis of propaganda discussed in Chapter 7) that quickly alert us to weeds growing in our social seedbeds so we can yank them out. If coping with the new propaganda were nothing more than recognizing such talk, it would be easy enough to do, although it would certainly take some of the fun out of living. One would scarcely be the life of the party by knocking every utterance as exaggerated, ambiguous, wandering, wavering, figurative, or wily. Skepticism can rarely go so far. Anyway, making grouches of ourselves will not assure that we detect the palaver of new propaganda. For there is something else at issue in that palaver that we must take into account if we are to recognize it and fend off its guile and charm.

Philosopher Harry Frankfurt provides intriguing insights into a practice of communication that is closely akin to what we have labeled in this book as palaver. Frankfurt uses another term, one that is descriptive of the excrement of the adult male bovine.[14] Since Frankfurt's term might offend the sensibilities of some readers (although it is a term widely used among persons of all ages), we shall simply summarize his argument here by employing *palaver* where he uses a far more malodorous word. In so doing we plead guilty to ambiguity and vacillation, but—of course—in the name of a higher [sic] calling! Frankfurt begins by observing, "One of the most salient features of our culture is that there is so much" of, let us say, palaver-like talk.

> Everyone knows this. Each of us contributes his share. But we tend to take the situation for granted. Most people are rather confident of their ability to recognize [palaver] and to avoid being taken in by it. So the phenomenon has not aroused much deliberate concern, nor attracted much sustained inquiry.[15]

Certainly Frankfurt could be speaking directly of palaver: it too is a salient feature of our culture; we take it for granted, contribute our share, think we can recognize and not be taken in by it, and thereby don't think seriously about it.

After devoting a brief discussion to setting off "it" from such practices as humbug, lying, bluffing, and so forth, Frankfurt reaches the heart of the matter: "the essence of [palaver] is not that it is *false* but that it is *phony*."[16] By "phony" he is not speaking of something that is defective. To be sure, phonies are copies, counterfeits, or fakes of persons, places, events, and so on. Yet, facsimiles may be so exact as to be in no way inferior to the "real thing" (as the Coca-Cola commercial claims). The document that comes out at one fax machine differs not at all from that put into another. The image of a candidate, the sizzle of the steak, or the "IBM compatible" personal computer may not be *the* candidate, steak, or IBM, but that does not make any one of them less authentic.

Instead, in speaking of "phony" Frankfurt is stressing *how something is made*. Take palaver as a case in point. The new propagandist fashions guile and charm without a concern for truth. This does not mean that the palaver is necessarily false; it may indeed be accurate and true to the situation. Remember that the masters of propaganda discussed in Chapter 2 were not always concerned with the truth-value of their messages, but heartily approved of being truthful whenever possible. Palaver, in short, is made neither to tell the truth nor to lie, *but to fake*. The difficulty with academic political correctness, for example, is not that the language and the curriculum is a lie or is true, but rather that it is phony.

Think of another example. As a reader of this book it is likely that you are a college or university student. Suppose you enroll in a course in history, political science, sociology, or communication. Midway through the term you have an essay exam. Although you have prepared well, when you get the exam you have a sinking feeling in your stomach. You simply don't understand the question and don't know what to write. Your essay can't reflect the "truth" of the matter, because you don't know it. It can't be a lie, that is, full of false information, because the instructor will detect it (perhaps). If you are like many other students, however, you don't panic. You decide to fake it! You do what Ellul said happens throughout society, you *reduce the substance of the question to technique*. Since you have prepared for the exam, you can, for instance, rephrase the question asked (that you can't answer) into one that you can answer. Your answer to the question is not true because you don't answer the question; your answer is not false, because the information you provide is accurate. Instead your answer is a counterfeit, a facsimile of an answer to what might have been but was not asked. You hope the instructor will give some credit for the answer you have faked.

Here, with *palaver* inserted for what Frankfurt is actually talking about, is his view:

> What [palaver] essentially misrepresents is neither the state of affairs to which it refers nor the beliefs of the speaker concerning that state of affairs. Those are what lies misrepresent, by virtue of being false. Since [palaver] need not be false, it differs from lies in its misrepresentational intent. The [palaverer] need not deceive us, *or even intend to do so*, either about the facts or what he takes the facts to be. What he does necessarily attempt to deceive us about is his enterprise. His only indispensably distinctive characteristic is that in a certain way he misrepresents what he is up to.[17]

Frankfurt goes on to note that an honest person and a liar have one thing in common. For a person to lie, that person must know the truth, just as an honest person must know the truth to tell it. Lying presumes that one says something is so that one knows not to be so. But the artist of palaver sides neither with the truth nor with lies. In many instances the purveyor of palaver may not know the truth (as exemplified in the example of the essay exam). Herein lies a problem. Since a liar knows the truth but does not tell it, being a liar does not, to use Frankfurt's phrase, "unfit a person for telling the truth." But an emphasis on the technique of guile and charm in the absence of knowing the substance of things is another matter. "Someone who lies and someone who tells the truth are playing on opposite sides, so to speak, in the same game," writes Frankfurt. Each responds to facts as understood—the honest person guided by the authority of truth and the liar refusing to meet the demands of truth. The counterfeiter, fake, palaverer, or other artist "ignores those demands altogether." Continues Frankfurt, "he does not reject the authority of truth, as the liar does, and oppose himself to it. He pays no attention to it at all. By virtue of this [palaver] is a greater enemy of the truth than lies are."[18] The college administrator who defends political correctness with the argument that there are higher considerations than free speech or an impartial curriculum is a [palaver] artist.

Frankfurt suggests that faking it is unavoidable whenever circumstances make it necessary for people to speak without knowing what they are talking about. If Ellul's thesis is correct, this accounts for the tendency in society for politicians to reduce the substance of candidacies, problems, policies, and so forth, to the technique of palaver. The complexities of substantive issues require highly specialized knowledge and skills to understand them. Not possessing such knowledge or skills, the politician relies on those who do, then puts a gloss on his or her efforts to speak about issues by faking it, that is, by resorting to guile and charm to dictate the new propaganda.

How does Frankfurt's view assist us in coping with the new propaganda? How does it go beyond merely recognizing exaggeration, ambiguity, wavering, wandering, guile, and charm? He tells us two things. First, we must go beyond the recognition of palaver to ask what it is that the new propagandist is up to that is being misrepresented through faking. Second, we must judge the palaver not on the basis of truth or falsity but by whether it reduces a substantive problem to technique alone. Propaganda, we have argued, may or may not be intentional. But if a politician's message misrepresents, to use Frankfurt's phrase, "what he is up to," then we are alerted that things are not as they seem. If palaver exists for palaver alone, then like the king without any clothes standing in his "altogether," things are not only not as they seem, they are nothing at all!

A Paradox: Piety Plus Incredulity Equals Skepticism

Detecting palaver and coping with it is, of course, not easy. Propaganda is so much a part of our lives and so taken for granted that it is far easier to form habits of acceptance than habits of skepticism. If, however, we wish to cope it will help to replace acceptance with a *habit of discursive piety*. As we have seen, the artist of palaver has no concern for correct and honest discourse—what people read, see, say, and hear. But languages of communication are certainly one of humankind's most magnificent inventions, to be used with tough-minded thought and embraced with tender-minded care in pious ways. Conversely, prolix, extended, ambiguous, confounding discourse that does not inform, evaluate, or express—in short, palaver—deserves scorn. Orwell argued that "if thought corrupts language, language can also corrupt thought." By allowing the "invasion of one's mind by ready-made phrases," one risks suasion by propaganda, since "every such phrase anesthetizes a portion of one's brain," and in the long run contributes to "the decadence of our language."[19] Orwell speculated that the decadence of language corresponds with the decadence of political culture, thus discursive piety may not reverse or even retard the decay. Yet such a habit of mind can do no worse than one of ritualistic acceptance of the palaver in our political and personal lives.

We have seen repeatedly in this book that we take propaganda for granted not because it is true or false, but because it seems credulous. Fending off palaver requires a different habit of mind, the *habit of incredulity*. The ancient philosopher Zeno of Elea argued that knowledge advances through refutation, in effect decreasing the amount of things we believe we "know." Propagandists depend upon certitudes affirmed by magic and myth. The habit of incredulity disputes the certainty of propositions, doubting those things represented to us as certainties. As with the habit of discursive piety, however, there are no guarantees. By disbelieving so much we do not necessarily enlarge what we know to be true or to be false; yet we can perhaps progress toward reducing the sizable expanse of what Frankfurt calls the "phony."

A CONCLUDING CONFRONTATION WITH THE CONFIDENCE-MAN

People could argue for hours the question of who is America's greatest writer of fiction. Certainly one name that would come up is Herman Melville (1819–1891). Much of Melville's fame rests on his novel *Moby Dick*. Here, however, we are interested in another of his works, *The Confidence-Man: His Masquerade* (1857).[20] In everyday language a confidence man is one who uses guile and charm to win the confidence of other people, then swindles and defrauds them. Melville's confidence man is that, and much more.

The story takes place on a steamboat, the *Fidele*, that leaves St. Louis on April Fool's Day to travel down the Mississippi River to New Orleans. During the course of the trip and tale the reader meets a variety of convincing characters, each colorful, a little mysterious, and, in one way or another, charming and beguiling. Included are a deaf-mute preaching biblical charity; a cripple begging for money; a man in mourning soliciting aid from strangers; a man dressed in a gray coat and white tie promoting "World's Charity," an asylum for widows and orphans; the president of a coal company encouraging speculative investments; an herb-doctor promoting "Omni-Balsamic Reinvigorator and Samaritan Pain Dissuader"; a man representing the "Philosophical Intelligence Office" promoting faith in the goodness of humankind; and a cosmopolitan urging trust in one's fellows on all levels from the philosophical to the mundane.

We need not summarize details of the plot of *The Confidence-Man* here. It suffices to say that one reads the book and asks what each of the fascinating characters is up to: *are things really as they seem*? A reader marvels at each character's effortless, fluid, smooth ways of conversing; distinctive costume, appearance, and savoir faire; and appeals to basic human desires—to comfort grief, alleviate suffering, acquire money, be healthy, discover goodness, and love and be loved. Talk, costumes, appeals—a rich diversity of techniques that win the confidence of fellow passengers. Indeed it is as though Melville were providing a textbook instructing the new propagandists that would follow almost a century later in guidelines for faking it.

The reader of *The Confidence-Man* must be alert, pay close attention, be painstaking in examining the conversations of the characters, and remain steadfast in incredulity. If so, that reader does not move far through Melville's novel before a suspicion grows. The characters are richly diverse, yet they seem alike. And well they should. For they are not separate characters at all but separate characterizations of the title character, "The Confidence-Man." With the techniques of a chameleon he slips from one guise to another. He assumes *appearances* gracefully in keeping with shifting demands, times, and situations.

Like Frankfurt's artist of fakery he deceives not about morality and immorality, truth and falsehood, but about his enterprise. And who is this confidence man? Lo and behold, it is The Devil. The closing line of the novel is "Something further may follow of this masquerade." Critic James Miller interprets that as follows:

> The action cannot end, for the devil is still among us, testing his tricks as we travel on the *Fidele*. Indeed, he may very well be in the chair across from us as we close *The Confidence-Man* and look about with a slight feeling of discomfort and expectations.[21]

We are not saying that new propagandists are simply The Devil in differing guises. But they do share with The Devil the practice of reducing all matters of substance to those of technique, the technique of palaver. Recall that early in this concluding chapter we took note of Harold Lasswell's expressed hope that "the study of propaganda will bring into the open much that is obscure, until, indeed, it may no longer be possible for an Anatole France to observe with truth that 'Democracy (and, indeed, all society) is run by an unseen engineer.' "[22] Given our penchant in this book for treating propaganda not as a mechanical process but as one akin to propagating plant life, we close with a similar, albeit differently worded thought: the study of the new propaganda will indeed bring into the open much that is obscure; perhaps then it will no longer be possible to say that democracies (and indeed, all societies) are tended by an unseen gardener—one with a pitchfork for a tail.

NOTES

1. Harold Lasswell, "Propaganda," in Dwaine Marvick, ed., *Harold Lasswell on Political Sociology* (Chicago: University of Chicago Press, 1977), p. 228. The selection originally appeared in the *Encyclopedia of the Social Sciences* in 1934.
2. Jacques Ellul, *Propaganda: The Formation of Men's Attitudes* (New York: Vintage Books, 1973), p. xviii.
3. Wilson Bryan Key, *Subliminal Seduction* (New York: New American Library, 1974).
4. Eric J. Zanot, et al., "Public Perceptions of Subliminal Advertising," *Journal of Advertising* 12 (1983): 38–45.
5. See Edgar H. Schein, *Coercive Persuasion* (New York: Norton, 1971); J. A. C. Brown, *Techniques of Persuasion: From Propaganda to Brainwashing* (Baltimore: Penguin Books, 1971).
6. One of the first, and a classical, effort to integrate the findings from studies in this tradition of persuasive effects is Joseph T. Klapper, *The Effects of Mass Communication* (Glencoe, IL: Free Press, 1960).
7. Aldous Huxley, "Letter to George Orwell," in Irving Howe, ed., *Orwell's Nineteen Eighty-Four*, 2nd. ed., (New York: Harcourt Brace Jovanovich, 1983), pp. 373–374.
8. Robert L. Heilbroner, *An Inquiry into the Human Prospect* (New York: Norton, 1980), pp. 172–173.
9. Aldous Huxley, *Brave New World Revisited* (New York: Perennial Library, 1958), pp. 36–37.
10. See radical critic Michael Parenti, *Inventing Reality: The Politics of the Mass Media* (New York: St. Martin's Press, 1986).
11. Neil Postman, *Amusing Ourselves to Death* (New York: Penguin Books, 1986), pp. vii, 155.
12. Mark Crispin Miller, "Big Brother Is You, Watching," *Georgia Review* 38 (Winter 1984): 710, 719.

13. Andrei Codrescu, *The Disappearance of the Outside: A Manifesto for Escape* (Reading, MA: Addison-Wesley, 1990).
14. Harry Frankfurt, "On Bullshit," *Raritan* 6 (Fall 1986): 81–100.
15. Ibid., p. 81.
16. Ibid., p. 94.
17. Ibid., p. 96 (emphasis added).
18. Ibid., p. 98.
19. George Orwell, "Politics and the English Language," in Irving Howe, ed., *Orwell's Nineteen Eighty-Four*, p. 257.
20. Herman Melville, *The Confidence-Man: His Masquerade* (New York: Norton, 1971).
21. James E. Miller, Jr., *A Reader's Guide to Herman Melville* (New York: Farrar, Straus and Cudahy, 1962), p. 192.
22. Harold Lasswell, "Propaganda," p. 228.

Index